Contents

THIS BOOK WILL HELP YOU:

Contents

Foreword

The authors of this study skills book would like to congratulate you on deciding to go on to further study; you will find it a true 'rite of passage' for your personal development, both socially and professionally.

Your time in higher education should be seen as an opportunity to develop yourself through both study and new friendships. The authors have designed the chapters to enable you to get the most out of your business and management studies subjects. There are plenty of activities in the book to help you focus on key intellectual skills to improve not only your studies but also your approach to being a professional in later life. If you can develop a self-reflective and 'can do' approach, this will mark you out as an independent lifelong learner – a vital attribute for anyone today.

Being able to reflect on all the skills you are developing during this period, be they through your studies, sports, volunteering or part-time work, enables you to become aware of the employability and professional skills you are developing. You can record this information in your personal development planner (PDP) that you will be given by your tutors. The PDP enables you to reflect on your developing skills, make your learning explicit and becomes a good aide-memoire when you come to that important interview. The PDP at the end of each chapter is a start.

Finally, we would like to wish you all the best with your studies and beyond.

Paul Ramsay
Pat Maier
Geraldine Price

How to use this book

Why this book?

The academic and study skills that you develop during your degree will set you up as a lifelong learner and equip you to progress your business or management career. The tone of the book is one of personal development, encouraging you to reflect on your skills, develop a 'can do' attitude and know what you need to do to improve. These are the qualities that will increase your employability and mark you out as a high flyer, and help you achieve your aspiration to be a business leader.

The book can be used by individual students or tutors wishing to embed these skills in the curriculum and link into personal development planners. We are living through a period of rapid change where our knowledge needs updating regularly throughout our lives in order to remain current. Lifelong learning skills therefore become important and enable us to improve and keep up to date throughout our working life.

For you – the student

This book explores the challenges of university life and how you can move from being a novice to becoming an experienced learner in your field. The challenges for you are at many levels: your engagement with the subject, your ability to manage your time and your motivation to take responsibility for your own learning. Those of you who take up the challenges and develop a deeper understanding of your subject are more likely to succeed and do well. The book helps you to take control of your own learning, with self-management being an overarching skill underlying in each of the chapters. Self-knowledge and reflection will improve your grades and give you the qualities employers seek. It is an interactive book which prompts and guides you to more effective and efficient working habits.

To help you do this, each chapter provides *activities* which enable you to increase your skills. The activities in the book are not a once-and-for-all activity and should be revisited throughout your stay at university as your skills develop. It is important, therefore, that you reflect on your stages of learning by completing the *personal development planner* section at the end of each chapter. These PDPs can be used with your tutor, or linked into your department's own PDP to encourage you to move ever forward and onward.

It is advisable to start with the first chapter as this will give you that broad-brush view on getting started in Higher Education. If you are already in later years, you will also gain from the focus in this chapter.

For you – the tutor

Tutors wanting to use this book may be working centrally as learning advisers or with a department as a subject tutor. As a learning adviser you may be working individually with students, outside their curriculum or collaboratively with subject tutors. Whichever role you have, this activity-focused book could be adapted to your own circumstances and to slot in easily with other material.

The authors, as subject and skills tutors themselves, have developed this material from their own practice and tested the material with their students. Some suggestions for using the book are as follows.

Induction for first years. It is useful to include information from 'Learning in Higher Education', which gives a broad-brush view of moving into Higher Education. Chapters 1, 'Time management', 2, 'Managing your stress' and 3, 'Learning part time, online and on a work placement' are also useful for adaptation in induction sessions, both at undergraduate and postgraduate level.

- **Personal development planners**. Every chapter encourages students to reflect on the skills they are developing. You may expect students to carry out some of the activities in this book for initial proof of their reflective ability.
- **Reading and thinking critically**. As tutors we are all aware of the difficulty students have in rising above writing simple descriptive texts. Criticality is a skill that is valued, and encouraging criticality in later study years becomes an issue. The sections on reading, thinking and writing critically and reflection could be used in a project unit, or could be articulated across units to provide a sequential long, thin approach to embedding the relevant skills into the curriculum. Individual activities, such as Activity 7 in Chapter 7 'Reading critically', could be used as warm-up exercises to encourage more engagement in seminar or group discussions.
- **Presentation skills**. The chapters on teamwork and presenting your work have proved very useful for giving students guidance on poster preparation, oral presentations and working in real teams.
- **Work placement and professionalism**. For those students who undertake a work placement year, we know all too often that they

return to their final year having lost the 'edge' in terms of their learning and study practices. The final section of Chapter 3 could be used in a Year 2, Semester 2 workshop to look at strategies to offset this. The chapters on thinking critically, reflection, and ethics and integrity are suitable for adaptation to help students establish a personal framework for ongoing professional development and to explore the meaning of 'professionalism'.

- **Learning outcomes**. Each of the chapters conforms to academic practice and includes learning outcomes. There is no assessment, but informal reflective exercises at the beginning and the end could serve to 'assess' increased awareness.

Getting the most out of the book

Each chapter opens with a *navigation page* giving a brief overview of the sections within the chapter along with the learning outcomes. This means that you can easily dip into the sections and activities you want. Each chapter begins and ends with your reflection on how you feel your skills are developing. It is valuable to reflect on your skills prior to reading the chapter and then see how you have increased your awareness as a result of working through the activities. These mini PDPs are intended to be used as part of your institution's own system.

Some of the *activities* require you to take stock of your own skills while others give you valuable practice, i.e. putting into operation what you have read. Towards the end of each chapter you will find a *summary map* combining all the parts of the chapter into a visible whole. Finally, each chapter also gives you advice on where you might go for further help if you still feel unsure of your performance

Today's business and management studies students and practitioners need to engage with a range of truly global issues which include ethical and socially responsible business practices, real-world strategic orientation, and diverse and intercultural working. This book is designed to be used whilst you are a student, whilst you are on a work placement and as you move into your graduate employment.

Unlock your potential

You have the potential to do well, obtain good grades and be employed in an area that interests you. So, use this book as part of your strategy for personal development and realise your potential.

In times of change, learners inherit the Earth, while the learned find themselves beautifully equipped to deal with a world that no longer exists.

Eric Hoffer, an important social thinker/writer of the twentieth century

Publisher's acknowledgements

We are grateful to the following for permission to reproduce copyright material:

Figures

Figure 3.2: Adapted from *Integrating Technology in Learning and Teaching*, London, Kogan Page (Maier, P. and Warren, A. 2000).

Tables

Page 49: Adapted from *First Things First: Coping with the Ever-increasing Demands of the Workplace*, London, Simon & Schuster (Covey, S. R., Merrill, A. and Merrill, R. 1994).

Text

Page 236: Example adapted courtesy of David Brown.

In some instances we have been unable to trace the owners of copyright material, and we would appreciate any information that would enable us to do so.

Learning in Higher Education

Learning in Higher Education is, and should be, challenging. The challenges for you are at many levels: your engagement with the subject, your ability to manage your time and your motivation to take responsibility for your own learning. Those who take up the challenges and develop a deep understanding of their subject are more likely to succeed and do well. Those of you who do the minimum work and take a 'surface' approach to learning are more likely to fail or drop out. Although your tutors and advisers are there to give you the support you need, the decision to take this responsibility, to reflect and act on your development, is yours and yours alone. Take it and succeed.

We don't receive wisdom; we must discover it for ourselves after a journey that no one can take for us or spare us.
Marcel Proust (French novelist, 1871–1922)

In this chapter you will:

1. recognise what makes you a proficient learner;
2. understand what plagiarism is and how to avoid it;
3. identify the key documents that describe your programme and units;
4. know how to start thinking about your employability.

USING THIS CHAPTER

If you want to dip into the sections	Page	If you want to try the activities	Page
1 Become a proficient learner	2	1 Your motivation to learn	3
2 Academic integrity – plagiarism	12	2 Create a concept map	7
3 Understand your programme or course	15	3 How do you feel about reflecting on your progress?	10
4 Your employability	16	4 Why do some people plagiarise?	14
5 Going forward	19	5 Update your personal development planner	19

Estimate your current levels of confidence. At the end of the chapter you will have the chance to re-assess these levels where you can incorporate this into your PDP. Mark between 1 (poor) and 5 (good) for the following:

I understand what I can do to become a proficient learner.	I know what plagiarism is.	I understand the key documents describing my course.	I know why I should consider employability throughout my studies.

Date: _____

1 Become a proficient learner

You may not think this, but being a good learner is a skill. It is not just about sitting in front of your book and reading and hoping something will 'stick', or about completing yet another problem sheet or exam. Of course, you can go through your studies just doing this. However, your learning will be fairly shallow and often crammed in before the next exam. In order to become interested and proficient in the topic you are studying, you will need to go a bit deeper and your ability to do this makes you a skilled and lifelong learner; a learner that not only knows 'what', but also 'how' and 'why'.

Knowing 'how' and 'why' is increasingly important as knowledge has a shelf life, like so many other things. This is referred to as the **half-life of knowledge** and, to give you a flavour of this, 95 per cent of the drugs in use in 1978 were unheard of in 1950 (Smith, 1978, p. 914). Environmental Science, for example, probably has a half-life of 1–3 years, especially in relation to environmental law and aspects of climate change. Since knowledge is an economic resource in a knowledge economy, having up-to-date knowledge is vital for a company. Employers therefore will want employees who are prepared to be lifelong learners. Having the skills to do this, with study skills being a prime example, becomes an important employability skill.

Your degree of motivation for your subject will determine how you study and how much effort you put in. If you are not very motivated you will more than likely be someone who will memorise enough facts to get you through the coursework and exams; you will be what is called a 'surface learner', take little time to reflect on your learning, have a 'make-do' attitude to your studies and have difficulty managing your commitments. As you can imagine, this is not the ideal student, or the ideal employee. This lack of motivation is very evident both to your tutors and to potential employers.

Therefore, learning is something that is not restricted to your time at university. It is more than likely going to be part of you for the rest of your life. In order to do this you need to:

- be responsible for your own learning;
- know yourself as a learner;
- reflect on your learning.

Be responsible for your own learning

The first thing you must do is to get to know yourself as a learner. It is important you are honest with yourself. Your mode of learning in the past may have served you well, but now you need to make a step change in order to get the most out of your studies. Activity 1, below, indicates some of the features that characterise dependent and independent learning. As you can see, the 'independent learner' shows a greater responsibility for his or her learning.

ACTIVITY 1 Your motivation to learn

At this point in time, where would you place yourself?

Your learning	A	B	Generally me (A or B)
Motivation to learn	I am motivated to get my degree and as long as it is a respectable grade I don't mind. I expect my tutors to provide me with interesting material to keep me on track. I will do work only if I am going to get assessed. If I get a bad degree mark it is probably due to a bad course.	I expect a well-organised course and good teaching, but I know this is a two-way process and I have to find out information myself in order to complete assignments as well as seek support from various people. I know my final degree will reflect not only the course organisation and teaching but also the amount of work I have put in myself.	
Learning resources	The content and resources are determined by my tutors and I limit myself to what is provided for me. I think exams are passed by memorising facts and I have a good memory.	Although my tutors have given me guidance on the resources I need, I happily seek out my own resources. I really want to understand the principles and concepts of my subject, not just a load of facts.	

Your learning	A	B	Generally me (A or B)
Time	Tutors tend to set coursework deadlines too close together, so when I try to get the work done I am having to cram everything in at the same time to meet these deadlines. I prefer working to tight deadlines and this means I leave all my work to the last minute. It would be better if tutors spread out the deadlines as that would suit me better.	Although we get coursework deadlines set close together, we are told in advance and I try where possible to set my own staggered deadlines so that I am not working on all coursework at the same time.	
Reflection on learning	I find little opportunity in my studies to do this and we are generally not encouraged to do it either, so why bother? I had to do this in school and feel that it should be left there.	I am keen to reflect on what and how I learn. Tutorials and seminars are good for this as discussion helps me see what I understand and don't understand. I always want to know how I can improve.	

Are you predominantly A or B? You may have guessed that A represents a dependent learner while B is an independent learner.

How independent and responsible do you feel you are with regard to your learning? What might you do to improve this – write three things in the box below. Read the remainder of this chapter and identify the later chapters you think could be relevant to you.

1.

2.

3.

NOTE Your tutors can only do so much. It is up to you to be prepared to take full advantage of what is on offer.

Know yourself as a learner

At this stage of your studies you are really preparing yourself for work and part of that, as indicated earlier, is about being a lifelong, independent learner. Increasingly employers will expect you to learn on the job, take further study or follow a continuing professional development programme. Being able therefore to reflect on how best you learn, on the skills you are acquiring and on improvements you need to make will be vital as you progress your career. Take a look at some of the relevant later chapters in areas you feel you could do with checking.

What kind of learner are you?

In Chapter 5, 'Working in a real and diverse team', you are asked to identify the kind of learner you feel you are based on the learning styles proposed by two psychologists, Peter Honey and Alan Mumford (1992):

An activist: you like to learn by doing things. You are happier with project work and all kinds of active learning. You are less happy reading long papers, analysing data and sitting in lectures.	**A reflector:** you are more cautious and like to weigh up all the issues before acting. When you make a decision, it is thought through. You are probably happy to work on a project if you are given time to observe all the facts before making a decision. You dislike having work dumped on you and get worried by tight deadlines.
A pragmatist: you like taking theories and putting them into practice and you need to see the benefit and relevance of what you are doing. If you are learning something you feel has no practical value, you lose interest. You may want to ask your tutor: 'why are we learning this?' If you are a student who says 'I don't like this course as it is all theory' then your learning preference is probably 'pragmatist' or 'activist'.	**A theorist:** you like to understand what is behind certain actions and enjoy working through issues theoretically and in a well-structured way. Whether you apply it or not doesn't interest you so much. You may be the one to ask questions as to why and how something occurs. You dislike unstructured sessions and dislike it when you are asked to reflect on some activity or say what you felt about it.

Each of these learning styles represents a point on the learning cycle proposed by David Kolb in 1975 (see figure that follows) showing that when we learn something we need concrete experience, and time to observe and reflect on abstract concepts and theories before we apply these ideas in new situations. We can start this learning cycle at any point, and as a learner we are happier in some of the stages than others and it is this that gives us our learning preferences.

Which part of the learning cycle do you feel more comfortable with and how might this affect your learning? Can you find ways of working around other aspects of the learning cycle that you don't feel so comfortable with? To be a successful learner you will need to be able to at least function on all points of the learning cycle, even though you may be happier in one area.

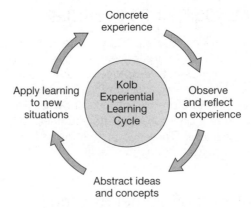

Kolb's experiential learning cycle
Adapted from Smith (2001)

Move from novice to expert

Knowing how novices see things and how experts see things is a help-ful shorthand in understanding how we learn. No one is expecting you to become an expert overnight, but you will see your tutors as experts and wonder why you can't understand things that appear so simple to them, and vice versa they may be puzzled why you can't understand something. But just remember, you are probably much better on mobile phone technol-ogy than any of your lecturers!

How often have you felt that you just don't know what your brain can do with yet another piece of information? These pieces seem to be all uncon-nected. You feel frustrated as you panic about trying to remember it all. This is because you haven't yet been able to process this information into chunks and store it away ready for retrieval when you want it. The more you learn, reflect and revise a subject, the more you will start to see patterns in the information and you can start to group things. At that point, these chunks of information become knowledge and you can then start applying it.

One of the major things that experts do that you won't do as a novice is find order and patterns in information and they do this by chunking pieces of information together; they know how to make these chunks and identify the patterns. This means that, unlike novices, they are not working with discrete pieces of information, they already know how it fits into a larger jigsaw. Experts therefore have that bigger picture.

One way to help you integrate these pieces of information, and start to build the bigger picture, is to draw a concept map (see Activity 2). This technique was developed by Joseph Novak in the 1960s and is a visual method of showing linkages between ideas, concepts or topics. Each topic is linked by a line that indicates the nature of that relationship. See the example below.

Concept maps can be drawn as hierarchies, flow charts or networks (as in the figure below). If you prefer a more linear approach, use an indented list that indicates at least a hierarchical relationship. However, a list on its own is less useful as you need to see the relationships between things.

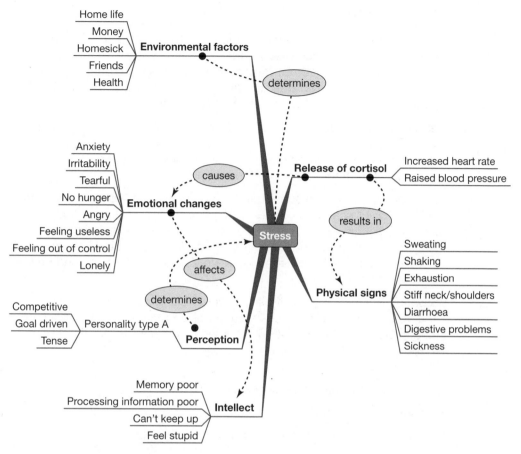

Home life
Money
Homesick
Friends
Health
Environmental factors

determines

Anxiety
Irritability
Tearful
No hunger
Angry
Feeling useless
Feeling out of control
Lonely
Emotional changes

causes

Release of cortisol
Increased heart rate
Raised blood pressure

Stress

results in

affects

Competitive
Goal driven
Tense
Personality type A
determines
Perception

Physical signs
Sweating
Shaking
Exhaustion
Stiff neck/shoulders
Diarrhoea
Digestive problems
Sickness

Memory poor
Processing information poor
Can't keep up
Feel stupid
Intellect

Produced using MindManager

Concept maps enable you to see the relationship between concepts and how chunks of things belong together. You may find this difficult at the beginning of a topic, but if you persist it will pay off and you will develop an integrated view of your topic and start to mimic the experts. Also, for each topic you are revising for an exam, finalise your revision with a concept map. Then use your concept maps for quick revision prior to the exam.

ACTIVITY 2 Create a concept map

Look at Chapter 1, 'Managing your time', and develop a concept map for your current approach to time management using the concepts in that chapter. How well can you piece together information into a set of related topics? Try using this technique when you are note taking. You may first have to take a set of linear notes as you read through a text, but then afterwards you can link it together through a concept map. If you really don't like creating concept maps, write out a hierarchical list or flow chart.

Get organised

In order to be an effective learner you need to understand how you learn and how you manage yourself in order to learn. Sue Drew from Sheffield Hallam University carried out a piece of research in 2001 asking students what helped or hindered their academic achievement (Drew, 2001). She reported that students came up with four main areas:

- self-management, including taking responsibility for their own learning;
- motivation to study;
- understanding and reflection of their learning experience;
- support from their tutors and the institution.

These findings were also supported by a report on the first-year experience of UK Higher Education students (Yorke and Longden, 2007). Some of the features that first-year students do not like are workload and time management, confusion about assessments and lack of feedback. If you are a first-year student, you need to work on your time management and be prepared to ask for feedback.

Motivation to study is your primary driver in being successful in your studies. If you don't feel motivated to study, or you feel you have chosen the wrong subject, stop now and consider what you want to do. Select one of the following questions to answer privately:

1. I want to study this subject because …

2. I know I want to study, but I'd prefer to study …

3. I don't really know why I am here, I would rather do …

From now on, it will be assumed that you are motivated to study.

Self-management is an overarching skill you need to develop. As an 18-year-old first-year student this may be the first time you have left home and you have to sort out accommodation, finance, new friendship groups and understand all the documentation associated with your study programme as well as start to learn something. If you are a mature or international student you will have additional issues to contend with. So, being able to manage all these aspects of your 'new life' can be daunting.

You need to quickly identify where you can get support for your needs. The Students Union is an excellent place to start. They will have an overview of all the services available to you at your institution. Your teaching department will probably have a student office where you can sort out specific things relating to your study. Get familiar with what is available and build a rapport with key people.

If you feel that self-management is an issue for you, take a look at the chapters on stress and time management and develop your own strategies.

Develop an attitude

The greatest discovery of my generation is that a human being can alter his life by altering his attitudes of mind.

William James (US pragmatist, philosopher and psychologist, 1842–1910)

Developing a 'can do' attitude is going to help you enormously. This will enable you to manage yourself and feel in control of events around you. Your confidence will develop and you will easily be able to manage your time and stress. Chapter 2, 'Managing your stress', will help you work through the concept of self-belief or 'self-efficacy', a term that was first coined by the psychologist Albert Bandura. For self-belief to gain a hold you need to:

1. be motivated in what you do;

2. believe in yourself;

3. recognise and deal with things that stress you so you can control your anxiety;

4. look for solutions, not obstacles;

5. organise your time so you feel on top of things and in control;

6. reflect on and recognise your strengths and weaknesses in order to make informed choices.

If you feel this is an issue for you, you may want to look Chapter 2 on managing stress now.

Reflect on your learning

If someone said to you 'Reflect on what you have just said for a moment ...', you know you would be expected to think about what you have just said, and then reconsider the implications of it and what you've learned from it. What you are actually doing is: (a) recapping on what you said (replay), (b) taking a more objective look at the implications of what you said (reframing your actions) and (c) learning from it (reassessing your actions and future actions). Activity 3 helps you reflect on your learning.

ACTIVITY 3 How do you feel about reflecting on your progress?

What I feel ...	Usually me	Think again ...
I find reflection difficult because I can't see what I am learning.		Work with a friend. Sometimes it is difficult when you first start to be objective about your own skills, especially when we are encouraged to be modest most of the time.
I find it a waste of time.		OK, don't call it reflecting, but make a list of the things you can do well, OK, or poorly and work out how you can improve. If someone asked you in an interview whether you were a good team player, how would you answer and if they asked what makes a good team player, what would you say?
I can't see where I'm developing skills in my courses.		Each course/unit should have a description of what you'll be expected to learn along with the assessment. Check the assessments and the learning outcomes (these should also include a list of skills you're learning) and from this you can see what skills and knowledge you are developing.
I don't know what to do with my PDP when I complete it.		Your PDP should be part of every year in your degree. In some degrees it is built into the first year and then vaguely mentioned in years after that. Try to keep it up to date, this is for you and you can use it to adjust your CV and keep you prepared for those interviews and even for part-time work.

Sum up your feelings about reflecting on your skills and knowledge

Reflection is important if you are to develop your understanding of your skills, yourself and your knowledge. You will be expected to work in teams, write essays and give presentations, etc., and through reflection you will be able to recap, reframe and re-assess your learning. Many students dislike the reflection aspect, but once they get used to doing it they see the value.

For most of the time we go about our business, interacting with people, developing skills and gaining knowledge without really being aware that we are doing this. A lot of what we learn is 'implicit', which means we are not aware that we are learning. Sometimes it takes another person to say what you have been learning in order to realise how you are developing. Implicit learning therefore comprises skills and knowledge you have, but you don't know you have. However, if you reflect on what you have been doing and you are able to objectively 'stand back' and think about it, you start to see the skills and knowledge you have and these then become 'explicit', i.e. we are conscious of them. Once these are explicit we are able to refer to them in our CV, talk about them at an interview and plan to use them again. While our skills and knowledge remain implicit, we can only react to our environment and when someone asks us what we can do, we tend to look a bit vague and trot out the usual 'I don't know'. Good reflection therefore enables us to be more strategic and create opportunities to improve ourselves, while having a better understanding of how we will perform in a similar eventuality. This is the hallmark of a good graduate.

Reflection is not just thinking about what happened at the end of some event; it occurs at various stages. For an assignment it is:

- at the beginning when you reflect on what you have to do;
- during the assignment where you adjust your plans in light of your experience;
- afterwards, and it is this reflection that you resent. However, post-reflection provides you with the strategic information you need to take forward to the next assignment and it also makes you articulate what you have learned.

Students in clinical practice for example will be familiar (if not now, then later) with 'reflection **in** action' and 'reflection **on** action', coined by Donald Schön (1930–1997), an American philosopher whose work has been adopted by many in the health professions in order to develop the 'reflective practitioner'.

When studying, reflection can take many forms, such as the following:

Personal development planner	This is a record of your own assessment of your developing skills, which should include any part-time or volunteering work you do.
Reflective aspects of coursework, e.g. working in groups	Sometimes a formal part of your coursework assessment.
Tutor feedback	Feedback from your tutors is important for your learning. Most students complain they don't have enough feedback. Try asking for specific feedback when you hand in your coursework if you feel you are not getting the feedback you want. Remember, good feedback enables you to make an action plan for improvement.
Peer feedback	Sometimes you may be asked to assess your peers, e.g. on an oral presentation, part of a report or their ability to work in a group. Once again, be objective and act fairly. Don't give marks on your likes or dislikes for that person. Be professional.

End-of-unit evaluation	This allows you to reflect on the whole unit, how coherent it was, how much you've learned, the organisation and how well you've been taught. Think about this objectively and professionally and reflect fairly. Don't give your tutor a low score because you simply don't like him or her or because you got some low marks.
Tutorials and seminars	An opportunity to go over difficult topics and discuss.
A student representative on a department committee	A chance to represent fellow students and reflect on your educational provision constructively.
Study groups with friends	Informal opportunity.

The PDP is the key document for recording your reflections. Ensure you keep this up to date, whether your tutors ask you or not. This is primarily **for you** and the more explicit you can be with what you know and can do, the easier it is to talk about it to a potential employer. All the chapters in this book have been designed to incorporate reflective aspects; try using these activities to get you in the habit of reflecting. Activity 3 asked you to consider what you know about reflection; Chapter 10 will explore reflection further.

2 Academic integrity – plagiarism

A Times Higher Education UK survey (March 2006) found that one in six students admitted to copying from friends, one in ten to looking for essays online and four in ten said they knew someone who had passed off someone else's work as their own. This is now recognised as an international problem and universities across the world are starting to tackle it. The main problem with academic cheating, particularly if it escalates, is that it is unfair to those students who don't cheat and eventually will undermine the value of degree awards, as the standard cannot then be guaranteed. Would you like to be treated by a doctor or a nurse who you knew cheated throughout their degree? Would you like to walk over a bridge where the structural calculations were checked by the structural engineer who cheated through his/her degree? I am sure the answer is a resounding 'no'.

Violating academic integrity can take several forms.

1. No referencing

- You must have read some authors' work, even if it is in a textbook, to give you ideas for your paper. Make sure you have the correct reference at the back of your paper. Ensure you use the correct referencing style for your subject. If you are not sure, ask your tutor or a librarian in your institution.

2. No in-text referencing (citations)

- If you report a fact, or some information from an author, you need to put that person's name as close to the statement as possible and use the following convention:

  – Barlow (2001) discovered that ...

  – The term 'flight or fight' was first used by Cannon (1920) when he ...

  – Innis and Shaw (1997) surveyed students' study habits and found ...

You still need to put the full reference at the end of your paper.

3. Taking chunks of text without attributing it to the original author

- This happens quite frequently. You may find a really good website and just copy and paste chunks of information into your text. You can take chunks of text from another author if you put it in quotes and make an in-text reference next to it.

4. Buying an essay online or from a friend

- This is quite simply cheating and unethical.

5. Taking part of your work from a friend (colluding)

- It is easy for your tutors to see if you and your friend have handed in essentially the same work, even if it is only in parts. You are both liable and could be accused of colluding. Similarly, if a friend asks to see your work, you may not know if he/she is copying it or not, so it is better not to share your work before you hand it in.

6. Feeling your English is not good enough

- Sometimes if you are not a confident writer you feel that you just cannot write out that idea better than the author. No one is expecting you to write better than the author and it is important that you put down ideas in your own words and then attribute the idea to the original author. If you feel your writing is very poor, you should consult your institution and get support.

Are you at risk of plagiarising?

The first two instances, in particular, are very often due to the fact that you don't fully realise what plagiarism is. In your first year, you should be given a talk by your tutor or someone from the library explaining what plagiarism is and what happens if you are accused of it. If you aren't given any advice, carry out a web search: there's plenty of information to select from. The other violations of academic integrity are more associated with cheating and the most serious one relates to buying essays which you then pass off as your own.

If you find that you can't meet all your deadlines, whether because of part-time work, family, parents, sickness, lectures or coursework load, then you are at risk of cutting corners somewhere. If it is your coursework, and you feel tempted to buy an essay, or copy chunks from a website or your friend, then beware, as your institution may have strong penalties. Poor referencing is a lesser offence than buying an essay, but once you have been given a warning, you will also be subject to penalties relating to plagiarism. If managing time and stress is a problem, check later chapters in this book. Activity 4 helps you to consider why some people plagiarise.

ACTIVITY 4 Why do some people plagiarise?

Look at the following scenarios and identify why plagiarism could occur: (a) poor writing skills, (b) poor time management, (c) poor note-taking skills. Once you have done that, consider how that student could improve the situation to avoid falling into the trap of plagiarism.

Scenario	What would you recommend?
1 Sam is a first-year student. He is having difficulty organising himself and suddenly finds that several pieces of coursework are due. Time is not on his side so he asks a close friend if he can just look over his work so that he has some ideas. When the work was marked the tutor found these two pieces of work very similar and called them both in. They were both given an official warning.	Reason: a b c
2 Sally has been reading for her assignment for a few weeks and put in a lot of work. The work is due on Monday and it is now Friday. She has taken lots of notes and wants to start writing, but she realises she has a lot of information, but no references as to where she got it from. She has a vague idea of what the references are and decides to take a guess at the references; she is sure the marker won't notice.	Reason: a b c
3 Jamal feels that he doesn't write very well and whenever he reads anything he feels he can't put it better himself so tends to take chunks of information from books or a good website. The more he reads, the more inadequate he feels his writing ability is. This next coursework is an essay and he has decided to put in bits of text he has found on the web without putting it in quotes or making an in-text reference.	Reason: a b c

NOTE   When you take chunks of text and place them in your own work, it is obvious as the style changes dramatically. You don't have to be a forensic linguist to notice it.

In all of the scenarios above, there was no malicious attempt to cheat, but be careful, plagiarism is on the rise and institutions are under pressure to crack down. Some tutors are using anti-plagiarism software; the most well known for UK universities is 'Turnitin', which highlights potentially copied work (see www.plagiarism.org).

For more information on plagiarism, or academic integrity as it is now called, see Chapter 12, 'Understanding academic integrity: learner ethics and plagiarism'.

3 Understand your programme or course

Your institution and lecturers will have spent a surprisingly large amount of time preparing programme and course information for you. You might just see it as a heap of information that you may get round to reading one day, and then when you do get around to reading some of it, you don't understand all that educational mumbo-jumbo. So let's try to dissect some of the things that go into these documents for the UK.

The programme specification

The programme refers to the degree you are studying for, whether it is an FdA in Business & Management, a BA in Business Studies or an MBA. The programme specification tells you the aim of the programme as a whole across the three or four years of your study. It also gives you some idea of what you will learn through a list of learning outcomes. The learning outcomes indicate what you should know and be able to do at the end of your studies. If you read nothing else, read the learning outcomes. There will also be information on how you get support while at the institution.

This document should be available to you either on request or on your department's website. Ideally you should look at this before you sign up for your degree, but not many students realise that this document exists.

Module/unit/course description

Every programme will be supported by units, modules or courses (each department seems to have different names for these). The unit is where the learning and teaching takes place. You may find you have core units and elective units. Each of these units also has a description outlining the aims of the unit, the learning outcomes and the assessments.

It is important to read the unit description, as your assessment will be based on the learning outcomes stated there.

About credits

In the UK, institutions of Higher Education use a Credit Accumulation and Transfer Scheme (CATS), sometime written as credits. This system allows us to value and measure the size of a unit. A three-year honours degree will accumulate 360 credits (120 each year). Each institution will package the number of credits you have to do in different ways.

NOTE It is a good idea to ask your tutors how many hours of learning (this includes face-to-face teaching and private study time) a credit is worth. This will give you some idea of the credit value of the unit. For example, if one credit equates to ten hours of learning, you are looking at 100 hours of learning for a ten-credit unit. Check how many face-to-face hours you have and then you can see the amount of work expected of you as private study for this unit.

As the European Higher Education systems become more aligned, we shall be moving to a European Credit Transfer and Accumulation System (ECTS), and currently 10 UK credits are worth approximately 5 ECTS. If you go on an exchange visit with the Erasmus/Socrates scheme and have to collect credits for your course, make sure you check out how many you have to do.

4 Your employability

If you are in your first few years of study, you may wonder why you should be thinking of employability now. Well, you should be. Employability is about you consciously developing your knowledge and a wide range of skills even if you still don't know what you want to do later. You record your developing skills in your PDP, which will enable you to see your progress across the years. You should take advantage of what is on offer now, be that sponsorship schemes, volunteering, work placements, career talks, talks from past students, career sessions or full career management courses (with or without credits), as this will help you develop yourself and focus on what you really want. It will also help you with part-time work.

If you are in your final year of studies, you may still not know what you want to do, you may want to take a gap year or you may have found the job you want. Make sure you complete your PDP as this will enable you to articulate what you know and can do as well as remind you where the evidence is to support this. You should visit your Careers Service for advice – most institutions allow you to use this service for several years after graduation.

What is the difference between employability and employment?

Employability refers to your personal qualities, your attitude to work, the knowledge you have and the skills, both practical and intellectual, that you have developed. This refers therefore to your ability to find a job, stay in that job and progress to the next step. Employment refers to simply 'getting a job'. One of the aims of Higher Education is to make you more employable and by doing that also develop your interests in a particular topic.

What do employers want?

Your degree is only the first tick in the box. For the graduate jobs that you will be expecting to do once you have finished, your degree will just enable you to apply, not necessarily get the job. A 2007 government report (Leitch Review, 2007) stated that 40 per cent of the adult population should have a first degree by 2020. So if you want to get noticed, you will have to develop some aspect of yourself that marks you out individually.

Some employers want graduates with discipline-specific knowledge while others are interested in the graduate quality regardless of discipline. The graduateness qualities that employers refer to are knowledge of a subject area, analytical skills, interpersonal skills, communication skills, time-management skills, personal belief, taking responsibility for your own learning, and the ability to reflect and improve yourself. You will be able to work on all of these areas while at university if you take the opportunities available.

What's the knowledge economy – and why should it concern me?

We are living through a knowledge explosion. New communications technologies enable research and new knowledge to be exchanged much faster than ever before. Knowledge becomes a valuable resource and since it is moving so fast, the life span of knowledge, especially technologies, is ever shortened. We are all in a vicious circle of trying to 'keep up' with the latest knowledge.

During your studies, therefore, you will acquire knowledge that could be out of date in five years, and sometimes less. It is important, therefore, that you learn a set of skills that enables you to update your knowledge and make you a proficient lifelong learner. The whole purpose of this book hinges on this point. This book aims to help with personal development where you can enhance your skills rather than immediate quick-fix tips. It is valuable, therefore, to understand the current thrust of Higher Education worldwide.

Look at the map below and see whether you can add any more aspects of employability that apply to you.

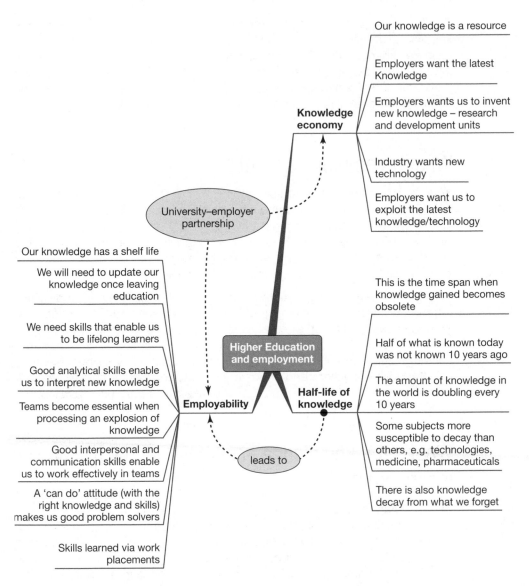

Source of information on half-life of knowledge from Peter Knight-Moore (1997)

What should I be doing now?

You will probably have been given a PDP by your department. Some departments will fully develop this with you, while others will have it very much on the side. The PDP is for *you* and regardless of how your tutors feel about this, it is in your interest to keep it as up to date as you can.

This really is your evidence of how you are developing, within and outside your studies.

Use your part-time job to your advantage and include what you are learning in your PDP. If you are alert to what you are learning, you will be able to articulate it. Even sitting at a checkout in a supermarket will mean that you have to learn to deal with difficult customers. Take note on how you do this and how effective (or not!) you are. How have you improved this skill?

Take advantage of volunteering and other similar schemes, career-management sessions or courses, talks and visits from employers.

Once you have left your university, you will find that most offer access to the Careers Service for a few years after graduation.

5 Going forward

This chapter has set the scene for the remainder of the book, and from working through it you may know now which section to dip into next. Before you do that, take time to assess how prepared you are to take full advantage of learning in Higher Education. How does your current assessment compare with your assessment at the beginning of the chapter?

ACTIVITY 5 Update your personal development planner

Grade your confidence on a scale of 1–5 where 1 = poor and 5 = good.

Moving into Higher Education – my plan	Confidence level 1–5	Plans to improve
I understand what I can do to become a proficient learner, e.g. be responsible for my own learning, understand myself as a learner, get organised, see the value of reflection (via PDPs). *Section 1*		
I understand the principles of plagiarism and realise why it has to be controlled. *Section 2*		
I understand the key documents relating to my programme and courses. *Section 3*		
I understand why employability is something I should consider throughout my studies and what to do about it. *Section 4*		

Getting extra help

- Your local students union as well as the National Union of Students at www.nusonline.co.uk.

- If you have any kind of condition that you feel could interfere with your studies, check out your own institution. There are usually units within student services that are available for all kinds of help.

- If you feel you aren't coping, first check with your personal tutor (or someone in your department), then go and get help from one of the specialist units in your institution.

- There is always someone in student services, or the Students Union, to show you where to get help with finances.

- If you feel you are on the wrong course, talk to your personal tutor and see whether you can change. Do this early in your first year if possible.

- If you want to do some volunteering, first go to your Students Union – they will know of schemes within your institution.

- Don't forget the library. Staff are usually very friendly and more than happy to help you. Libraries can appear daunting, but don't be afraid to ask.

References

- Drew, S. (2001) 'Student perceptions of what helps them learn and develop in Higher Education', *Teaching in Higher Education*, 6(3), 309–31.

- Honey, P. and Mumford, A. (1992) *The Manual of Learning Styles*. Maidenhead, Peter Honey.

- Knight-Moore, P. T. (1997) 'The half-life of knowledge and structural reform of the education sector for the global knowledge-based economy', Paper prepared for the Forum on Education in the Information Age, organised by the Inter-American Development Bank and the Global Information Infrastructure Commission and hosted by the Universidad de los Andes Cartagena, Colombia, 9–11 July 1997. Available at: www.knight-moore.com/pubs/halflife.html [last accessed December 2009].

- Kolb, D. A. and Fry, R. (1975) 'Toward an applied theory of experiential learning', in C. Cooper (ed.) *Theories of Group Process*. London, John Wiley.

- Leitch Review (2007) *Prosperity for all in the Global Economy: World Class Skills*, H.M. Treasury, UK Government, available at: www.hm-treasury.gov.uk/leitch [last accessed December 2009].

- Schön, D. A. at Informal Education (Infed), available at: www.infed.org/thinkers/et-schon.htm [last accessed December 2009].

- Smith, E. P. (1978) 'Measuring professional obsolescence: a half life model for the physician', *The Academy of Management Review*, available online at Jstor, pp. 914–17. Available from: www.jstor.org/search/ArticleLocatorSearch [last accessed December 2009].

■ Smith, M. K. (2001) 'David A. Kolb on experiential learning', *The Encyclopedia of Informal Education*, available at: www.infed.org/biblio/b-explrn.htm [last accessed December 2009].

■ Yorke, M. and Longden, B. (2007) *The First-year Experience in Higher Education in the UK*, Higher Education Academy, available at: www.headcademy.ac.uk/resources/publications/exchange/FYEFinalReport.pdf [last accessed December 2009].

Behaving professionally

> *'Today's labour market is bringing home to students the need to take personal responsibility for developing the skills and attributes that will help make them employable and their employers competitive. It's also teaching them the necessity of presenting themselves and what they can offer to a prospective employer well.'*
>
> David Lammy, Minister of State for higher education and intellectual property
> (CBI, 2009)

How you look, talk, write, act and work indicates how professional or amateur you are. Society has tended not to emphasise the importance of professionalism, so people tend to believe that amateur work is normal and as a consequence 'just getting by' is an attitude many people accept. But things have changed, as Lammy's statement makes clear.

Out of the top ten things that matter to business leaders when seeking to recruit graduates, honesty and integrity are at the top of the list (IoD, 2007). Other top ten things include being reliable, being hardworking, being punctual and being able to meet deadlines as well as having a good work ethic and a positive 'can do' attitude. These things are not achieved with a 'just getting by' attitude. These employability skills form the core of what it takes to be a professionally oriented graduate. Your time at university can be one in which you learn to be professional, or remain an amateur.

In this chapter you will:

- learn about professional behaviour and why it is important;
- explore some ways of auditing your professionalism;
- examine how the synthesis of university and practical knowledge contributes to professionalism.

USING THIS CHAPTER

If you want to dip into the sections	Page	If you want to try the activities	Page
4 Using this book to support your professional development	32	4 Working with 360 feedback* (*see note in section about this activity)	32
5 On reflection	33	5 Update your personal development planner	34

Estimate your current levels of confidence. At the end of the chapter you will have the chance to re-assess these levels where you can incorporate this into your PDP. Mark between 1 (poor) and 5 (good) for the following:

I understand the importance of professional behaviour.	I know what the key attributes are of someone who behaves professionally.	I can audit my professional behaviour skills.	I know how to manage my professional behaviour development.	I understand how to apply professional behaviour to my university studies.

Date: _____

1 Why is professional behaviour important?

'Our people make us stand out as a firm. So we chose the best and invest heavily in them.'

(PwC cited in Realworld, 2009)

In Chapter 3, Section 3, we look at maintaining your learning whilst on a work placement and emphasise how important this is. We end that chapter by suggesting that it is the start of the rest of your life. As the PricewaterhouseCoopers quote makes clear, graduate employers want the best. If you have the mindset that once you are in graduate employment your learning days are over and all you have to do is turn up, do some work and get highly paid, then you will fall far short of your aspirations. The reality of today's complex globalised environment means that if you want to do well and earn the respect, and the income, you think you deserve, you will have to be **proactive** in maintaining your learning, knowledge and skills set (see 'Learning in Higher Education', Section 4, 'Your employability'). As the Institute of Directors research shows, however, it is **more** than this: the professional mindset also includes honesty, integrity, reliability, punctuality, hard working, 'can do' attitude, and results orientation (IoD, 2007). Simply put, professional behaviour is important if you are to achieve your personal goals and contribute both to the success of your employer and to that of a more sustainable and ethically driven future world.

2 What do we mean by 'professional'?

One specific meaning of 'professional' is someone who belongs to a profession (for example, a lawyer) and can practise only if they are registered with their profession's governing body and are subject to its formal regulation. The broader meaning of 'professional' is the adoption of attitudes and behaviours that are **professional** in nature. These attributes will in part be governed by values, expectations, principles and policies that come from your employer, from the legal and regulatory framework that all business has to operate within, and from the broader social context within which this takes place. Fundamentally, however, it is your 'internalised' governance (e.g. attitude, values, behaviour, responsibility and social skills) that will identify you as truly professional. Explore this in Activity 1.

ACTIVITY 1 Do I have professional attributes?

Consider each set of statements in the table below and rate yourself by circling where you think you currently lie on the scale, left to right. You can do this in relation to your university experience or your work/employment experience, as the mindset issues apply equally to both. The most important thing is that your self-appraisal is **honest and considered**.

When faced with a new task I try to learn every aspect of it.	+2	+1	0	−1	−2	When faced with a new task I skip the learning process whenever possible.
In any context I try to discover what is needed and wanted.	+2	+1	0	−1	−2	In any context I assume what others need and want.
I try to look, speak and dress like a professional.	+2	+1	0	−1	−2	I think others should just accept my casual appearance and speech.
I have a clean and orderly desk/work area.	+2	+1	0	−1	−2	I have a messy, disorganised or dirty desk/work area.
I tend to be focused and clear-headed.	+2	+1	0	−1	−2	I tend to be confused and distracted.
I try not to let mistakes slide by.	+2	+1	0	−1	−2	I ignore or hide mistakes.
I am willing to take on difficult assignments.	+2	+1	0	−1	−2	I try to avoid difficult work.
I complete projects as soon as possible.	+2	+1	0	−1	−2	I am surrounded by unfinished work piled on unfinished work.
I tend to remain level-headed and optimistic when the going gets tough.	+2	+1	0	−1	−2	I tend to get upset and assume the worst when the going gets tough.

I handle money and accounts very carefully.	+2	+1	0	−1	−2	I am 'easy come, easy go' with money or accounts.
I face up to other people's upsets and problems.	+2	+1	0	−1	−2	I avoid others' problems.
I produce more than expected.	+2	+1	0	−1	−2	I produce just enough to get by.
I produce a high-quality product or service.	+2	+1	0	−1	−2	I produce a medium to low-quality product or service.
I work hard to be respected and don't take anything for granted.	+2	+1	0	−1	−2	I expect the world to respect me whatever.
Add each column						
Total these 5 scores =						

Now total the circled scores in each column and then add up these five scores to produce an overall total.

See the feedback on activities section for further comment on this activity.

In an examination of a number of business and financial scandals of the time, Fassin (2005) summarised business ethics as 'doing the correct things, and doing the things correctly; doing honourable business, and doing business honourably'. Since then, other examples of unprofessional and unethical business and financial behaviours have created global economic problems; hence the priority employers now place on professional behaviour. If 'behaving professionally' is substituted for 'business ethics', then Fassin's statement becomes a useful summary of the idea of internalised governance, in other words the personal responsibility we must each take for how we behave as professionals.

Mapping professional attributes

There is a fair degree of agreement about what the attributes of professional behaviour are. This point of view from Professional Practice for Sustainable Development, albeit from a science perspective, is one expression of this:

1. The ability to engage customers in discussion about sustainable development with the aim of gaining a higher profile for sustainability in project plans.

2. The ability to communicate good science appropriately and effectively to other professionals and the public alike. Professionals need to get the public on the side of science. Good communication could overcome some of the scepticism of science.

3. The ability to view their professional activities in a holistic way and apply systems thinking skills when finding solutions to specific problems.

4. The motivation and ability to set a good example.

5. Recognition of the need and the ability to take account of ethical considerations when offering solutions even though these may not be 'scientific'.

6. The ability to make decisions based on incomplete information.

7. The ability to integrate learning with working.

Source: Professional Practice for Sustainable Development (PP4SD, 2006)

Hall and Berardino (2006), writing in a business ethics context, variously identify the following attributes of professional behaviour:

> 'Professional behaviors may include time management skills (e.g., regular and punctual attendance), making ethical decisions, participating in professional organizations, appropriate professional appearance, and appropriate meeting behaviours (e.g., limited cell phone use) ... the abilities to demonstrate self-discipline, act ethically, work co-operatively, work alone, and accept criticism (Otter, 2003) ... the appropriate use of office computers for personal business' (pp. 407–13)

Although there are different emphases in these examples, we can nonetheless identify the attributes of professional behaviour from these examples and others. These attributes range from aspects of our personal presentation through skills, attitudes, values, behaviours to the approach to knowledge we take. These are summarised in the figure below.

The main attributes of behaving professionally

This raises a number of challenges for all of us, for example when we have to consider how we dress and the language we use. This is where the value of Schön's reflective practitioner ideas (see 'Learning in Higher Education' and Chapter 10, 'Understanding the value of reflection') can help us resolve these possible dilemmas.

ACTIVITY 2 Is it ethical and professional?

Look at each of the following brief scenarios and consider whether the behaviour is ethical or professional.

1. John, a new graduate employee, wore trainers, jeans and a hooded sweatshirt to work on the day he knew the European CEO was visiting.

2. Sally used her employer's internet access to download pirated music files.

3. Tariq didn't draw his client's attention to the small print on a contract that specified the cooling-off period during which the client could withdraw from their contractual obligations. This was contrary to the organisation's fair trading policy.

4. Ingrid gave her brother some general information about the company she worked for when he was bidding for a contract it had put out to tender.

See the feedback section for further comment.

3 Synthesising university and practical knowledge: a professional process

'I did this internship over the summer. A couple of the people I worked with kept saying that theories were alright but they had nothing to do with the 'real' world. Although I disagreed, I found it hard to say why.'

Alex, third year Business Administration student

As we have suggested, a key thing that makes someone professional is their commitment to maintaining up-to-date knowledge. It is not uncommon, however, to find people questioning the value of 'theoretical' knowledge in the way Alex encountered. Underlying this is a problem with the assumption some people make about the way 'university' knowledge is connected with 'practical' knowledge – see the figure that follows.

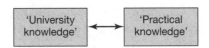

University vs. practical knowledge

This model makes the assumption that the two types of knowledge are at opposite ends of a spectrum. The difficulty Alex experienced came from her colleagues' assumptions about this 'oppositional' relationship and the fact that there is no place in it for 'professional' knowledge. However, if we see professional knowledge as distinct from university and practical knowledge, yet as a combination of them both, we can see a very different relationship model, as in the figure that follows.

Professional knowledge: the product of university knowledge and practical knowledge

This follows, in a much simplified way, the ideas of John Biggs, a respected UK educationalist. He suggests that university knowledge and practical knowledge (which he calls 'declarative' and 'procedural' knowledge respectively) actually connect at a higher level which he calls 'conditional' knowledge. He then proposes the highest level of knowledge, 'functioning' knowledge, which he suggests is about knowing how to put knowledge to work, solve problems and perform at a level of complete understanding (Biggs, 2003). The important things about the model in the university vs. practical knowledge figure above are firstly, that it represents one way in which professional knowledge can be visualised as a product of the two other knowledge bases and secondly, that it illustrates that professional knowledge has to be **actively** developed. It is a synthesis that won't happen on its own.

This active development of professional knowledge comes from understanding the contributions university and practical knowledge make:

- Practical knowledge is knowing 'what', in other words the **competencies** that are required to perform a task accurately to required standards.
- University knowledge is knowing 'why' and 'how', in other words the **reasons** (i.e. the theories, evidence, models) that things are done in a certain way, or the case for alternative ways of doing things.
- Professional knowledge is knowing 'when', 'where' and 'who' in relation to a given situation or problem, in other words judging and evaluating the optimal ways of achieving the best results and solving problems through the **application** of practical and university knowledge.

One way to visualise this is like the structure of an onion: with successive rings building out from the centre – see the figure opposite.

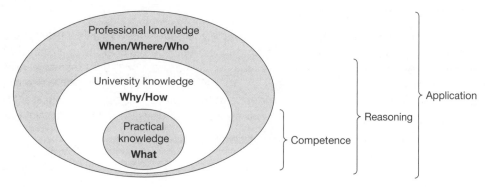

An 'onion skin' model of professional knowledge development

Chapter 9, 'Thinking critically', looks in detail at some of the meta-cognitive skills associated with the process of building professional knowledge.

How do I develop a professional approach to my practical knowledge?

'It is encouraging to see that students are increasingly aware of what will help them succeed in the workplace but they must take the development of their wider competencies as seriously as they take their studies.'

Richard Lambert, Director-General, CBI (CBI, 2009)

According to the Management Standards Centre (MSC), the National Occupational Standards (NOS) are 'relevant to anyone for whom management and leadership is, to a greater or lesser extent, part of their work' (2007). It also suggests that the NOS apply to all sectors and industries. These standards cover a key range of performance areas:

- managing self and personal skills;
- providing direction;
- facilitating change;
- working with people;
- using resources;
- achieving results.

If you want a real-world tool then this framework is a useful one for you to use to appraise your current practical knowledge position in a disciplined and professional way. You can find out more by using this weblink: www.management-standards.org/content_1.aspx?id=10:5406&id=10:1917

NOTE If your degree is vocationally oriented, perhaps with a professional body validation, student status or dispensation towards registration, you will be introduced by your tutors to the professional standards that body requires. You may prefer to use these in the following activity.

ACTIVITY 3 Appraise my competencies

Using the competence or standards framework you have chosen, review the indicators or performance measures for each competence area. You need to make a record of both how you rate yourself at this time (you can use a scale of 1–5 for example) **and** any brief comment about the grounds you use to make that rating judgement. Remember that whilst you might not have any evidence at the moment for some areas it identifies, this review will allow you to better describe where your development needs might lie.

You may find this template a useful framework for doing this task:

Competency:	
Measures/indicators	**Rating**
■	
■	
Brief review of development need	

You will be able to refer to some of the PDPs you have completed in this book to help you. See the feedback section for further comment on this activity.

How do I develop a professional approach to my university knowledge?

'A professional student is someone who grasps the fact that whilst they may only have 18 hours 'contact time' a week, they still have to put in the rest of the hours, maybe 25 or more hours a week, week-in week-out, to do well.'

Tutor's comment

No one is expecting you to start wearing suits to lectures or seminars (although there is nothing wrong in this if you choose to do so)! However, if you are going to be professional then all of the guidance in this book applies and you will start by committing yourself to undertake the PDP activities at the end of each chapter. You will then review them at the end of each semester on an ongoing basis as you get more evidence from your assignment feedback. This is the professional process of review and reflection (see 'Learning in Higher Education', section 'Reflect on your learning' and Chapter 10, 'Understanding the value of reflection'). Whilst there is no specific activity set here, if you wish to ensure a **professional approach to developing your university knowledge** then start with the following commitments:

■ You will do and review the PDP activities routinely.
■ You will need to apply the same measures of patience, persistence, practice and repetition that the problem-solving strategy of Chapter 11, 'Approaching numerical problems' identifies to all your study activity.
■ You will need to constantly improve your time management (see Chapter 1, 'Managing your time').
■ You will need to manage your integrity and ethical approach to study (see Chapter 12, 'Understanding academic integrity: learner ethics and plagiarism').
■ You will need to develop teamworking and awareness of diversity and cultural issues (see Chapter 5, 'Working in a real and diverse team').
■ You will take advantage of all the feedback opportunities on your assignments and seek further support and guidance to turn this into your improved practice as a scholar.
■ You will approach the whole of your studies with a developing sense of criticality and embrace the commitment this demands of you (see Chapter 9 'Thinking critically' and Chapter 14, 'Improving your business and management studies writing').
■ You will take every opportunity to become a reflective learner and practitioner (see Chapter 10, 'Understanding the value of reflection' and Chapter 15, 'Developing your reflective writing').

How do I develop a professional approach to being professional?

Throughout this book the guiding principle is **your** personal development. Each chapter has personal development planning embedded in it, and most of the chapters are concerned not just with your learning development but also with your professional development. In the 'How to use this book' section 'For you – the student' we stated, 'the activities in this book are not a once-and-for-all activity and should be revisited throughout your stay at university as your skills develop'. Knowledge is constantly renewing itself. A professional knows this and is prepared to invest in themselves: they do not 'just get by'. Behaving professionally and developing yourself professionally are two facets of the same thing.

If you are using this book to facilitate your professional development on a work placement year, internship or in your first graduate position, you have the opportunity to benchmark your current level of professionalism from other people's perspectives. One way to do this is to do a 360° feedback. According to CIPD (2009), 'Done well, 360° feedback challenges the recipient's perceptions of their skills and performance, and provides the motivation to change'.

NOTE Activity 4 is intended for people who are on a work placement year, internship or in their first graduate position. You may be able to use this tool if you have suitable term-time work, but it is not recommended under any other circumstances. You might wish to consult with your tutor as to whether this activity is appropriate for you at the moment.

ACTIVITY 4 Working with 360 feedback

Consult the CIPD web page at www.cipd.co.uk/subjects/perfmangmt/appfdbck/360fdbk.htm to find out more about the process of 360 feedback. You may decide to use a rated set of questions or simply to ask for free text comments to a set of questions such as:

- In what ways does my behaviour meet your expectations of a professional practitioner?
- What do I do that is particularly professional?
- What do I do that I can improve to be more professional?

Remember to provide a suitable explanatory letter with each of the questionnaire sheets you send out and you will need to ensure anonymity of the appraiser. Remember also that you are asking for genuine, candid responses that challenge and motivate; this means that you must expect and accept critique as a driver for your improvement.

4 Using this book to support your professional development

This section offers you an alternative index to content which you might find helpful in relation to managing the key elements of your professional development.

Academic development	Professional development
Manage yourself	
1 Managing your time	
2 Managing your stress	Preparing yourself for work placement
3 Learning part time, online and on a work placement	

Academic development	Professional development
Improve your work	
4 Getting the most out of lectures	
5 Working in a real and diverse team	Being aware of issues around diverse groups especially with regard to cultural differences
6 Presenting your work	Presenting your ideas professionally both visually and orally
7 Reading critically	Reading 'between the lines' and evaluating what you read
8 Excelling in exams	
Apply your thinking skills Intro	
9 Thinking critically	Making rational decisions and synthesising knowledge
10 Understanding the value of reflection	Reflecting on your actions as a strategic tool
11 Approaching numerical problems	Developing your problem-solving strategies
Develop your writing skills	
12 Understanding academic integrity: learner ethics and plagiarism	Ethics in practice
13 Taking control of the writing process	Communicating through effective writing
14 Improving your business and management studies writing	
15 Developing your reflective writing	Reflecting on your actions as a strategic tool

5 On reflection

This chapter has looked at the importance of behaving professionally in the complex global world in which today's business and management activity takes place. It has identified what graduate employers are looking for in graduates in terms of professional and ethical behaviour, and it has encouraged you to appraise yourself as part of developing a more professional approach to being a student. This includes optimising the opportunities around you at university and in the community within which your campus is located, to stretch and challenge yourself to develop professional behaviour. If you are working, then you have the opportunity to take control of your professional development in a number of ways, including those suggested in this chapter.

Summary of this chapter

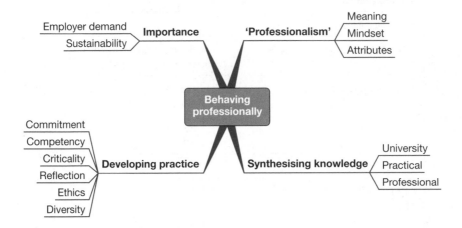

ACTIVITY 5 Update your personal development planner

My developing skills	Confidence level 1–5	Plans to improve
I understand the importance of professional behaviour.		
I know what the key attributes are of someone who behaves professionally.		
I can audit my professional behaviour skills.		
I know how to manage my professional behaviour development.		
I understand how to apply professional behaviour to my university studies.		

Getting extra help

- Go to your careers or employability service to get further advice on working generally.
- Your department or faculty may have a work placement team who can offer general and specific information about behaving professionally.

- Your students union may have an active programme designed to help student volunteers to get essential transferable skills.

Consult the following:

- For an interesting discussion on sustainable development and CPD: www.pp4sd.org.uk/downloads/pdf/CanEFSchange.pdf

Feedback on activities

ACTIVITY 1 I have professional attributes?

If you haven't been ruthlessly honest with yourself, go back and redo this activity. No one claiming to be professional would cheat themselves on a task such as this.

If you **have** been honest with yourself then whatever your score, you have the right attitude.

- If you score a positive number, then your professional attitudes and values are already showing. Your task is to take every opportunity in the way you conduct yourself as a student, in part-time work, work placements/internships and so on to enhance and refine these attributes.
- If you flat-line at zero then whilst you have a way to go, you are on the journey. But you have to take positive action to put an improvement strategy in place. You need to consider what opportunities will allow you to push forward. This might include the options suggested above but it could also include taking on a formal committee role at a university club, or something similar in a volunteering capacity, for example.
- If you score a negative number, the fact that you have been honest is your real asset. However, you need to do some serious thinking and reflection about your priorities and personal responsibilities. Perhaps in the past well-intentioned people took responsibility for you and you have developed a comfort zone based on that. Maybe you haven't had the range of experiences that turns us into fully mature adults. Maybe you are complacent. However this has developed, you now need to use your time at university to move beyond this point. Consider how you can engage with the actions suggested in the feedback above.

To help inform your improvement strategy, however you scored, look at the key issues where you score lowest and target those. You may need to get further advice or guidance, but as a developing professional you will research where and from who this is available. You can start with your university or college career or employability service.

Remember, this is not a validated assessment tool; its purpose is to make you consider some aspects of what being professional entails and where you currently sit in relation to these, in order to enhance your professionalism.

ACTIVITY 2 Is it ethical and professional?

1. On the face of it this is probably unprofessional and a misjudgement by John as to the proper way to present himself. However, the organisation might practise a 'dress-down' day once a week for all staff, or there may be no set dress code. If this were the case, how would you make a judgement on a day-by-day basis as to how to present **yourself** to managers and clients/customers?

2. This is illegal and both unethical and unprofessional. A company may have a fair use policy for private internet access, but it won't permit illegal activity.

3. Although the client ultimately is responsible for checking the terms of any contract they enter into, as the company had an explicit policy to work to this is unprofessional. It would also be unethical if it was driven simply by personal gain (i.e. commission or performance-related benefits) rather than being a genuine oversight.

4. As it is general information it is likely to be in the public domain, so potentially this isn't a problem. However, if it wasn't in the public domain, unless Ingrid could demonstrate she would offer the same information to anyone who enquired then she could be deemed to have acted unprofessionally and unethically.

ACTIVITY 3 Appraise my competencies

This is a major task and you may wish to consult with your course tutors on how best to integrate this into your learning whilst at university. You may find that there are alternative tools that your course uses to achieve the same task; if so, use those in preference to the one here. The overriding objective is to be able to identify what you do and to what level of achievement you do it. If you aren't currently doing it, you should now be able to describe what you need to do to develop. Overall you are aiming to action plan for improvement based on this self-appraisal.

References

- Biggs, J. (2003) *Teaching for Quality Learning at University* (2nd edn). Buckingham, Open University Press/Society for Research into Higher Education.
- CBI. (2009) *Future fit*. Available from http://highereducation.cbi.org.uk/uploaded/HRE_091_Future%20Fit%20AW.pdf [last accessed 21 November 2009].
- CIPD (2009) *360 Feedback*. Available from www.cipd.co.uk/subjects/perfmangmt/appfdbck/360fdbk.htm [last accessed 21 November 2009].
- Fassin, Y. (2005) 'The reasons behind non-ethical behaviour in business and entrepreneurship', *Journal of Business Ethics*, 60, 265–79.
- Hall, A. and Berardino, L. (2006) 'Teaching professional behaviors: differences in the perceptions of faculty, students, and employers', *Journal of Business Ethics*, 6, 407–15.

- IoD (2007) *Graduates' employability skills*. Available from www.iod.com/intershoproot/eCS/Store/en/pdfs/policy_paper_graduates_employability_skills.pdf [last accessed 21 November 2009].

- MSC (2007) *Standards*. Available from www.management-standards.org/content_1.aspx?id=10:1917 [last accessed 21 November 2009].

- PP4SD (2006) *Skills for Sustainability Report.* Available from www.pp4sd.org.uk/downloads/skills_Nov06.htm [last accessed 21 November 2009].

- Realworld (2009) *Graduate case studies – PricewaterhouseCoopers LLP (PWC).* Available from www.realworldmagazine.com/pricewaterhousecoopers [last accessed 20 November 2009].

1 Manage yourself

We all have a multitude of things to do at work, at home, with friends and for our studies. We are all juggling these aspects of our lives and we may find at times that one of these areas starts demanding more of us. Many Business and Management Studies students balance part-time study with full-time commitments at work and at home; if you are someone with this 'management' challenge, then you know that you have to juggle priorities and commitments. Even if you are a full-time student without home commitments, you are likely to have a part-time job. Either way, your ability to manage task and time has a direct connection with the results you achieve **and** the value you extract from the learning opportunities your tutors make available to you. The first two chapters in this part refer to stress and time management; we have included them from another book in the series because we think the guidance they offer is too important to miss out here.

As a part-time learner, you will have particular pressures from the demands made on you. You may also be learning apart from your fellow students, which increases your need to develop a virtual learning community that can sustain you through difficult patches. If you are a mature student, you may not know about some of the new technologies that can help you do this. You may also be less certain about the types of assessment you may be required to do, yet feel that this is not something you should bother other people about. Familiarity with these aspects of part-time study will help to reduce the sense of distance you may feel.

If you are a full-time student who takes a year out on a work placement, there is the new challenge of maintaining your learning in preparation for return to university to complete your studies. Your final academic year will go by very quickly, so knowing how to hit the ground running and not waste time getting up to speed will make a big difference to how well you do.

Although it is targeted at part-time learners and year-out students, much of the information in the third chapter will be of interest to all students.

This section will help you focus on developing the key skills of managing time and learning part-time, at a distance and whilst on work placement, that will enable you to juggle your busy life and come out on top.

1 Managing your time

Managing our time is something like dieting. We know what we should eat, we know why we should eat that way and we know the benefits it will bring. However, how often do we start with good intentions and then let things slip? Time management can be similar. We know why we should manage our time, we often know what to do, but we just can't keep to it.

In this chapter you will:

1. identify your relationship with time and understand how this affects your time management;
2. consider your life goals as part of your time management;
3. manage your time efficiently and effectively.

USING THIS CHAPTER

Estimate your current levels of confidence. At the end of the chapter you will have the chance to re-assess these levels where you can incorporate this into your personal development planner (PDP). Mark between 1 (poor) and 5 (good) for the following:

I can identify my relationship with time and understand how this affects my time management.	I can identify my life goals as part of my time management.	I can get the best out of my time.	I can manage my time effectively.

Date: _____

1 Introduction

How many of us have started each day by stumbling from lecture to seminar to the café, to the pub, and then to bed, only to do the same the next day with little thought of what we are doing? How many of us start the day by looking at electronic messages and using that as a driver for the morning's activities? At the end of the day you get to bed exhausted because you have been so busy 'reacting'. But what have you actually done that is important in moving you forward? Are you a proactive time manager or a reactive one?

Our relationship with food, stress and time is very personal and in order to move on in all these areas we need to identify our relationship with them. This chapter enables you to identify your relationship with time and recognise how you time manage now. You will look at the importance of the whole picture in order for you to fulfil all aspects of your life, not just your studies. Finally, we shall look at the mechanics of time management in order to make things happen.

Seeing time as a resource

We have only to look at the number of idioms in English that relate to time to see that we regard time as a resource. Most of these idioms refer to either spending, wasting or saving time, as shown in the figure below.

We are living in an increasingly global world with technological communications that give us instant access to information and we find ourselves in an environment that demands even quicker responses from us than ever before.

We are living in social cultures, be this industry, college or social spheres, where the volume of activity each week has rocketed. This can result in us feeling controlled by time. In a study of how North Americans use their time, the researchers found that 61 per cent of the population reported never having excess time, with 40 per cent feeling that time is a bigger problem for them than money (work by Robinson and Godbey, 1997, cited in Boniwell, 2005).

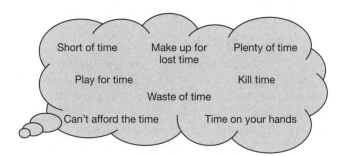

The life of a student is tightly constrained by deadlines, time slots and time-tables. How many times have fellow students you know complained about the amount of coursework they have to do and the bunching of deadlines? We increasingly work and play in environments that demand multi-tasking, and that suits some and not others. Time affects us all, but how we **perceive time** and handle it varies between individuals.

2 Recognising your relationship with time

We can get an insight into how we deal with time by recognising if we generally 'look forward', 'look to the past', 'work to the wire' or finish one thing before starting the next. When we look at time like this, we realise there can be no 'one size fits all' as we have individual preferences.

First let us look at our preferences for particular time perspectives, as this is one aspect that affects our motivation to study.

Time perspectives

Professor Philip Zimbardo, an award-winning social psychologist from the University of Stanford, looked at how our dominant orientation to the past, present and future influences our behaviour and especially our ability to manage our time (Zimbardo and Boyd, 1999). Activity 1 helps you to identify different time perspectives in other people.

ACTIVITY 1 Recognising different time perspectives in others

In this activity there are no absolute answers, and it is used to prepare you for recognising your own relationship with time later. Use the scenarios to give you a flavour of the characters and then estimate the following:

1. What time perspective dominates these students' lives at present: past, present or future? There could also be a mixture of these time perspectives.

2. Who do you think are multi-taskers and single-taskers?

3. Estimate their motivation to study.

Adrian is a second-year student living in a house with other students. He is very sociable and really enjoys his time with friends. The highlight of his week is Thursday night when he goes out with friends until the early hours of the morning. These Thursday nights have been so enjoyable he has started extending them to a few more nights as well, as Adrian's philosophy in life is 'to live for today'. Now, in the second semester, coursework and work difficulty are increasing and he is finding it hard to cope with everything, apart from his social life. He has had several warnings from tutors for late hand-ins, but just can't get around to doing more work, but he knows he has to. He finds it quite difficult to juggle social life and coursework.

Ismet is someone you can rely on to have a good time. He often arranges great evenings that are cheap but great fun. He is now in his third year and knows exactly what he wants to do when he finishes studying. His great planning abilities have helped him manage a busy social life and a challenging course. However, he knows he could probably have got a better degree grade if he had put in more work, but he gets such a buzz from juggling all these parts of his life that he is prepared to accept that. Although, having said that, he is heading for an upper-second degree classification.

Rachael always wanted to be an engineer and as a child was fascinated by those Victorian civil engineers who laid the foundations of our cities today. She knows it is tough, and is determined to get a good degree. She works very hard and is setting up volunteering and vacation work to get as much hands-on experience as possible. She also manages to have several pieces of coursework on the go at the same time and seems to be able to cope with it, although she gets a little irritated if she is interrupted while working. Her friends think she needs to relax a bit and at least take some time to enjoy herself now.

Student	Time perspective (past, present, future)	Preference for multi-tasking or single-tasking	Motivation to study (high, medium, low)	Estimated time management skills (poor, OK, good)
Adrian				
Ismet				
Rachael				

Check the feedback section at the end of the chapter.

Now, think about some of your friends. What time perspective dominates their lives? Do you think they are multi-taskers?

What's your time perspective?

Sometimes it is easier to recognise characteristics in others than ourselves, so now you've looked at others, it is time to take a look at yourself and see if you can identify which time perspective dominates you during semester time: in Activity 2 you can select several time perspectives. It would be interesting to see which one feels like you **now**.

ACTIVITY 2 Identifying your own time perspective

Look at the different time perspectives – which one(s) do you feel dominate(s) you during the semester?

Time persective 1	Time persective 2
I tend to be impulsive and love excitement. I am happy to take risks as this makes life exciting. My motto is: 'Live for today because I don't know what tomorrow will bring.'	My past life was not very pleasant and I too frequently recall events or things I regret doing and it can sometimes affect me now.
Time persective 3	**Time persective 4**
I know where I want to go and I put plans in place to help me get there. I am prepared to work through boring pieces of coursework as I know it is laying a foundation for later work.	My motto is 'Whatever will be, will be.' I generally feel that I shouldn't worry too much about the future as it will take care of itself and luck plays a large part in how successful one is anyway.
Time persective 5	
I get a warm feeling when I think about the past, my family or cultural traditions. It makes me know who I am. It is very important for me to keep track of my old friends.	

Check the feedback section at the end of the chapter.

Consider how these time perspectives could affect your time management behaviour. Do you think you need to make adjustments to enable your studies?

Ideally we should be balanced between the different positive time perspectives, but not perspectives 2 and 4 as they have a negative effect on our life. Most successful people have a tendency to be 'future oriented' (perspective 3). When you are engaged in your academic studies this should motivate you sufficiently to encourage you to be future oriented. If you are not motivated, then it is going to be hard to engage with your learning or manage your time effectively. However, too much of this orientation can make you a workaholic, so you need a balance.

We have seen that our time perspective affects our behaviour and our motivation to study and subsequently how we manage time. Our preference to being a multi- or linear tasker reflects our perception of time and how we manage time to complete tasks.

Are you comfortable multi-tasking or not?

An important anthropologist, Edward T. Hall, observed that different cultures had particular preferences when structuring their time. Cultures that see time as linear tend to emphasise the usage of time in discrete slots and complete tasks in a linear manner. Those cultures that see time as more fluid and less exact tend to carry out their tasks in a more non-linear manner and do lots of things at the same time. Work has continued in this field and these characteristics are also observed in individuals and particular jobs.

Different jobs have different time cultures where different time personalities can thrive. Those working with disaster teams, transport crews and surgical teams need people who can estimate time accurately and know what has to be done, when it has to be done, and do it. Those working in more creative fields may find such colleagues stifling. The academic time culture is deadline driven and many institutions will penalise you if your work is not handed in on time. If working to deadlines is not your preferred style then it is important to acknowledge that first and devise ways of coping.

With regard to individuals, those preferring to do one task at a time are seen as 'linear taskers' while those happy to juggle lots of tasks at the same time are seen as 'multi-taskers'. If you see time as being discrete then you are able to identify slots in which to work and control your time. If, however, you see time as fluid and continuous, you may not see much of a separation between work and your social life and you carry out tasks when the mood takes you rather than working to rigid time plans. How you think of time therefore can influence your tendency to multi-task or not. Activity 3 helps you to identify whether you are a multi-tasker.

NOTE If you want to learn some jargon, a multi-tasker is a **polychron** (a term first coined by Hall, 1959) and someone who focuses on one task at a time is a **monochron**. Can you recognise monochrons and polychrons in your friendship group?

ACTIVITY 3 Are you a multi-tasker?

Some of the key time management behaviours that can distinguish multi-taskers from others are: planning, focus and attention, reaction to change, and performing under pressure. You may already know if you are a multi-tasker, but have a look at a few of these statements and check the feedback. Remember, we can all be multi- or linear taskers, but we prefer to operate in one or the other. Your preference will determine how you manage your time and how you meet your deadlines.

	Ideally me	But in practice ... I do/ don't do this ...
Planning		
1 I like to plan what I am going to do. Although I find it hard, I need to plan my time quite carefully. Without a plan, I feel a little bit lost. [linear tasker]		
2 I don't like working to a detailed time plan. It makes me feel constrained and irritable. [multi-tasker]		
Focus and attention		
3 Once I start on a task I give it my full attention and I dislike it when I am interrupted. [linear tasker]		
4 My focus and attention tend to be spread across lots of different tasks I am doing. It doesn't bother me if I am interrupted, I just deal with that and then carry on. [multi-tasker]		
Reaction to change		
5 I can make rough plans, but happily change them too. [multi-tasker]		
6 Once I have worked out my plan of action, I get annoyed if I have to change it. [linear tasker]		
Performance under pressure		
7 I like to keep track of the tasks I have to do and can prioritise very well. This gives me breathing space and so I can do the work before the pressure gets too strong. [linear tasker]		
8 I work best when I feel under time pressure. I am usually juggling several pieces of work to meet my deadlines. Prioritising is a last-minute approach for me, but I tend to get everything done. [multi-tasker]		
Is your preference multi-tasking or linear tasking?		

Check the feedback section at the end of this chapter for more information

NOTE These characteristics are just some indicators of multi- and linear tasking.

Advantages for the multi-tasker

You will probably feel less intimidated by the time pressure as you are able to juggle your coursework. You will probably find this stimulating. You may be a procrastinator as you are happy to leave things to the last minute and get started on many things simultaneously, but make sure you finish them! You have a very flexible working style and can deal with interruptions and changes to your schedule.

Dangers for the multi-tasker

Your preference for working under pressure and leaving things to the last minute does not allow for any mishaps. What if you suddenly realise you don't understand something the night before you hand in your coursework or that you should have completed a set of data before now? Since you can juggle lots of tasks, you may react to all your tasks in the same way. You must remember to plan and schedule and prioritise your activities, at least to some degree. If you try to do too much at one time you can be inefficient as you may just get overloaded and find you don't do anything very well. It may be better to allocate quality time for particularly difficult or important tasks. You may find you are a multi-tasker because you are an urgency addict (see Section 3 below). Now is the time to reveal your true colours!

Advantages for the linear tasker

You consciously want to have control over your time and if you are able to plan and identify time periods when things should be done, you can probably deal with the pressure. As a result of your prioritising and planning, you will be able to focus on key pieces of work.

Dangers for the linear tasker

Studying and the bunching of coursework deadlines can lead to a sense of time stress and the feeling that you can't do anything properly. You need to break down your tasks into smaller chunks and schedule at that level so you feel you are working in a linear mode. You may also need to be flexible enough to find those quality slots at short notice.

Checklist: dealing with your relationship with time

1. Identify your time preference.
2. Recognise whether you are a multi- or a linear tasker.
3. Note if you can improve your relationship with time.
4. Recognise how this impacts on your time management.

3 Addressing your life goals: getting a balance

Time management is more than just organising ourselves and writing 'to-do lists'. We also need to make room for our wider goals in life, relationships, friends and family – we need a balance. Just planning and prioritising the tasks we have been given can be rather reactive; in order to account for all aspects of our life that are important to us, we also need to be proactive and ensure we work at them too. In our busy world there is a tendency to be 'urgency driven', reacting to all those demands that cross our path rather than those things that are important. We need to make sure we can plan, create and fit in all the things that are important to us in our life.

Traditionally time management training has been concerned with giving us tips to enable us to organise our time and deal with those ever increasing urgent activities, generally in a very linear manner. Stephen Covey, father of nine children, professor of business management and author of one of the most influential business books, *First Things First* (1994), believes that we need to change our paradigm of time management from being addicted to dealing with what we perceive as urgent to proactively determining what is important. 'Importance' then becomes the new framework for managing our time.

The framework below was devised by Covey *et al.* (1994) to enable us to clarify what is urgent, not urgent, important and not important. Activity 4 asks what is important in your life.

	Urgent	Not urgent
Important	I	II
	Lectures, seminars, etc.	Preparation – long-term goals
	Coursework preparation	Planning – long-term goals
	Assignment deadlines	Relationship building
	Crises	Creating
		Personal development
Not important	III	IV
	Interruptions (some)	Trivia
	Meetings (some)	Junk mail
	Some e-mails	Time-wasting activities

Source: Adapted from Covey *et al.* (1994) with permission.

Quadrant I

Activities here are important and urgent; they have to be dealt with. To deal with activities here, we have to organise and prioritise what needs to be done. If we procrastinate with activities here, there will be serious consequences. In this quadrant we can feel driven and constrained by time, resulting in feeling stressed.

Quadrant II

This quadrant is where we deal with important issues such as planning (to keep quadrant I in check), creating new ideas and working towards our goals for both university and life in general. Keeping fit, doing exercise, broadening our mind, making intellectual leaps in our studies, volunteering, reading, helping friends and family, and developing meaningful relationships are all part of quadrant II. In this quadrant, we feel empowered and we need to proactively deal with items in this quadrant. Don't neglect to do so.

Quadrant III

Many of us who are urgency addicted will deal with items that seem urgent but are not important. You may find you are reacting to other people's priorities at the expense of your own – try to keep a balance, and say 'no' to a few more non-urgent things.

Quadrant IV

This is where we generally waste our time. We might slump in front of the television, read trashy novels, etc. We are all in this quadrant from time to time, but try to limit how much time you spend here. You will find yourself in this quadrant often if you are driven by urgency as you will be stressed and exhausted and this is where you 'drop'. Also, when you procrastinate, you will find yourself in this quadrant.

ACTIVITY 4 What's important in your life?

You may feel very tempted to skip this activity. Please take time to think about it. The questions are quite challenging, but answers will come.

1. What things are important to me across my life?

2. What gives me a buzz?

3. What kind of work would I like to do after my studies? Do I need to be getting experience in place for that?

Now think of some of the steps you need to take in order to operationalise these goals. What could your plan look like if you include some of these things? Remember, these are your quadrant II activities and you need to be proactive in order to make them happen. Quadrant II activities are easier for those with a future time perspective.

This activity is something you need to do on an annual basis as your views do change, and it may need to be revitalised.

NOTE You should be motivated to study and successfully completing your degree should be one of your life goals. If this does not appear in your list, you need to ask yourself why you are studying or if you are studying the wrong subject.

4 Organising yourself

Organising yourself involves planning your time and organising your study space. Your plan tells you what you should do and when you should do it and for how long. Your study space enables that to happen. If you are a multi-tasker you may want to skip this section, but stop and read this as you may be able to maintain your spontaneity and couple this with some degree of planning that can help you. In addition, you should be able to determine the kind of environment that gets the best out of you. Linear taskers will probably be competent planners by now, but check where you best learn and ensure you can make that happen.

Of course, your degree of motivation for this will depend, to some extent, on your time perspective. Planning encourages the development of a future orientation. If you are dominantly oriented towards the present, you will find it hard to fufil your plans even if you make them. Be careful of this.

How do you organise your time through planning?

Even the worst students of time management don't lurch unconsciously from one thing to another during the day, every day. There is always some degree of planning. However, what is your general pattern on time planning during a week? A plan will give you some idea of where all that time is going and how effective you are at getting those important things done (see Activities 5 and 6). Interestingly, a study in 1997 found that students at a particular university had more study work activity on Monday, Tuesday and Thursday, and fewer studied at weekends. It found that typically students spend 38.8 hours on study-related tasks (the range was 34–48 hours depending on age, gender and year). Of that study time, 35.5 per cent was spent on assessed work, 12.8 per cent in lectures, 8 per cent on non-assessed work, 7.6 per cent of time in tutorials and 3.2 per cent searching books in the library (Innis and Shaw, 1997).

ACTIVITY 5 Developing a weekly schedule

Look back on a typical week during semester time and try to remember how you spent your time. Include sleep, going out, paid work, private study, group/course work, etc. as well as attendance at lectures/seminars. Note it down on the schedule below and estimate the time for your activities, using time slots. Are you happy with this or would you have liked it to be different? Is it similar or wildly different to the research above?

A typical week

Approx times	Mon	Tues	Wed	Thurs	Fri	Sat
8.00–10.00am				9.00–10.00 Lecture		
10.00–12.00		11.00–12.00 Lecture	Seminar			
12.00–2.00pm						Paid work
2.00–4.00pm			**Sport**			
4.00–6.00pm			**Sport**			
6.00–8.00pm			Paid work			
8.00–10.00pm			Paid work			
10.00–12.00pm						

Now think of next week and plan how you should spend your time, given the deadlines you have.

Approx times	Mon	Tue	Wed	Thurs	Fri	Sat
6.00–8.00am	Sleep	Sleep	Sleep	Sleep	Sleep	Sleep
8.00–10.00am				9.00–10.00 Lecture		
10.00–12.00		11.00–12.00 Lecture	Seminar			
12.00–2.00pm						Paid work
2.00–4.00pm			**Sport**			
4.00–6.00pm			**Sport**			
6.00–8.00pm			Paid work			
8.00–10.00pm			Paid work			
10.00–12.00pm						

Next week my main goals are: _____

ACTIVITY 6 Balancing your time

Look at the activities on your weekly plan:

1. Can you identify the quadrants? Label them: QI, QII, QIII and QIV.

   ■ Are any of your activities labelled QI really QIII? You can gain time by weeding out QIII type activities.

2. Make a new empty weekly planner and start by putting in events/activities that are time sensitive, e.g. a lecture, as these are immovable.

3. Add QII type activities in the free slots (these may not be on a weekly basis, but possibly a monthly basis). These will be taken from Activity 4, above, 'What's important in your life?.' Remember to use the time slots to free up time to do things you want to do.

Organising your study space

You may have read in time management books that you need to have a clear desk (represents a clear head!), be somewhere quiet and not be disturbed. However, when you actually talk to students and ask them their organisational preferences, they vary. What do you prefer? See Activity 7.

ACTIVITY 7 Your current and ideal study space

Imagine you have to complete a piece of coursework, which could, for example, be an essay or a laboratory report. You know you have to begin this piece of work today and so you sit down to start. Answer the questions in the table below. The examples are just prompts, you can also add your own. You may be happy with what you do, then say so; if not, say what would be ideal for you.

	What you do currently	Is this ideal? If not, what is ideal?
1 Where do you prefer to work?	At home, in the library	
2 Generally, how is your work space organised?	Cleared desk, work on top of other things, work on floor, have papers in a folder, have loose papers	
3 When you sit down to work do you find yourself getting up soon afterwards?	You are hungry, thirsty, just need to sort something out quickly. Check the ritual you have before you finally get started	
4 How long do you think it takes you to feel settled and start work?		
5 Do you like to have music on at the same time as studying or have other people around you?	Some people need to be alone and quiet and others need a certain background noise. What is your ambient preference?	

There are no correct answers for this except to say that it is advisable to have all the papers you need to start an assignment at hand, as well as knowing **exactly** (not roughly) what you have to do and how long you have to do it. Having a messy desk and working with music and people around you may be what works for you. If so, then keep to it, but do check you get the best out of this and it is not just a habit. The essence of this activity is for you to identify how you currently organise yourself, recognise your rituals (this is like doing stretches in the gym prior to your workout; you prime yourself for activity) and recognise that you are getting ready for work. However, if your 'rituals' go on for too long, you may be procrastinating. So be aware. If you are currently working in a space that is not conducive to your learning, now is the time to identify what the problems are and make changes.

Making a piece of work manageable

Some pieces of coursework can be rather daunting, so you need to create smaller chunks that are easier to manage:

- clarify what is needed in your coursework;
- identify any data you need from experimental or practical work;
- identify the pieces of information you need;
- make a list of all the parts/chunks you need to complete;
- order the list;
- check your hand-in date for your coursework;
- add a time frame to each chunk.

If you are a multi-tasker you may be happy with the main points. If you are a linear tasker, you may want to develop the sub-points in your list.

5 Time management strategies

In the earlier sections we have looked at individual preferences with respect to our perceptions of time and how this influences the way we organise our time. In some cases time may be handled well and for others, the majority of us, there will be room for improvement.

Time is a resource that cannot be reused or recycled as with some other resources. We have a fixed number of hours in a semester and the only way of doing all those things we want to do and need to do is to manage this resource more efficiently. If you consider how much effort you put in each day you need to ask yourself what the net effect or outcome of all this effort is.

Mechanics of time management – planning, scheduling and using to-do lists

To do this effectively you need to take different time frames and the most appropriate is the semester, the week and the day. Your semester plan enables you to see the overall picture for your studies and plan those important things that can get lost once the semester starts, e.g. develop a new sport, start up a new hobby, do some volunteering work or attend the careers advisory talks/workshops.

The weekly schedule fills in those time-constrained activities like lectures, etc., leaving you slots for other important activities.

The 'to-do' list relates to each day and is where all your planning stops and the 'doing' takes place. This time frame is critical. If you consistently don't deliver within this time frame and you are predominantly a linear tasker, you start to feel overwhelmed and out of control. Multi-taskers may condense their 'to-do' lists in a flurry of activity, possibly at the last minute.

The table below gives some idea of how these time management aids work for your studies, but remember this should also include important things you want to do outside of your studies.

NOTE To-do lists are where the action happens and they should have a time frame and be able to support your goals. Make them SMART: specific, manageable, attainable, relevant and timely.

Long-term planning Planning	Mid-term planning	Short-term planning Doing (outcome from your time planning)
Semester plan	*Weekly schedule*	*Daily to-do list*
Identify your academic goals for this semester. Read unit descriptions to see what is expected of you. Select options.	This is similar to the weekly planner in Activity 5, above. Ensure items identified in your semester plan get transferred to appropriate weekly planner.	This is your present time perspective. Apart from your time-sensitive slots, you should prioritise your other activities according to their importance.
Note assignments and hand-in dates for your courses. Find out who you need to see regarding possible work placements, Erasmus exchange, etc.	Enter your time-sensitive items like lectures, tasks/events that satisfy your key goals and those urgent things that must get done.	Start your day by setting your to-do list and then **prioritising** tasks according to their **importance** and 'due date'.
Note any software you need to learn or will be expected to know and find out how you can train yourself.	Make sure your weekly planner includes your whole life and not just your studies. Many people are increasingly turning to electronic means for this through mobile phones or PDAs.*	PDAs usually have a 'to-do list' function, you may want to use that. Highlight the high-priority tasks.
Promise yourself to complete your personal development planner as this will enable you to articulate what you are learning and identify where your strengths and weaknesses are.	Carefully estimate the time it will take you to complete tasks. This takes experience, but it is a characteristic of good time management.	

*PDA is a personal digital assistant. It can be integrated in your mobile phone or as a standalone tool. There are also several desktop tools that can be used like a PDA, e.g. Google has a selection of tools and Microsoft Outlook has a PDA-like function built into it.

Recommending a time management strategy

Good time management is about working smart and not about working long hours. Your time is precious and you don't want to squander it on things that are not important, so be:

1. **Specific**. Quieten your mind and focus on what needs to be done now, later this week and this month. Concentrate on the first two. Make sure your work space is organised for best effect.

2. **Manageable**. Manage your time so that it **suits you**. Break large pieces of work into manageable chunks that enable successful/staged completion.

3. **Attainable**. Don't set yourself goals that are going to be difficult to achieve as this will only sap your self-confidence. Set sizeable goals that may be challenging, but attainable with the resources you have.

4. **Relevant**. Don't just rush into any job, this will make you 'urgency driven'. Remember to be driven by what is important and reduce those activities that just waste your time.

5. **Timely**. Your time management should be organised in a way that enables you to work through important tasks within a given time frame. Your plan can be rough or detailed, depending on your preference, but whatever your style, the hand-in date is just that.

Checklist: developing good time management strategies

1. Balance short-term with long-term (life) goals.
2. Be importance rather than urgency driven.
3. Plan – in detail for linear tasker and roughly for multi-tasker.
4. Know how and where you learn best.
5. Understand your relationship with time.

ACTIVITY 8 Recommending time management strategies

How should these students improve their time management skills? Can you identify their issues with regard to time management? A concept map summary of time management is included below to help you work through this activity.

Jane is the first of her family to study at university and she is very excited by it. She lives with a long-term boyfriend who is just finishing a modern apprenticeship scheme. She is in her first year and, although she has worked before, she was not prepared for the amount of independent work she would have to do in addition to keeping her 'old life' together. Jane knows what her goals are, but finds the juggling of tasks difficult as there seem to be so many demands on her time.

Winston has been in the UK for about a year and is enjoying his studies. He knows what he wants to do when he finishes but has difficulty around exam times. He is fine during the year and manages to get his coursework in on time. Revision for exams is somehow different. He doesn't have a set place to revise and some days goes to the library, other times he sits on the floor of his bedroom or in the kitchen. He knows that when he starts to revise he will suddenly feel hungry and then goes to make something to eat. He will come back, ready to start, and then realises he hasn't made a promised phone call, so he does that. He is now ready to start, and a friend calls and they have a chat. By late afternoon he gets some work done, but then his friends ring up and invite him out. Since he feels that his day is already wasted, he decides to go. He feels bad about this, but promises himself he will start revising properly tomorrow.

Can you write your own scenario?

See the feedback section for suggestions.

NOTE If you are dyslexic you may have difficulty putting things (mentally and physically) in order. It is important for you to try to identify what you need to do and create a slot for it. If you have persistent problems with this, it would be advisable to consult a learning differences unit at your institution as it is essential you find a strategy that suits you.

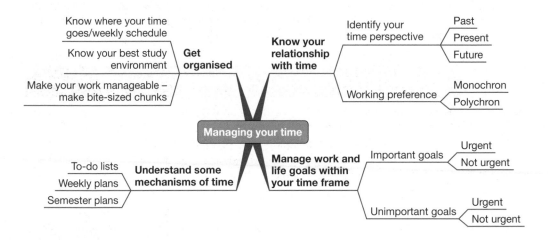

6 On reflection

Time management is about understanding your relationship with time and how that affects your ability to manage time. Looking forward motivates you and enables you to identify your life's goals. Keeping up with old friends, and enjoying yourself now, also balances your life.

Planning, scheduling and to-do lists are mechanisms you can use to keep yourself on track, but ensure that your track is for important issues and not trivia. This will give you a sense of achievement and a feeling of control over your time.

Now, reflect on your relationship with time and how you intend to adapt your behaviour so that you can spend your time more effectively. You may want to transfer this information to your institution's personal development planner scheme.

ACTIVITY 9 Update your personal development planner

Having read this chapter, gauge your confidence again. How does this compare with your confidence levels at the start of the chapter? What can you do to improve? You can incorporate this into your personal development planner. Add anything else you feel is appropriate.

Grade your confidence on a scale of 1–5 where 1 = poor and 5 = good.

My time management plan	Confidence level 1–5	Plans to improve
I recognise that my relationship with time affects how I manage my time. *Section 2*		
I recognise that my life goals are as much a part of my time management as course deadlines. *Section 3*		
I know how to get the best out of my time as I know how I study best. *Section 4*		
I now know how I can manage my time effectively and can develop strategies that suit me. *Section 5*		

Date:_____

Getting extra help

At your institution:

- Consult the Careers Advisory Service or Student Services as they often hold key skill workshops on topics such as time management.
- Attend your institution's learning support unit (or similar) if you feel this is an issue for you.
- Check out your local students union as they often provide help in this area.

Books:

- Covey, S. R., Merrill, A. and Merrill, R. (1994) *First Things First: Coping with the Ever-increasing Demands of the Workplace*. London, Simon & Schuster.

A useful website:

- Mindtools, at: www.mindtools.com [last accessed December 2006].

Feedback on activities

ACTIVITY 1 Recognising different time perspectives in others

There are no absolute answers to this feedback. Here are some interpretations. If yours are different, it may be worth articulating your reasons.

Adrian

His time perspective is very much in the **present**, especially with respect to his social life and having a good time. From his short description, we might conclude that he is happier doing **one type of activity** at a time (his social life doesn't seem to vary much) rather than juggling a lot of different activities. His **motivation** to study appears to be **low**. His **time management skills** may be doubtful (poor).

Ismet

His time perspective is dominated by **present** and **future**. He is prepared to live now, but keeps his eye on coursework so that he doesn't fall behind. He seems to be a good organiser, and that takes some juggling. He has to do this as well as keep up with coursework, although I suspect he pulls back on his social life to get some of his coursework completed. He seems to be a **multi-tasker** and quite **motivated** in his studies as well as **good at time management.**

Rachael

Her time perspective is very much in the **future** and very much at the expense of living now. She should be careful that she doesn't experience burn-out and she needs to re-balance her life. She appears to be a **multi-tasker** when it comes to her studies, but the fact that she gets irritated when interrupted could mean that she prefers to focus on single aspects of her coursework – doing one piece at a time and liking to stay focused. She is **highly motivated** and probably a **good time manager** (motivated people usually manage their time better than non-motivated people).

ACTIVITY 2 Identifying your own time perspective

If you are dominated by time **perspective 1**, you are '**present oriented**'. You really focus on having a good time. For you, it is the now that counts. This is really a hedonistic perspective and we should all spend time in this perspective at some time during a week. If, however, it dominates you, you may find that you will be prone to giving up your work in favour of the addiction to seeking excitement and having a good time. Being permanently in this time perspective is very unhealthy for your studies or career in the future as you succumb to temptations that appear more exciting at the time.

If you are dominated by time **perspective 4**, you are also '**present oriented**' but in a negative, fatalistic way. You feel that life is outside your control and nothing you do will change that. You have a general feeling of helplessness. Being predominantly in this time perspective zaps your motivation. You see no point in putting in the effort so your studies and future work will really suffer.

If you are dominated by **perspective 5**, you are '**past oriented**' in a positive way. Your happy memories have helped you develop a positive view of life and given you the stability to move on; we all need this. Research has shown that those in this perspective have a high sense of self-esteem (Boniwell, 2005).

If you are dominated by **perspective 2**, you are '**past oriented**' in a negative way and you may not be able to get over something that was unpleasant in your past. If that is the case, and you feel it is an issue, you may be advised to seek professional help. It is important to deal with negative experiences so they don't ruin your life. In terms of your studies, you may find you are not meeting your full potential. Negative past events don't have to be traumatic; getting consistently bad marks for essay writing or maths tests, for example, could be enough to determine how you deal with these now.

If you are dominated by time **perspective 3**, you are **future oriented**. You have set out your goals and you make plans so that you can fulfil them. You seek out new challenges and opportunities where you can. Research has shown that this time perspective is associated with well-being, persistence and self-confidence (Boniwell, 2005). You can, however, be so concerned with achieving that you forget to enjoy yourself, become a workaholic, experience burn-out and forget to live in the present. You need a balance.

ACTIVITY 3 Are you a multi-tasker?

You will probably find academic life is very much a polychronic culture. More than likely your coursework assignments will be bunched towards the end of your course just when you are thinking of revising for your exams. In some cases you are finishing coursework and writing exams in the same week. It is important to identify what your working preference is so that you can make adaptations to fit in with the actuality of student life.

If you have identified yourself as a multi-tasker then you will probably fit in well with academic structure. Be careful, however, that you give important pieces of coursework enough attention and don't leave things to the last minute.

If you have identified yourself as a linear tasker, then you need to prioritise your tasks, break them down into small tasks, create a time plan and carry out these smaller tasks in a linear way. You need to work in small chunks so you can get that piece of work finished within your schedule. This will keep you on track in a polychronic environment while you work in a linear fashion!

Multi-taskers (polychrons) prefer ...	Linear taskers (monochrons) prefer ...
time to be unstructured	structured time
not to make detailed plans	to work to detailed time plans
to work on tasks when they are in the mood	to work to their prioritised list of activities
to spread their focus and attention across lots of things	a very focused approach
to go with the flow and if they are interrupted it doesn't matter.	to work without interruption.

ACTIVITY 8 Recommending time management strategies

Jane may have sorted out her major goals and planned well, but she does not seem to be handling her to-do list well. She needs to prioritise, and that includes her home life, and stick to her daily tasks. If she carries on like this, she may feel that she can't cope with her studies and leave. She must work smart and really do what is important and work on the 20/80 rule.

This is also called the Pareto Principle and means that only a small percent (20per cent) of what we do is important while the majority of what we do (80per cent) is trivial.

Winston has problems revising for exams whereas structured assignments seem to be OK for him. He seems to be a classic procrastinator. He needs to first accept that this is what he is doing and then set himself small tasks. He should concentrate on the task at hand and not take or make phone calls during this period. He can then reward himself with a couple of hours out with his friends. He will feel good about himself and enjoy his time out a lot more.

References

■ Boniwell, L. (2005) 'Beyond time management: how the latest research on time perspectives and perceived time use can assist clients with time related concerns', *International Journal of Evidence Based Coaching and Mentoring*, 3(2), 61.

■ Covey, S. R., Merrill, A. and Merrill, R. (1994) *First Things First: Coping with the Ever-increasing Demands of the Workplace*. London, Simon & Schuster.

■ Hall, E. T. (1959) *The Silent Language*. New York, Garden City.

■ Innis, K. and Shaw, M. (1997) 'How do students spend their time?', *Quality Assurance in Education,* 5(2), 85–9.

■ Northgate, S. (2006) *Beyond 9–5: Your Life in Time*. London, Orion Publishing Group.

■ Robinson, J. P. and Godbey, G. (1997) *Time for Life: The Surprising Ways Americans Use Their Time*. State College, PA, The Pennsylvania State University Press.

■ Zimbardo, P. and Boyd, J. (1999) 'Putting time in perspective: a valid, reliable individual differences metric', *Journal of Personality and Social Psychology*, 77, 1271–88.

2 Managing your stress

Most of your time at university will be a happy and enjoyable one. There may be times, however, when you feel things are getting out of control and you feel uncomfortably stressed. This can be related to your studies, your personal life, or both. Knowing what stress does to our bodies, our own tendencies towards being stressed and the approaches we use to handle stressful events is an important life skill.

In this chapter you will:

1. identify signs of stress in yourself and others;
2. develop proactive strategies for dealing with stress;
3. recognise a personal tendency to be more stressed;
4. recognise what your stressors are and how to manage them.

USING THIS CHAPTER

Estimate your current levels of confidence. At the end of the chapter you will have the chance to re-assess these levels where you can incorporate this into your personal development planner (PDP). Mark between 1 (poor) and 5 (good) for the following:

I can recognise my own signs of stress.	I can recognise what stresses me.	I can apply proactive strategies to combat stress.

Date: _____

1 Introduction

Of students surveyed for the Student Experience Report in 2006, 98 per cent said that university life was a happy one. You may well be one of those and may look at the title of this chapter and feel that you are not particularly stressed and that, if you were, you could cope with it. However, 56 per cent of those students also said that since being at university they were under a lot more stress than before.

If you are thinking of not reading this chapter because you currently don't feel stressed, **stop now** and consider the following: I know what happens to my body when I am stressed, I can recognise the symptoms and I fully understand what stresses me. I have also reflected on my attitude to things in my life and realise this plays a role in how stressed I feel and I have enough belief in myself to solve any issues that cause anxiety. If you are happy with all these statements, move on. If not, and you wish to develop or hone this life skill, read on.

2 What happens to our bodies under stress?

Richard Lazarus, an eminent psychologist who won the prestigious award of 'American Psychologist' in 2002, claimed that stress and anxiety mainly occur when we believe we can't cope with the problem we perceive as stressful (Lazarus and Folkman, 1984). When we see this problem as overwhelming and feel we have no way of escaping or solving it, we experience anxiety or stress. However, we don't all see the same events as stressful. We have different perceptions of what is stressful, we have different levels of confidence in dealing with it and different ways of coping with it. There is therefore no one solution, but in general it is the feeling of being out of control that makes us anxious and stressed.

How do our bodies respond to stress?

When we perceive an event as stressful, our bodies react physiologically to it. The Harvard physiologist Walter Cannon coined the term 'fight or flight' in the 1920s to refer to our body's physiological response to a threatening situation, be this physical or emotional. When we feel threatened our heart rate speeds up, our blood pressure rises and our muscles tighten. At the same time our body releases the hormone cortisol that increases the flow of energy to our muscles. This makes us ready for action: we either stay and fight or run. Once we have dealt with the threat our body returns to normal. However, if our perceived threat doesn't result in action, then cortisol takes longer to disappear. If we 'run away' from a piece of coursework, for example, it isn't going to help very much. We may find ourselves even more stressed. 'Running away' from many of our stressors often means making excuses, and this can make things worse in the long run, making us feel even more stressed. If this continues over a long period of time, it attacks our immune system, cardiovascular system, digestive system and musculoskeletal system until we are exhausted and eventually become ill.

Excess cortisol also affects the part of the brain that is central to learning and memory by interfering with how our brain cells communicate with each other. In a crisis, we often don't remember what went on exactly; it is as if our 'lines are down' and we react only to that which is vital. So, not handling stress well, or being under constant stress, will affect our ability to learn.

Being alert to what creates stress in our lives, and developing techniques that can enable us to cope with this, and reduce excess flow of cortisol, is therefore an essential life skill.

NOTE   Although stressors increase the amount of cortisol in our bloodstream, we also have 'daily shots' of cortisol throughout our daily cycle (circadian rhythm). This helps to keep us alert by maintaining our blood pressure and enabling us to react to our environment.

3 What are the symptoms of stress?

When we feel stressed we notice changes in our emotions and our behaviour. Activities 1 and 2 help you to identify stress in yourself and others.

ACTIVITY 1 Identifying signs of stress

Look at the scenarios below and complete the table.

Carlos is an outgoing and confident person and has decided to study abroad. He is now reaching the end of his first semester. He is gregarious and has a good friendship group. However, his friends are noticing that he is becoming increasingly withdrawn, is not eating properly and appears 'on edge' a lot of the time. When they try to talk to him he becomes irritable and no one feels they should pry any further.

Lucy is a third-year student and has always had a very full social life. Her tutors have spoken to her many times for handing work in late and missing classes. However, she always seemed to pull things together at the last minute. Just recently, however, you have noticed that she has started drinking more and when you pointed this out to her she said she wasn't sleeping well and needed some alcohol to help. You have also noticed that your fun-loving friend has little interest in the things you used to do together. She is also getting into difficulties with her third-year project group who are complaining of her forgetfulness and lack of interest in the project.

	Signs of stress	What he/she might be feeling	What he/she should do
Carlos			
Lucy			

Check the feedback section for more information.

ACTIVITY 2 Recognising your own symptoms of stress

When you feel stressed, what symptoms do you have? List them under how you feel, including physical characteristics (e.g. heart pounding, feeling sick, tired) and how you act (e.g. irritable, lack of interest, get emotional).

How do you feel? (Include physical and emotional characteristics)	How do you act and behave?

Check the feedback section for more information.

Let's keep things in proportion. We all get stressed at times. Most of the time symptoms are uncomfortable but short-lived and manageable. Sometimes we aren't even aware of feeling stressed until someone points out how irritable we are. However, we can get chronic stress symptoms and this needs to be dealt with.

Activities 1 and 2 have been included so that you can see the importance of being aware of your own and your friends' behaviour as an initial step in dealing with stress.

Is all stress bad?

Stress can be both positive and negative. Positive stress is having just about enough stress to motivate and challenge us. It can give us a buzz. However, generally when we hear the word 'stress' we associate it as a negative state, as our symptoms above show. So, for some a group project, an essay or a presentation may be seen as positive and challenging while for others it could be seen as negative and worrying.

Also, we need some stress in our lives to keep us alert and ready for that challenge. We have probably all experienced a rise in our heart rate just as we are about to do something we find challenging or stressful, but often that is what we need to get us up and running – a healthy dose of cortisol that dissipates quite soon afterwards. How many of us have put off a task because the deadline is just too far away? As the deadline approaches, we get the 'rush' and this stimulates us into activity. The trick is knowing when this can flip over from being the kick-start you need to being stressful.

Reflect on how you deal with deadlines: are you generally operating too close for comfort or just about right? You will probably find you have a particular tendency (see Chapter 1, 'Managing your time'). You need to identify this so that you can tackle it if you need to.

Some symptoms of positive stress are:

- I feel excited.
- I get motivated.
- It gives me a buzz.
- It stretches me intellectually or physically.
- It enables me to learn.

4 Personal development in handling stress

Broadly speaking, our attitudes will affect how we relate to others, how we cast blame when things don't work out, how we go about our tasks and the degree of control we feel over our lives. We need to develop our self-awareness in identifying stress and stressful events as well as confidence (self-belief) in being able to regain control over our lives.

Making personal changes – developing emotional intelligence

Daniel Goleman, author of the popular book *Emotional Intelligence* (1995), claims that intellectual IQ alone does not give us all the skills needed to be successful in everyday life. We need to develop self-awareness and recognise what others are feeling (empathy), know how to handle our emotions and have self-discipline. This, Goleman claims, is emotional intelligence or emotional quotient (EQ). Group work projects, for example, if taken seriously, develop our interpersonal skills (emotional literacy). Similarly, effective use of the personal development planner (PDP) enables us to reflect on our progress and personal development. These aspects of the curriculum therefore have good reasons for being there.

Emotional intelligence comprises, in essence, three areas: know yourself, choose yourself, give yourself. These are summarised in the next table.

By developing your emotional intelligence, you have the grounding to develop your self-belief and self-confidence, which gives you confidence to become more in control of your life. You also become aware of your own behaviour and how this can limit you as well as increasing your empathy towards your friends' troubles.

Emotional intelligence categories	Questions	Application to your studies
Know yourself	■ What makes you think and feel the way you do? ■ What parts of your reactions are habitual or consciously thought through? ■ What are you afraid of/anxious about?	Being honest with yourself enables you to reflect on your qualities and faults. You learn from your experiences. Reflect on this through your studies, part-time work, etc., and make notes in your personal development planner. This reflection should alert you to habitual actions – possibly fear of exams, particular coursework, etc. When you become aware of this you can then try to prevent yourself being a hostage to previously learned negative reactions.

Emotional intelligence categories	Questions	Application to your studies
Choose yourself	■ How do you know what's right for you? ■ If you were not afraid or anxious, what would you do? ■ Can you increase your awareness of your actions?	Manage your feelings. If something starts to stress you, identify exactly what it is and objectively assess why this is a stressor for you. Can you manage it yourself or do you need help?
Give yourself	■ Am I helping or hurting people? ■ Am I working interdependently with others? ■ Have I developed empathy? ■ Do I work by a set of personal standards?	Be aware of your fellow students. When working together, be alert to their needs as well as yours (be empathic).

Source: Adapted from the Emotional Intelligence Network, www.6seconds.org.

Making personal changes – developing self-belief

As we have mentioned, an important aspect of dealing with stress is this ability to feel you can control your life. The modern-day reaction to the 'flight or fight' is our ability to change things that stress us and to do that we need to have confidence in ourselves (see Activity 3).

Albert Bandura, a famous Canadian professor in psychology, began to see personality as an interaction between psychological processes, the environment and our behaviour. He noticed that those who felt more in control of their lives (had high self-efficacy) behaved differently and personally achieved more (Bandura, 1997).

ACTIVITY 3 Is it all down to fate?

Look at the following statements – do you agree with them or not?

	Agree	Disagree
When things go wrong for me, it is just bad luck.		
It doesn't matter how well I plan, what's going to be, will be.		
Friendships are a result of chemistry – they work or they don't.		
Some people have all the luck.		
When things go wrong, I can usually find out who is to blame.		

As you probably realised, these are statements that reflect someone who has little self-belief in their ability to make changes. Take a note of where your tendency lies. Check the feedback section for comments on these statements.

Write a new list of statements below that reflects someone who has self-belief.

	Generally me	Generally not me

Check the feedback section for some more examples once you have written your own.

Strategies for improving self-belief

1. Select a specific task/activity you want to improve and feel confident about. Think of a specific task.

2. This activity needs to be important to you as this will give you the motivation to work on it.

3. Has your previous experience of doing this activity been negative? If so, identify the specific negative aspects so you can work on them (don't generalise because you can't work with generalisations).

4. Develop a picture of yourself, or someone, doing this activity well. What makes it good? Make sure you 'see' your negative aspects performed well. Keep that picture in mind.

5. Set yourself specific and short-term goals to deal with aspects of the activity you have identified. See the section below on approaches to dealing with stressful events.

6. Seek feedback and work with it positively. If you feel you 'can't do something', always say 'I can't do that YET'. It has a powerfully confident feel about it.

7. Verbalise (write out) your strategy for achieving your short-term goals. This way you have articulated your success and you can 'hear' it, and it primes you for action.

8. Small successes breed overall success.

NOTE   Being 'in control' of events in your life is not about being a 'control freak'. It is about feeling that you can DO something to help. The higher your emotional intelligence, the better you will be at trusting others in order to give and receive help. Recognise when you need support and be proactive in seeking it out.

71

Checklist: signs of stress

Take the list of symptoms here as a warning signal. If these symptoms become chronic, you must seek help.

Physical

Headaches, backache, exhaustion, insomnia, pounding heart, diarrhoea or constipation, stiff neck and shoulders, rashes, nausea.

Emotional

Feeling useless, worthless, not confident of abilities, not recognising your strengths, talking yourself down, feeling lonely, feeling 'out of control', feeling irritable and angry.

Intellectual

Feeling you can't learn another thing, you can't remember things, you don't process information very well in class, you have to keep going over something to make it 'stick'.

As a result of some of these symptoms you may find that you have negative reactions, such as withdrawal from friends, mood swings, angry outbursts, inability to make decisions, feeling weepy, not hungry or eating too much, feeling sick when you open 'that' book or go past the library, possibly excessive drinking, drug abuse or self-harming.

NOTE   If things have gone on too long or have become worse you may start to show more serious symptoms such as obsessive behaviour, suicidal feelings or depression. If you feel your symptoms are getting worse and you are worried, you must get professional help from either your doctor or the counselling service at your institution. If you do this, make sure you tell your personal tutor so that he/she can make allowances for late work or postpone certain assignments.

5 Do I have a personality that stresses me out?

We are all aware that some of our friends get more stressed out than others and we may envy them if we are the one who gets stressed out while they remain calm. We should be aware by now that there are (a) individual differences in how stressful or challenging we see particular events, and (b) individual differences in our perceptions of our own ability to deal with these events, once we see them as stressful. One of the factors for these individual differences is our different personality styles.

How does your personality affect your stress levels?

In the 1950s, two cardiologists, Dr Meyer Friedman and Dr Ray Rosenman, observed that there was more heart disease in their male patients with high-pressured jobs. This may seem obvious to us now but it wasn't at the time. They also noted that particular personality types were also more prone to heart disease. The personality type they felt was more 'at risk' was their so-called 'Personality A' person. Incidentally, Friedman regarded himself as a 'recovering type A'. The type A personality has now become synonymous with 'driven' people, obsessed with time and perfection. The counter to that is the type B personality that is laid-back and easy-going.

Are you a type A or a type B?

Type A and type B is essentially a continuum of personality traits from being uptight to laid-back. It is not an intricate measure of your personality but serves to give you a guideline of where your tendencies are.

Type A personalities tend to:

- be very goal driven (in the extreme often at all costs);
- be competitive;
- need recognition and advancement;
- multi-task when under time pressure;
- be keen to get things finished;
- be mentally and physically alert (above average).

NOTE There is continuing debate as to whether type A personality people are more at risk from heart disease. But the potential anger and hostility aspect of this personality type does seem to be a factor.

Type B personalities tend to:

- be more relaxed;
- be more easy-going;
- socialise a lot;
- be less competitive;
- set realistic goals that don't overstretch them.

If you are not sure which personality type you are, the Science Museum has a short online fun quiz that allows you to find out. This can be found at: www.sciencemuseum.org.uk. Search on 'stress' from the search engine.

Help! I'm a type A personality and I'm already stressed out about it

Not all characteristics of type A people are bad. You will know yourself if you feel too driven or uptight. If you feel you are a type A person you may feel stressed out, for example, if you can't achieve what you set out to do, or if you see coursework deadlines looming and you think you are going to be late. You may need to readjust your personal standards and become a little more relaxed if you feel you are overdoing things. Some of your friends may hint at your behaviour and you may want to consider whether you are being too 'driven'.

Think about yourself and develop your emotional intelligence. Are there ways you can tone down your type A characteristics? Identify some of your characteristics you think you can work on. Also, check out the stress-busting techniques to help you when you need them.

Why bother? I'm a type B personality

Not all the characteristics of extreme type B personalities are good. You may find yourself too laid-back where nothing stresses you until things get out of hand. You need to submit work tomorrow and suddenly you have got to get into action and you may not have the time to give your best. But, if you are an extreme type B, this may not worry you either! However, try to balance your relaxed style and ensure you are keeping to the goals you have set.

We need to get a balance

As with everything, we need a balance of drive and relaxation. Ideally you should be halfway between a type A and type B person. This way you can deal with unexpected deadlines and other stressors by calm planning. You feel in control and not stressed out.

So once you have become self-aware, emotionally literate and believe in yourself, how do you approach stressful events?

6 Proactive strategies for dealing with stress

Stress-busting techniques are one way of coping with stress (see Section 8), but they are just that, 'techniques', and they are good to have. However, a more fundamental way of dealing with stress is to be **proactive** in your management of it. Psychologists have identified two broad types of coping strategy:

- problem-focused strategy;
- emotion-focused strategy.

Problem-focused strategy	<ul><li>Know your stressors.</li><li>Analyse what stresses you about an event.</li><li>Break down the various components of the situation into manageable chunks.</li><li>Identify which part is the problem.</li><li>Look at the options.</li><li>Develop an action plan.</li><li>Check your resources – do you need help?</li></ul>
Emotion-focused strategy	<ul><li>Know your stressors.</li><li>Reflect on how you *feel* when confronted with this stressor.</li><li>Resist your feeling to avoid thinking about this.</li><li>Reflect on how you can start to change this emotion.</li><li>Trust in others and discuss with a friend or counsellor.</li></ul>

Source: Coping strategies from Lazarus and Folkman (1984)

If you are already a proactive stress-buster, you may find you have a preference for one or other of the strategies above. Ideally, you should be using both strategies as they tap into your self-belief and your emotional intelligence. Activity 4 asks you to think about how you solve problems.

ACTIVITY 4 Problem solving as a way of dealing with stress

Think of an example that is pertinent to you. How would you use this problem-solving strategy?

1. Identify a stressful problem.

2. What makes it stressful?

3. How do I feel about it?

4. What can I do now to manage it?

Checklist: proactive coping strategies	
	Need to work on this ✓
Personal development: ■ Self-belief (I am a 'can do' person) ■ Emotional intelligence (I know myself and trust others)	
Personality type: ■ Type A (perfectionist, driven, high standards) ■ Type B (relaxed)	
Strategies: ■ Problem-focused (analyse, action plan) ■ Emotion-focused (realign emotions)	

7 What makes studying stressful?

Learning does cause stress and your ability to handle some degree of stress will help you. You may well find you are in your comfort zone at the beginning of a course where you feel in control of your learning and you can predict what is going on. However, very soon you may find that as the difficulty increases you feel less in control of what you know and don't know and very soon fall outside your comfort zone. At this stage you are learning! It is important to recognise that you must go through this stage in order for your new knowledge to find its place and become your new comfort zone. It is important to get back into your new comfort zone, although for some students this takes until the exams before everything starts to fall into place. Look at Figure 2.1.[1] Where do you feel you are now? Are you happy to be outside your comfort zone while you learn?

Becoming a student can be seen as a 'rite of passage'. It is something you probably feel you want to do; it certainly matures you. You leave home, make a new home for yourself, make new friends and learn about something you are interested in. These are all exciting challenges and can give

---

[1] Thanks to Professor Mark Lutman from the University of Southampton who discussed these ideas. He feels that a good learner is one who can cope with being outside their comfort zone – as long as it is not for too long.

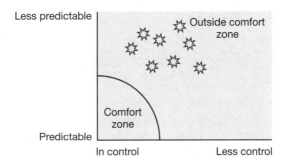

Figure 2.1 Are you in your comfort zone?

you such a buzz – **or** – completely stress you out. Which is it for you? Activity 5 asks you to identify stressors in academic life.

ACTIVITY 5 Stressors in academic life

Identify some of the stressors in academic life from this typical scenario. What do you think Joanne should do? Then identify academic stressors that particularly affect you.

Joanne was the first of her family to go on to further study and she was very excited at studying engineering. She made friends quickly through her studies and the clubs she joined. However, now in her third year, money, or lack of it, is an increasing worry. She has taken out several loans but has now decided to take a part-time job to make ends meet and has found herself a job in a local restaurant. She works two evenings a week on four-hour shifts finishing at midnight. She has also taken on another small job in the local supermarket working a busy afternoon shift. While her bank balance is now looking healthier, she feels that the late nights and the extra supermarket job are beginning to affect her work. Her studies are increasingly complex and she has several projects to complete. As this is her third year she needs good grades to get the degree she wants. She is beginning to feel there are too many demands on her life and doesn't know how to cope, especially since her boss is pressurising her to work more shifts.

	Academic stressors	Coping strategies
Joanne		
You		

Will I/do I fit in?

When you leave home to study you leave behind everything you are familiar with: your friends, your town, your boyfriend/girlfriend and your family. This familiar environment has helped make you and support you. Although you are excited by leaving all this behind, you may find that once you are away things do not feel as comfortable or safe as they did at home. You are basically homesick. Many of your fellow students will be feeling the same and you know you have to make an effort to fit in, find new friends and belong. The best time to do this is right at the beginning of your studies when everyone is looking for new friends. You may find that you don't mix with the right group in the first instance, but by the second semester you will be feeling confident enough to know who you'd like to be with and how to go about it. Being shy may make this process slower, but try to join clubs you are interested in and that should automatically link you with like-minded people.

I never seem to have enough money

The Student Experience Report 2006, carried out by MORI (Unite, 2006), conducted more than 1000 face-to-face interviews with undergraduate and post-graduate students. It found that of those sampled, over half reported difficulties managing their finances and one-third had already asked their families to help them out in a crisis. Postgraduate and mature students, however, were least likely to turn to their families for financial support.

Finances are an increasing source of stress for students and finding part-time work is an obvious solution. The trend towards part-time work when in full-time education is growing. The Student Experience Report 2006 reported that four in ten of those interviewed had done part-time work during their studies, and this is set to increase. In a *Guardian Unlimited* article in 2002 it was reported that the National Union of Students in the UK estimated that approximately 42 per cent of students worked part time, whereas the Trade Union Council's survey in 2000 claimed that 60 per cent of students needed to work to meet basic living costs (Hennessey, 2002). Although working gives you added experience and responsibility, too much can damage your studies. The Government recommends that you spend no more than ten hours/week in part-time employment.

Lack of money is the root cause of other stressors, e.g. poor accommodation, cheap food and lack of course materials. So getting your finances right is crucial (see Activity 6).

ACTIVITY 6 Budgeting

Budgeting is something we have to do all our lives. However, if finance is a particular stressor for you then you must get to grips with budgeting. This is rarely anyone's favourite activity, but to prevent debts building up you need to know what comes in and what goes out and work within that budget as much as you can.

How do your finances look? Work on a weekly or monthly basis, whichever suits you best.

	Amount incoming weekly/monthly	Amount outgoing weekly/monthly
INCOME:		
Loan		
Part-time work		
Family		
Savings		
Other		
ACCOMMODATION:		
Rent		
Electricity		
Gas		
Water		
Telephone		
Council tax		
Other		
	Amount incoming weekly/monthly	Amount outgoing weekly/monthly
STUDIES:		
Tuition fees		
Field trips		
Stationery		
Project costs		
Other		
LIVING COSTS:		
Food		

	Amount incoming weekly/monthly	Amount outgoing weekly/monthly
Eating out (evening and day)		
Toiletries		
Mobile phone		
Travel: car		
Travel: bus fares – daily		
Travel: long-distance trips (home?)		
Clothes		
Other (dentist, doctor, prescription, etc.)		
SOCIAL LIFE:		
The pub		
Cinema, clubs		
Sporting activities		
Other		
TOTAL		

Do the incoming and outgoing columns balance?

What should you do if you find yourself in need of financial support? Your institution will have a student support centre where you can find information on the student hardship fund that it operates. There may be other schemes to help you budget more effectively. These are people in your institution whose job it is to help you; you should be proactive and seek them out.

I don't know what my tutors expect of me

A problem for first-year students is that move into Higher Education. You may have come from an 'A' level course in the UK, be an international student or a mature student returning to full-time education.

Always check your programme and course documentation (see 'Learning in Higher Education') as this describes the aims of your course and the learning outcomes. Always make sure you know exactly what is needed in an assignment, never assume. Remember, you will be expected to develop an independent style of learning (see 'Learning in Higher Education'). If you are in doubt regarding what is expected, ask either your tutor or a student in the second or third year.

If you have a study buddy or peer mentoring scheme in your institution, take full advantage of it. If not, you may want to ask if one can be set up. See the Peer Assisted Learning website at Bournemouth University in the UK (http://pal.bournemouth.ac.uk, last accessed 13 January 2010).

I just can't learn everything I am expected to

The academic load and demands of coursework are another area that has been identified as a cause of stress. You may find that your assignments are bunched towards the end of the semester and you struggle to hand them in by the deadlines.

Assignment deadline bunching is a problem. But, if you are given the task way ahead of time, you will be expected to time manage all your assignments (see Chapter 1, 'Managing your time'). Plan when you can fit in each assignment given the amount of knowledge you have at the time. Sometimes you may have to get started before you have had the lecture, seminar or laboratory class. You can make an outline plan and fit in as much as you can as you go along.

Academic load in terms of sheer quantity of what you are expected to learn will mean that you need to develop some effective academic skills. The chapters in this book are designed to do just that. Actively take what you need from each chapter and **act on it** and this will start to reduce your stress as you begin to feel in control. Activity 7 asks you to identify your stressful events.

The complexity of the material you have to learn will also increase with the years and this has been shown to be another stressor. Don't suffer in silence over something you are struggling with. Ask your tutor and possibly a postgraduate teaching assistant who may be helping on the course. Don't forget you can ask your friends, or student mentors if you have this set up in your programme.

In 'Learning in Higher Education', we discussed the characteristics of a novice and an expert; you may want to check this out again later.

ACTIVITY 7 Identifying your stressful events

Which of the following, if any, do you find stressful:

■ bunched assignment deadlines;
■ the sheer quantity of work to get through;
■ complexity of the work;
■ anything else?

How can you be proactive in managing these potential stressors?

Complete the concept map below with the different types of study stressors and list ways of dealing with them. Place each study stressor on the first branch and the ways of dealing with it on the lower branches.

See feedback section for a map of the result of stress on study.

Dropping out: a response to stress?

Dropping out from your studies can be a response to stress, but not necessarily. If you feel that you really have chosen the wrong subject, the wrong place to study and you now know exactly what you want to do and it is not studying, then leave. You will become even more stressed if you stay and will be staying only because you want to save face or not offend someone. According to a BBC article (BBC News, 2004), one in seven students in the UK drops out. However, this varies greatly across institutions. Learning how to keep stress under control and not letting it ruin your life is vital.

If you want to leave because you feel you can't cope or you are generally unhappy, **think again**. With the help of your personal tutor, a student adviser, a friend, or a religious leader, discuss why you are unhappy and what your options really are. You will find there are various options and one could be just right for you, enabling you to go on and graduate. **Don't let wanting to leave be a flight reaction to stress**.

Who gets more stressed out?

As we should know by now, being stressed out varies between individuals. However, some groups of students are more likely to feel the pressures than others. Stressors can be external or internal. External stressors refer to things outside of us that we have to deal with, e.g. exams, coursework, finances, etc. Internal stress refers to our personality characteristics, or if we are dealing with some incapacity or illness. So, all stress is an interplay between what we bring to the event and the event itself. The imbalance between internal and external stressors can affect our psychological and physiological well-being and cause stress (Lazarus and Cohen, 1977).

Since external factors play a role in stress, certain students may find themselves under additional pressures.

Are you a mature student?

This refers to any student coming back to study after some time out of Higher Education. You may find that you are unsure about how you will:

- fit in with youngsters;
- be able to cope academically;
- be able to juggle home life and study;
- be able to cope financially.

Are you an international student?

As an international student you have additional things that bring pressure. You will have to deal with:

- setting up home in another country;
- being homesick;
- understanding the cultural differences (socially and academically);
- working in a language that is not your native tongue;
- facing, possibly, racist comments. Do report this if within the university.

External pressures are discussed in Activity 8.

NOTE You are probably a happy and well-adjusted student even though you may have these added pressures. Please don't feel you have to be stressed out. If you are coping well, you may want to be alert to students in a similar situation to you who are not coping well and you may be able to give them some support (develop your emotional intelligence).

ACTIVITY 8 My external pressures

	Applies to me	Do I need to do anything?
Just returning to full-time education after many years and wonder how I will cope.		
I'm homesick (or may become).		
My English is not good enough.		
I'm not giving enough time to my family.		
I miss my friends back home.		
Can I cope?		

List more pressures that apply to you and check whether you think you need to do something about it to keep it in check. What personality type are you – could this influence your reaction to stress? Are you proactive and use problem- and emotion-focused coping strategies (see Sections 4, 5 and 6 above)?

8 Stress-busting techniques: a maintenance strategy

In addition to the personal development and proactive strategies above, we can develop a maintenance programme that enables us to cope with on-going stress that hits us once in a while. Some basic techniques are as follows:

- **Exercise**. This will help the physiological aspect of stress and the release of endorphins will give you a feeling of euphoria as well as help your heart. It is also ideal for getting rid of anger and frustrations. If you want to choose only one stress-busting technique, then choose this one.
- **Relax**. When you are feeling stressed out it is difficult to unwind. You may find you have to make a big effort to do this. It may be better to go to classes such as yoga or tai-chi. Exercising also helps you to relax. If you want to develop your own relaxation techniques, try deep breathing or meditation. Go out with friends and have a good laugh.

- **Eat well**. Avoid junk food and too much alcohol – both of these can sap your energy and make you feel low.
- **Talk**. Open up to friends and family. They will feel honoured that you trust them enough to discuss your problems. Talking allows you to see things in perspective and get another view.
- **Stress diary**. By keeping a diary you start to articulate what your feelings are and what stresses you out. Once you do this you become conscious and self-aware, which is where you must start in order to cope. You can couple this with talking to your friends.
- **Focus**. When we are stressed we start to feel overwhelmed. Go back and look at the strategies above for developing self-belief and focus on each part of your plan.
- **Get support from others**. There are some problems you can't and shouldn't face on your own. Don't try to be superman or superwoman. Most Higher Education institutions are caring and will have support in place for you. You should make yourself familiar with what is available, for example student services, Students Union, religious chaplains, counselling services, medical services, your personal tutor and, of course, your friends and family.

Exams – the special case

During revision:

- plan a realistic revision timetable – this will help you stay on top of things;
- summarise your notes, make key points, highlight important information and use concept maps for quick overviews;
- take breaks so you can stay alert.

During the exam:

- 'feel' calm – breathe slowly and deeply;
- feel in control;
- read the instructions carefully (very often students don't do this);
- read the questions calmly – underlining key aspects;
- mark the questions you want to do first;
- allocate time for each question;
- allow time to check your work.

9 On reflection

Stress management, as you have seen, is much more than learning a few techniques: it is life changing. It cannot guarantee you a stress-free life, and would you want one? But it will enable you to manage it and keep the health-threatening aspects of stress under control.

Summary of this chapter

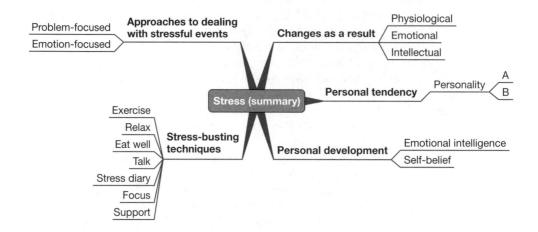

Now reflect on your current abilities to work through a stress-management plan and consider what you need to do to improve. You may want to transfer this information to your institution's personal development planner scheme.

ACTIVITY 9 Update your personal development planner

Having read this chapter, gauge your confidence again – how does this compare with your confidence levels at the start of the chapter? What can you do to improve? You can incorporate this into your personal development planner and of course add anything else that you feel is appropriate.

Grade your confidence on a scale of 1–5 where 1 = poor and 5 = good.

My stress management plan	Confidence level 1–5	Plans to improve
Recognise my personal tendency to being stressed (personality type A, B). *Section 5*		
Identify what stresses me. *Section 7*		
Recognise how I react to stress. *Section 3*		
Check my self-belief. *Section 4*		
Improve my emotional intelligence. *Section 4*		

My stress management plan	Confidence level 1–5	Plans to improve
Identify proactive strategies in dealing with stress that suit me best. *Section 6*		
Identify and use the best stress-busting techniques for me. *Section 8*		

Date:_____

Getting extra help

■ Talk to your university counsellor. He or she will be able to give advice on how best to deal with the common problems associated with the stresses of studying.

■ Ask friends how they cope with stress – not only will you discover that it's more common than you think, but also they may have some useful stress-busting tips for you.

Consult a few interesting websites:

■ **Student Mental Stress: DStress.** This site is produced by Loughborough University and is full of useful information. It is a good interactive site. See: www.d-stress.org.uk [last accessed December 2006].

■ **Mind: How to Cope with the Stress of Student Life**. Mind has a guide and a series of tips for getting help if you need it. Search on 'student stress' using its search engine: www.mind.org.uk [last accessed November 2008].

■ **Channel 4, 4Health, Student Stress, Wendy Moore**. Search on 'stress' using the search engine. 'Most students will feel the effects of stress at some point in their studies and a small number of students may feel stressed or depressed for a lot of the time.' See: www. channel4.com/health [last accessed November 2008].

Feedback on activities

ACTIVITY 1 Identifying signs of stress

	Signs of stress	What he/she might be feeling	What he/she should do
Carlos	Becoming withdrawn Not eating properly On edge/ irritable	Emotional. This can be weepy or aggressive. Emotional exhaustion.	Notice that things aren't right and something needs to be done before you get too behind with your studies. Talk to someone you trust – friend, tutor or counsellor. Make sure this doesn't go on for too long.
Lucy	Heavy drinking Not sleeping well Disinterested, forgetful	Feeling unwell and possibly depressed from too much alcohol and not enough sleep. Mental exhaustion.	Be alert to a change in behaviour that is unhelpful. Identify the first thing that needs to be done, i.e. stop drinking. Seek help from a friend or counsellor to prevent serious alcohol damage.

NOTE In these case studies the key to moving on is being alert to your own stress patterns and recognising when they are becoming overwhelming. Seek help and allow your friends to help you. As a friend, you may have to help someone who is trying to push you away. Be patient and try not to abandon him or her during this difficult phase of your friendship.

ACTIVITY 2 Recognising your own symptoms of stress

Here are some symptoms of stress. Check the ones that you have identified. You may recognise more symptoms that you didn't realise indicated stress.

How do you feel? (Include physical and emotional characteristics)	How do you act and behave?
Feeling overwhelmed	You are disorganised and forgetful. You are over-cautious and have difficulty making decisions. You panic. You have lost your confidence. You can't concentrate on your work. Mental exhaustion.

How do you feel? (Include physical and emotional characteristics)	How do you act and behave?
Feeling tired and exhausted	You have no or little interest in things. You don't sleep well. You cry about things easily.
Feeling anxious and nervous	You are moody, irritable, aggressive and get angry easily. You may resort to recreational drugs to alleviate symptoms.
Feeling very emotional and tearful	You react emotionally and are often near to tears … emotional exhaustion.
Feeling sick/tight feeling in stomach/ not hungry	You have diarrhoea and/or lose interest in food.
Heart is pounding	You perspire more than usual.
Feeling homesick	You withdraw from your friends.
Being anti-social	You want to be on your own. People irritate you and you get short tempered.
Feeling depressed	Everything becomes too much and you have little interest in doing anything.

NOTE If your list was rather short, you might now recognise some of the symptoms you have. Add them to your list in this activity. Being aware of our stress symptoms is very important, as we saw in Activity 1.

ACTIVITY 3 Is it all down to fate?

	Comments
When things go wrong for me, it is just bad luck.	This means that you feel your behaviour doesn't contribute, or contribute much, to things that go wrong for you. You are placing the blame on something external – 'bad luck'.
It doesn't matter how well I plan, what's going to be, will be.	You feel you have no control as your whole life is already mapped out for you.
Friendships are a result of chemistry – they work or they don't.	Chemistry is definitely part of friendship, but not everything. If you don't work at finding and keeping friends, you will be on your own. Social well-being is very important in controlling stress.
Some people have all the luck.	See the first statement above. In this case you assume other people's successes are a result of 'good luck' rather than their efforts.

When things go wrong, I can usually find out who is to blame.	See the first statement above.
Statements of self-belief	
I can influence what happens to me.	
If I make specific short-term plans I know I will be able to keep to them.	
I know friends are attracted to each other, but I can still influence how well I integrate with my friends. I have the interpersonal and emotional intelligence to do that.	
When things go wrong, I work out why and sort it out so that it doesn't happen again.	

ACTIVITY 7 Identifying your stressful events

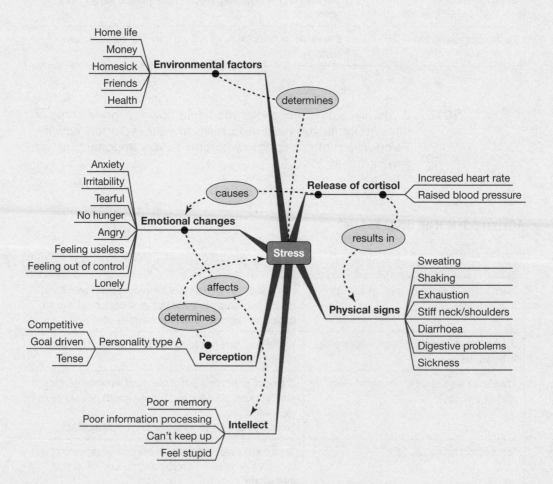

References

- 6Seconds: Emotional Intelligence Network, at http://6seconds.org/index.php [last accessed December 2009].

- Bandura, A. (1997) *Self Efficacy in Changing Societies*. Cambridge, Cambridge University Press.

- BBC News (2004) 'One in seven students to drop out', 30 September, available at: http://news.bbc.co.uk/1/hi/education/3703468.stm [last accessed December 2009].

- Goleman, D. P. (1995) *Emotional Intelligence: Why It Can Matter More Than IQ for Character, Health and Lifelong Achievement*. New York, Bantam Books.

- Hennessy, K. (2002) 'All work and no play makes ... a student', *Guardian Unlimited*, 30 September, available at: http://education.guardian.co.uk/students/story/ 0,,802009,00.html [last accessed March 2009].

- Lazarus, R. S. and Cohen, J. B. (1977) 'Environmental stress', in I. Altman and J. F. Wohlwill (eds), *Human Behavior and Environment*, Vol. 2. New York, Plenum.

- Lazarus, R. S. and Folkman, S. (1984) *Stress, Appraisal, and Coping*. New York, Springer.

- Science Museum, www.sciencemuseum.org.uk [last accessed December 2009].

- Unite, Student Experience Report 2006, MORI, available at: www.ipsos.com/researchpublications/researcharchive/poll.aspy?oItemId=578 [last accessed December 2009].

3 Learning part time, online and on a work placement

The distinction between full time on-campus students and those studying part time is becoming blurred. From a 2008 survey of student lifestyles conducted by Sodexho – Times Higher Education, it was found that 'almost half of the students with a job in term-time undertake paid work for between 11 and 20 hours a week, and 10 per cent devote between 21 and 30 hours a week to their job' (Attwood, 2008). As a part-time learner, you may also feel that you are missing out on all those facilities on campus but, again from the same survey, 67 per cent of full-time students socialise off campus, 63 per cent study in their own accommodation and 91 per cent spend ten hours or less in the library. So, don't feel you are necessarily missing out on a great social life on campus or are at a disadvantage in terms of accessing resources.

If you plan to take, or are on, a year out in work placement you will have even less direct contact with your university campus. Despite the opportunities a work placement gives you, you face the double challenge of maintaining the learning you have achieved in your (typically) first two years, and continuing to develop your learning skills to prepare for your return to university. Much of the general guidance to part-time and distance learners is useful to you, but you will need to have a personal strategy to help you maximise your learning whilst away from your course.

In this chapter you will:

1. be familiar with the key administrative documents on your course;
2. understand how to prepare yourself for part-time learning;
3. know the range of learning technology that could help you;
4. know the online skills you need to develop in order to exploit those technologies;
5. consider how to maintain your learning on a work placement.

USING THIS CHAPTER

Estimate your current levels of confidence. At the end of the chapter you will have the chance to re-assess these levels where you can incorporate this into your personal development planner (PDP). Mark between 1 (poor) and 5 (good) for the following:

I am well prepared for my studies.	I am familiar with the learning technologies I can use.	I am a competent online learner with a set of skills to help me.	I know what to do to keep up my university learning whilst on a work placement.

Date: _____

1 Being a successful part-time learner

As a part-time learner, whether enrolled as a full-time student or not, your main issue will be the competing demands on your time. You can succeed if you prepare yourself and recognise how you learn, remain well motivated, network well with fellow students, know how to deal with the potential stress of it all and manage your time effectively.

Different ways to learn part time

Being a part-time learner can mean several things: you study at home with a book, work to a learning agreement and evidence your learning through work; have day release to attend classes; study part time most of the year, but once or twice a year you have a residential week where you meet everyone. In all of these variations you will probably have some element of online learning, so understanding how to use learning technologies will be vital.

Distance learning

This is a generic term for learning 'off campus' or part time, and it can be paper-based, entirely online or a mixture of both. You will need access to a PC so you can log in to your institution. Apart from your course materials you should also have remote access via the Internet to library facilities, the Students Union, the library and most other facilities available to students on campus. You may need to check this out. Your course will have a set of documents that you need to familiarise yourself with (see 'Learning in Higher Education', section 3 and information below). Since you may not meet your fellow students, you need to network online in order to feel part of a study community (see 'Prepare yourself' below).

Work-based learning

Through this approach you will have registered to study and probably been given a list of things you are expected to show competency in at the end of your studies (learning outcomes). You will be expected either to complete coursework and learning outcomes through your everyday work activities or to present a comprehensive portfolio of evidence showing the competencies you have developed. It is very important therefore to ensure that the experience you are gathering does map to the learning outcomes of the course. If it does not, your tutor will not be able to give you a 'pass' as they have to match your developing competencies against the learning outcomes for that course. Understanding what is required on the course therefore becomes vital. Even though the course will be based on your job, you will still be expected to read academic literature and place what you are learning within conceptual frameworks that align with that literature.

Compact courses

These can also be distance-learning courses, with a week of face-to-face study at your institution. You will probably be given work to do during the semester so you are prepared for this intensive week. Arranging time off from work and family duties is essential and you will probably need to find a week's accommodation. If this is while your institution is closed to traditional students, you may be offered student accommodation.

Day-release scheme

Sometimes your institution organises courses that allow you to study one or two days a week. If this is the case, you will be local to your institution and in this mode of learning you will probably have arranged day release from work. You may also be joining a class of students who are studying full time and you may feel under time pressure as your reading and coursework will have to be fitted in. However, good planning and time management will see you through (see 'Prepare yourself' below).

Prepare yourself

At the start of your course take time to prepare yourself by identifying why you are doing it, recognising how much you want it and arranging your life to get you through those inevitable dips. Preparing yourself for study is not just for part timers, it is something all students should be doing.

Understand your course

Although you should look thoroughly at the course you have enrolled on beforehand, you will probably find that you have given the study detail only a fleeting glance. Once you have registered, you must take a closer look at your course. This is particularly important when learning at a distance as you don't have that easy back-up that you normally have when with fellow students on campus. Look at the checklist below and ensure you understand this information at the beginning of your course. If you don't know the answers now, make a point of finding out as soon as possible.

Checklist: proactive coping strategies	
	Need to work on this ✓
Regulations ■ I know the pass mark, marks needed to gain certain grades. ■ I know what my options are if I fail a unit or module.	
Learning outcomes ■ I understand this is what I should know at the end of the course, and I will have to evidence this through my coursework, portfolio and/or exams.	
Learning materials ■ I know where they are stored and how I can access them.	

Checklist: proactive coping strategies	
	Need to work on this ✓
Reference materials ■ I know how to get key texts and access the library remotely.	
Coursework ■ I know what is expected, when and how to hand it in.	
Assessment ■ I've made a note of the dates and what is expected. I have access to old exam papers so I can practise.	

Also check information in 'Learning in Higher Education', at the beginning of this book.

Your approach to learning

To get the most out of your studies, you need to understand yourself as a learner and through this you can exploit your strengths and work to improve your weaknesses. As explained in 'Learning in Higher Education', Section 1, David Kolb, in 1975, proposed a four-part learning cycle that we still use today: (a) gain experience, (b) observe and reflect, (c) work with abstract ideas and concepts and (d) apply learning to new situations. As we learn new things, we go through this cycle with the end result that we are able to apply our learning to new situations. As learners, however, we tend to feel happier in particular areas of this cycle, but not all of them. So, if you are happy in the 'gaining experience' part of the cycle, then you are more likely to be an activist and happy to get going quickly on a project and not 'hang about'. Similarly, you may not be too happy to 'take time out' to reflect on what you are doing. 'Know yourself as a learner' in 'learning in Higher Education' expands on this.

As a learner you also have a preference for processing information, and one popular way of looking at this is VARK© (Visual, Auditory, Reading/writing, Kinaesthetic). This proprietary tool, developed by Neil Fleming, an educational researcher from New Zealand, and Charles C. Bonwell from the USA, considers the four sensory ways we can get information: looking, hearing, reading/writing and hands-on. The authors say that as learners we have preferred senses for taking in information.

Look at the following – which do you think applies to you best and least?

Visual learners learn best through:

- Taking notes and making lists to read later.
- Reading information to be learned.
- Learning from books, videotapes, filmstrips and printouts.
- Seeing a demonstration.
- Working with concept maps.
- Seeing the overview of what is to be learned.

Strategies for visual learners

- Use highlighters in texts.
- Create concept maps/ flow charts.
- Use videos.
- Format your texts to visually lay out your information.
- Underline and circle text as you read.

Auditory learners learn best through:

- Listening to lectures and audio sources.
- Arguing and discussing ideas.
- Giving oral presentations as they can generally talk well.
- Using speech recognition software like DragonPlus© or Via Voice©.

You may be distracted by a lot of noise so your learning environment should be quiet.

Strategies for auditory learners

- Record your notes through speech-recognition software.
- Read aloud.
- Revise by recording your thoughts and playing them back.

Reading/writing learners learn best through:
- Handouts from lectures.
- Good textbooks.
- Writing essays.

Strategies for reading/writing learners

- Take a good set of notes in lectures.
- Learn for exams through practice essay writing.
- Learn through your own writing (you often don't know what you know until you write it down).
- Learn through writing out things that you have to learn (often again and again).
- Create lists.
- Create and answer your own Frequently Asked Questions.

Kinaesthetic learners learn best through:
- Doing and practising.
- Taking in information through labs, field trips, excursions, etc.
- Demonstrations.
- Using examples to learn concepts and principles.

Strategies for kinaesthetic learners

- Walk about while you are learning.
- Take frequent study breaks.
- Learn by handling materials, using models, doing things.
- Create models, posters, images.
- Skim-read books to get an overview first.

NOTE For more information on learning styles see: http://www.stud-yskills.soton.ac.uk/studytips/learn_styles.htm or an internet search on VARK.

Take care when using learning-style questionnaires. There are very many of them and they all measure something different. Always listen and reflect on how you learn best and use that if in doubt. The VARK© approach above will give you some ideas and you can always add your own.

Motivation

Learning part time and/or at a distance will mean that you need a lot of motivation to keep going. Learning can be difficult and you will hit low spots where you have to pick yourself up and keep going. Without a lot of motivation to study, you may 'lose your way'. Motivation comes from various sources.

Motivation to learn	
Extrinsic	**Intrinsic**
External motivation from parents, employer, partner, friends, etc. and possible rewards such as bonus, promotion, new job. The subject you are studying may or may not interest you that much.	Internal motivation results from something you really want to do and can also be linked to new job prospects. You are particularly interested in the topic.
Success and reward	

Your motivation will probably be a mixture of intrinsic and extrinsic. However, when the going gets tough, you need a good dose of intrinsic motivation and self-belief to 'stay the course'. To keep your motivation up it is important for you to feel reasonably well in control (see Chapter 1, 'Managing your time'), chunk up your work into manageable bits, set short goals that allow you to succeed and recognise your achievements as you go along.

Confidence

When you are studying part time you have to juggle lots of things in your life and as your studies become more difficult and make more demands on you, you may feel your confidence drop. This is a natural response. However, it is important it doesn't become too critical. All true deep learning will, at some time, put you outside your comfort zone. If you find your confidence ebbing away and you are not recovering, email your tutor or fellow students and get it sorted out. It is important to talk about it as then you can start to find solutions. Many general study skills books offer further advice on how to manage stress and it is worthwhile consulting them.

Hot Tip

Your university or college will have a range of student support services which will be able to help with your confidence (for example, academic or study skills units, counselling guidance services). These will be available to all students, whatever your mode of study. As well as on-campus support, you will be able to access these services by telephone and email.

Family and work commitments

This will be the greatest competition for your time. You need to establish a regular time and place to study and, as with all your other activities, this should become a fixture in your diary. As soon as possible establish critical dates for family, work and study and get them in your diary. If there are any clashes, be pro-active and negotiate with your family, employer or tutor.

Network and keep in touch

Learning is based on an inner dialogue with yourself in relation to the learning materials and coursework and through interpersonal dialogue with your fellow students and tutors. You need both! It is important therefore to make sure you know who may be studying on your module at the same time as you so you can support each other. Don't forget your tutor is also part of this network.

Identify a learning space

Find a place where you can study. If you are studying at home and have to move your papers after each study session, make sure you have a handy box that you can put everything into so that nothing gets lost. Also, identify where you can learn best: a quiet place, a busy place, a tidy place or a messy place. We all have our own preferences. Whatever you do, try to establish a learning routine, pace yourself and set reasonable goals.

Hot Tip

Since you will need to have internet access at home, invest in a wireless-enabled laptop so you can sit anywhere in your house and be online. This will give you maximum flexibility regarding your learning space.

Skills for part-time learning

All learners need to understand themselves as learners and develop skills that best suit them. This is the whole purpose of this book. It is more critical, however, for part-time learners to understand how they learn best as they have to make the most of the small amount of time they will have available. The crucial skills for you as a part-time learner will be your ability to:

- manage stress and time;
- motivate yourself during difficult times;
- take responsibility for your own learning and
  - be self-disciplined and set your own deadlines;
  - reflect on your progress and do something about it if necessary;
  - ask if in doubt;

- exploit learning technologies.

2 Using technology to learn

Whether you are learning part time or full time, you will probably need to have some technology to keep you going. Ideally you need:

- a broadband internet connection at home;
- a wireless-enabled laptop so that you can work in the most comfortable place in your house and be able to move around if others demand that space;
- a memory stick so you can back up your material and take your work with you as needed;
- a printer as you may be expected to submit work in paper format;
- an MP3 player if you have access to audio or video podcasts.

As we saw earlier, even a full-time student isn't necessarily on campus and socially there. The Sodexho – Times Higher Education survey (Attwood, 2008) also found that 88 per cent of students use social networking sites every week, so take a look in this section to see how you can benefit from them educationally. Increasingly students are using social network sites to break down distance and location by setting up online study communities that cross both campus boundaries *and* modes of study.

Access to information

You will be given a set of materials, such as these: lecture notes, problem sheets, case studies, textbooks or journal articles. Whether you are a campus or a distance student, you will probably have access to a 'virtual learning environment' (VLE). This is an online repository for all the learning materials as well as other online tools. Generally, these systems are now available via the Web and through internet access on your own PC. With a password from your institution, you will be ready to access all your material. Apart from written texts, you may find that increasingly your tutors provide you with audio and/or video podcasts which enable you to download on to an MP3 player, for what is now called 'mobile learning'. You should also be able to get remote access through your library to online journals as well as the university catalogue. Most university libraries are investing in electronic book resources, so you may find that your core textbooks are already available online. File-sharing video applications on the Web, for example YouTube, have also become a host to educational videos. The Open University in the UK, for example, has launched a set of YouTube videos – you may want to check this out: www.youtube.com/ou (Times Higher Education, 2008).

Collaborate with others

Online tools for collaboration, information sharing and networking are loosely known as Web 2.0 technologies. Some examples of these technologies are email, chat rooms, blogs, sites such as Facebook, office-type documents on Google, and wikis.

Wiki

The most famous wiki of course is Wikipedia, the online encyclopaedia that gets its information from the general public (which is why you should use it with care and never as your primary source of information). A wiki allows you to create linked pages of text and multimedia 'assets'. Your tutor may ask a group of you to create a wiki on a topic and this will enable those with permissions to upload and edit information. You may also want to create your own wiki as a study guide or a portfolio. If your institution does not have a wiki feature on the VLE it uses, you can always try some of the free services that are available, such as PB Wiki. However, since it is a free service, it does have limited capacity. You can see how to use this through a YouTube video.

Blogs

A blog is a short-hand version of 'Web log' and is set up by an individual to publicise their views on a particular topic. Blogs tend to be text based but they can also take multi-media items. Blogs can also be used for online seminars where your tutor will set a topic for discussion.

Google Docs

Web 2.0 technologies have increased our ability to learn from anywhere and with anyone; we don't necessarily need to be sitting at our own PC. However, when we have our documents on our own PC then we need to be at that PC in order to access them (unless you have emailed them to yourself, or put them on your memory stick). If you use Google Docs, for example, you can access your documents (text, spreadsheet or presentations) from anywhere and you can also allow your colleagues to see and work with them if you want. If you don't have a PC with all the relevant office software, or you want to be able to access your documents from anywhere, you may want to consider exploring this. Check out 'google docs' on a Web search engine and follow the video tour. A good place to start if you are interested is:

www.google.com/google-d-s/tour1.html

Social bookmarking

This is a way of marking Web pages you (and others) are interested in. The standard 'add to favorites' feature on your Web browser allows you to save an interesting site in a hierarchical structure that you have created. You also have to go back to the same PC in order to access your 'favorites'. Social bookmarking software 'Del.icio.us' allows you to post interesting sites to your Del.icio.us account (it is a free service), add key words that help you organise the information (a bit like putting in folders except you can have many key words) and share this with others if you wish. To access your sites, you search on the key words you have used and all sites with those 'tags' appear. You are also able to see whether anyone else has used that key word for other sites – giving you a wider view. There are several things you need to know about social bookmarking:

1. You need to 'tag' the sites you post to, let's say your Del.icio.us account. These tags, or key words, relate to how you will use the information and you may be able to use it in several ways, so you will have several tags. The tags will enable you to search for the group of sites you have marked with these tags. Knowing how you want to tag is important. All resources in a library are tagged, but they use a standard set of tags, e.g. Library of Congress, and this formal tagging system is called a taxonomy. Because it is formal it enables everyone to find the same information using the same search words. However, when we tag our websites in social bookmarking applications, we tag in an informal way and the same website can be tagged in numerous ways by different people. This way of tagging is called a 'folksonomy', a term coined by the information management architect Thomas Vander Wal (www.vanderwal.net/about.php).

2. In these applications you have the option of viewing your tags as a list, you can bundle them (like grouping in folders) or you can view them visually as a 'tag cloud' (see Figure 3.1). Words appear in cloud format, with some words in larger font if they have more websites tagged using this word. Tags are on single words, but the author in the example below has grouped words that go together to ensure an easier retrieval. However, this does limit your return when using this term to identify similar sites tagged by others.

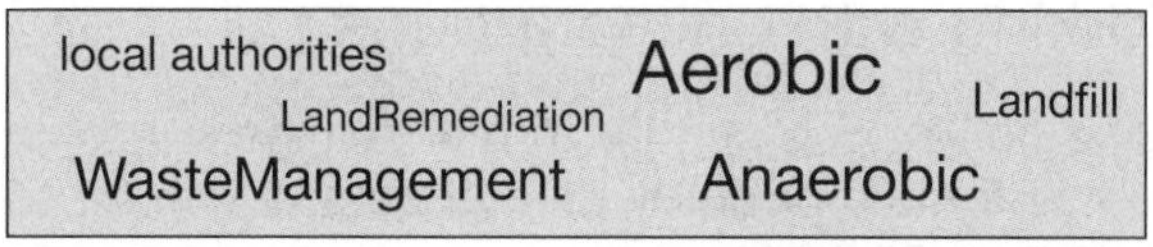

local authorities	**Aerobic**	Landfill
LandRemediation		
WasteManagement	Anaerobic	

Figure 3.1 An example of a tag cloud

For more information on social bookmarking and a list of online tools, see Netsquared organisation at: www.netsquared.org/choosingsocialbookmarking

Skills for online learning

Using learning technologies in your learning is not just for part-time learners. Increasingly full-time students are finding that a lot of their work is online. However, as a part timer you will find that you have to rely more on e-learning as your main source of literature, learning materials and online activities. All students then need to develop a set of skills that enables them to exploit these technologies to the full.

Netiquette

Netiquette is simply 'etiquette for online communication'. Email-type communications do have certain social rules that you should adhere to:

- **Write clear subject headings**
  - Be precise – the heading should reflect the content of the message.
  - Keep the header when forwarding or answering so a chain of messages can be identified.

- **Organise your message effectively**
  - Don't be too verbose; keep your message to the point.
  - Itemise key things where you want a response. Don't hide key information in verbose text, particularly at the end of the email. It will almost definitely be missed.
  - Avoid sending attachments if you can. Remember you can use applications like Google Docs which allows you to direct people to a document or Flickr if you are using photographs.

- **Be aware of your tone**
  - Don't use capital letters as it feels like YOU ARE SHOUTING.
  - It is easy to mis-read the tone in an email and respond in an aggressive way. If you feel offended, wait and respond when you feel calmer.
  - Don't send 'flaming' angry emails yourself as it can appear more aggressive in this medium.

Working with online groups

Online networking can be formal seminars, groups working on a project, informal forums or study help groups. It can be tricky working in a group online, especially if you have to make a decision about something. When you are sitting face to face in a group, you know where everyone is and that sets up an expectation of how the interaction will be; for example, a person at the apparent head of the table has a greater tendency to dominate or lead the discussion. Similarly, how people sit in the meeting, the tone of their voice and facial characteristics give you clues as to how engaged they are with the discussion. When you are working online, these physical cues are not available to you and you need to apply a bit more structure to the proceedings in order to move forward. Figure 3.2 gives you an idea of some of the structures that you and your group may want to consider.

Online seminars/discussion groups

In formation (a) of Figure 3.2, your tutor holds centre stage and most of the interaction will be from tutor to student. Here the tutor is 'in charge'. You 'listen' to what others say and contribute as you see fit. In this pattern there is rarely interaction between students.

In formation (b), your tutor is one of you, part of the group, but this can be difficult to achieve as you will always feel that the tutor is 'in charge'. More mature students can cope with this better.

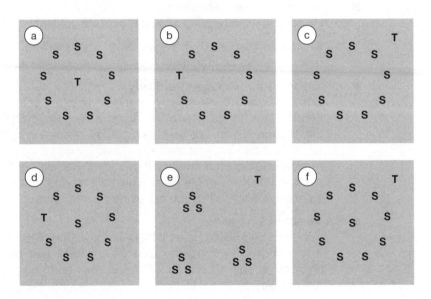

Figure 3.2 Online group structures (S = student, T = tutor)

Source: Maier and Warren (2000). Reproduced with permission.

In formation (c), the tutor is the quiet observer. He or she may be 'listening in' on the discussion and you may have an uneasy feeling about this. It is easy to feel a little paranoid in an online environment. If this mode is used it is important for the tutor to say so and be explicit about his or her role.

In formation (d), your tutor may select someone to lead the discussion and then be part of the group. If you are selected to lead, you also need to bring your tutor in along with everyone else. This is quite difficult, as you may feel nervous about handling it. Again, this is easier for more mature students.

In formation (e), student sub-groups would have been set up to discuss some aspect of an issue or problem with a view to re-assembling to see what others have said or decided. Your tutor may only 'listen in' at the end phase.

In formation (f), your tutor will select someone to lead the discussion as in (d) above. This is a very good skill to learn, as you need to know who is in your group, who has said what, whether there are people who have said nothing yet and how you can bring them in. You need to know from your tutor what the goal of the discussion is, how long it should last and what the output should be.

Group projects online

In a group project, you will be working together to produce a report, a wiki, an online presentation or some other kind of coursework your tutor deems necessary. You need to be well structured and you may want to think ahead of time how you might structure your group. Take some of the ideas from Figure 3.2 and develop your own structure. One thing you need to consider is who will direct – either the sub-groups and/or/ the whole group. Having the attitude 'we will all muck in' isn't enough for an online activity where you need to finish with a product.

Evaluating a website

Since you will be looking at a lot of information online, it is important for you to know the quality of what you are looking at. Your tutors will be quick to mark you down if you get your information from sites that cannot provide evidence for what they say. Ask yourself the following:

What's the purpose of the website?

1 Is the site selling a product or services?
2 Is this an institution or a company promotion site?
3 Is this a self-promotion site?
4 Is this a collection of information/links of interest to the author and others?
5 Is it instructional material?
6 Is it a collection of papers, like e-prints or an online journal website?

What information is there about the origin of the site?

1 Who is the author? Identify the authority of the site.
2 What organisation is the author affiliated to?
3 What is the domain of the site? For example, .edu, ac.uk (education, academic), .gov, .com., etc.
4 When was the site produced or last updated? Determine the currency of information on the site.

What can you deduce from the content?

1 What is the focus of the site?
2 What is the potential readership?
3 What impression do you get from the language? Does it use 'persuasive' language or is it objective and backed up by evidence/references?
4 Can you detect any biases?

Websites which naturally have academic integrity are those for online journals. Check out 'Web of Knowledge', but make sure your institution has given you access. If you are a UK student in Higher Education, this will be your 'Shibboleth' login (if you have studied previously, Shibboleth is the protocol replacement for 'Athens' accounts). Remember, any information you get from general websites needs to be backed up by work that is based on evidence (i.e. research). You need to apply critical reading and thinking skills to all sources, particularly web-based sources. See Chapters 7, 'Reading critically' and 9, 'Thinking critically' for more about these skills. Remember also to cite your websites properly.

Hot Tip

To search the web for more academic sites try using Google Scholar (http://scholar.google.co.uk) or Intute (http://intute.ac.uk). Google Scholar ranks a site according to, for example, its original publication source and citations. The websites listed on Intute have similarly been scrutinised for their academic integrity. However, in both cases, you still need to check for yourself.

Assessment

Assessment comes in two basic forms: **formative** and **summative**. Summative assessment is probably what you think assessment to be, and it contributes to your final grade. Formative assessment, meanwhile, is there for you to take advantage of tutor feedback to test how you are getting along and identify any areas where you need to do more work. Very often students won't do assessments that don't 'count'. This is very short-sighted and you should take every opportunity given to you for formative assessment. As a part-time learner this can give you a real boost as well as identify where you need to concentrate your efforts to achieve better grades.

Quizzes and tests

A quiz sounds very much like something you see in a magazine; however, it has now become associated with formative assessment in online learning. Tests are more formal and often seen as summative assessment.

Tests and quizzes online tend to be (although not exclusively) multiple-choice questions (MCQs). You will be given a statement and then expected to select the correct answer from a list. You can also have tests where you are expected to match two parts, label diagrams and so on. If you know you are going to have online tests you need to know what kind they are and practise using the software. Very often these tests are timed and some may apply a negative marking rule (in other words, penalties for random guesses). The point is that you need to read the instructions to establish exactly what to do and not assume you know.

Coursework

You will have larger pieces of coursework to do on your course and in fact you may only have coursework as your summative assessment. Make sure you check this at the beginning of your course, together with how it should be presented and the submission date.

You may be asked to submit it electronically through your institution's VLE and if you do this you usually get an electronic 'stamp' to verify that you have handed it in. If you send by email, ensure you set up your email to ask for a receipt once your email is opened.

Once you hand your work in electronically, it can be checked for plagiarism. In the UK, generally the Turnitin software is used for this. Make sure you understand what plagiarism is (see Chapter 12, 'Understanding academic integrity: learner ethics and plagiarism').

Hot Tip

The excuse 'my PC crashed' for not handing in your coursework on time is no longer a valid one. You are responsible for backing up your work. Save your work at short and regular intervals while working, save to your memory stick or send it to yourself by email..

Exams

Check at the beginning of the course whether there are any exams, or if it is all coursework. If there are exams you need to know whether they are in the form of computer-aided assessment, i.e. online, or if you have to go to your institution to 'sit' the exam under strict exam conditions.

If you are on day release, or have any other form of contact with your institution, you will probably be expected to attend a formal exam hall if you have to do exams.

Make sure you know how to study well for your exams so you can recall the information when you need it (see Chapter 8, 'Excelling in exams').

3 Maintaining your university learning whilst on placement

I had a great placement year, but I didn't think about my university work at all. When I returned to university I had forgotten a lot of things, like how to write an essay!

Ryan, final year Business with Accounting student

You are already a successful student who has progressed in their university education. You already have some credits towards your final degree. If you are one of the many students taking a placement year, however, you face a particular challenge in keeping up your university learning during your year out. Many students find that their university skills get rusty. Although they are reading, writing and thinking, they are doing so in a specific way to meet the needs of their employer. Whilst this is invaluable learning in its own right, it can mean the return to university with exams, a dissertation or an independent study project to deal with *is* the culture shock Ryan describes.

Your final year will be a major contributor to your final grade so if you have to spend time getting 'up to speed' with your reading, writing and thinking skills when you return, you will lose valuable time *and* valuable marks if you leave this to chance.

If you are currently on, or are preparing to start, a placement year you need to consider your learning progress and plan a strategy to maintain and enhance your skills in preparation for your return.

A strategy to maintain your learning

One way to maintain your university skills is to ask yourself three straight-forward questions every week, and then do something in response to these. The questions are:

- What text are you **Reading** this week?
- What previous work are you **Reviewing** this week?
- What learning are you **Reflecting** on this week?

Reading

It is very tempting and very easy to put down your university books and journals once you are on your work placement. However, this is the ideal time to develop the **breadth and depth** of your reading, particularly as you don't have a specific assignment to read for. In other words, you can read more on the topics that interested you, but that you didn't have the time, then, to explore. If you set yourself the standard of reading **one text a week**, then you will achieve several positive outcomes. First, you will maintain your *academic* reading skills, second, you will broaden your knowledge and understanding, and third, you are likely to trigger interest to do further reading. Use Chapter 7, 'Reading critically' to help you.

Whether directly or indirectly, the intellectual stimulation you get from this will feed into your workplace performance. This in turn will be reflected in the reference you might be relying on to get that first graduate job.

Reviewing

You have two major sources of information that, through systematic review, will maintain and develop your learning: your **marked assignments** and your **notes**.

Assignments. It is easy to forget or ignore last year's assignments and the feedback that your tutors gave you, but they offer you a fantastic learning opportunity. Now is the ideal time to look in more depth at the feedback you got by considering the following questions:

- What are the common themes to the tutor feedback?
- What are the improvement suggestions they make?
- What did you do about it then?
- What will you do about it now?

If you follow this process rigorously, you *will* gain an overall insight into the strengths and weaknesses of your academic performance so far.

To deal with the last of these review questions, you need to attack your essay or report assignment in a detailed and targeted way. You have the benefit of critical distance now, so take advantage of this. One technique that you can try, as you reread your work, is to annotate each paragraph in the margin with a key word or phrase that sums up the point that you were trying to make in that paragraph. When you've completed this step, transfer each annotation on to a separate sticky note. Now stick these all on a blank wall/mirror/door in the original sequence:

- Is the assignment structure this reveals coherent?
- What would you do differently?
- What do you think would have made this piece of work first class?
  - Does it use sufficient evidence and reasoning to make its case?
  - Does it analyse, discuss and evaluate the quality of that evidence and fully deal with the range of debate about the topic in question?
  - Is the writing clear and cohesive?
  - Does it comprehensively answer the question?

You might want to leave the sticky notes up for a couple of days to see if or how your view changes. Use Chapters 13, 'Taking control of the writing process', 14, 'Improving your business and management studies writing' and 9, 'Thinking critically' to help you work through the analysis you are doing.

Notes. You will have a lot of notes from two years of lectures, seminars and course reading. Again, it is a mistake to assume that they are redundant. If you have used a technique such as the Cornell Method discussed in Chapter 4, 'Getting the most out of lectures", then you already accept the value of active learning. You need to continue this active approach but at a 'meta' level, i.e. review all your notes' summaries with a view to **resummarising** the key learning points, themes, concepts, theories and ideas they contain. In other words, you are now looking at the big ideas in your subject area and the connections between them.

It is important that you don't just read your notes uncritically. You need to think about the significance, content and consequences of the big idea:

- What are the implications of this big idea? (For example, does it move understanding forward? Can you explain this?)
- What is problematic or troubling about it? (For example, it is a good theory but in practice it raises equity or ethical issues; it doesn't translate easily to real-world implementation. Can you say why?)
- What other problems might it be applied to? (For example, you identify an innovation opportunity. Can you identify the benefits of this?)

Now relate them to the pragmatic real world of your work place.

For each set of module or unit notes make a resummarisation template similar to that shown in the table below.

Big idea (for example, theory/concept/model)	Commentary (for example, implications, concerns, innovations)	Real-world context (based on your work place experience)
Your notes here	*Your notes here*	*Your notes here*

This review approach will help you both consolidate and develop your subject knowledge and your approach to learning by maintaining a good background level of knowledge and enhancing your overview of how the framework of your subject links together. You are also laying the foundations for a more confident approach to the coursework assignments (including a dissertation or independent study project) and exams that you will face on your return to university.

Hot Tip	If you haven't used an organised approach to your note making so far, now is the time to do something about it!

Reflecting

The value of reflecting on your learning generally is explored in Chapter 10, 'Understanding the value of reflection'. It is really a development of the systematic review step we have just considered and your work placement will give you daily challenges and opportunities to relate and connect your university knowledge to the real world. If you take these challenges and opportunities at face value you will learn something. However, if you *actively* engage with these using a purposeful, reflective approach you will **add value** to the learning you gain.

One step you might take is to keep a **learning log** (see Chapter 15, 'Developing your reflective writing') to help you develop an active engagement with the experience of the work placement. Another step might be to see if you can arrange some form of mentor relationship to facilitate your reflective thinking. In fact this might be a good thing to ask for before you commit yourself to a particular employer!

Will I have the time?

You may have read this section and started to think that you haven't got time to do all of the things it recommends. Figure 3.3 puts the ingredients of the strategy into a simplified form to show that with the right mindset you can achieve a significant outcome. In our experience you will be able to do all of the things suggested in the previous section with less than three hours a week application. This is a small time commitment for a large, long-term gain, but it is a matter of what you prioritise as important. According to the Sodexo-Times Higher Education survey, 40 per cent of students 'watch television for two to three hours a day' and '88 per cent of students use social-networking sites every week'. If you don't know where your time goes, audit it for a week and then make an *informed* judgement about whether you can afford three hours a week maintaining your learning.

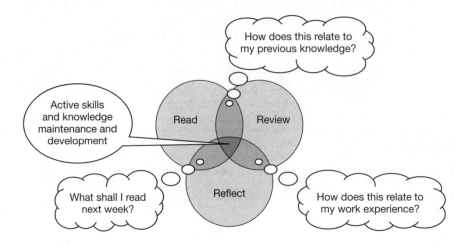

Figure 3.3 An active strategy

One of the things most students develop during their work placement is a new relationship with independence and responsibility. This is a personally transforming time and is, as the saying goes, the start of the rest of your life. Why wouldn't you want to make the most of something as significant as this and invest in it now?

4 On reflection

In this chapter you have looked at what it means to be a successful part-time learner and the kind of technology and subsequent skills you will need. You have also considered some ways in which you can maintain your university learning whilst on a work placement and the longer-term benefits of such an approach.

Summary of this chapter

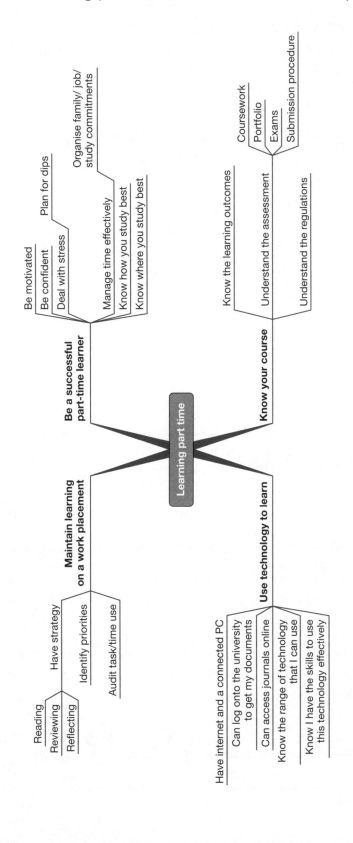

Learning part time

Be a successful part-time learner
- Be motivated
- Be confident
- Deal with stress
  - Plan for dips
  - Organise family/ job/ study commitments
- Manage time effectively
- Know how you study best
- Know where you study best

Know your course
- Know the learning outcomes
- Understand the assessment
  - Coursework
  - Portfolio
  - Exams
  - Submission procedure
- Understand the regulations

Maintain learning on a work placement
- Reading
- Reviewing
- Reflecting
- Have strategy
  - Identify priorities
  - Audit task/time use

Use technology to learn
- Have internet and a connected PC
- Can log onto the university to get my documents
- Can access journals online
- Know the range of technology that I can use
- Know I have the skills to use this technology effectively

ACTIVITY 1 Update your personal development planner

Now reflect on your current abilities and consider what you need to do to improve. You may want to transfer this information to your institution's personal development planner scheme.

Grade your confidence on a scale of 1–5 where 1 = poor and 5 = good.

My developing skills	Confidence level 1–5	Plans to improve
I am well prepared for my studies.		
I am familiar with the learning technologies I can use.		
I am a competent online learner with a set of skills to help me.		
I know what to do to keep up my university learning whilst on a work placement.		

Date:_____

Getting extra help

- Check with your institution whether they have online tutorials or training material for the software or technology they may expect you to use.
- Find out whom you should ask if things go wrong with your technology; there is usually a telephone number you can ring. Check you have this before things go wrong.
- Search the web for a wide range of tutorials on topics you are finding difficult.
- Use your student network to get support.
- Know how to get in touch with your Students Union.
- Identify a supportive colleague, or arrange a mentor relationship, in your work place.

Consult the following:

- *Effective Study Skills* by Geraldine Price and Pat Maier (2007) (Pearson Education) has useful chapters on making notes.

References

- Attwood, R. (2008) 'Survey finds it's all work, less play for the top-up generation', *Times Higher Education*, 11–17 September.

- Fleming, N.D. and Mills, C. (1992) 'Not another inventory, rather a catalyst for reflection', *To Improve the Academy*, 11, 137.

- Intute Collection Development Framework and Policy at http://intute.ac.uk/policy.html [last accessed December 2009].

- Maier, P. and Warren, A. (2000) *Integrating Technology in Learning and Teaching*. London, Kogan Page.

- Times Higher Education (2008) 'The Open University – YouTube opens a video eye on OU', 21 August.

- Vander Wal, T., Wanderval.Net at www.vanderwal.net/about.php [last accessed December 2009].

2 Improve your work

This part emphasises what you can do to get the most out of some of the basic components of your education: lectures, team work, presenting your work, reading and exams. Lectures are often seen as a passive activity but you can get more out of them if you know how to be an active listener.

At some time during your studies, team work, oral presentations and poster presentations will be part of your assessment. Your tutors may refer to these as key or transferable skills. This means that once you are aware of how to improve these skills, you can transfer it to other contexts.

You may think reading is something you learned in primary school and you don't need to look at it again; this is not the case. At this level you need to be more aware of how texts work, be critical of what you read and develop efficient strategies. This increased awareness will also improve your writing.

Exams are inevitable, so within your busy schedule it is important to know how to organise the revision process, identify the best ways to present the information you need to learn and recognise how you best remember things.

Take time to reflect on the skills you are developing in this part through the questions in each chapter.

4 Getting the most out of lectures

If you have to take notes in a lecture, the pace, rate of delivery and framework for presenting the information are all out of your hands. The pressure is on to think on your feet, to try to make sense of the thinking which has gone on behind the scenes in the preparation of the lecture and to be able to record information at speed – in other words, the ability to multi-task. Thus, it is vital that your listening skills and your note-making abilities are in tip-top condition to enable you to get the most out of lectures.

In this chapter you will:

1. assess your interaction during lectures;
2. explore the skills needed to get the most out of lectures;
3. examine how to prepare for lectures to develop efficiency;
4. develop keener listening skills.

USING THIS CHAPTER

Estimate your current levels of confidence. At the end of the chapter you will have the chance to re-assess these levels where you can incorporate this into your personal development planner (PDP). Mark between 1 (poor) and 5 (good) for the following:

I know the skills needed to get the most out of lectures.	I know the different types and purposes of lectures.	I can listen effectively and differentiate the information I am listening to in lectures.

Date: _____

1 Are you a lecture sponge?

Lectures are a waste of time.

Angela, first-year student

A **sponge** learner is ready (or not so ready) to **soak up** information from tutors and lecturers. This sounds comfortable and relatively relaxing, but it is an ineffective way of learning. Did you know, for example, that if you listen to someone (for example, a lecturer) without actively making notes or participating in some other activity you will be doing well to remember 20 per cent of what's been said?

There are many reasons why some students do not get as much out of lectures as they should. Often this is because they have not prepared sufficiently and have inappropriate expectations of lectures.

What do you expect to get out of a lecture?

Pitching your expectations high is one of the ways you can yield good results. If you intend to interact with the information you will receive during lectures, you need to have the right mindset (see Activity 1).

ACTIVITY 1 Am I a lecture sponge?

Answer true or false to each of the statements.

	True	False
1 The lecture (or series of lectures) should teach me all I need to know on that subject/topic.		
2 I want to go into the lecture and get all the information I need for my assignment.		
3 I should not need to take notes because the information is provided as handouts or online.		
4 I do not need to think in lectures; I just need to listen carefully.		
5 Lectures should contain pictures, video clips, etc. as well as written and oral communication.		

If you have answered 'true' to most of these statements, you will find that there is a gap between your expectations and what lectures offer. This is the fault of neither your lecturer nor you; it is simply that the rules of the lecture game do not match what you expect. Most students want value for money from the lectures, but it is important to understand the purpose of lectures as a teaching tool. This will help you to get the most out of them.

How to increase your capacity during lectures

Activity 2 explores some of the problems that students have expressed about lectures. Identify your problems and look at the solution hint so that you can go immediately to the appropriate section of this chapter.

ACTIVITY 2 What do I do in lectures?

Problem	Solution
Your expectations for the purpose of the lecture are inappropriate.	Look at the purpose of lectures so that you adjust your expectations.
You are unable to cope with the volume of information because it is all new to you.	You need to do some pre-lecture preparations.

Problem	Solution
You quickly go into information overload and give up taking notes.	You need to do some pre-lecture preparations to ensure that you are ready for listening and understanding the information more effectively and at greater speed. You need to sharpen up your listening and selection skills.
You do not recognise or understand some of the new terminology.	You need to do some pre-lecture preparations.
You cannot follow the gist of the lecture and seem to become muddled.	You need to have a tentative information framework upon which to hang the information. You need to do some pre-lecture preparations.
The information seems very detailed and in great depth.	You need to do some pre-lecture preparations so that you have your own framework or skeleton of information before going to the lecture.
Your questions are not answered during the lecture.	This may be the result of a misunderstanding of the lecture format. Have a look at the purpose of lectures.
You are distracted easily by other students who are talking or by rustling of paper.	Either choose where you sit very carefully (if possible) or learn how to cut out extraneous and unwanted noise. Develop more effective listening skills.
The lecturer's style may not match the way you take in information.	You need to be more aware of the way academic tutors present information so that you can choose an appropriate method to take in more information and also to get the information down more effectively. Try to increase your listening skills. Try to vary the format of the presentation of your notes.
Your lecture notes are not used later on.	Match up the purpose of the lecture, the type of lecture and your presentation format so that the notes will be helpful. Develop more effective listening skills.

2 The purpose of lectures

Lectures are not the same as seminars and group tutorials. They serve a different purpose, and consequently the anticipated outcomes for students are different. Lectures last 40–50 minutes. As a teaching tool, they are intended to give information to groups of students. In some ways they are cost effective in that they can deliver information to large student cohorts. The size of the student group will depend upon the subject and the individual university. Some undergraduates are taken aback when they walk into a lecture theatre and there are up to 500 students present. The size of the group can vary between 25 and 500.

Most departments organise a series of lectures to coincide with specific units of study. At the start of the unit, some students seem unaware of the purpose of lectures. However, this may be a case of crossed messages and that the lecturers' intentions are not made explicit to students. For example, many lecturers do not usually expect to be interrupted by students' questions during a lecture. Some academics will tell you that they have set aside a little time at the end for questions, but many will give their 'speech' and disappear. This is down to individual teaching style and delivery. However, be alert to the lecturer who sets aside time for questions. This may change your note-taking tactics during the lecture in terms of making your questions stand out in your notes as a memory jogger for later. Usually, you are expected to listen to the talk. Many lecturers use PowerPoint slides on a large screen to get across their points. Some lecturers may use an overhead projector (OHP) with transparencies (OHTs) containing information. These may be typed or handwritten. In some subjects, notably Mathematics, lecturers provide examples by writing mathematical workings at speed on a board.

There are various types of lectures, and the efficient student is aware of these types so that most use can be made of the information, format and style. This means that you may need to think on your feet quite quickly to spot the type and be flexible in your response in terms of expectations and note taking.

Type of lecture	Purpose	Outcomes
Keynote	Intended to raise issues/questions. Setting the scene and giving a broad overview.	To get you to question information and research. To inform you of the main issues.
Introductory	Introducing a series of lectures. Setting the scene and giving a broad overview.	To provide you with a framework of knowledge/concepts upon which everything else will hinge.
Sequential	Each lecture builds upon the previous one.	An assumption of prior knowledge from previous lectures.
Focus	Takes a specific aspect of a topic and goes into detail. Provides information and detail about specific research.	To fill in or put flesh upon the framework which was provided in the introduction.
Conclusion	Sums up the key points of previous lectures. Draws all the threads together.	To give an overview which can be used in conjunction with introductory lecture notes.

The biggest problem for students is that often the lecturers do not specify which type of lecture they are delivering so you will have to think on your feet at the beginning of a lecture. Of course, you can make some judgements prior to the lecture. If you look at the unit/course handbook this will help you to work out the type of lecture you are listening to. By reading between the lines of the departmental guidance information you can decide upon the type.

Most experienced lecturers follow a logical framework for delivery. There will be a brief introduction, the main part of the lecture and summaries or conclusions. However, these components are discrete and many lecturers do not signal explicitly what is happening. However, you need to be alert to this hidden structure so that you can be prepared. For example, the introduction will help you to anticipate what is to come. Some lecturers will provide a quick overview of the structure which will help you to be aware of when they are moving on to another section or sub-topic. It is worth making sure that you take down the summaries and conclusions so that you can use these as a check to find out whether you have teased out the main points of the lecture. This alerting system will be examined in more detail in the section about listening skills.

3 What skills are involved?

Getting the most out of lectures hinges upon your ability to make connections. The efficient and effective student is able to take in and select the information, while at the same time fitting this into some internal scheme or mental jigsaw. The lecture sponge soaks up the information but does not realise that the facts and knowledge are part of a big picture and so has not developed the flexibility to fit new information into previous knowledge – so the connections are not made and the jigsaw is often incomplete. This will result in notes gathering dust in files or having to spend time trying to make sense of why you made the comments.

There are seven main skills which you need if you are to get the most out of your lectures:

- good listening skills;
- concentration skills;
- summary skills;
- note-taking skills;
- organisational skills – both on paper and in your thinking;
- critical thinking skills;
- multi-tasking skills – the ability to do many of the above at the same time and at speed.

Of course, lectures do not suit all types of learner. Some students' knowledge and understanding are increased by listening to someone tell them about a topic or explaining a concept. However, others do not get as much out of this oral method of getting information because it has no hooks to help them remember and process the information. Thus, you must ask yourself how you are going to bypass your preferred learning style if you rely upon visual and written note cues. Perhaps it is worth considering how you can develop greater efficiency so that lectures are a true source of information. See the sections on pre-lecture preparation and templates for taking down information – in particular the Cornell Method.

As was stated earlier, students who simply turn up for the lecture and listen for 40–50 minutes are missing opportunities. Some work in preparation for lectures is not time wasted. Similarly, reflection and consolidation after the lecture will reap benefits for revision and in helping you to obtain better grades in your coursework and examinations.

Efficient pre-lecture preparations

Time preparing for lectures is time well spent and will ensure that you learn more when you go to the lecture and that your note taking is more effective and meaningful. Your preparation will pay off because you will be able to recognise and begin to understand new terminology and ideas. This means that you know which key words to listen out for. This will help you to **focus your listening skills** so that you can take better notes. You will, therefore, be able to listen for the clues which are in the lecture to help you make sense of new information and concepts.

There are many sources of information which you can use to help you prepare effectively to get the most out of your lectures:

Source	How to make use of it
Course handbook	
Unit/session overviews	To give you an overview. To give you an idea of what to expect. To inform you of the purpose of specified lectures.
Lecture series titles	To help you to start building that framework or jigsaw of information.
Lecture titles	To enable you to make the connections and links.
Unit glossaries	To help prepare you for new terminology. To improve your listening skills – you know what to listen for. To help you to understand new concepts.
Indicative reading lists	Get hold of some of these and look at the sub-headings in chapters to get a sense of a new topic and to help you to develop your own internal map or jigsaw picture. See if there are any definitions of new terminology so that you are prepared for your lecture.
Department site	Check electronic information which is available. This may be in the form of PowerPoint notes or information sheets. Read this information in advance of the lecture to put you in the right frame of mind and to prepare you for key concepts and ideas.
Internet searches	Download background information to help you understand what the lecturer is getting at.

Source	How to make use of it
Library site	Check the subject section to find out what your subject librarian has loaded up for different courses/units.
Yourself	
	Make a list of questions which spring to mind about the topic. See if you can get the answers in the lecture. (If not, at least this is a check-list of things you need to find out.) Get your file/notes organised in advance to save time on the day (see the section on notes organisation in Chapter 4). Anticipate some sub-headings for your notes.

Making effective use of pre-lecture notes and downloads

In the long term, pre-lecture preparations will help you to understand new concepts and ensure that you are ready to take in new terminology because you have had to engage with the information and have had to think about it. Think about athletes. They always perform warm-up activities to ensure that their muscles are flexed beforehand and performance is high. Pre-lecture preparations have the same main purposes and act as a warm-up for the brain or to get you into the right frame of mind to absorb the lecturer's information more efficiently and effectively. The hidden side effects are explained in the following table.

Pre-lecture activity with collected or downloaded information	Purpose/use
You can go through them carefully and high-light with a coloured marker pen important information.	This will increase your understanding. This will improve your memory skills. This will help you to retrieve the information later because crucial information stands out and provides a quick-access short-cut for the brain.
You can also annotate those notes – make your own comments or questions in the margin.	This will increase your understanding. This will improve your memory skills.
You can highlight key terminology (and put a definition of meaning alongside if necessary).	By putting the definition in your own words, this will increase your understanding and memory – much more so than if you simply copy out someone else's definition.

Pre-lecture activity with collected or downloaded information	Purpose/use
You can scan the lecture notes into your computer.	You can customise the layout so that you can make your own additional notes during the lecture alongside the lecturer's notes. (Some students prefer to customise printed lecture notes by double spacing for ease of access; or make space for your own notes parallel to the lecturer's notes.) Once again, reading and making decisions about what to do with the layout will provide valuable reinforcement.
You can scan the notes into your computer and make up your own concept map.	This is useful for those who prefer to have information in this alternative format rather than the traditional linear format. Making yourself do this activity can help you to develop your own map of the information.

Cautionary tale

I haven't got the time to do all this before each lecture. It's bad enough having to keep up with everything as it is.

Sharon, first-year History student

It is short-sighted to think that there is not enough time to do this type of pre-lecture preparation. It will save you time in the long run because you will get more out of the lecture in terms of your understanding, your notes will be of a better quality and this in turn will boost your chances of producing a better assignment or remembering information for examinations. It boils down to ensuring that you organise your time as effectively as you can and add this element into your weekly schedules. Try out some of these activities over a semester and reflect upon your grasp of the topic and your ability to cope with the process of writing an assignment.

Supposing I did all of this beforehand. What would be the point in actually going to the lecture!

Jim, second-year English Studies student

Jim is not the only student who has made this comment. However, the point he is missing is that during lectures, tone of voice, emphasis and other body language will strengthen your understanding. Remember, some lecturers try to provoke thought by their tone of voice and this does not come across in the impersonal notes. You can't get all of this from the two-dimensional downloads and information on screen. It is true that some lecturers are more memorable in their delivery than others, but this human interface may spark off discussions with your friends, and you will not be able to participate in this further dimension to the purpose of lectures – to generate discussion and questions.

Post-lecture activities: what to do with the information after lectures

What do **you** do with your lecture notes after the lecture? Many students toss the notes into a file, often in a haphazard way. Some have a number of file pads which are used randomly for various lectures, and the notes are left there for filing at a later date. But what happens when you drop your bag and the notes are scattered everywhere?

If your notes are of real value, you will need to do some work on them as soon after the lecture as you possibly can – while the information is still fresh in your mind. Your notes will be vital for assignment and examination success, so why not spend some valuable time in reviewing, consolidating, tidying up the loose ends and reflecting?

- The organisation of your filing system is personal, but the system has to be maintained and each set of lecture notes needs to be carefully filed away into your system.
- Take time to read through your notes to make sure they make sense to you. You may have to write in full some of the abbreviations you were forced to use in the lecture because of the speed of the lecturer's delivery. Tackling this soon after you have taken the notes means that you can draw upon recent memory of what the lecturer said to improve your notes and make them more understandable.
- Highlight key words and phrases so that they will stand out when you come back to the notes at a later date.
- If you have not had time to do sub-headings, read through a section and put a succinct title to it. Check your sub-heading titles and consider whether you need to change these so that the notes have greater cohesion and you will be able to immediately recognise the framework of the information at a later date when your memory of the lecture has faded.
- Write the key concepts in a different colour in the margin next to important information. This is termed annotating your notes.
- A4 Summary Sheet – if you can discipline yourself to do this, you will reap greater benefits. This is a bullet-point summary of the information and key points. By doing this, you will have to review, reflect and consolidate the knowledge and information and most importantly you will have to put it into your own words. This can be placed at the beginning or the end of each notes section so that you can get a quick reference to what is contained in the notes to help you decide whether you need the information for an assignment at a later date. These Summary Sheets are also useful for revision purposes.

4 Lecture alerts: behind the scenes

Obviously, lecturers have their own style of delivery and quirky ways. However, there are some features that you might like to look out for in order to alert you to possible outcomes which could affect your concentration and selection of information.

Body language cues	Alert
Speaks very quickly	Need to have good listening skills. Look out for key words/information. It may simply be a sign of nervousness.
Speaks very softly at the beginning of the lecture	This may be used as a ploy to get students' attention and to calm down the 'audience'. If used for this purpose, what they say at this point may not be vital.
Reads from notes	This type of lecture places greater pressure on your concentration skills because it can often be delivered in a monotone. The lecturer may be nervous or unsure of the information and needs to rely heavily on notes.
Says some things very slowly	This is a verbal method of underlining and putting information in bold. It is likely that the information is important so you need to record it in your notes.
Repeats phrases and sentences	It could be that the lecturer has lost his place in his or her notes! More often it is a way of emphasising important information so you need to record it in your notes.
Pauses occasionally	You have to decide whether this is an individual, stylistic feature or not. It could be that the lecturer has lost his place in his or her notes! It may be a ploy to make a point that some students are talking during the lecture. It may be the lecturer's way of emphasising important information so you need to record it in your notes.
Turns to screen to go through slide information (be it OHT or PowerPoint)	This is the sign of an inexperienced lecturer. Sound levels will naturally drop so you need to be listening carefully.
Paces up and down in front of 'audience'	This style of lecturing is often accompanied by lack of notes. The lecturer knows his stuff! It can be distracting for some students, so you must ensure that your concentration levels are high.
Use of rhetorical questions	You are not expected to answer these either by shouting out the answer or raising your hand. They are used to get students to be critical or to demonstrate the current debates and issues. The lecturer then proceeds to answer his or her own question. At times they are a device to vary the delivery so that students do not fall asleep in lectures!

Environmental features	Alert
PowerPoint slides	Where are the notes? Are hard copies available in the room? Was I expected to download them myself prior to lecture?
PowerPoint slide usage	■ As information handouts only (usually six slides per A4 page) to start off your notes. ■ As an aide-memoire for note taking (usually three or four slides per A4 page with lines for you to personalise the information). ■ Some slides are for information only and are not talked about by the lecturer; others are brought up on screen and additional information is given. If a lecturer uses this style, you must be alert and concentrate so that you do not lose your place.
Overhead transparencies (OHTs)	This is an alternative to PowerPoint. It probably means that there is no electronic version available for download. Each slide contains succinct information which you are expected to record in some way.
Writes information on board	You need to take down this information because it may not be contained in any other source of notes.

An awareness of these features will ensure that you get even more out of your lectures.

5 Template for note taking

Taking notes in lectures relies upon the expertise of the lecturer. Style of delivery and expertise varies and this can have an impact upon your ability to keep up with the notes, but more importantly you need to be flexible. This applies to all formats of note taking.

Your note taking should ensure that you leave spaces for the lecturer's afterthoughts and revisitings. Lecturers are only human and at times suddenly remember information that should have gone with an earlier section. At other times, lecturers can be imparting information from their notes and at the end of a section they want to bring you up-to-date information which they have just read about. This information has to be tacked on and you will need to try to place it in the appropriate section of your notes. If you have left no room, you should ensure that you link the information by arrows or colour coding when you are involved in the post-lecture activities.

One of the problems with making a note of what the lecturer has said in a linear manner is that there is less room for flexibility. A template for lecture notes could solve your problems.

The Cornell Method

This method was developed more than 40 years ago by Professor Walter Pauk to help his students at Cornell University (Pauk, 2000). It was intended to increase efficiency and originally consisted of six stages. It was his intention that students:

- record information from lectures;
- reduce their notes;
- recite the information to aid recall and memory;
- reflect;
- review the information to make sure they understand it;
- recapitulate and make a summary.

The following table shows how you could organise your note taking, the Cornell way. As you can see, it is a template which could be prepared beforehand, using your word processor. Section A provides vital information to help you to identify your notes at a later stage. Section B is the space where you write your information during the lecture, while Section C will allow you to reflect upon what you have learnt during the lecture and give you space to write up distilled and useful information. This could be essential for use in gathering information for your essay or as a start to producing effective revision notes. Of course, the active student will come away from the lecture with some questions unanswered and Section D will provide space for you to summarise the lecture to get a global or overview picture.

A. Lecture title: Date: Lecturer's name: Page number:	
B. Space for information taken down **during** lecture	
	C. Additional notes in post-lecture phase: key words; key concepts; key theorists/names. Additional information which you have remembered from the lecturer's talk which you didn't have time to record in lecture.
D. Follow-up: Questions you might have Commentary	

Uses

Its main advantage is that it is possible to cut down on redoing notes. Again, you have to be well prepared in advance for this way of taking notes. However, once you have got into the routine of preparing your pages in this way, you will quickly adapt and the lecture workspace (B) will not seem restricted or limited. It will also provide you with more useable notes for revision. Similarly, if you are searching through your files for information to put into your essays, you need only glance at the summary section to find out if there is anything worth using.

6 Using a laptop during lectures

Electronic notes are now part of a student's life. Writing electronic notes during lectures is down to personal preference but also to the facilities which are available in your college or university. If you have a laptop computer with wireless connections you will have access to many facilities. However, not all lecture rooms are set up in this way at the moment. To help you to decide whether electronic notes are viable for you, consider Activity 3.

ACTIVITY 3 Should I use a laptop in lectures?

Which of the following statements apply to you? Answer true or false.

	True	False
1 I prefer not to work straight on to screen.		
2 I do not feel confident working on a computer under pressure.		
3 My keyboard skills are slow.		
4 I am not sure about basic functions of my word processor.		
5 I do not like to read information straight from the screen.		
6 I feel embarrassed using a computer in front of other people.		
7 I am worried that I might press the wrong keys and wipe all my lecture notes.		

If your answers are mainly true, you really ought to consider whether you are ready or really want to make electronic notes during lectures and seminars. You need sophisticated skills of listening, summarising and multi-tasking when coping with lectures. Making electronic notes adds another dimension to this complexity. You need to ask yourself whether using an electronic format during the lecture is the right approach for you. The crucial questions you have to ask yourself are:

- Do I have the necessary skills?
- Is this way of note taking going to support me or be a barrier to my learning?
- Do I want to take notes in this way?

Of course, if the answer to the final question is 'no', then you will eliminate this mode of 'writing'. However, you need to make sure that in the long term you are not closing doors for more efficient ways of working both at university and beyond.

You need to have good **typing speed** if you are going to stand a chance of keeping up in lectures. This may seem a trite remark, but spending some time in a vacation or before you embark upon your course learning how to touch-type or improving your typing speed will be time well spent. The old adage 'practice makes perfect' has never more been true than in these circumstances. The more time you set aside to practise your skills, the quicker you will become. The best-case scenario is that you are able to **touch type**. This means that you can look at the slides and still type in your information. Being at this level of expertise also implies that you will not be slowed down looking for a specific key. If this happens, the lecturer will be three sentences ahead of you and you will be constantly chasing your tail. Touch-typing does not imply that you use both hands – though this is better. Many students can type at speed only using two fingers on each hand. You need to ensure that your typing speeds and your knowledge of the word-processing program are automatic so that you are not slowed down grappling with the technology.

Reviewing and consolidating your notes is easier on computer and the final product will be clearer to read at a later date. However, a small amount of forethought can reap excellent rewards when you are under pressure to find information for an essay, for example. Thus, setting up a template on your laptop can be done in advance so that you can move around the document, placing the lecturer's information in its appropriate box or section.

7 Critical listening: ways to increase your listening skills

Listening to a lecture requires skills which you may need to practise in order to increase your efficiency. The student who develops **active listening** skills is the one who will understand and deal with new and challenging information more effectively and will also be able to remember the information for longer periods of time before having to rehearse the information in some way (see the section on exams in Chapter 8).

Baseline skills

These are:

- concentration
- anticipation

- questioning
- selection/elimination
- analysing
- summarising.

If you are questioning, selecting and summarising spoken information, you will be actively involved in the lecture. The result will be higher levels of **concentration** because you are being critical – not in the sense of negatively criticising your lecturer's voice or clothes but, more importantly, critical of what is being said. You can improve your concentration skills. It is all very well to be told not to daydream during lectures – it is natural for the mind to wander – but you must make sure that you keep yourself in check. Prompting yourself with questions is a way of keeping your mind on the job in hand. Thus, if you think you are getting bored, instead of doodling, start analysing the information you are listening to.

Mental joggers – asking the right questions

These are:

- Why has the information been included?
- How does it link with the rest of the information?
- Is it essential or exemplar information?
- Is this a new section?
- Does what the lecturer is saying fit in with what you have already read or is it controversial?
- What point is the lecturer trying to make?

In addition to concentration, a vital skill to use is that of anticipation because it will set off your own questions, make you listen for the answers you need, and in this process you will be selecting information and tagging some parts of the lecture as being of higher priority than other parts (selection and elimination).

What to anticipate/what to listen out for	What is its use?
Introductory statements	May indicate an overview of the lecture structure so that you can be ready to organise your sub-headings and branches of information.
Signal language	This could get you ready for lists, for example. For more specific examples, see below.
Summaries/conclusions	These will help you to develop a framework of information. They can be used as a checklist when you review your notes to make sure you didn't miss anything out. They can deepen your understanding.

8 How to hone your listening skills: we hear what we want to hear

The warm-up

You can double your listening capacity by doing the pre-lecture activities. These activities will make you aware of **key terminology** and give you a broad framework of information so that you go into a lecture with some hooks upon which to put the new and sometimes challenging information. Although these activities will increase your ability to make sense of new concepts and ideas, you need to do something slightly different to ensure that you prepare yourself for **hearing the information**.

- Pick out and list key terms, terms with which you are unfamiliar and terminology which seems to be used in a very specific way in the subject. (You will be aware of this because your understanding of the meaning of the word does not make sense in the specialist texts.)
- Check your understanding by defining the terms in your own words. Then, cross-check in a subject glossary to find out whether you got them right.
- Say the words aloud or better still record them on to a disk and listen to them. This way you will be prepared for hearing the terms and your brain will not have to slow down to process the information when you are in the lecture.
- If you are working electronically, you can enlist the help of your computer if you have appropriate software. You can type in your list (or cut and paste if you are working from departmental, electronic information) and get the computer to speak the words to you so that you hear them. Voice-recognition software such as Text Help has this facility and will even let you decide whether you want to hear a male or female voice!

Now you are in a better position to listen out for the key words in the lecture because your mind has heard them and is looking out for them (Activity 4).

ACTIVITY 4 Listening for key words

Here is the script of part of a lecture. Get a friend to read the text to you or scan the text into your computer and get your computer to read the information to you and see if you can pick out the key words.

The topic of the talk is 'The Dangers of the Sun'.

This is a general talk by the Health Services and is open to all and any students.

Jot down what you would anticipate you will hear about this topic:
1
2
3
4

You will find answers at the end of the chapter.

Now jot down the key words/terminology which you would anticipate:
1
2
3
4
5
6

You will find answers at the end of the chapter.

Text extract: 'The Dangers of the Sun'

Pick out the key words and points while you listen to this extract:

For many years dermatologists have warned the public about the dangers of staying in the sun without protection. Exposure to the sun can have dramatic results, apart from the treasured tanned skin. There are three points which I wish to bring to your attention in this talk. Firstly, the sun can damage the layers of the skin. The outer layer can change its appearance. The texture can become leathery with a loss of elasticity. This can result in premature ageing of the skin, causing wrinkles and brown blotches. Secondly, over-exposure can result in skin cancer. The brown blotches may be the outer indicator of cancer. They appear as moles on the skin. Next, extreme exposure to the sun increases the possibility of breaking down our natural protection from the sun's radiation. The effects of UVA and UVB are becoming more well known. Tanning shops promise their customers that they can provide 'safe' tanning. They try to convince us that UVA is a lower level of radiation and therefore less harmful. This is not true! In fact, UVA has been proved responsible for damaging the deeper layers of the skin which destroy structural proteins and thus harming the immune systems.

Check your notes with the answers at the end of the chapter to see if you picked out the main key words and points.

Listening for main points/ideas

This exercise will help you to improve your skills of selection and elimination. The task is best tackled as a listening exercise so get a friend to read the text to you or scan the text into your computer and get your computer to read the information to you and see if you can pick out the main points.

Text extract: 'Is a bulky diet of eucalyptus leaves the best option for the tiny Koala?'

Should Koalas change their diet? Are eucalyptus leaves a sensible choice in the changing environment? Is the Koalas' diet appropriate for the modern world? All these questions and more have been asked by biologists in their study of this diminutive and appealing little animal.

The diet of the Koala is limited almost entirely to eating eucalyptus leaves. Environmental issues and the decrease in natural habitats apart, there are drawbacks and advantages to such a restricted diet. The size of the Koalas' digestive system, their metabolic structures and chemical make-up of eucalyptus leaves combine to provide a fascinating forum for discussion.

The dichotomy lies in the leaves and the digestive system. On the one hand the leaves are rich in fibre but contain high levels of lignin. Fibre is not conducive to digestion, and lignin, a woody material found in the cell walls of many plants, is indigestible. So why does the Koala have such a voracious appetite for this source of fuel? Another drawback is that the ratio of an animal's gut volume to its energy needs is dependent upon animal mass. Thus, this tiny creature does not have the capacity and its metabolic system has difficulty coping. The quality of the food is poor so this means that large quantities are needed in order to extract sufficient nutrients. So how does it manage to digest and process poor-quality food for its metabolic needs?

It would appear that the Koala has adapted its digestive system to cope with its roughage-laden diet. Scientists in New South Wales conducted a study in the early 1980s and uncovered three major factors.

Firstly, the Koala can regulate the passage of food through its system, like a rabbit. In this way it has developed a system which discriminates between different sized particles so that the smaller, more easily digested ones can be digested first while the coarser, indigestible matter is expelled almost immediately. This space-saving exercise allows the Koala to increase the rate at which the 'good' material can be put into the system.

Secondly, the Koala is a relatively slow-moving animal compared with others of a similar size so it is able to reduce the fuel it needs. It can be compared with the slow-moving, three-toed sloth.

Finally, eucalyptus leaves have hidden fuels. Although the woody, indigestible lignin is present, there is also a wealth of lipids and phenols which are rich sources of energy. However, the Koala's system cannot cope with phenols so these are excreted, leaving the lipids, which provide useful carbohydrate energy in the form of starch and sugar.

So what seems an improbable system has been adapted to take account of animal size, metabolic rates and energy-saving adaptations.

See if you have picked out the main points in the answers at the end of the chapter.

Verbal cues and signals

Your listening skills can be greatly improved if you know what triggers to listen for and the significance of these signals.

Signal	What to expect
Start with	This may be signalling the introduction which will give overviews.
Lecture is divided into ...	Tells you the structure.
However, on the other hand, but, conversely, on the contrary, despite	This signals contrasting or opposing information and evidence.
In addition, in other words, put another way, also, as I said previously	This signals repetition of information or provides you with another definition or explanation.
For example, that is to say, furthermore, another example, such as	These alert you to the fact that what follows will be examples of a main point.
Especially, specifically, most importantly, I cannot stress enough	Lecturers will use these to signal emphasis so listen very carefully because they obviously think the information is vital/important.
Firstly, secondly (etc.), next, then, penultimate (last but one), ultimate, finally, in conclusion	Be ready for a number of points or lists.
Therefore, thus, because, consequently, accordingly, if ... then, as a result of this	Cause and effect.
I'll expand on this later on ... I'll give you more detail about this later in the lecture ... I'll take this point up later ...	This means that you must be on the alert to link up later information with this earlier point. You might even leave space in your notes to accommodate this.
In conclusion, let me summarise, let's recap, in short/in brief, to wrap up, the main points covered were ...	These are useful because they will help you to get the global/big picture because the lecturer has summarised the information for you.

The significance of knowing about these signals when you are listening to someone speak is that you are expecting and anticipating certain types of information to follow. This will aid your understanding and speed up your processing of the information so that ultimately your notes will be of a better quality.

Thus, by a more focused and active approach to your listening, you will be able to make more effective notes and overcome the problem of forgetting what you have heard.

9 Recording lectures

This section explores the use of electrical and electronic devices to record and store information from lectures and seminars. Before you rush off and buy some gizmo, you need to consider its uses, the advantages and disadvantages of different devices and likely academic tutors' attitudes and responses to usage (see Activity 5).

ACTIVITY 5 Recording lectures: myth or reality?

Look at the following comments made by students and decide whether you think they are true or false.

Statements made by students	True	False
If I use some sort of recording device …		
It will take all the hard work out of lectures.		
It will save me time.		
It will mean I do not have to do anything.		
It will help me remember information.		
It will ensure that I understand my lectures.		
I can sell the information to other students who didn't make the lecture.		

To find out if you are correct, look at the answers at the end of the chapter. The implications for these statements are discussed in this section. Some students have been encouraged at school and sixth-form college to use Dictaphone-type devices. They may have been useful and appropriate at that stage of study, but you need to consider your academic demands now and whether this type of method of recording is most suitable and appropriate to your individual needs.

Devices

There is a baffling array of gadgets available on the market. Which one you choose largely depends upon what you want to use it for:

- tape recorders
- mini-disk recorders
- mobile telephones
- PDAs (personal digital assistants).

The pros and cons of these gadgets are discussed in the table below.

Device	Pros	Cons	Additional features worth considering
Tape recorders	Cheap to buy. Small and portable. Tape cassettes are inexpensive.	Not very versatile. Information on tape is not easily transferred to other systems. A one-hour lecture takes an expert two hours to transcribe. Sound quality is variable and can be dependent upon where you are sitting in relation to the lecturer.	Variable-speed playback enables you to slow down playback so that you can take in information more effectively. There are different sizes of tape cassettes. If you intend to share with others, you need to consider compatibility. Is there an advanced facility to 'mark'information while someone is speaking – aids retrieval later.
Mini-disk recorders	Sound quality on playback is excellent and not reliant upon sitting at the front for best results. Fairly cheap to buy. Small and portable. Mini-disk capacity is larger than tape cassette. Navigation is easier – therefore searching for specific information is quicker and less time consuming. Can be used for other purposes – e.g. recording music.	Attractive gadget and therefore stealable. A one-hour lecture takes an expert two hours to transcribe.	Variable-speed playback option enables you to slow down playback so that you can take in information more effectively.
Solid-state recorders	Record information on to RAM chips or cards. Easier transfer of information from one system to another. Recording time is longer than both the above. Small and portable.	A one-hour lecture takes an expert two hours to transcribe.	

Device	Pros	Cons	Additional features worth considering
Mobile telephones	You probably already have one so no additional cost.	Recording space is limited. Use only in emergencies.	Check the memory capacity. Is there an option to plug in memory cards to boost facilities?
PDA	Small and portable. Voice memo is available on more expensive models.	Expensive if you get one with the options you need for this type of activity. Limited capacity for recording speech. Need to be well organised and to back up information regularly on to another, more permanent system. Attractive gadget and therefore stealable.	Look for MP3 facility to enable you to listen to text.

A final consideration – some machines can record information in a way that is compatible with speech-recognition software on your computer. However, your machine has to be set up to recognise the voice before it will download and transcribe recorded speech. This may seem like an excellent solution, but the practicalities are such that **all** of your lecturers would have to take time out of their busy schedules to go through the voice-recognition program. If you have one lecturer for a lot of your time, it might be worth considering, but be ready for your lecturer to refuse, stating time pressures, etc.

Recording protocols

If you wish to record the lectures in some way, apart from cost, utility and meeting your needs, you must bear in mind other factors. It is important that you get **permission** to use your machine. This means that you might need to email lecturers before the start of their unit to ask for permission. It is also worth briefly reassuring your lecturer about the purpose to which you intend to put the recordings. Some students explain that they are auditory learners and take in information more readily if they hear it while reading handouts and notes. It might be that you need to request a temporary use of a recorder because you have broken the hand/arm with which you write. Many lecturers are uneasy about students recording their lectures; some are openly hostile. You need to be aware of this so that you are not frustrated or upset by responses to your request. The reasons some lecturers do not want you to record their lectures often relate to copyright of intellectual property or the fact that they can no longer control how their information is used.

'What are they going to do with this information?' is a question frequently asked by lecturers. Some academic tutors are wary of giving permission because a lecture may contain off-the-cuff comments and responses which the lecturer would not want to be used for future purposes. It may be a reflection of the litigious society in which we live that lecturers are on their guard concerning recording of lectures because of the notion of 'evidence which could be used, etc.'. That is not to say that this is commendable, but it is certainly understandable.

If you seek permission at the beginning of a unit, this usually means that you do not have to make the request at each lecture. Of course, if there is a stand-in lecturer, it is only polite to inform them that you have been given permission to record the lecture.

At university you will be expected to cope with the recording and the machine so that it does not interfere with the smooth running of the lecture. Academic tutors do not expect to be given the machine so that they can turn the recording on and off. This may have been the system at school but it is different in Higher Education settings. You will need to think about the ethics of selling your recordings to other students.

10 On reflection

Organisation and management are key factors to success. Getting the most out of lectures is up to you. Preparing properly, organising your note taking and developing effective listening skills will help you to gain the added value you need to ensure that your understanding and knowledge of your subject are deepened.

ACTIVITY 6 Update your personal development planner

Now reflect upon how you go about getting the most out of lectures and how you intend to change and adapt your habits so that you can spend your time more effectively. You may want to transfer this information to your institution's personal development planner scheme.

Grade your confidence on a scale of 1–5 where 1 = poor and 5 = good.

My developing skills	Confidence level: 1– 5	Plans to improve
I know the skills needed to get the most out of lectures.		
I know the different types and purposes of lectures.		
I can listen effectively and differentiate the information I am listening to in lectures.		

Date: _____

Summary of this chapter

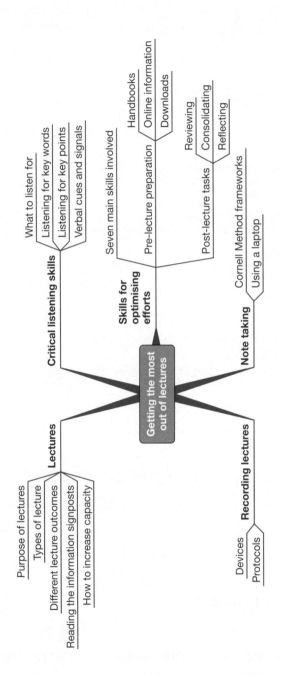

Getting the most out of lectures

Lectures
- Purpose of lectures
- Types of lecture
- Different lecture outcomes
- Reading the information signposts
- How to increase capacity

Critical listening skills
- What to listen for
- Listening for key words
- Listening for key points
- Verbal cues and signals

Skills for optimising efforts
- Seven main skills involved
- Pre-lecture preparation
  - Handbooks
  - Online information
  - Downloads
- Post-lecture tasks
  - Reviewing
  - Consolidating
  - Reflecting

Note taking
- Cornell Method frameworks
- Using a laptop

Recording lectures
- Devices
- Protocols

> ## Getting extra help
>
> ■ Go to the students union to find out where to go for skill development. Many universities and colleges have tutors who provide this service.

Feedback on activities

ACTIVITY 4 Listening for key words

The talk: 'The Dangers of the Sun'

Jot down what you would anticipate you will hear about this topic:
1 Problems of over-exposure
2 Skin protection and radiation
3 Skin cancer
4 Ageing process

Now jot down the key words/terminology which you would anticipate:
1 Skin cancer
2 UVA/UVB
3 Dermatologist
4 Skin layers.
5 Over-exposure
6 Cancerous moles

Sample notes

Dermatologists warned about the dangers of over-exposure without protection.

1. Sun damages layers of the skin, changing appearance:

   (a) texture – leathery with a loss of elasticity;
   (b) result – premature ageing of the skin, causing wrinkles and brown blotches.

2. Secondly, over-exposure – skin cancer:

   (a) brown blotches indicator of cancer;
   (b) appear as moles.

3. Extreme exposure – skin's natural protection from the sun's radiation destroyed:

   (a) effects of UVA and UVB more well known;
   (b) tanning shops – UVA is a lower level of radiation and therefore less harmful; Not true!
      (i)   UVA responsible for damaging the deeper layers of the skin;
      (ii) structural proteins destroyed;
      (iii) immune systems damaged.

Text extract: 'Is a bulky diet of eucalyptus leaves the best option for the tiny Koala?'

Should Koalas change their diet? Are eucalyptus leaves a sensible choice in the changing environment? Is the Koalas' diet appropriate for the modern world? All these questions and more have been asked by biologists in their study of this diminutive and appealing little animal.

   Koala diet: limited – eucalyptus leaves.
                 + & – to restricted diet

The size of the Koalas' digestive system, their metabolic structures and chemical make-up of eucalyptus leaves combine to provide a fascinating forum for discussion.

Leaves and the digestive system

Leaves	■ rich in fibre;
	■ fibre not easily digested by Koalas;
	■ but high levels of indigestible, woody lignin.

Digestive system	■ gut volume to energy needed = animal mass;
	■ Koala capacity = small;
	■ eucalyptus nutrients poor so large quantity needed.

System adaptations

1. Koala can regulate food in system:

   (a) differentiates types of food;
   (b) expels coarser indigestible matter;
   (c) left with smaller, more easily digested particles.

2. Cut down on energy requirements:

   (a) slow moving;
   (b) needs less energy;
   (c) unlike other small animals;
   (d) like three-toed sloth.

3. Koala extracts energy fuel carbohydrate from eucalyptus:

    (a)   lipids – rich source of energy;

    (b)   expels phenols;

    (c)   gets starch and sugar for energy.

Feedback

ACTIVITY 5: Recording Lectures: Myth or Reality

Look at the following statements and decide whether you think they are true or false. If I use some sort of recording device ...	True ✓	False ✗
It will take all the hard work out of lectures.	Yes it will take some of the hard work out of lectures in terms of recording notes. You still have to listen and it will be beneficial for you to make a note of things that YOU HAVE THOUGHT of during the lecture.	
It will save me time.	Not really as you will still have to take notes from the lecture at some point in order to have something to revise from. It means that you can take your time listening though.	
It will mean I do not have to do anything.	You may think you have nothing to do and that is the danger. See feedback on the first point. It is always preferable for you to make notes of how you understand things as they develop.	
It will help me remember information.	If you are an auditory learner this could be a really good way to learn. However, you still need some concise notes for revision – at some point you will have to write out what you know! Use the recording to top up your knowledge again once you have a good set of notes.	

Look at the following statements and decide whether you think they are true or false. If I use some sort of recording device ...	True ✓	False ✗
It will ensure that I understand my lectures.		Not necessarily. You have the opportunity to listen several times and that can help if you are struggling with a concept. Lecture notes can also help here.
I can sell the information to other students who don't make the lecture.		Forget it. You may want to look at the chapter on ethics.

Reference

■ Pauk, W. (2000) *How to Study in College,* 7th edn. New York, Houghton Mifflin.

5 Working in a real and diverse team

Working with others is always a balance between maintaining our individuality and becoming a member of a group to which we are proud to belong. The more we join with people 'like us', the more confident we feel in being able to maintain that balance. This balance is often a result of being able to predict how each of us will behave, which in turn builds up trust within a team. However, once we work with people we don't know or with those from different cultures, we are less able to comfortably predict how we will react with one another or what our expectations are. Many companies work in multicultural environments, with flatter hierarchical structures on increasingly complex issues, where you will be expected to work in very diverse teams. Being a member of such a team therefore needs more skill and you need to know the components of team building in order to make this work. Hoping to muddle along because you have had experience of working with your friends on many projects is no longer sufficient.

In this chapter you will:

1. understand what a real team is;
2. identify the learning styles of your team in order to allocate key roles;
3. engage with the mechanics of setting up a real team;
4. increase your sensitivity towards cultural differences;
5. reflect on your developing skills.

USING THIS CHAPTER

Estimate your current levels of confidence. Mark 1 (poor) and 5 (good) for the following. I can:

Understand what a real team is.	Identify the profile of your team in order to allocate key roles.	Engage with the mechanics of setting up a real and diverse team.

Date: _____

1 Introduction

We work and play together in a variety of groupings which are brought together for a variety of purposes, such as sports teams, informal learning groups, mentoring groups, buzz groups for creative solutions, virtual groups and project teams. We generally lump this all together as 'group work'. However, each of these groupings operates differently. This chapter will develop our understanding of the team project as opposed to a loose gathering of individuals, a key employability skill for your future.

As business is increasingly global in substance and recruitment, working with mixed cultures, either as a manager or a colleague, will become increasingly crucial. It is important to challenge our prejudices and identify the cultural filter that influences our behaviour. Group projects at university should be seen as a training ground for not only applying what you have learnt through your studies but also for recognising your behaviour and improving your interpersonal skills. Without this reflection, it is very difficult for you to become the manager and colleague your company would expect of you.

The Association of Graduate Recruiters' chief executive, Carl Gilleard, said to the BBC News (online, 2006) that, 'Employers are likely to be looking to graduates who can demonstrate softer skills such as team-working, cultural awareness, leadership and communication skills, as well as academic achievement.'

There is generally no doubt that being an effective team player and/or leader of a team is an important skill and its development starts during your studies. However, you undoubtedly have a view of group work that may not be all that positive, so let's start by revealing that position now.

ACTIVITY 1 Annoying things about working with others

Below is a series of statements that students often make about group work. How would you deal with these annoying things? Answer these questions now, but you may want to change your answers after reading the remainder of this chapter.

Annoying things	I would deal with this by ...
There are always free-riders in a team and their marks are boosted by those who do the work.	
Teams slow me down and that irritates me.	
I have difficulty with the topic the team has to work on and I'm afraid I'll keep the others back.	
Sometimes team members won't complete their tasks (at all, or on time!).	
Sometimes teams don't divide up the work fairly.	
I sometimes have difficulty working with students from other cultures as they have such different ways of working and it takes so long to get anything done.	
Sometimes you get students who just don't care about their grades, but I do.	

Check the feedback section at the end of the chapter for more information.

2 What is a team?

A team is a group of individuals who work together for a particular purpose. The individuals in a team are interdependent in order to get the job completed. Teams therefore have outputs. However, just coming together with a group of friends does not mean that you are automatically a team. Most employers know that we have to work at becoming a team and this is reflected in the significant amount of staff development that goes into team building.

Teams are able to deal with complex problems and come up with more creative solutions than individuals alone. In the work place, teams are increasingly cross-disciplinary, drawing on the expertise of many. More than likely, your student project will be confined to those on your course, but remember that working together with different kinds of people is a preparation for future work. Good teams also enhance commitment and a feeling of community among their members.

Friendship groups and teams

We all automatically want to form a team with our friends and if you are told to form a team, you would probably do just that. The advantages of this are that you are comfortable with each other, you want to support each other and it makes you feel good. The main disadvantage of friends as teams is that your relationship is built on socialising and having fun. The project team could put a strain on the relationship as you may have to behave in a different way with a particular friend in the team than you would do socially. If someone outside your friendship group joined your team, it might also be difficult for him or her to feel accepted.

Moving from group to team

The main issue for student project groups is to move from being a group of individuals to being a team. Two management consultants, Jon Katzenbach and Douglas Smith, wrote a best seller entitled *The Wisdom of Teams* (1993), in which they look at the difference between a group of individuals working together and high-performance teams (see Figure 5.1).

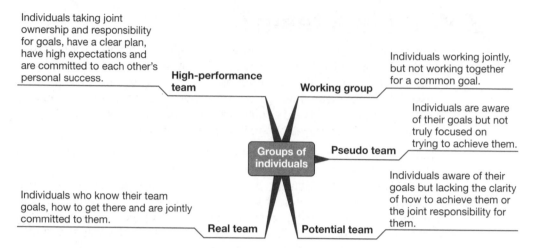

Figure 5.1 How individuals work together

Source: Adapted from Katzenbach & Smith (1993)

Identifying team characteristics

Characteristics	Grouping*	Issues
You are working together as a group to share information, understand assignments and learn together. Each of you will take away information from the group, which will help your own understanding of a topic. The group has no accountability for its output.	Working group	As an informal grouping this can be very productive and supportive during the learning process. Recognise that you are an informal group and that you have no output as a team.
You are in a group that has been assigned a task. As a group you are responsible for the output. However, as a group you are not working collectively in order to try to achieve this. The group appears to have no interest in setting goals, working collectively and coming up with a plan even though you may call yourselves a team.	Pseudo team	This is a real problem grouping because you think you are team when you're not. At this level you have not developed team skills or fully understood how teams work. You need to understand the task, work collectively, identify skills within the team and be mutually accountable for the outcome.
You are in a group that has been assigned a task. You understand that as a group you are responsible for the output. You understand that you need to work together, develop a plan and be collectively accountable. You are trying to do this but it can be very frustrating because the ' team' becomes unfocused and members are not always moving together in the same direction.	Potential team	As the label for this grouping suggests, there is potential here but it is not yet fully realised. By the end of year two you should at least be carrying out teamwork at the 'potential team' level. You will further develop your skills in the following year(s). Most problems with student project teams are identified with this kind of grouping (including pseudo teams). Take stock of the team skills you need to develop and make notes in your PDP.

Characteristics	Grouping*	Issues
You are in a group that has been assigned a task. As a group you are responsible for the output. All members of the group are committed to the project and understand that they hold themselves mutually responsible for the outcome. As a group you have identified the resources you have in your team, i.e. the skills and knowledge you can bring to the team in order to make your plan more effective. You are also aware that all team members need supporting.	Real team	If you are working at this level you understand how teams work, including the collaborative work and accountability that are needed for the output. By the end of year three you should be working on team projects at this level. Student projects working at this level should do very well. Critically reflect on the team skills you are developing. Don't forget to evaluate and evidence your developing skills in your PDP and incorporate in your CV.
You are in a group that has been assigned a task. As a group you are responsible for the output. All members of the group are committed to the project and understand that they hold themselves mutually responsible for the outcomes. As a team you know the strengths of your members and work with those strengths. In addition, you are truly interdependent and aware that each member of the team needs space and encouragement for personal development, and the team values everyone's contribution.	High-performance team	This is what you are aiming for. You work with mutual interdependence that reflects the group's skill mix and personal preferences. Your language is aligned to the goals of the task and you have a strong sense of mutual responsibility for the output of the team. Team members feel fulfilled and proud to be part of this team. If you have got to this level before your final year of studies then you are doing very well, but it is a rare occurrence. Aim to be in at least one high-performance team before you finish your studies. Update your PDP with an evaluation of how your skills have developed in this area.

* Terms in this column used by Katzenbach and Smith

Checklist: creating a real team

Members of a team ...

■ are absolutely clear about the team's goals;
■ take joint responsibility for the goals;
■ plan how to achieve goals;
■ allocate tasks to all members;
■ are good time managers;
■ value everyone in the team;
■ identify and deal with hidden agendas;
■ trust each another to be dependable, honest, fair and objective in their dealings with each other.

As you work towards being an effective team, you need to consider the various functions that teams perform in order to work well together. John Adair (1986), a leading authority on leadership and the first to be appointed as a professor in Leadership Studies, says that teams need to consider how they achieve the task, build/maintain the team and take care of individual needs – see Figure 5.2.

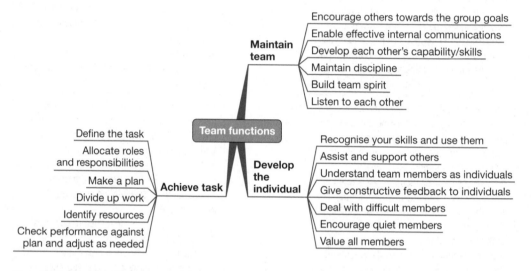

Figure 5.2 Team functions

Source: Adapted from John Adair's model of how teams function (Adair, 1986)

NOTE   If you are working in a culturally diverse team, your team members may not see team functions this way at all. It may be worth talking this through with your team to see if you have a joint understanding of how teams function.

ACTIVITY 2 Understanding team patterns – what's your view?

Each of the three areas identified by Adair (achieving the task, building the team and responding to individual needs) should be addressed if your team is to work effectively and harmoniously. Just imagine these scenarios and identify the functions missing from John Adair's model and estimate the kind of group you think they are (working group, pseudo team, potential team, real team, high-performance team).

Check the feedback section to compare your answers.

Scenario 1

You are working with a great group – they are all your friends. You often meet in the pub as it gives a good informal atmosphere and you can enjoy the work. It is good because no one in the group nags or bosses anyone else around. You have done some reading around for this project and written a few things down and you hope that it will be useful. You assume everyone else is doing that too; after all, they all turn up and seem engaged.

Assume it is now two weeks before your final deadline.

	Jot down some ideas
What are the dangers for individuals working in a group like this?	
How might such a 'team' appear during the project presentation if they don't change?	
Take stock – what does the group need to do NOW?	
What would you have learned about team work from such a group?	
Which function(s) of the Adair model is missing in this example? What type of group do you think this is: (see ' Identifying team characteristics' earlier in this section)? working group I pseudo team I potential team I real team I high performance team	

Scenario 2

You are working with a group of people – they are all your friends. You all sat down and worked out what you had to do and you think someone made a list, but you haven't seen it. A couple of your friends have become really bossy and they tell everyone else what to do, constantly adjusting and fiddling with things and even controlling what you are doing. They have told you to do something that you have no expertise or interest in and you do not like how tasks are allocated. You never expected these friends to be like this. You'll be glad when it is all over.

Assume it is now two weeks before your deadline.

	Jot down some ideas
What are the dangers for individuals working in a group like this?	
How will you all be feeling right now? Who will do those last-minute tasks if you all feel fed up?	
How might such a 'team' appear during the project presentation if they don't change?	
Take stock – what does the group need to do NOW?	
What would you have learned about team work from such a group?	
Which function(s) of the Adair model is missing in this example? What type of group do you think this is: (see section on Project Teams)? working group I pseudo team I potential team I real team I high-performance team	

Scenario 3

You are working with some people you know and some you don't know. Things are going well and you have even developed ground rules, appointed a group coordinator and have regular meetings. However, as time goes on problems arise as two group members aren't pulling their weight; one has even stopped coming to meetings and hasn't produced anything yet. The group is getting annoyed as they see all their hard work being compromised by those who aren't contributing effectively.

Two weeks to go – what would you do from the following? Select 'yes' or 'no' if you would carry out this action.

Action	Yes/No	Possible reasons
Find out if person X has a genuine reason for not doing the work.		He/she may be ill, have family problems or just be finding life pressures difficult at present. Depending on the answer, as a group you could give that person support or you may need to encourage him/her to seek help. Other reasons?
Ignore person X and do his/her work yourselves.		It is the only way to complete the project. The tutor is giving only one mark for the completed project, so we have to. This is not ideal and it will only cause resentment. Other reasons?
Assuming there are no mitigating circumstances, contact person X and say you need him/her to do their share – refer to ground rules and what she/he has to do to complete the project. Discuss with the person and then put it in writing – email or letter – from the whole group. Ensure a date for reply/action – retain a copy.		Person X realises the group is serious. Keep a record of your communication – you may need to say what you will do if you get no/little response. Other reasons?
Report person X to your tutor, explaining which part of the project person X is responsible for.		This should be a last resort, but may be necessary in extreme cases. If you do this, you should tell person X and give him/her a chance to put things right. It should all be transparent and business like. Your reason?
Some of your ideas …		

Which function(s) of the Adair model is missing in this example?

What type of group do you think this is: (see section on Project Teams)?

working group | pseudo team | potential team | real team | high-performance team

3 Getting started as a team

Before looking at the task or problem:

- everyone introduces themselves (often seen as an ice breaker);
- everyone agrees a set of ground rules;
- estimate the learning styles you have in your team as this will impact on the tasks and roles your team members are happy to assume;
- allocate roles.

Set your ground rules

Ground rules are vital if you want to establish an effective team. Ground rules will be the basis for a strong working relationship based on trust, honesty and an awareness of each other's expectations. Social groups also have ground rules, but these tend to have developed over time and are very often unspoken. However, if someone in a social group violates these 'rules', they are often made to feel acutely aware of it. In a team, where individuals come together to start working as a team, making ground rules explicit is very important and forms the agreement of how you will work together. Make sure this is the first thing you do so that when any member of the group feels things are going wrong, he/she can refer to them and remind everyone of their agreement. Be honest with the group and say what is important for you when working with them.

ACTIVITY 3 Establishing ground rules

Develop ground rules that can be used by a team – some examples are below. List three more that would be important *to you* when working with a team. If you are already working in a team, do this together and make sure you make a note of your rules.

Ground rules
1. Take responsibility for your own learning, actions and reactions (i.e. accept accountability).
2. Be honest and open (especially if you don't understand or agree with something).
3. Carry out your work on time.
4.
5.
6

Determine your team profile

Teams start with a group of individuals who need to become a team. You need to recognise each other's individual differences as a resource and in order to do that it is useful to look at your individual learning styles.

Peter Honey and Alan Mumford, two British psychologists and leading experts in learning and behaviour, have developed a set of learning styles that determines whether you are an activist, a reflector, a theorist or a pragmatist (Honey and Mumford, 1992). See the diagram below. Activity 4 asks you to identify your team's profile.

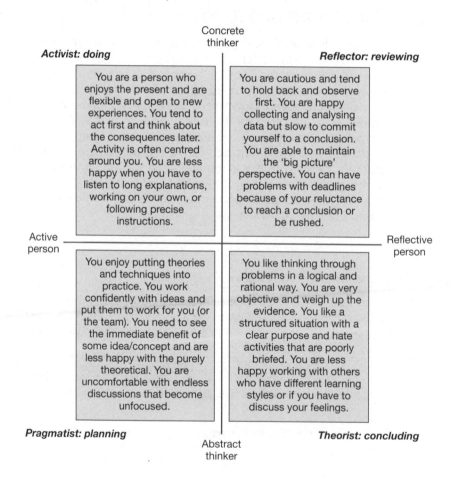

Concrete thinker

Activist: doing

Reflector: reviewing

You are a person who enjoys the present and are flexible and open to new experiences. You tend to act first and think about the consequences later. Activity is often centred around you. You are less happy when you have to listen to long explanations, working on your own, or following precise instructions.

You are cautious and tend to hold back and observe first. You are happy collecting and analysing data but slow to commit yourself to a conclusion. You are able to maintain the 'big picture' perspective. You can have problems with deadlines because of your reluctance to reach a conclusion or be rushed.

Active person

Reflective person

You enjoy putting theories and techniques into practice. You work confidently with ideas and put them to work for you (or the team). You need to see the immediate benefit of some idea/concept and are less happy with the purely theoretical. You are uncomfortable with endless discussions that become unfocused.

You like thinking through problems in a logical and rational way. You are very objective and weigh up the evidence. You like a structured situation with a clear purpose and hate activities that are poorly briefed. You are less happy working with others who have different learning styles or if you have to discuss your feelings.

Pragmatist: planning

Theorist: concluding

Abstract thinker

ACTIVITY 4 Identifying your team's profile

What's your team's profile? Using the diagram above, identify which quadrant most describes you when working on a project. Try to do this as a team so you can identify your team's profile. If you are not working in a team currently, identify the profile that usually suits you when working in a team.

Look at the descriptions in the quadrants above. You may find you can identify yourself in several quadrants. However, rank order the descriptions where it is:

1. = like me most of the time } Dominant profile
2. = like me some of the time }
3. = rarely like me
4. = never like me

Put your rankings in the table below:

Team member	Activist	Reflector	Theorist	Pragmatist
Example: person A	4	1	2	3
Me				
Number of members ranking 1 or 2 on a given type				

In the example above, person A is predominantly a reflector/theorist. If most of the other members of your group also have this profile, you may have difficulty producing your goals on time. Knowing this in advance can alert you to the potential weakness of your team. This allows you to take corrective action early on.

According to personal rankings our team predominantly comprises:

Type	Number of members with this tendency/ profile
ACTIVISTS	
REFLECTORS	
THEORISTS	
PRAGMATISTS	

Ideally, a team has a member from each of these categories, but more than likely you cannot change your team members, so use this exercise as a guide to consider how best to achieve your task with the individuals you have. You need to consider who is best suited to lead on:

1. coordinating/leading the team;

2. keeping on schedule;

3. analysing and suggesting how the problem can be broken down into tasks;

4. analysing sets of data;

5. carrying out research of the various theories that underpin your project;

6. applying theory to practice in your project.

Remember, as a team you still will all need to consider how you will fulfil other functions like maintaining team spirit and ensuring that everyone is valued (see team functions, above).

Working in a cross-cultural team

In the early 1990s, Professor Geert Hofstede, working at the University of Tilburg in Holland, developed a framework identifying how different cultures interact in groups and teams within an organisation. He developed five dimensions:

1. **Low vs. high power distance**. This refers to how well individuals accept unequal power distribution in an organisation. Cultures with a low power distance would expect working relationships to be more consultative and inclusive. In cultures with a high power distance, individuals perceive any unequal distribution as acceptable.

2. **Individualism vs. collectivism**. This measures the value placed by a culture on being identified with a group or series of groups affiliated with you. These are termed collectivist cultures. Individualist cultures expect you to display your individual personality and determine your own groups.

3. **Masculinity vs. femininity**. This refers to societies that value male characteristics such as competitiveness and assertiveness or female characteristics such as quality of living and the development of relationships.

4. **Low vs. high uncertainty avoidance**. This refers to how well a society copes with uncertainty. Where there is a tendency for uncertainty avoidance, that society may put in place a series of explicit rules that people can follow to reduce uncertainty. Opposite societies prefer more implicit and flexible rules.

5. **Long- vs. short-term orientation**. This refers to societies along a time continuum. Those that have a long-term view are predominantly future oriented (see Chapter 1 for a similar interpretation) and value behaviour such as perseverance, deferred gratification and planning. Short-term societies tend to respect tradition, want stability and reciprocate with gifts in order to maintain a balance in relationships.

Source: www.geert-hofstede.com

ACTIVITY 5 Reflecting on the cultural dimension

Look at the five dimensions above and consider how these could influence misunderstandings in an intercultural team. Remember, these dimensions are not individual traits but a potential filter through which we view the world. This filter can be very subtle and we need to sensitise ourselves to how our own cultural filters work. Look at these dimensions in relation to (a) yourself and then (b) with members of your group and add it to your team profile. You may also want to critique Hofstede's dimensions. Are they too general? Are you tempted to apply this at an individual level? What about personal traits?

4 Becoming an effective team

Now you have the basics in place, you can start planning, allocating roles and making good decisions.

Develop team roles

Use the information from this section and the one above to establish the kind of roles you would like in your team. You may find you have to split up along thematic lines as you may be expected to hand in work as a team, but with identifiable parts for each participant's grade. However, you do need to establish who does what and whatever you decide, you will need to have a coordinator as someone who keeps the team on track and on time. There will be other roles and some people may have two roles, one on the task and another related to some element of team maintenance.

First allocate your coordinator, then develop your plan (see below) and return to complete your team roles later.

ACTIVITY 6 Allocating team roles

Name	Role(s)

Develop a plan of action

Without a plan you will not be able to work as a team. Once you have identified a coordinator/leader, you can start working on your plan. The plan includes not only a list of activities but also protocols for the team, e.g. dealing with meetings and what to do if individuals don't fulfil their tasks, etc. The designated coordinator needs to ensure there is a workable plan and **everyone** understands it and is committed to it. You can then develop the team roles.

When planning:

1. Read carefully the brief given to you by your lecturer.

2. Agree what you have to do, by when and in what format(s).

3. Divide the brief into various sub-tasks.

4. Allocate team members to the various tasks.

5. Set a timetable with milestones.

6. Set out how you will handle meetings: regularity, minute taking/storing, decisions taken and actions set.

7. Establish reporting procedures and mechanisms for revising the plan, and keeping records and minutes of meetings.

8. Have a mechanism to ensure open communications with the ability to resolve conflict.

9. Plan how you will present your work.

Make good decisions

Decision making can be difficult in teams. You may be more of a risk taker than others, look at evidence selectively, have certain prejudices (often unknown to yourself) and be swayed, or not, by group pressure. All these lead to a flawed decision-making process.

There are various ways for teams to come to an agreement and make a decision:

1. **Consensus**. This agreement means alignment of the team as a whole with the goals set. Those who may have disagreed are prepared to cooperate for the success of the team and not take up defensive positions.

2. **Unanimous**. Here everyone has to agree before a decision is taken.

3. **Majority**. This can be, for example, if 51 per cent agree then the decision is taken, but this can split your team.

Ideally you want to have a consensus decision which means you are all prepared to accept the decision made. A fairly simple technique you can use as a team to air the issues during the decision-making process is the Six Thinking Hats proposed by a leading authority on creative thinking, Edward de Bono (1999).

Each 'hat' looks at an issue from a particular point of view. This can also reduce confrontation as people are working within the confines of their 'hat'. You don't physically have to wear different hats, but they are used to symbolise a different viewpoint. It is more objective if you adopt a hat that does not directly correspond to your own position.

White Hat: With this hat you focus on information, reports and any data that are available. It is an objective position.

Red Hat: With this hat you make a decision based on your opinion, intuition and feelings. It is a subjective position.

Black Hat: This is a pessimistic and critical review of the decisions being taken. You focus on what may not work with this decision and what could go wrong. You are essentially looking for the weak points and the team should be able to address and counter these points. This position will help you make more reliable decisions. This is an objective position.

Yellow Hat: This is an optimistic viewpoint and helps you see all the benefits and value of a decision.

Green Hat: This is the hat for creativity and intuition. This position is very important when the team feels it can't move forward. Sometimes you need to harness this creativity and take risks.

Blue Hat: This is the overview position or the 'meta-hat'. The team coordinator or a person chairing your meetings may want to have this hat. The person wearing this hat should know when to call on the other hats in order to come to a decision.

Once the team has heard all the views from the different hat perspectives, a decision is made.

NOTE Only take time to use a technique like this for important decisions. Also consider your cultural differences when you come to decision making and reflect on how you arrive at a decision with respect to other cultures.

ACTIVITY 7 Being your own troubleshooter when teams go wrong

It is usual to go to your tutor when things go wrong in your team. This is invariably around someone not fulfilling their part, or you feeling that you are doing too much or being left out. It is easy to turn to someone else, but before you do that, try troubleshooting your problems. In the table below there is a list of things that can go wrong. You may want to add your own as well and consider how you could put things right.

If you are expected to reflect on your team work as part of your project, then do reflect on how you sorted out your problems. This can only gain you marks for initiative and being an independent learner.

Tick what might be going wrong in your team and think how to remedy it.

What's happening in the team?	Tick	Possible remedies (and make cross-references to places in this chapter that could help)
Not clarifying what your task or objective is.		
Not checking on progress.		
Not checking on time.		
Not clarifying or recording what has been decided.		
Not clarifying who is going to do what.		
Not clarifying what has to be done by when.		
Not establishing procedures for handling meetings.		
Not keeping to agreed procedures.		
Not listening to each other.		
Allowing individuals to dominate and others to withdraw.		
[some are] Not turning up for meetings.		
[some are] Not doing the work allocated.		
[some are] Not doing the work allocated very well.		

What's happening in the team?	Tick	Possible remedies *(and make cross-references to places in this chapter that could help)*
[some are] Not recognising the feelings of members of the team.		
[some are] Not contributing equally to the progress of the team.		

NOTE Teams can work well and then go wrong. Make sure you keep communication channels open as your team develops, so you can keep it working well. Bruce Tuckman (Tuckman and Jensen 1977) suggests that teams go through a repetitive cycle of:

- forming – characterised by dependence on the coordinator, but little consensus on the aims;
- storming – where members take up positions, establish themselves within the group, form sub-groups and challenge other team members;
- norming – where agreements are met and adhered to, members feel they have their role and can make decisions, and the coordinator can work without major challenges;
- performing – where the team knows what it has to do and all members are committed and feel accountable for the outcome.

You may find that you cycle several times through storming, norming and performing as your project develops. Be aware of these cycles, see them as part of the process and find a way to deal with it. If you feel inclined to seek help from your tutor, check to see if you are just in a storming phase which you need to work your way out of as a team.

Working in a diverse team

There are various aspects to working in a diverse team and this section is just a brief discussion of some of the issues. We live with diversity across our lives from different types of people, different abilities, different subject disciplines and different cultures. Diverse teams make the working with diversity more formal and it is this aspect of team working that requires more attention as we have to work harder at creating the trust necessary for effective team work.

The diagram below will give you a snapshot view of some of the issues to consider.

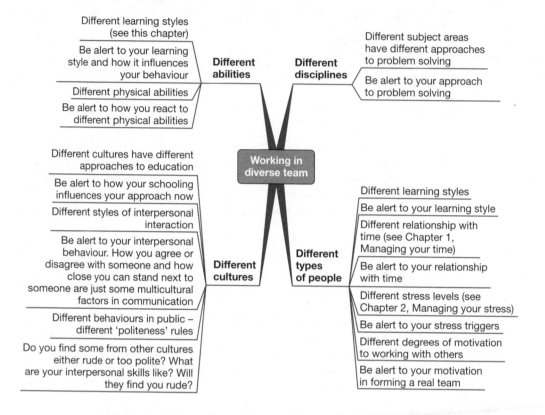

Different learning styles (see this chapter)

Be alert to your learning style and how it influences your behaviour

Different abilities

Different physical abilities

Be alert to how you react to different physical abilities

Different disciplines

Different subject areas have different approaches to problem solving

Be alert to your approach to problem solving

Working in diverse team

Different cultures have different approaches to education

Be alert to how your schooling influences your approach now

Different styles of interpersonal interaction

Be alert to your interpersonal behaviour. How you agree or disagree with someone and how close you can stand next to someone are just some multicultural factors in communication

Different behaviours in public – different 'politeness' rules

Do you find some from other cultures either rude or too polite? What are your interpersonal skills like? Will they find you rude?

Different cultures

Different types of people

Different learning styles

Be alert to your learning style

Different relationship with time (see Chapter 1, Managing your time)

Be alert to your relationship with time

Different stress levels (see Chapter 2, Managing your stress)

Be alert to your stress triggers

Different degrees of motivation to working with others

Be alert to your motivation in forming a real team

Checklist: a copper-bottomed approach to team work

1. **C**ommitment: You all take joint responsibility for the success of the team and be inclusive to all.
2. **O**bjectives: You take time to make the objectives and goals for the team clear to all.
3. **P**urpose: In order to keep the team motivated you all need to be clear why you are involved with this team and have clarity of purpose.
4. **P**lan: You need to plan how to solve the problem by breaking down the task into sub-tasks *and* establish how you work together as a team.
5. **E**xpectations: As a team, state what your expectations are and work towards a set of high expectations.
6. **R**oles: Make sure you allocate roles to your team members so that you can act on your plan. Recognise individual differences when allocating roles.

5 Tools of the trade

While students on campus and living close can easily work face to face, not all students are full time or living close enough to do this. Forming a *virtual team* for those off-campus students is the only way to progress this. Although it is easier to make decisions face to face, virtual teams will gain experience of working together in an approach to teamwork that is becoming more common in the work place.

Both virtual and face-to-face teams should be using technology. The virtual teams will be using it to communicate and store information, while the face to face-to-face group will probably limit it to file storage, the odd email and mobile calls. Virtual groups should ensure that the technology they use offers a mix of synchronous and asynchronous communication possibilities.

There are various pieces of technology that can help groups keep on track:

- **Mobile phone (synchronous communication)**. Use your phone for confirmation or cancellation of meetings. This is too awkward for arranging meetings.
- **Email (asynchronous communication)**. Make sure you have each other's email addresses. You can keep in contact easily, share documents and arrange meetings.
- **Online chatting facilities (synchronous communication)**. Computer conferencing software usually means that you are communicating as you would in email. This is referred to as asynchronous communication and is unlike telephone or face-to-face chatting which is in real time (synchronous communication). Sometimes it is fine to communicate asynchronously, but there are times when you just have to work in real time. The best way is always face to face, but if this is impossible, consider using online chat facilities through software at your institution or facilities in MSM. Remember, decision making is always best when face to face, so try to get together for key moments in your team. If you are a virtual team, you may find your institution has a computer conferencing facility. Check this out as it could be a useful tool to learn.

Using electronic group facilities: 'a must' for virtual groups

Many institutions now have portals or similar software where you can set up your own groups. You can use this to keep in touch, upload key documents and generally use for team administration. Also, if you are a team who either study part time or live far away from each other, you can use an online group facility to store all your documents. If you are a virtual group, you will also want to check whether your institution has software for online chat room facilities or online conferencing software so you can have real-time conversations. If your institution does not have these facilities, you could investigate using MSN Messenger.

Developing a good filing system

You will have your documents on your own PC, but you also need a joint filing system for all the team's documents and this can be done using some online group facilities at your institution. Also, remember to organise your files to reflect your team's plan and keep well-labelled versions of your documents so that you know which document you are working with.

NOTE   Make sure you back up all your documents regularly. 'I couldn't hand my work in because I had a computer crash' is becoming an increasingly lame excuse and your tutor will view it like that. Be responsible and back up your work as you go.

6 On reflection

Through this chapter you should be able to articulate the essentials of working in a real team, reflect on your experience of working in student project teams and know what you need to do to improve the next team. At an interview for a work placement or once you leave your studies, you may be asked how well you work in groups. Now you have started to reflect on and articulate your skills, it will make this kind of question a lot easier for you to answer.

Go back to the first activity, 'Annoying things about working with others', and see if you would now answer them differently. You should have developed some more awareness on how you would deal with these potentially annoying aspects of working with others.

Take time to reflect on your experience in project teams and the skills you feel you need to develop to make yourself a more effective team member. You may want to transfer this information to your institution's PDP scheme.

Consider how you work with students from other cultures. What annoys you? Be honest and discuss this rationally with that person and you will also learn what makes you annoying!

Having read this chapter, gauge your confidence again. How does this compare with your confidence levels at the start of the chapter? What can you do to improve? You can incorporate this into your own PDP. Add anything else you feel is appropriate.

ACTIVITY 8 Update your personal development planner

Grade your confidence in your ability on a scale of 1–5 where (1 = poor and 5 = good).

My team work skills plan	Confidence level 1–5	Plans to improve
I understand what a real team is and I am developing my skills to achieve this. *Section 2*		
I understand how to identify my own skills, learning style and cultural filter in order to work effectively within a group. *Section 3*		
I know the mechanics of setting up a real team and put those steps in place when I work in a team. *Section 4*		
I understand that a major challenge is working in a diverse group. My team is aware of the issues involved and alert to possible problems. *Section 2, 3, 4, 5*		

Date: _____

Getting extra help

- Your institution or course possibly offers team-building training. Take advantage of this and take time to reflect on what you are learning.
- See references at the end of this chapter.
- A general web search on 'team building' or 'working in teams' will provide a host of information.
- For cross-cultural information, carry out a web search using 'cultural awareness' as a search term.
- When searching the web try using academic search engines like Intute or Google Scholar, ISI Web of Knowledge to find more academic sources.

Feedback on activities

ACTIVITY 1 Annoying things about working with others

Annoying things	I would deal with this by ...
There are always free-riders in a team and their marks are boosted by those who do the work.	Starting with ground rules for the team. Agree what we will do in advance if someone doesn't do their share. If the situation persists, let the tutor know (rationally, not in a whingeing manner) what we have done and that it has not improved.
Teams slow me down and that irritates me.	Listening to what other team members are saying rather than assuming they can't contribute. Recognise the different types of contribution they bring. If I am better at the technical side, I am happy to share this with the team as we are all interdependent.
I have difficulty with the topic the team has to work on and I'm afraid I'll keep the others back.	Letting the team know of my worries and offering to do some things that I know I am good it.
Sometimes team members won't complete their tasks (at all, or on time!).	Checking if our ground rules are being flouted. Enforce our rules and if this does not improve, inform our tutor. State the measures taken in order to improve this ourselves.
Sometimes teams don't divide up the work fairly.	Seeing whether the team may be working as sub-groups within the team. This has to be stopped. This issue has to be talked about so that everyone feels they are being heard and valued.
I sometimes have difficulty working with students from other cultures as they have such different ways of working and it takes so long to get anything done.	Working out what the intercultural tension is: is it time keeping, work ethic, feeling isolated? Identify the main issue and try to discuss and deal with it. This is very much 'reflection – in-action'. Also take a look at Hofstede's cultural dimensions in Activity 5.
Sometimes you get students who just don't care about their grades, but I do.	Convincing the team that they are interdependent and let others down if they don't work. This is part of the ground rules and if it cannot be solved by the group, it needs to be discussed with the tutor

ACTIVITY 2 Understanding team patterns – what's your view?

Scenario 1

Type of group

This is more of a 'working group', i.e. a group of people who are not really pulling together as well as they could. These individuals are probably working informally as a working group without realising it and possibly see themselves as a team. They have assumed that since they all worked well together before, it would be successful. However, as a team they have to work differently and very often working with friends is not a good idea as old and established ways of getting along may not be appropriate for this task.

Adair group functions

The group lacks a focus on the task and they aren't building their team, although it is working at a very social level. The group needs to redefine itself as a team.

Scenario 2

Type of group

The group is more of a 'pseudo team'. You started out identifying your goals but you don't seemed to have shared that. Why didn't you ask to work on the identified goals rather than just moaning that you haven't seen them? Some of your friends realise they need to behave differently if they want to get the job done, but seem to be doing this in a unilateral way. It appears they have taken the lead instinctively, without discussion, which makes them appear bossy. If this group wants to stay together as a group of friends *and* a team, they need to openly discuss how they can achieve the task set and the different roles they will have to adopt in order to do that.

Adair group functions

This group is basically lacking the team-building function. Some of you are trying to achieve the task while others are still operating as a social group. This group needs to think of itself as a team and of ways to bring everyone together on task and to be mutually dependent.

Scenario 3

Type of group

This group is more of a 'pseudo team' now, but with a little effort and the development of interdependence and joint responsibility for the goals you could be a 'potential team'. It may be that this team didn't fully discuss the task and identify the resources within the group at the very beginning. Management theory refers to the importance of frank discussions within a group so that all are in agreement (aligned) with what has to be done, how it has to be done and who has to do it. Remember, a 'real team' has shared responsibility and is moving in one direction towards the goal.

Adair group functions

This group appears to be achieving most of the Adair functions but not as effectively as it could. As the group develops, it may need to reassess some of its earlier decisions as to the needs of individuals in the team and how the team spirit should be maintained. Keep lines of communication open so that problems can be ironed out before they become obstacles to achieving the task.

ACTIVITY 7 Being your own troubleshooter when teams go wrong

What's happening in the team?	Tick	Possible remedies *(and make cross-references to places in this chapter that could help)*
Not clarifying what your task or objective is.		You haven't gone through the planning process. See section 4.
Not checking on progress.		You haven't developed a mechanism for checking how things are going. You can't leave everything to your coordinator. Go back to your planning document and put something in there that you can all sign up to. This is very important.
Not checking on time.		As above. It is part of your progress-checking mechanism.
Not clarifying or recording what has been decided.		Include as part of your planning mechanisms for recording your decisions. See Sections 4 and 5.
Not clarifying who is going to do what.		You don't seem to have allocated roles (see Section 4) and in order to do that you need to understand the learning styles of your group (see Section 3).
Not clarifying what has to be done by when.		This means as part of your planning you have not established a timetable with milestones.
Not establishing procedures for handling meetings.		Again this is part of your planning process (see Section 4). Devise an electronic method for storing your decisions/actions from meetings (see Section 5).
Not keeping to agreed procedures.		Check you have your ground rules in place (Section 3) and how you deal with individuals who flout them (Section 4).
Not listening to each other.		If you remember, being a real team means collaborating and appreciating all in your team. Look again at the team functions from John Adair, Section 2.

What's happening in the team?	Tick	Possible remedies (and make cross-references to places in this chapter that could help)
Allowing individuals to dominate and others to withdraw.		See above and this relates again to the functions in a team.
[some are] Not turning up for meetings.		Your ground rules and procedures for making them work should be applied here. This is why it is important to set these up *before* things go wrong. See Sections 3 and 4.
[some are] Not doing the work allocated.		As above. However, you may want to check that this person did actually agree to do this work. If it really is a problem, you may need to reallocate tasks. Be flexible enough to do this.
[some are] Not doing the work allocated very well.		It is quite likely that you will get some high-flyers in your team and others who are struggling. If you feel the work some do is not up to standard, bring the team together and work out a way of resolving this. Should someone else do that aspect, does he/she need some quick coaching? Find out the problem.
[some are] Not recognising the feelings of members of the team.		This relates back to the 'develop the individual' aspect of John Adair's model. Everyone in your team is an important member and all your team needs to recognise the value of all.
[some are] Not contributing equally to the progress of the team.		First check why this is happening. Maybe those concerned feel they are contributing well. Be honest and clarify the situation. Again, with a good plan and clear milestones you should be able to go back and identify where things are going wrong. You may need to make adjustments.

References

- Adair, J. (1986) *Effective Team Building*. Aldershot, Gower.
- BBC News (2006) 'Graduate demand outstrips skills', 7 February, available at: http://news.bbc.co.uk and search on the title of the article.
- de Bono, E. (1999) *Six Thinking Hats*. London, Penguin.
- Hofstede, G. (1991) *Cultural Organisations*. London, McGraw-Hill.

- Honey, P. and Mumford, A. (1992) *The Manual of Learning Styles.* Maidenhead, Peter Honey.

- Katzenbach, J.R. and Smith, D.K. (1993) *The Wisdom of Teams.* New York, HarperBusiness.

- Tuckman, B.W. and Jensen, M.A.C. (1977) 'Stages of small group development revisited', *Group and Organisational Studies,* 2, 419–27.

6 Presenting your work

Being able to present your work well as a student, and later on in your job, is an invaluable skill. You have probably sat through countless talks already and looked at many posters, so you instinctively know the kind of presentation that bores you. Now is your opportunity to articulate your instincts and hone your presentation skills for both posters and talks.

In this chapter you will:

1. prepare information for posters;
2. design posters for visual clarity and coherence;
3. design slides for clarity;
4. recognise what makes a good and bad oral presentation;
5. know how classic mistakes in oral presentations affect your audience and how to avoid them.

USING THIS CHAPTER

Estimate your current levels of confidence. At the end of the chapter you will have the chance to re-assess these levels where you can incorporate this into your personal development planner (PDP). Mark between 1 (poor) and 5 (good) for the following:

I can understand the key elements of poster design.	I can understand key elements of slide design.	I can understand the characteristics of effective oral presentations.

Date: _____

1 Introduction

Being able to give a good and clear presentation to a public audience is a skill that you and your future employer will value greatly. Prospective employers invariably ask for your experience in using these key skills during interviews. You need to be able to articulate what makes a good and poor presentation and offer evidence for your knowledge. So, when you are asked to give a talk or produce a poster as part of your studies, recognise the importance of developing the skills of delivery as well as conveying the content.

Posters and oral presentations are forms of presentation that enable you to develop your confidence in different ways. Posters check your ability to succinctly present information and present it in an attractive and message-focused way, while oral presentations allow for more information and a more in-depth delivery. In both modes you will probably find yourself taking questions and explaining your ideas.

2 Poster presentations

Assessed coursework can take the form of a poster presentation. This can be, for example, an individual piece of research, a group project or a visual essay where you present the ideas of a particular topic. Whatever the content of your poster, a poster is a visual presentation format and as with any other form of communication, it should 'tell a story'.

Before you do anything, start with a checklist.

> ### Checklist: clarify what is expected from your poster assignment
>
> 1. The purpose of the poster and the intended audience.
> 2. The size of the poster required.
> 3. Any specifications for the production, e.g. does it have to be through particular software, can you produce it by hand, or use a cut-and-paste method?
> 4. Expectations regarding display, e.g. do you need to print it out or display via a PC/laptop?
> 5. Printing quality, i.e. can you print out in draft form as this is much cheaper?
> 6. The presentation, e.g. in a conference setting with your posters set up around a room or as part of an oral presentation.
> 7. The assessment criteria.

Information regarding the checklist is discussed in this section.

Planning what you want to say

Identify your audience

Establish who your audience is. Your tutor should give you guidance here. Don't just assume that you are writing for your tutor because there is a tendency to think he or she knows this material already and you don't need to explain it in such detail. So, it is better to assume your audience is an intelligent 14 year old.

NOTE Researchers are now asked by some Research Councils to write an abstract of their research that could be understood by an intelligent 14 year old.

Identify your message

The key to any poster is deciding **what** your message is. In order to do this you need to distil the key points of your work on to some rough paper and arrange the order of your 'story'.

If you are reporting on work from your individual research project or a group project it is good to write a short section at the beginning (approximately 200 words) which outlines:

- why you did this research (gives a context);
- how you did it (method);

- issues it raised (there may be some interesting things to solve on the way);
- key findings/conclusion/recommendation.

This is similar to an 'abstract', which is found at the beginning of a journal article in order to prepare the reader for the content of the paper. Once you have the abstract, you have the key ideas for your poster and your introduction.

If you have not carried out any data-gathering research, you may be asked to present a poster on a topic. This is something like a visual essay and you will also need to start by jotting down a summary of your reading by:

- stating the importance of this topic (gives context);
- listing the key points/issues/positions (as theoretical positions, key researchers, key solutions, etc.);
- offering critical reflection on what you have read and a concluding remark.

Once you have summarised what you have found, you have the key ideas for your poster and they can be part of your poster introduction.

Second, your poster must have a clear message. The information in your abstract or introduction can be developed in the boxes on your poster (see 'Designing your poster' below).

How we read a poster

A poster is not a jumble of things that can be read in any order (unless you are using the poster as a form of art). Generally, we read a poster from the top left and work our way down to the bottom right, as with any page we read. However, you can break this rule if your route through the poster is clear and logical.

Coherence (progression of ideas) is important in any written document and a poster is no different. Make sure your start and end points are obvious. More creative subjects may want to flout this rule and offer a more visually demanding display. If this is the case, you need to decide if your reader needs to come away with key pieces of information and how you will visually identify them.

Remember, readers will probably spend no more than about five minutes reading your poster. In that time you have to convey your message through words and images. Identify key pieces of information (see 'Identify your message' above).

Designing your poster

Layout

A fairly transparent way to design your poster is to allocate text and picture boxes to the size of paper you have. Your first decision is the size (A1?) and the orientation (portrait or landscape?) of your poster. Figures 6.1–6.3 show different layouts.

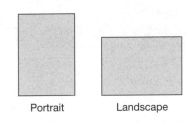

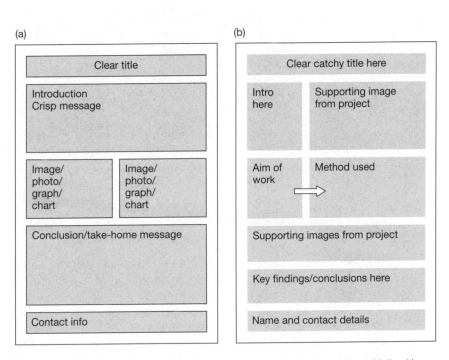

Figure 6.1 Portrait: mixed column solutions. (a) Predominantly single column with lined boxes (b) Predominantly double column with or without lined boxes

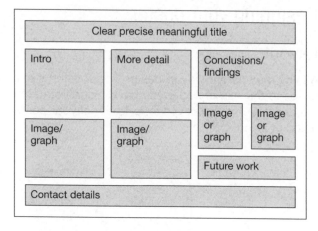

Figure 6.2 Landscape: a more visual poster

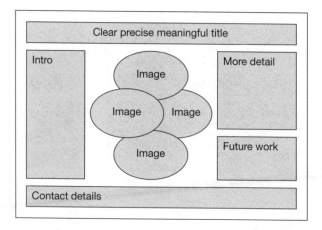

Figure 6.3 Landscape – collage effect

You need to play around with ideas on how you want to set out your text and images and the kind of information you want to include. Remember to think of how your information will flow, so it is obvious to the reader. Also, make sure your colour scheme enables easy reading. Your colour scheme should enhance the message, not dominate it. Pastel-coloured backgrounds with dark text are easy on the eye. Dark backgrounds with light text can look effective, but be careful it doesn't become too garish and difficult to read. Your topic should also give you a feel for the colour scheme you want to adopt.

Poster size

Paper sizes are standardised and the ISO (International Standards Office) paper sizes we use are labelled as 'A' size papers ranging from A7 to A0;

the smaller the number, the larger the paper size. The paper size we use most often is A4. Most student writing blocks are A4 size and it is also the standard size for most photocopiers and printers. The usual size for a poster is A1.

Some paper sizes are as follows:

A5 + A5 = A4 *(height 29 cm × width 21cm)*

A4 + A4 = A3

A3 + A3 = A2

A2 + A2 = A1 *(height 84 cm × width 59 cm)*

Text: size and choice of font

Remember people will be standing some distance away from your poster, so make your text easy to read from about 1.5 m. You may want to use fancy fonts, but be careful – simple, clear and well-proportioned fonts are better. Try to use a point range between 20–35, but the size you choose will depend on the font as some can appear clumsy when too big.

Some of the options you have are as follows.

Typeface: serif or sans serif?

The basic choice is between serif and sans serif fonts. Many studies have shown that sans serif and a wide letter look are easier to read.

Times New Roman is a serif font but with a rather narrow letter look. This generally rates poorly on readability tests. This is also now considered rather old fashioned.

Garamond is also a serif font but the letters look a lot wider and this makes it easier to read. If you prefer to use a serif font, this is probably better than Times.

Arial is a sans serif font and the letters combine a narrow look with an uncluttered letter shape.

Verdana is also a sans serif font but the letters have a wider look which makes it easier to read.

Font size

It will depend on the typeface you use, but as a guide: the main title at approximately 100 points, sub-headings 50 points and the main text 25 points.

Emphasis

You may want to emphasise key points. Below are some possibilities. However, use only two, at the most, in one poster. You can:

- use bold, italics, underline or capitals;
- change the text colour;
- put text in a graphic or box.

Alignment

The human eye can detect very quickly if text is not aligned and this can make it look unprofessional. It is like wearing clothes that are not ironed. Make sure your text does align and if you have a list ensure that all the first words in your list start the same, i.e. don't use a mixture of capitals and lower case.

Line length

Lines that are too long or too short in length interfere with the speed of reading. A good average line length to work with is approximately 39 characters long.

Graphics

Select graphics that enhance your text. Some stray images will look very odd.

Checklist: do's and don'ts

- **Don't** have lots of different typefaces.
- **Don't** use lots of different point sizes.
- **Don't** use your emphasis features for a large block of text.
- **Do** have a consistent layout.
- **Do** include white space around your text as this gives contrast to text and rests your eyes.
- **Do** print a draft copy to check before the final print.

Hot Tip Don't use an unusual font as the printer may not recognise it.

Tools to use

You can prepare a poster by freehand drawing, writing text in a word processor, printing and then cutting and pasting on to your paper or using a software package. Check with your tutor how he or she wants you to prepare your poster. Part of your assignment may in fact be the use of a particular piece of software.

Microsoft PowerPoint is a natural choice for most as it is already part of Microsoft Office. As a UK student (of recent years) you will probably have used this software for school coursework. Before you start you need to set up the page size and orientation you want to use. To do this in PowerPoint for an A1 poster, open a new file and click **File > Page Setup > Custom**, select a **Width** of 60 cm and a **Height** of 84 cm, and choose either portrait or landscape orientation.

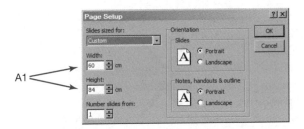

You can then save your PowerPoint file on to a CD or memory stick and take it to someone who can print it the size and weight of paper you require. Try to get an A3 (twice as big as A4) draft copy of your poster to check the layout and colour scheme before printing at A1 size.

NOTE If you have had no experience of PowerPoint, check to see if your institution is running any ICT sessions or tutorials.

Displaying your poster

There are several ways of displaying your poster:

- on a display board;
- hanging from nylon thread (need heavier weight paper for this or mounted on card);
- with sticky tape on a lecture room wall.

NOTE If you are going to present your paper outside your institution, you may need to have it laminated (your institution should have facilities for this). You will also require a cardboard roll to transport it safely to your venue.

> ### Checklist: your poster
>
> There is nothing worse than hanging up your poster only to find an obvious spelling mistake. Poster language must be correct. You (or better still someone else) need to:
>
> 1. Check your message for clarity.
> 2. Reduce the number of words and still keep it clear.
> 3. Check for spelling mistakes.
> 4. Check your images support your text.
> 5. Check the order of information for cohesion.
> 6. Get a draft A3 copy to check layout and colour (see Figure 6.4 for a summary of posters).

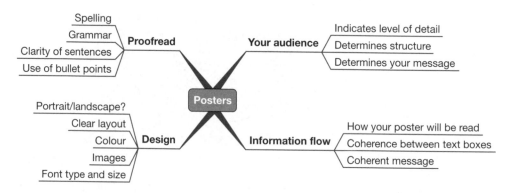

Figure 6.4 Poster summary

Talking about your poster

Although your poster sits there for all to read, you will probably be close by and may be asked some questions. You should practise explaining in a simple way what your work was about, why you did it, any problems you had to overcome on the way, and the outcomes and conclusions. If your poster is an 'ideas poster' on a topic, you need to be able to explain the central message and issues of the topic presented in your poster. Your poster may be the visual aid for an oral presentation in preference to slides.

See Section 3 for some information on oral presentations.

Having your poster assessed

Your tutors will tell you how they are going to assess your work. Some of the things that they may look for are listed below:

Criteria	Description
Knowledge	The knowledge presented is accurate, relevant to the title, key points clearly evident.
Structure	The poster has a clear beginning and end. The text boxes have clearly defined pieces of information.
Language and images	Language is clear, concise and easy to understand. It is appropriate for the intended audience. No spelling or grammatical errors. The images enhance the text.
Amount of information	There is enough information to inform the audience of the topic and not too much to require lengthy reading.
General impression	The poster is visually attractive. The content presents new information or information from a different angle. It has some novel/interesting things to say.

3 Oral presentations

Giving a talk can mean standing up alone or with a group and presenting your ideas or your project work. You can use visual aids like slides or, if you are presenting a small paper in a seminar context, have no visual aids.

Before you start you need to consult the following checklist as this will influence what you do.

> **Checklist: identifying what is expected in your oral presentation**
>
> 1. The topic – identify and present the key issues.
> 2. The talk – group or individual.
> 3. The purpose of the talk and the intended audience.
> 4. The length of time you have to talk.
> 5. The length of time for questions.
> 6. The method of presentation, e.g. overhead projector, via a computer, with no visual aids at all.
> 7. The handouts – are you expected to provide them? If so, how many?
> 8. The room layout: where will you stand? Where can you put your papers? If you are a group, how will you arrange yourself in the space?
> 9. The running order for presentations – are you one of many that afternoon?
> 10. The rehearsal – use to decide who says what in a group talk.
> 11. The assessment criteria – address them in the preparation.

The oral presentation assignment

Once you have provided answers from the checklist above, you can start preparing your talk.

Organising what to include

The amount of detail you put into your talk will be determined by the purpose and the audience, but your talk must always have a **beginning**, a **middle** and an **end**.

If you are presenting on an individual or group project you need to:

- contextualise the project – lead in;
- state how you carried out the project;
- mention problems you may have experienced;
- state your findings and conclusions.

If you are presenting an idea you need to:

- contextualise the issues;
- state where you researched the issues (a broad-brush approach to show where you have your evidence);
- discuss controversial issues;
- state any conclusions.

NOTE　A common mistake with many student presentations is that the talk fails to have a proper introduction that contextualises and introduces the audience to the topic. Many students jump straight into the fine detail of their work. **Don't do this**, as the audience has to work hard to catch up in order to understand you. You have to assume that your audience may not know as much about the topic as you do and providing an introduction is a key element in a talk.

Timing

Check how long you have for your slot and confirm if this includes question and feedback time afterwards. As a rule of thumb work on the following for a 15-minute slot:

- ten minutes talking;
- five minutes questions and/or feedback.

Again, as a rule of thumb, if you assume one slide per minute then you should have a **maximum** of ten slides for a ten-minute talk.

The method of presentation

The most common ways of giving a presentation are as follows:

- via a computer using presentation software;
- using an overhead projector;
- with no visual aids at all.

When using an **overhead projector** you will need transparent slides to either write on, with a marker pen, or to print to from your computer. You can use a presentation package, like Microsoft PowerPoint, and print directly on to OHP slides. It is not recommended that slides are handwritten as this can appear messy, unless you have particularly clear handwriting. Graphics would also have to be hand drawn and that is not a good idea.

When using a piece of software you can **present via your computer**. This gives a clearer presentation and enables you to add graphics easily, include colour and use hyperlinks if necessary. If part of your work was to produce a website, then this would be vital, as you would be able to show it.

Giving a talk with **no visual aids** is quite difficult. The traditional example of this is reading a paper in a tutorial. This can be very tedious. If you were expected to use this mode of delivery, it would be wise to put your key ideas on cards and talk around the ideas, rather than reading directly from your paper.

Slide design

As with posters, the design of your slides is important. Your audience will not want to read a lot of text from your slides. You are not there to read from your slides; that is pointless and tedious. Your slides are there as visual aids to set the scene for the topic you are talking about and give a visual anchor around which you can talk. Therefore, the more visual you can make your slides, the better – as long as it doesn't look like a comic! We all remember:

- images;
- diagrams that show connections/processes;
- key words and phrases (especially if they are repeated often enough).

We don't remember dense text or bullet points very well.

Software like PowerPoint has built-in slide designs, but there are only a few that are really usable and not too fussy. We have all seen those designs too often and this can create boredom in the audience before you start. So, avoid the template designs in the software and create your own, if you can (Figure 6.5).

Try using more images than text, but make sure your images are related to your work.

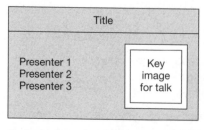
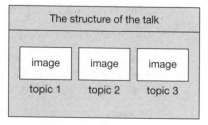

Body of talk: topic 1 [mixture of images and text]

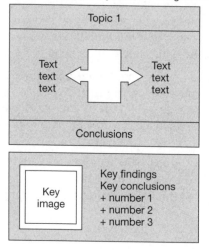
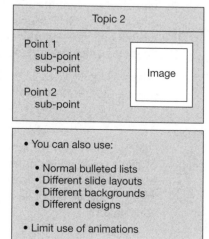

Figure 6.5 Slide designs

Your slides should be clear and uncluttered in order to be understood. Select a font that is easy to read and be guided by the suggested font sizes in PowerPoint (point size 32 for main bullets and 28 for sub-bullets).

Hot Tip

Take as many digital photographs as you can of your work while you are doing it so you can include them in your presentation. This can be, for example, your team, the equipment you used, the results (if visual) and simplified graphs. This will really bring your presentation to life.

What audiences remember

Your audience will hear what you have to say only once; they have no opportunity to go back and check. What you say at each point should be clear. We all remember how things 'fit together' better than a list of things. If you can show how things are connected (via diagrams), how processes work (flow diagrams) and how things look (images, pictures), this will make your presentation memorable. Identify your 'take-home message' and make sure you say this at the end in a clear voice with visual support.

Characteristics of oral presentations

Activity 1 will look at our experience of listening to and/or giving a talk.

ACTIVITY 1 Good and bad characteristics in oral presentations

For a moment, consider the numerous talks and lectures you have listened to and complete the table below.

Characteristics of talks you have enjoyed	Characteristics of talks that bored you ...	Your strong and weak points when giving an oral presentation
		I'm happy with ...
		I'd like to improve ...

Were any of your strong and weak points in the feedback section at the end of the chapter? Check to see the effect they can have on an audience.

Dealing with nerves

Many people get nervous when they have to speak in front of others, even if they have been presenting for years. You may think your lecturers are fine at giving talks, but invariably the first few lectures of a semester cause a few 'butterflies' even to long-standing performers. Having some nerves is good as this gets the adrenaline flowing and keeps you alert and on top of the subject. You may find that you are nervous at the beginning of the talk, until you get into the swing of it, and then you are fine. This is very common. Problems occur only when your performance nerves overtake you.

Some of the things you may be nervous about are:

- an overwhelming feeling of being watched;
- feeling that others will think you're stupid;
- forgetting what you want to say;
- losing your thread and getting muddled.

Some of the signs that tell you that you're nervous are:

- shaking;
- forgetting certain words;
- stuttering;

- sweating;
- your voice becomes higher than normal;
- you speak too quickly;
- being tongue-tied.

You may be able to recognise some of these characteristics when you give a talk, and the effect can be distressing.

Dealing with performance nerves

The first thing you need to do is take back control and you do this by increasing your confidence in your ability by being well prepared and in control of the topic you are presenting. Rehearse your talk so that you practise the words and phrases you are going to use and assess how long your talk will last so that it is within your time limit. Most student project presentations are approximately 15–20 minutes, but if you are presenting as part of a group you may have only five minutes for your part. Never go over your time limit. When you rehearse, you should identify areas that don't flow, where you are unsure of the point, or where you've included something that you are now unhappy with. A rehearsal will also identify the key sentences you need to link between slides.

The next thing you need to do is deal with your emotions. As stated before, some nerves are good, but not too many. Your aim is to calm yourself down so that you can think and speak clearly. Try visualising a speaker you admire. Identify why you admire that speaker and try to visualise yourself presenting like him or her. You need to do this regularly so that it becomes a habit and when you stand up, there you are 'in character'. If that doesn't work for you, deep breathing is often recommended in order to lower your heart rate and reduce your nerves. Finally, reflect honestly with a friend on your performances. You may feel, for example, that you were hesitating a lot, but more than likely the audience didn't notice it. Your perceptions of your performance are therefore often different from the audience's. Essentially, you have to find out what works for you, and it is important to be proactive in achieving that.

Activity 2 helps you to recognise if you have performance nerves.

ACTIVITY 2 Recognising if you have performance nerves

Indicate for yourself: 1 = rarely me, 2 = sometimes me, 3 = always me.

Characteristics of performance nerves	This is me: 1–3	What I plan to do
An overwhelming feeling of being watched		
Feeling that others will think you're stupid		
Fear of forgetting what you want to say		
Fear of losing your thread and getting muddled		

Check the feedback section at the end of the chapter.

Delivering your talk confidently

First, remind yourself that giving a talk is not the same as writing an essay that you then read out. Reading aloud from a script will result in poor marks for the communication skills aspect of your assessment (see feedback for Activity 1). So, writing an essay or long-hand notes and then reading it is not an option. What you will need is some form of notes – perhaps prompt cards, unless you are confident enough to rely on PowerPoint slides or transparencies to act as prompts for you.

When written text is read aloud it always sounds monotonous, and it is easier to read it than to listen to it. Free speech is much more interesting and it does not matter about the odd 'um' or 'er' – that's natural and allows some 'processing time' for your audience.

The key features that you need to consider during the delivery of a talk are your:

- voice and pace – vocal formatting;
- engagement with the audience;
- manner of handling questions.

Voice and pace

In Activity 1 you may have identified some voice characteristics that illustrate a poor talk. Being alert to your voice and pace is a key attribute in public speaking. Check out Figure 6.6 and, when you rehearse your talk, check your voice and pace characteristics.

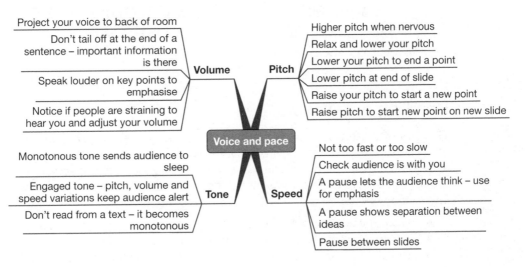

Figure 6.6 Voice and pace summary

NOTE   Use language markers, e.g. and now ... the next point ... in contrast ... in conclusion ... and finally ... plus voice tone to indicate a change or a new point. This can be done by raising your voice, speaking more slowly and pausing slightly before moving on, which helps the audience to follow the flow of your talk. Don't use clichés or empty, worn-out phrases.

Engagement with the audience

For those of you in the process of developing your oral presentation skills, you can tend to focus on yourself as the speaker and forget about the audience. This is a cardinal mistake. Once you accept that the audience is there and you want to engage with them, your talk will become an interactive event and you will enjoy it. To engage your audience therefore you should:

- stand for eight seconds at the beginning of your talk looking at the audience. Just scan across the room and don't look at anyone in particular – this cues the audience that you are ready to speak;
- introduce yourself while scanning the audience;
- start positively and not with an apology because something didn't work – your audience are interested only in what you have to say now;
- look and sound interested in your talk and the audience;
- tell your audience the structure of your talk;
- maintain the right pace and use voice features mentioned above;
- thank the audience for listening and invite questions.

NOTE   If you read from a paper you will not be able to engage with the audience as you will lose eye contact, start to mumble into your paper, be monotonous and read too fast. If you find that slides are not enough and you feel quite nervous, use notes on a card, or a paper with large print – around **verdana point size 16**. Add notes to tell yourself to look at the audience, pause or stress a point.

Handling questions

This is always harder for the individual presenter. However, you need to prepare for questions as well as you can. Make a list of your key messages and look at the questions that could be asked for each. If you are in a group, you should answer questions relating to your contribution to the talk. Question areas to prepare for include the following:

- Why did you choose to research the topic using a particular method?
- Did the work of a key author influence you in any way?
- How did you arrive at your conclusions (possibly the choice of statistics used)?

- What difficulties did you find during your research and how did you overcome them?
- If you did this work again, what changes would you make?

NOTE If you get questions you can't answer, be honest. It is always obvious when a speaker tries to invent an answer. You can always thank the questioner for that question as it will move your thinking on.

Planning a talk

Whether you are planning your talk for yourself or with a group, the key features remain the same. However, group presenters have the added task of deciding how each presenter contributes to a coherent talk (see Chapter 5, 'Working in a real and diverse team').

ACTIVITY 3 Oral presentation: time check

If you are involved in preparing for a presentation use Activity 3 to check your progress.

14 preparation time-check tasks	To do	Doing now	Done
In the weeks or days before the talk			
1 **Understand your research topic** and ensure you know enough background to feel confident with your particular angle on it. This will also give you confidence at question time.			
2 **Structure your talk** by identifying key messages and points for development within those sections. If you are presenting as a group you will divide the sections between you. Make sure you have a beginning (stating what you will do), a middle (develop your arguments) and an end (present a conclusion). Remember, group presentations need to allocate responsibilities.			
3 Decide on the **visual style** you will use and prepare your slides well. Make sure they are uncluttered and easy to read.			
4 **Decide on a title** for your talk. Try to make it short but informative. Use the 'Baked Beans' approach – 'it says what it is' – you can always have a fun strap line (like a sub-heading), but it must be catchy.			

14 preparation time-check tasks	To do	Doing now	Done
5 **Write brief notes** on prompt cards to help make sure that you cover the ground you intend to, and in the right order.			
6 **Practise** giving your talk and timing it – either to friends or between yourselves.			
7 **Check the room layout for the talk** and make sure that you know where you will stand or sit, where your audience will be and the equipment you will use.			
8 Identify your **'take-home message'** and how you are going to deliver it.			
9 **Assessment criteria:** do you think your talk will meet the assessment criteria? If not, what changes do you need to make?			
On the day of the talk			
1 Re-read your prompt notes and any supporting material, such as handouts you may have prepared for the audience, to make sure you 'get on message'.			
2 Get to the venue early and check the equipment, if you can.			
3 Remind yourself of the simple but vital rules for delivering your talk confidently (voice, pace, audience, questions).			
4 Support each other in a group presentation. Identify where you will all stand and how you will link between speakers.			
5 Relax, breathe deeply to keep those nerves in check (see above) and remember that your audience is on your side!			
You're on! Go for it!			

4 On reflection

This chapter has looked at only two aspects of presenting your work: posters and oral presentations. Essays, reports, making and producing things and portfolios are examples of other ways you can present your work. In all of these, be clear what is expected of you, how it should be presented and what your message is. You should also pay attention to the coherence of your message, with regards to the general look and feel of the product. When you present your work you should feel proud of the content and how it looks.

ACTIVITY 4 Update your personal development planner

Having read this chapter, gauge your confidence again – how does this compare with your confidence levels at the start of the chapter? What can you do to improve? You can incorporate this into your personal development planner and of course add anything else you feel appropriate.

Grade your confidence on a scale of 1–5 where 1 = poor and 5 = good.

My presentation skills development plan	Confidence level 1–5	Plans to improve
I can condense information relevant for poster presentation.		
I can design a good poster using the key elements of design.		
I can identify key messages when giving a talk.		
I am gaining confidence in recognising and reflecting on my strengths and weaknesses when giving a talk.		
I understand the principles of slide design.		
I can engage the audience when I give a talk.		
I know how to deal with questions.		

Date:_____

Getting extra help

- Check your institution as most universities have web pages giving you support for a range of study skills. These are usually there to provide brief tips.

- On the *Mind Tools* website you will find a wide range of self-help tips. The material is directed towards business people, but advice is suitable for anyone wishing to develop their skills in these areas. See www.mindtools.com/CommSkll/PresentationPlanningChecklist.htm.

- If you are expected to use ICT and a presentation software you are unsure of, check your institution. Your options should be a paper, virtual or hands-on tutorial.

- Look for books on public speaking.

Feedback on activities

ACTIVITY 1 Good and bad characteristic in oral presentations

Some of the key factors that determine the quality of a presentation are shown in the following table.

Characteristic	Effect on the audience	Solution
Little or no eye contact	'Hello' we are here as well!	Make every effort to look at your audience. Look around and try not to look at just one person. If you look at one person all the time it becomes embarrassing and the new focus of attention for the audience.
Mumbling	What is he/she talking about? After trying to understand for a while, the audience will give up.	Practise your talk beforehand and either record it or get a friend to listen. You need to project your voice. Always talk to the back of the room rather than those at the front.
Monotonous voice	A monotonous voice becomes a drone and the audience can't work out what is important in your talk. If this goes on for too long they start to daydream, go to sleep or just wish they were somewhere else. Avoid the EGO effect (eyes glaze over).	The message in a piece of written text is delivered via headings, sub-headings and paragraphs. Your voice has to format your text for you. You can use **pitch**, **loudness** and **pauses** to create effect. Use these to show movement between ideas and emphasise important points.
Reading from the paper	Your audience feels bored. If you read from the paper, first you tend not to look at the audience very much and second, your reading speed will be faster than free speech.	Read from cards if you feel you have to read something. Make the font large as it is difficult to read large font quickly. Also put notes on your card telling you what to do, e.g. 'look at audience', 'make reference to diagram on visual', etc.
Little or no structure	Your audience feels 'what is this all about?'. Audiences are very forgiving at the beginning of a talk and usually assume it will get better. But if after five minutes it is not clear how you are going to structure your talk, they will get annoyed and only have you to focus on instead of the content.	Remember, if you get lost in a book, you can flick back through the pages. You can't do that when listening to a talk, so you must provide visual and oral help to reinforce the structure. Pause between sections and speak louder at the start of a new section. See these as vocal formatting techniques.
Too much information	Oh no, not another graph I can't read or another slide full of tightly packed bullet points. The audience can take very tightly packed information for only a few minutes, then there is overload and they switch off.	Identify your key messages for your talk and expound them. Better to present too little rather than too much. What is the 'take-home message' from your talk? Make sure they at least remember that.
Bad visuals	Your audience feels annoyed. Poor graphs, small images, tightly packed text all add up to 'noise'. The audience can't read it so why use it?	If you are using graphs, create a visual of the trend for your presentation. If you want them to see detail, give it as a handout and talk around it.

ACTIVITY 2 Recognising if you have performance nerves

Characteristics of performance nerves	What you can do
An overwhelming feeling of being watched	Once you engage with your audience and start looking at them, you should start to reduce this feeling. Try to think how you feel when you are having a conversation. If you don't look at people, this feeling could intensify.
Feeling that others will think you're stupid	This is a confidence issue. Make sure you practise your talk, know how to explain difficult things and be comfortable with the order and content of your slides.
Fear of forgetting what you want say	This is also part of a lack of confidence and something that you fear when you get stressed. If you practise you should have the key phrases and concepts ready for use.
Fear of losing your thread and getting muddled	This happens when you feel stressed. You need to start by feeling positive about your talk. You have practised, you may not say everything in an ideal way, but no one will notice. If your structure is clear, you can't get muddled.

7 Reading critically

Critical reading is an essential aspect of academic study at university. It is more than reading all the entries on your reading list. Developing a critical approach to what you read will not only assist you in getting better grades, it will also be a skill that you will need for your professional career.

Critical reading involves flexibility and interactivity. It also requires you to apply yourself and not expect it to be easy. This chapter will help you take control of your reading in a way that enables you to develop your thinking in your subject.

In this chapter you will:

1. learn the key elements of a text and how to navigate them;
2. discover how to develop strategies to identify and select texts relevant to your study need;
3. find out what skills are involved in critical reading;
4. learn how to develop a strategy to build a critical engagement toolkit for different text types.

USING THIS CHAPTER

Estimate your current levels of confidence. At the end of the chapter you will have the chance to re-assess these levels where you can incorporate this in to your Personal Development Profile (PDP). Mark 1 (poor) and 5 (good) for the following:

I understand how features of a text can help me read more effectively.	I know how to critically select what to read.	I know what skills are involved in critical reading.	I know the best questions to interrogate texts.	I know how to judge information I read on the internet.

Date: _____

1 Finding your way around texts

As a reader you may not have taken note of how texts are constructed before because you were concentrating on the message contained in the text. However, if you are to engage with texts **critically**, you also need to know how they are put together. A critical reader reads for content *and* for form.

Reading for 'form' lets you improve your critical comprehension by becoming familiar with the way text is written for your subject. This is called 'genre' or the style of the text. You might also examine how the text is organised and how the author has analysed (broken down) the material in order to set up an argument. Be aware that different disciplines (e.g. marketing, accounting, management) may have different ways of arguing, so the text may be set out in a different format and adhere to different 'rules'. The two common types of text business and management students will encounter are summarised below:

Type of text	Key purpose	General features
Discursive	To argue or persuade the reader	Thesis or hypothesis Arguments Examples/back-up information Conclusions
Report (operational/ research)	To classify information To present findings To record data and/or procedures To justify and recommend changes	Objective account Review literature Contain data/statistical information Data analysis/interpretation Discuss findings Make recommendation

Be aware that elements of these text types may overlap in some contexts.

Key features of a text

The SMART reader (**S**kill **M**anagement in **A**cademic work through **R**easoning and **T**hinking) is well placed to become a critical reader. Knowing that different types of texts have different features is important. Understanding these features can help you get a quick overview of a text. Most of the features you will know, but do you have a critical approach to using them effectively? Use Activity 1 to explore this.

ACTIVITY 1 How do you use text features?

Text features	What do you do?
1 How do you use headings and sub-headings?	1 I don't really think about it; I just start reading to the end. 2 Skim through text to see what it is about 3 Use them to structure my notes.
2 Do you read the abstract?	1 I don't know what this is. 2 I don't bother with this as it is outside the main text where all the information is anyway 3 I always read it before deciding if I should read any further.
3 How do you use summaries in texts you read?	1 I just read; I don't think about it being a summary or not. 2 I read an abstract or summary first to get an idea. 3 I understand a summary can be at the beginning or the end of a text, so I look for it.
4 Do sub-headings help you understand how the writer thinks	1 I have not really thought about it. 2 I know they are there and take notes under sub-headings. 3 I use sub-headings to get an overview of the text before I start reading properly
5 What's a paragraph for?	1 It breaks up the text on the page so it doesn't look too dense. 2 It is the writer's way of explaining something.
6 Do you use the revision section of a textbook (if it has one)?	1 I don't usually have time for this. 2 I do look at the revision section at the end. 3 I look at the revision section at the beginning and at the end.
7 Do you take any notice of key terms or concepts that are sometimes used in texts?	1 Generally no; I just read and take notes. 2 Yes, I take a look to give me an overview of what will be in the text.
8 What do you do with the references?	1 I've never really thought about looking at them 2 I use the references to see who the key researchers are in this area and how I can extend my reading.

See the feedback section at the end of the chapter for further explanation.

Thinking about the answers to the above points will mean that you have to examine the way text is put together for your subject. Not only will this help with comprehension and speed of access to the information the text contains, it will also encourage you to take it apart or deconstruct it. This is essential to developing critical reading skills, as we will now see.

Critical analysis of paragraph structure

All writers use the paragraph to build up their argument. How they do this depends on what they are talking about, for example: a process, a definition, a description. Analysing how the author is building up the argument, chunk by chunk, will help you to deconstruct what might otherwise be an impenetrable text.

Some simple ways that ideas are developed by authors are through the following:

- **Definitions** and/or **descriptions** using link words such as: *is defined as*, *comprises*, *refers to,* etc. The author may be looking at descriptions or definitions that are under dispute, adding his or her own definition, or referring to some standard definition.
- **Comparing and contrasting** using link words such as: *similarly*, *on the other hand*, *is different from*, *compared with*, *however,* etc. The author will be, for example, comparing results from various experiments or contrasting different views.
- **Cause and effect** typically use link words such as: *as a result, therefore, if ..., then ..., because*, etc. This is usually found when an author is discussing how things work.
- **Processes** or **sequences** typically use words that indicate a sequence of events such as: *first, second, then, next, finally,* etc. Processes can refer to the flow of an event and/or the time sequence.

It is important to look out for these link words and underline some of them as you skim through the text. You should prime yourself if the writer says: 'There will be four key changes to ...' Skim the text and underline the key link words that introduce these four changes. Understanding link words tells you how the text is organised.

In addition, a good writer will use the first or second sentence in a paragraph to indicate what that paragraph is about. This is called the topic sentence. Once you know this, you can use it to identify the key steps the author takes to map out the argument being made. Similarly, a good writer will use the last sentence in a paragraph to either conclude the point they have sought to make and/or set up the link to a more detailed development of that point or the next point they will set out to make, i.e. the topic sentence for the next paragraph.

Text ingredients

Look at Figure 7.1 to see how paragraph development operates.

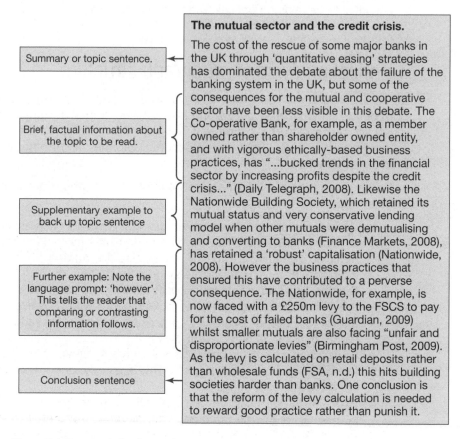

Figure 7.1 Paragraph development

As you can see, sentences have a function in the text and this is the way the author can guarantee that the text fits together or has coherence. We look at how *you* can develop these academic writing practices in Chapter 14, 'Improving your business and management studies writing'). Activity 2 asks you to analyse one of your unit/course texts.

ACTIVITY 2 Analyse one of your texts

Choose a paragraph from a chapter in one of the books on your reading list and fill in the table opposite.

Text ingredient	Write example from text
Topic sentence	
Introductory information	
Supplementary example information	
Further example/opposing view	
Conclusion sentence	

Hot Tip

Not all texts are perfectly written. Some writers do not always think of their readers so you might find a text does not follow these 'good practice' guidelines. Therefore, if you can't find your way around sections of text it might not be your fault at all. Of course, in the main your tutors will try to guide you to texts that are well written, but there may be an occasion when the only text available is not well written.

Reading journal articles

Many students find journal articles more difficult to read than textbooks and are daunted by the fact that journal articles are written by current experts in their field of study and sometimes their own lecturers. However, this source of information can be worth considering because many universities provide students with electronic access to journal articles. This can be useful when making notes about what you have read. (For guidance on note making see, for example, Price and Maier, 2007, Chapter 2.1, pp. 79–100.)

It is useful to adopt a twofold approach to reading an article.

1. Read quickly to find out the main ideas and findings of the article.

   – Read the **abstract**, which contains an overview of the article.

   – Read the **summary and conclusions**. If the article does not have a summary, look at the titles, sub-headings and the **discussion section** of the article. As you read ask yourself whether the information is relevant to your reading purpose or research. Will it be useful for your assignment?

2. Read more thoroughly to familiarise yourself with the details.

- Ask yourself questions and search for the answers in order to focus your reading.

- Read the article critically and analyse and evaluate the findings.

The abstract can be used not only to give you a snapshot of the article but also to guide you to the intended order or sequence of the article.

As soon as you told me that the abstract was a mini framework of the article, I was more prepared for what to expect and also for the order in which it would be presented. This made a big difference to the amount of time I spent reading the article.

Andy, second-year Psychology student

Locating the information you need quickly is part of your management technique as a SMART reader. For example, if you want to find out about the implications of the research, you would home in on the 'Discussion' section. Therefore, realising the hidden function of the different sections could save you valuable time and enable you to buy yourself some thinking time for critical reading. Look at the table below, then tackle Activity 3.

Article sections	Author's purpose
Abstract	A summary of the article. It should contain the rationale for the study as well as the main results and a statement about interpretation of the results.
Introduction/background	This section will put the context of the article. It will often contain the researcher's position or the premise of the article. If the article is exploring a new or specific point of view, the theoretical context will be introduced so that the reader can relate the author's findings/ideas to earlier research. The hypothesis or the main argument is usually set out in this section so that the reader has some sort of anchor for the subsequent sections.
Methods	Much will depend upon the type of article you are reading as to the presentation of information in this section. If the research describes and explains clinical experiments, then the design of the experiments will be detailed. For example, the number and type of participants will be described. This section should also indicate the different methods used, for example case studies, participant observation, etc. This is useful information when comparing two articles to interpret the reliability (or otherwise) of the research This section may be omitted if the article is not an experiment type of research. For example, the article may be a philosophical discussion of a theory or premise.

Article sections	Author's purpose
Results/findings	This section presents data (often in statistical format). However, social sciences research may present qualitative findings, for example pupils' perceptions of discipline in the classroom. This type of data may not be suitable for statistical analysis. This section is often descriptive.
Discussion	This section provides the reader with the researcher's interpretation of the results. In this section, the author may try to persuade the reader to a way of thinking. Sometimes, this section will be critical of the way in which the research was conducted so that the reader is aware of any flaws.
Conclusions/summary	This section will provide the reader with a snapshot of the research but also will give the implications of the research.

ACTIVITY 3 Navigating my way around a journal article

Armed with the information from the table above, now see how you can extract information efficiently from a journal article.

Name of article/article sections	Note down information
Abstract	
Introduction/background	
Methods	
Results/findings	
Discussion	
Conclusions/summary	

Hot Tip

You can enhance your reading speed and understanding by getting to grips with the technical terminology. The sooner you start to tackle this, the better. Key words are used as a sort of shorthand in communicating with others in the field. It is vital that you learn how they are specifically defined in your subject. Look out for glossaries of technical words and have these by your side when tackling new and difficult texts. You will be surprised how quickly you can get on top of this by frequent use and constant reminders of the meanings.

2 Critically judging what to read

What you read will depend on the purpose of your reading. When you look for a text, you need to be clear why you are reading. It can be quite general if you are just wanting to get an overview of an area, or it can be quite specific if it relates to a piece of coursework. Knowing what to read involves your critical judgement, and this can be enhanced with a question-based approach.

Identify suitable texts

Suitability of text is not just about choosing the right book for the assignment, it is also about choosing the right book *for you* at your stage in the learning process or your level of understanding. It is important for you to manage this (see also Chapter 10, 'Understanding the value of reflection').

Some books are too hard

Whilst choosing books to suit your needs depends upon what you already know and bring to the task, you must remember that sometimes your tutors put books on the lists which are too difficult for many students. They have introduced these books to stretch and challenge you. Their expectations are high!

If some of the books are too hard for you, you must draw upon strategies to cope with this. You need to start examining the suitability of the text for your purpose.

Is this text suitable for you?

Just because a tutor has placed a book in the Reserve Collection or on Short Term Loan does not always mean that you are ready to access that particular book. Some students forget that one of the elements of successful reading is the knack of matching your level of understanding with the relevant reading for your coursework.

You may become disheartened when you can't understand a text on the book list. This may be because you are still grappling at an early stage of understanding, of both the new concepts and the new terminology. Some books may be just too complex for you at this stage. If this applies to you, you should choose a text that gives you more of an overview. If the subject is new to you, the Idiot's Guides on the market are a must! However, there may be some excellent A-level textbooks which serve this purpose before you start reading more complex journal articles. It is important that you seek advice from your department, tutors and post-graduate students about what is available. You can of course always try your institution's second-hand bookshop and see what other students bought.

NOTE This advice may seem to contradict what your academic tutors tell you. There are few who would recommend 'The Idiot's Guide to …' or Wikipedia. This is because tutors expect their students to have a higher starting point. You need to assess the knowledge you bring to this activity and choose accordingly. However, use these resources **only** to get you started.

Is this text suitable for my studies?

The question you need to ask yourself is: 'Does this book or chapter or article contain the information or evidence I need for my assignment or task?' If it does then it is worth using. However, you will probably find there is no one book which conveniently and neatly contains all the information you need for your specific assignment. So you are expected to dip in and out of books, chapters and journal articles. Remember, the books or chapters or articles have not been written especially so that you can answer the question posed by your tutor! They may go into a lot of complicated depth, which is not relevant to your current needs, so read only what you need to read to gain an understanding and the information you want.

ACTIVITY 4 Selecting appropriate books

Try this out with a selection of **books** for one of your assignments. You will need to have a list of key words available. Mark it as 'a possible read' or 'discard it'.

Write book title:
Has this book been mentioned/recommended by my tutors?
Is it on the reading list?
Are there some of my key words (or equivalent) in the title?
Is the book fairly recent? Remember, if the publication date is too old, the information may be out of date.
Look at the back cover of a book. Do the summaries indicate that there may be some useful sections?
Look at the List of Contents at the beginning. Are there any of my key words in the titles?
If so, note the specific chapters in the 'Possible' column.
Look at the Index at the back of the book. Search for specific key words (or equivalent). Note the page numbers in your 'Possible' column.
Sample some of the chapter sub-headings. Do you think some sections may be of use? Make a note of page numbers in the 'Possible' column.
Sample a small section of a chapter. Is the information accessible to me? Remember, if the style of writing is too academic or filled with many technical words which you don't know, you may not be ready for it yet.

ACTIVITY 5 Is this the right journal article?

Try this out with a journal article you have come across, mark it as 'a possible read' or 'discard it'.

Write article name:
Has the article been mentioned/recommended by my tutors?
Is it on the reading list?
Are there some of my key words (or equivalent) in the title?
Read the Abstract. This gives an overview of the article. Does it contain any useful information for my assignment?
Examine the key words (usually located after the Abstract). Is there a high match factor?
Is the article fairly recent? Remember, if the publication date is too old, the information may be out of date.
Sample some of the sub-headings. Do you think some sections may be of use?
Sample a small section of the article. Is the information accessible to me? Remember, if the style of writing is too academic or filled with many technical words which you don't know, you may not be ready for it yet.

3 What is critical reading?

Selecting the right texts to read is a good start to reading critically, but for many students the next step, of critically *reading* and critically engaging with the texts, is troublesome. Consider this student's comment:

> *My tutor said I must read critically. Surely if a book or journal article is published it must be good?*
>
> Simon, first-year Business Administration student

In a survey of academic skills at Southampton University (Price, 2001), the gulf between what the academic tutors expected of their students and the skills the students thought were needed for study was great. Academic tutors expect their students to be able to interact with the texts. When your tutors talk about interacting with the texts, they are referring to readers who can question, reflect upon and evaluate what they are reading. You may even hear them talking about 'metacognition', which is simply a way of saying that you are in control of your learning and that you are making positive, reflective decisions at all times. A high level of reading autonomy is assumed (Barnett, 1997; Peverly *et al.*, 2002).

Gaining high grades for your assignments involves your ability to engage with text in **a critical manner**. Most tutors will tell you that you will be expected to:

- understand the content of a variety of texts;
- reflect upon what writers have said;
- evaluate what you have read from different sources;
- develop your own ideas;
- use reading to develop your thinking.

Quite a tall order when you are bombarded by information, recommended reading and electronic resources. Critical approaches to study are, therefore, vital. Much of this is to do with the way you interact with text, whether it is text which you have generated or text in books, journals, etc. Critical reading usually occurs when students have a working knowledge and understanding of the issues, theories or topics they are studying.

To read critically is to make judgements about *how* a text is argued. This is a highly reflective skill requiring you to stand back and gain some distance from the text you are reading. You might have to read a text through once to get a basic grasp of content before you launch into intensive critical reading.

These are the keys:

- Don't read looking only or primarily for **information** (surface approach).
- Do read looking for **ways of thinking** about subject matter (deep approach).

You might like to refresh your memory about the eight stages of reading development which will support critical reading. If you intend to change your reading habits and wish to become a critical reader then you must consider how you can engage more with your texts.

Hot Tip

You can find further helpful guidance in Price and Maier (2007) about using active reading approaches to engage with your texts. Alternatively, try the search string 'SQ3R Active+Reading' to find internet sources that may be helpful to you.

4 Getting started: becoming a critical reader

Now use Activity 6 to think about how you go about your interactive reading.

ACTIVITY 6 Are you using your critical skills?

Are you using critical reading skills?	Yes	No
1 Do you think about what you are reading and question what the author has written?		
2 Do you take what the author has said as gospel truth?		
3 What credibility does the writer have in the subject area?		
4 Do you challenge the ideas as you are reading?		
5 Are you able to distinguish different kinds of reasoning used?		
6 Are you able to synthesise the key information and make connections between what different authors are saying?		
7 Can you make judgements about how the text is argued?		
8 Can you evaluate how the information could be better or differently supported?		
9 Can you spot assumptions that have not been well argued?		

The above nine questions demonstrate what you are aiming for to become a critical reader. You should use these as keys to help you increase your criticality. Now you are in the right mind frame for approaching your reading in a critical manner, you need to practise and generalise your skills. Activity 7 presents some questions to get you to interact and think about your texts. Gathering the evidence is the first stage; weighing up what you have found is the critical thinking you will have to apply.

You need to consider whether the evidence or the way the author tries to persuade you is strong or weak. Ask yourself if it is substantiated (a) by the author's admission and (b) by other authors. This will give you a strength gauge. You will also have to consider whether the evidence you have looked at is flawed.

ACTIVITY 7 Weighing up the evidence

Choose a chapter or an article and find out answers to the following questions.

Your questions	Evidence from the text
Who is the author's audience?	
What are the central claims/arguments of the text?	

Your questions	Evidence from the text
What is the main evidence?	
Give examples of how this is substantiated.	
What assumptions lie behind the evidence or arguments?	
Is adequate proof provided and backed up with examples of evidence?	
What are the general weaknesses of the threads of the argument/evidence?	
What are the general strengths of the threads of the argument/evidence?	
Give examples of what other leading authors have to say on the same subject.	

5 Taking a critical look at a text

I find it difficult to do the critical thing. After all, who am I, a lowly undergraduate, to make judgements about the ideas of someone who is the leading researcher in cognitive psychology? Yet my tutors are always going on about 'you must be critical and analytical of the information'. How do I decide?

Susan, second-year Psychology student

Many students want to be critical in their reading but are faced with the same dilemma as this Psychology student. Your tutors want to see evidence of your ability to weigh up ideas and information. To do this effectively, you will need to interact with your text so that you get into the habit of questioning information and seeing links between what one author has written and what you find in another text. Do they corroborate each other or do the authors take a different stance?

Reading between the lines

All that glisters is not gold.
Often have you heard that told.

Shakespeare: *Merchant of Venice*, 11:vii

This quotation can be applied to texts you will come across. Texts may not be what they literally appear to be. Some authors hide their true meaning. Books cannot always be taken literally, i.e. word for word as a factual account. Being able to read between the lines is an important reading quality which you need to finely tune if you are to increase your critical approach to reading. Your tutors will mention **inference** skills which relate to reading between the lines. For example, an author, writing about the war in Vietnam, might state: 'The landscape was washed with blood.' This can be taken literally to mean that the fields had blood running in streams but it may be the author's way of depicting the horror of the situation.

Reading between the lines requires you to take an interactive approach to text. You are expected to put two and two together and come up with answers. However, you must take care not to come up with the wrong answers! At times, authors make assumptions about their audience and expect the reader to take for granted some information which is not explicitly stated. In these cases you will have to read between the lines to extract the full, intended meaning. For example: 'In Paris in the 1970s, the university students were revolting.' Here the author could be expressing a personal comment about what he thinks about students or he could assume that the reader knows about the tumultuous, political upheavals of the day when university students were actively involved in political change.

It is important to ask yourself questions about the information you are reading. It is also vital that you are aware of how the writer's use of language can give clues that help the reader to examine text critically.

Hot Tip

Remember that part of weighing up information, being critical, is your questioning ability. Can you ask yourself the right questions to ensure that you evaluate and analyse a text? Try Activity 8.

ACTIVITY 8 What to look for in a text

In the table below you will find some generic questions which you can apply to most texts you are studying at university. The table also provides you with ways of finding the answers to your questions and what to look out for in a text.

Question	Solution
Are these ideas the author's potted summary of someone else's research?	Look for words like: ■ according to ... ■ a research study by ... ■ evidence supplied by ... ■ (cited in Smith and Bloggs, 2007)

Question	Solution
Is the argument sound/strong?	■ Look for examples of other research/information which backs up the line of argument. You might have to dip into other sources to check this. ■ Look at other sources for disagreement. This will help you to decide which has the most convincing argument which is backed up by evidence.
Is the evidence reputable? Remember that evidence comes in many shapes: statistical/graphical/anecdotal/reports	■ What is the author's track record? ■ Be guided by what is said in lectures, course handbooks, etc. ■ Do a quick survey on the internet to find out about the author. Has she or he been involved in research? What sort of publications are there? Always question the type of publication. Remember that some have greater credibility than others.
Is the evidence refutable?	■ Do a quick survey on the internet to find out other people's views. ■ What methods were used to gather the evidence? If, for example, it was gathered from asking friends about the subject, you must question this.
Are there any threads in the text which have not been dealt with or any inconsistent statements?	■ Take each idea and check what the author has said. This is where colour-coding information is useful. ■ Use the 'find' facility to survey an electronic text.
Does the conclusion reflect the evidence/information in the text?	■ Take each conclusion statement and quickly scan the text to find out where this has been dealt with.

Hot Tip

The old saying 'practice makes perfect' applies to the way you can develop your critical reading skills. Some students have never been introduced to this way of handling the texts they read. It is worthwhile exploring one of your course texts and using the above questions to guide your critical reading skills. Try Activity 9.

ACTIVITY 9 Interrogating a text

Choose a chapter or section from one of the texts on your reading list.

Question	Your findings
Are these ideas the author's potted summary of someone else's research?	
Is the argument sound/strong?	
Is the evidence reputable? Remember that evidence comes in many shapes: statistical/graphical/anecdotal/reports	
Is the evidence refutable?	
Are there any threads in the text which have not been dealt with or any inconsistent statements?	
Does the conclusion reflect the evidence/information in the text?	

6 Critical evaluation of internet information

One of the advantages of the internet is that it is so accessible and a wealth of information is available. For academic purposes, however, not everything on the internet is considered valuable, and some students find that quotations they have found on an internet search are scorned by their tutors. The reason for this is that the information may have little credibility or the author is an inappropriate source. It is, therefore, important to apply your critical reading skills to this type of information.

For example, a search about perceptions of dyslexia yielded this information:

> *Dyslexia is often not identified at school. I had left high school before someone said that I might be dyslexic.*
>
> Barbara from Wisconsin, USA

If we unravel these statements, we can understand why using this as evidence in an essay would be thought inappropriate by your tutors. How much credibility would you set by it?

- Who is Barbara from Wisconsin?
- Has she conducted well-designed research into this subject to enable her to make the first statement that 'dyslexia is often not identified at school'?
- What evidence is there that dyslexia is often not identified at school?
- What is the frequency of identification? For example, how often is 'often' in this information? It is too vague.

- What was the status of the person who suggested assessment for dys-lexia? Was it a friend? Another dyslexic person? A trained assessor?
- You need to be alert to the fact that later in this information you find that Barbara is trying to sell you a product. Obviously, she will speak about it in glowing terms. You need to consider its worth and credibility.

Question credentials

The example in the previous section demonstrates that you must question the credentials of the person who has written the information, what evidence there is for the claims and what the ulterior motive is for making this information available free to the whole world.

I only search for articles or e-journals on www.scholargoogle.com.

Christiana, MSc student

Searching reputable sites is vital, so you may need to ask your tutors for guidance. Of course, you may need to analyse the information to see whether it gives you information you can understand. If it is too technical, you may need to find out some basic information first before going to more technical and subject-specific sites, for example www.ask.com. There are also online dictionaries and thesauruses to help you with getting to grips with technical terminology, for example www.askoxford.com.

Types of information on the internet

The array of sources can be baffling. Apart from the obvious e-journals which are available on your university site and in library databases (which are often divided into subjects by your librarians), there are many other sources. However, some types of information are more useful to certain subjects. For example, newspapers will give up-to-date editorial information for Politics students, while Social Studies, Education, History and Environmental Studies students can benefit from government statistical data. There are downloadable, video-streamed interviews of professionals' case study findings for Education students on www.teachers.tv/home.do.

7 On reflection

If you want to obtain a good degree, then this chapter is vital reading. You must develop and increase your critical reading skills. This section has explored ways in which you can interact more effectively with texts. Reading at university is stimulating. However, it requires more effort and energy on your part. You need to use your interrogation skills and adopt an enquiring approach to reading. As a SMART reader, you will be utilising the 'R' and 'T' – the reasoning and thinking – aspects.

Summary of this chapter

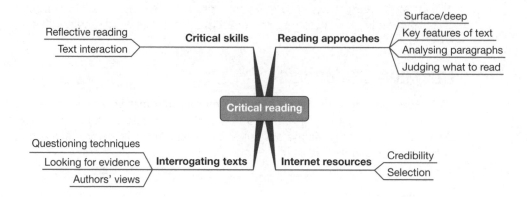

ACTIVITY 10 Update your personal development planner

Questioning what authors say and weighing up the information will ensure that you do not take what you read for granted and that you are more alert to reading between the lines. However, at the heart of critical reading is your ability to know what questions to ask and how you can find the answers to your questions.

Now reflect upon how critical a reader you are and how you intend to change and adapt your current approach to reading texts.

Grade your confidence on a scale of 1–5 where 1 = poor and 5 = good.

My developing skills	Confidence level 1–5	Plans to improve
I know what skills are involved in critical reading.		
I know how to interact with texts.		
I know how to read between the lines when reading.		
I know the best questions to interrogate texts.		
I know how to judge information I read on the internet.		

Getting extra help

- This web page will help you to evaluate and critically read qualitative research articles: www.bmj.com/cgi/content/full/315/7110/740.
- This web page will help you to understand in more detail how to critically read a journal article: www.oandp.org/jpo/library/1996_01_024.asp. It takes you through the elements of an article and gets you to think about questions to ask as you read.

Feedback on activities

ACTIVITY 1 How do you use text features

Text features	What do you do?
1 How do you use headings and subheadings?	a. I don't really think about it; I just start reading to the end. b. Skim through the text to see what it is about. c. Use them to structure my notes.
You should actively use the headings and sub-headings to skim a text and see what it is about. If you only use it to structure your notes then you will just get a summary of that text. Make sure this is what you want. If not, think how else you can take notes. A smart reader shouldn't being doing 'a'.	
2 Do you read the abstract?	a. I don't know what this is. b. I don't bother with this as it is outside the main text where all the information is anyway. c. I always read it before deciding if I should read any further.
You should always read the abstract if there is one. This gives you a quick overview and can prevent you reading something that is not appropriate.	
3 How do you use summaries in texts you read?	a. I just read; I don't think about it being a summary or not. b. I read an abstract or summary first to get an idea. c. I understand a summary can be at the beginning or the end of text, so I look for it.
Always look at the summary or abstract first to get a feel for what it is about. You should be doing 'b' and 'c'	
4 Do sub-headings help you understand how the writer thinks?	a. I don't really think about it. b. I know they are there and take notes under sub-headings. c. I use sub-headings to get an overview of the text before I start reading properly.
You should answer 'c'. Only take notes under sub-headings if you want a summary of the text to work from.	

Text features	What do you do?
5 What's a paragraph for?	a. It breaks the text up on the page so it doesn't look too dense. b. It is the writer's way of explaining something.
The answer is 'b'. Since each paragraph is an idea, you can see how the writer builds up his or her ideas/concepts/arguments.	
6 Do you use the revision section of a textbook (if it has one)?	a. I don't usually have time for this. b. I do look at the revision section at the end. c. I look at the revision section at the beginning and at the end.
You should really be doing 'c' if you want to understand fully what this text is about. Reading the revision section at the beginning can prime your reading.	
7 Do you take any notice of key terms or concepts that are sometimes used in texts?	a. Generally no; I just read and take notes. b. Yes, I take a look to give me an overview of what will be in the text.
The key terms are important as they give you the scope of the text and you see which terms are familiar and unknown to you in advance.	
8 What do you do with the references?	a. I've never really thought about looking at them. b. I use the references to see who the key researchers are in this area, and how I can extend my reading.
If you are carrying out a larger piece of work, like an extended essay, a large project or a dissertation, it is important you use the references to piece together who is doing research in this area. For smaller pieces of work, you probably won't need it.	

References

- Barnett, R. (1997) *Higher Education: A Critical Business*. Buckinghamshire, Open University Press.
- Peverly, S. T., Brobst, K. E. and Morris, K. S. (2002) 'The contribution of reading comprehension ability and meta-cognitive control to the development of studying in adolescence', *Journal of Research in Reading*, 25(2), 203–16.
- Price, G. A. (2001) Report on the Survey of Academic Skills at Southampton University. Southampton, University of Southampton.
- Price, G. and Maier, P. (2007) *Effective Study Skills*. Harlow, Pearson.

8 Excelling in exams

Examination success is the final hurdle. Examination marks often form part of your overall mark and thus count towards your final degree. Success depends upon knowing what is expected, good organisation, appropriate notes and effective memory techniques. This chapter will help you to explore what works and why. It will increase your skills and productiveness.

In this chapter you will:

1. examine the purpose of revision;
2. explore new and effective techniques for efficient revision;
3. learn about memory strategies;
4. learn how to organise yourself during the examination.

USING THIS CHAPTER

Estimate your current levels of confidence. At the end of the chapter you will have the chance to re-assess these levels where you can incorporate this into your personal development planner (PDP). Mark between 1 (poor) and 5 (good) for the following:

I can manage and organise the whole revision process effectively.	I can recognise which revision notes system to use for different purposes.	I understand how to control pressure and stress.	I understand the characteristics of productive memory strategies.	I can use effective strategies during the examination.

Date: _____

1 Introduction

What are the most common reasons why students do not get the marks they anticipate?

Some students dread examinations while others will admit that they enjoy the adrenaline rush. However, many students are at some time disappointed with their grades. Unexpected failure or low marks do not always mean that the student has not revised or that they do not understand the subject. A survey of tutors and examiners highlighted a number of common problems (see Activity 1).

ACTIVITY 1 Where do I stand?

Reflect upon your previous examination performance. What do you think could be improved? Look at the table below and be honest with yourself. In the right-hand column there are suggestions for methods to improve your performance and cross-references to some relevant sections in the book.

This chapter will take you through the solutions so that you can increase your performance and get better grades.

Problem	Has this happened to you? Answer yes or no	Solution
Failure to answer the question set.		BUG technique (see Chapter 13)
Misinterpreted the question.		BUG technique (see Chapter 13)
Answered the wrong number of questions.		Get to know what is expected of you (see Sections 3 and 4).
Insufficient examples to support ideas/ arguments.		Get to know what is expected of you. Improve your revision mapping techniques.
Insufficient knowledge.		Get to know what is expected of you. Distil information into manageable revision notes.
Illegible handwriting.		Practise writing at speed to maintain legibility.
Incoherent writing – long, rambling sentences which do not make sense to the reader.		Concept maps to connect information more effectively will have an impact upon your written communication and organisation.
Not all the questions answered. This may have occurred because you have run out of time or spent too long on the early questions.		Be strict and stick to time allocations worked out prior to the examination during revision. Memory-recall strategies and techniques need to be strengthened. Practise recalling information under timed conditions.
Forgot the information on the day.		Relaxation techniques. Have a good night's sleep. Do not drink large amounts of alcohol and caffeine before the examination.
Course materials not referred to sufficiently.		Get to know what is expected of you. Listen out for tips and guidance during lectures. More effective revision notes. Increase your memory techniques.
Irritating errors – spelling mistakes, weak and incomplete sentences, silly errors in calculations, etc.		Leave some time at the end of the examination to check through your work for irritating errors.

2 What is revision?

Perhaps this question is jumping the gun and the first question should really be: 'Why have examinations?' Examinations and revision are closely inter-linked. Examinations are a way of finding out what you have understood from your course. Many lecturers refer to 'learning outcomes' and exam-inations are a method of testing your grasp of those outcomes. Contrary to popular belief, examinations are not a fiendish method, devised by your tutors, to trick you!

The answer to the question 'What is revision?' may seem obvious, but it is important to make sure that you understand the purpose of revision so that you optimise your efforts. In its literal sense revision means 'seeing again', and this is what you will be doing when you go over your notes and look back on the information you have gathered over your units and mod-ules. However, if you want to be an effective reviser, revision is much more than reading your notes. You need to develop an active approach. This will ensure that you get better grades. So what makes a successful reviser?

- Preparation
- Organisation
- Memory and recall.

Activity 2 asks you to identify your problems with revision.

ACTIVITY 2 Common difficulties with revision

Which of these apply to you?	Tick ✓
1 I am often frustrated at examination times.	
2 I am often very nervous at examination times.	
3 I often find that I can't sleep properly at examination times.	
4 I seem to spend a lot of time revising and not getting good results.	
5 I am not sure if my techniques are the most efficient.	
6 I mainly leave revision until it is almost too late.	
7 I put off my revision and find myself looking for other things to keep myself occupied.	
8 I have vast amounts of notes to help me revise.	

Check the feedback section at the end of the chapter to find out how to start changing your working patterns.

3 Productive revision

Be prepared

Most students come to university with some ideas about how to go about revising for examinations. However, the strategies you have used in the past may have been effective for the type of examinations you did then, but are not necessarily the most efficient now. Preparation is not only about drawing up a timetable and arranging your files and books on your work space! Activity 3 asks you to reflect upon how you have tackled revision in the past; you should analyse what worked well (you got good results) and what didn't work well (you got poor results).

ACTIVITY 3 Productive working habits

Which of these revision techniques worked well for you and which didn't?

		Yes/No
1	Writing out my notes again and again helped me to remember facts and information.	
2	Reducing information into shorter notes helped me to remember facts and information.	
3	Memorising essay answers.	
4	Writing out sample essay answers under timed conditions.	
5	Using concept maps, mind mapping or diagrams helped me to remember facts and information.	
6	Putting important information on to audio tapes and playing this over and over again.	
7	Revising with friends.	
8	Using colour (coloured highlighters, for example) to help me to summarise and understand key points and to remember facts and information.	
9	Reading my lecture notes (without any other activity).	
10	Writing out essay plans from past questions.	
11	Spending long periods revising a week before.	
12	Using memory triggers to help me remember.	
13	Using key words as the basis for understanding.	
14	Any other method you have used.	

In certain circumstances, these are all useful techniques either on their own or, more appropriately, in combination. However, you now need to consider their role and value in the context of study at university level. Think about why and when certain techniques worked well for you and why others did not, and develop your own approach.

4 Countdown not meltdown

Be organised

Preparation, organisation and memory recall are the essential elements of good revision. It is important that you have a clear revision strategy leading up to examinations so that you do not experience 'meltdown' or excessive anxiety during your examinations. This section explores:

- how to develop the right mindset;
- the tricks of the trade, i.e. the best strategies for maximising time and results;
- dealing with examination nerves;
- last-minute countdown.

The right mindset

Preparing for examinations is not just about learning and memorising facts and information so that you can regurgitate them in a timed examination. It is also about:

- knowledge of what is expected of you by your tutors;
- consideration of the assessment criteria;
- selection of important theories, ideas and evidence;
- realistic self-expectations;
- development of efficient note-making systems;
- development of organisational strategies;
- increasing your memory capacity;
- ability to 'crack the code' of the examination questions;
- getting a buzz from understanding your subject.

Knowing what to expect and, equally importantly, what is expected of you are vital parts of the revision process. These two factors should drive your preparations and inform your strategies. See Activity 4.

ACTIVITY 4 Knowing what to expect

This table will get you actively involved with your revision right from the start of your unit/module. Use it as a memory aid and keep it prominently displayed at your workstation (wherever you do most of your studying) as a constant reminder. If you are studying for Joint Honours or have examinations set by more than one department, it is vital that you check each department's rules and regulations. Do not assume that they are the same.

What to expect	Source of information	Fill in your answers in this column
List the number and title of papers/examinations I have to take this semester.	Course handbooks. Departmental online information. Examination office – some of the larger institutions have a central office to deal with the organisation of examinations and have a section on the college/university website.	
What am I allowed to take into the examination room (e.g. calculators, statutes for law tests, course notes)?	Course handbooks. Departmental online information. Check with the unit tutor.	
What will be provided for me in the examination room (e.g. periodic tables, molecular models, scientific calculators, law statutes)?	Course handbooks. Departmental online information.	
What do I need to take into the examination room (e.g. pens, pencils, coloured highlighter pens, etc.)?	Examination officers (either departmental or institutional) will let you know the regulations.	
What type of questions can I expect in the various papers?	Past papers: take care that there are no changes for your year. Course handbooks. Departmental online information.	
How many sections are there in each paper?	Past papers: take care that there are no changes for your year. Course handbooks. Departmental online information.	
How many questions do I have to answer?	Past papers: take care that there are no changes for your year. Course handbooks. Departmental online information.	
Where are the instructions on each paper?	Past papers. Course handbooks. Departmental online information.	

What to expect	Source of information	Fill in your answers in this column
What is the length of the examination paper?	Past papers: take care that there are no changes for your year. Course handbooks. Departmental online information.	
What is the marking allocation for the questions in the paper?	Course handbooks. Departmental online information. Check with the unit tutor.	
What are the assessment criteria for the unit/module?	Course handbooks. Departmental online information. Cross-check with learning outcomes.	
What are the expected 'learning outcomes' for this unit/module?	Course handbooks. Departmental online information. Lecture notes from your tutor – some tutors display these at the beginning of units or lectures.	

As you can see, a lot of information can be gathered from your course handbooks. The library is another source of information. Many departments deposit past papers in the library (often in a reference section) and more and more are available electronically. Collecting photocopies of past papers of the relevant examinations that you will be taking is essential.

Hot Tip

Much of this information can be gathered before you start your new academic year because you will have discussed with your tutor which units/modules you will be taking. So before you dash off on holiday, why not get this information and store it in a safe place, clearly marked. October is always a hectic time and you will be bombarded with a lot of information at the start of your courses. Consequently, many students do not feel they have time to collect information for events that will not take place for months. This is short-sighted. The other advantage of getting the information before you are plunged into a new academic year is that libraries, in particular, are less busy at the end of June and early July and you will be able to gather your information more quickly.

What type of examinations will I have to take?

Your tutors use many different ways to test your knowledge and under-standing. Some subjects traditionally use essay questions, while others have always used multiple-choice questions. You may find that for some units paper 1 might utilise multiple-choice-type questions and paper 2 relies upon essay responses. Knowing a little about the different types of questions can inform your revision strategies because the different test types tap into different skills and memory techniques. These are summarised in the table below.

Type of examination question	Definition	Skills needed
Multiple choice	A statement followed by a choice of answers which are often short and succinct. They test your knowledge of facts.	Good memory for facts. Quick memory recall. Reading accuracy and fluency.
Short answers	These questions require you to write brief paragraph answers and test your knowledge of facts.	Good sentence writing. Succinctness and summary skills. Selection of information.
Essays	These are the same as your course assignments and require you to write coherently and convincingly. They test not only facts but your interpretation of them.	Cracking the code (question analysis). Summary skills. Selection of information. Paragraph/sentence writing. Good grammar and punctuation.
Open book	This type of examination allows you to take in course texts and notes. Some students are duped into thinking they do not test memory.	Selection of information. Location of information. Linking and mapping information.
Take-home tests	Students are given three or four essay titles and have to prepare for these in advance. They do not know which question they will have allocated to them until they enter the examination.	Good memory. Selection of information. Summary skills. Organising thoughts in coherent written format.
Problem solving/case studies	Some departments prefer to set these types of examination questions. Students are expected to marshal facts and put them into real-life, imaginary settings.	Cracking the code (question analysis). Selection skills. Linking and mapping information.
Practice tests	Medical and Health Professional students, for example, are often tested on their practical ability to apply knowledge.	Application of knowledge and understanding. Good memory. Speed of recall and assembly of information.

Some people have the knack of remembering vast amounts of facts and being able to regurgitate them quickly. These people can score highly on multiple-choice questions. There are others who need time to mull over information and gather their thoughts together. Without lots of timed practice, they will not score well on multiple-choice questions. In an ideal world it would be good if you could choose the type of examination format which suits you best. The reality is that the type of assessment and the ways in which examinations are traditionally set, as yet, do not reflect different learning styles. Besides, the variety of methods for assessing students test different skills, as you can see from the table on page 227. Sometimes your tutors want to find out if you have remembered important facts. This could be the case with the viva that medical students have to take: a sort of oral, fast-paced test of factual information. Multiple-choice questions also enable your tutors to test this type of knowledge. However, most examinations will demonstrate your understanding of the subject and your ability to draw out relevant information to answer the question which is posed. In other words, the ability to handle information which you have stored in your memory.

How organised are you?

The key to success in many circumstances is organisation – not just in your studies but also in the way you run your life. However, organisation pervades every aspect of revision. It relates to your physical environment – for example, where you keep your revision notes, how you categorise your information – as well as the information you have to remember. A well-organised student also has better control of his or her inner self and is thus able to deal with concentration, motivation, stamina and examination nerves.

When should I start my revision?

It is never too soon to start the revision process. Many students leave it too late to do a proper job. Have you ever said: 'If only I'd started earlier with my revision?' Revision is an activity which should be ticking over quietly throughout your unit or module, reaching a crescendo of activity in the weeks and days before the examination. Many students put themselves under unnecessary pressure in the last few weeks before the examination by trying to make their revision notes at the same time as learning and committing information to memory. It is no wonder that the brain and memory are overloaded and less effective. Try to pace yourself and start the revision process at the beginning of your units instead of at the end.

Overview of the revision process

The table below provides you with guidelines for pacing yourself and maximising your efforts. Once you get into the 'Before, During and After' routine you will find that you can improve your grades in examinations.

Before (the start of your unit)	During (while your lectures and the unit are taking place)	After (at the end of your unit in the time before the start of examinations)
1 Collect all the necessary past papers and store them in the appropriate revision file. It is useful to analyse the examination questions so that you can get an overview of the topics which are set and those which come up frequently.	5 After a series of lectures and seminars on a particular topic/theme, gather together all your information from different sources. These could be handouts, electronic information provided by your tutors, your own lecture notes and notes you have made for background reading (possibly in preparation for an assignment).	8 Read through your revision notes and information to ensure that they still make sense and that you understand what you have gathered together in (6).
2 Purchase some special files in which to keep your revision notes – these are different from your course and lecture notes as you will see later in this chapter.	6 Distil all this information into dedicated revision notes. (Note-making techniques are explained in Chapter 4.)	9 If you have gaps or your notes do not seem to make sense, you will need to go back to the original notes and information to improve your revision notes.
3 Section off your revision files with clearly labelled dividers. You will need to cross-reference these sections with the examination themes and topics.	7 It is a good idea to sub-divide your topic information into the following sections: <ul><li>key words in the chapter;</li><li>concept map;</li><li>list of important facts/ theories;</li><li>key theorists;</li><li>selection of quotations.</li></ul>	10 Begin the memory stage of your revision – memory techniques are explained later in the chapter.
4 This is for those who like to use technology to help them with revision. Set up a separate folder on your computer for revision. Divide the folder into files which match the topics/ themes that are to be assessed. Perhaps you could code the files with an 'R' for revision to make sure that they do not get muddled with ongoing course-work and lecture notes.		11 Practise recall of information under timed conditions. Various techniques are explained later in the chapter.

The multi-dimensional revision map

For some students, revision is like a journey. To reach your destination in good time, it is worth investing in accurate maps. You need to keep in mind your journey's end, even at the start of your revision. On a journey there are times when you have to plot and plan out the whole journey and for this you need to see all the road networks and how they link together. At other times you need to focus on the minute details of street plans. Thus, in the examination there will be occasions when you will need to have the big picture of a topic to help you to make decisions about which elements or networks are applicable to the question; at other times, when working on your essay answer, you will be dealing with individual facts. You need to be able to manipulate both the whole and the parts to answer questions effectively. These are the mental acrobatics you will have to employ when you are in the examination room. Good revision will help you to be in control of your map and to know when to switch from the big picture to the fine details. However, what makes examinations so special is that they put you under timed pressure.

Time-controlled conditions put an added dimension to the revision process. Not only are you expected to be able to recall factual information accurately, to manipulate this information to meet the demands of specific questions and to assemble information from different mental storage areas, but you also have to do this under the pressure of time. Think of each topic as a big map. The way you organise the storage of facts and figures, theories and quotations will determine how quickly you can assemble the relevant information for a given task or question. However, it does hinge upon good networks which are adaptable and can provide you with quick routes to get you to where you want to be. The better organised your information is, the smoother, and therefore quicker, it will be to map out your information effectively.

What is your filing/storage system like?

Use different coloured files to gather and store your revision notes for each of your examinations. Believe it or not, this simple start to your organisation will reduce stress in the final countdown to your examinations. You will have all the relevant information at your fingertips and will not have to waste time searching through lecture notes and various topics to carry out your memory routines. Keep your back-ups on a memory stick and in a safe place.

It is a good idea to stick to one system for organising each section of your files. You will need:

- Key words with your definitions
- List of important facts/theories
- Key theorists
- Selection of quotations
- Concept maps.

Suggestions for building up these sections in your files is given in Section 5, below.

Once your storage framework is in place, using either separate files or computer folders and files, you can start gathering and distilling information in readiness for storing it in your memory systems.

5 Tricks of the trade: good revision notes

This section provides you with ideas for techniques for formatting your notes. It also explores ways in which you can produce more effective revision notes which in turn will increase your memory capacity and strengthen your knowledge and understanding of the subject.

Examinations can help you to consolidate your knowledge and bring together lots of different strands from your unit. During revision time you may find that the 'penny will drop' for you on some topic that you found puzzling during the semester. Making effective revision notes will help in this process and will ultimately give you an indication of what you understand and where the gaps are in your knowledge. In Activity 5 you are asked to identify and analyse your personal preferences for revision notes.

ACTIVITY 5 My revision notes techniques

Have a look at the different types of notes systems presented in the table below. Decide upon your personal preferences for using the different types. Then analyse and evaluate whether they have been of real help in remembering information for examinations.

Note types	Preferences 1 = frequently used 2 = not often used	Memory lubricators Ask yourself if the note type has helped you remember information for examinations
Lists		
Linear notes in bullet points		
Diagrams (some subjects lend themselves more to this than others)		
Notes in prose format (sentences/paragraphs)		

Note types	Preferences 1 = frequently used 2 = not often used	Memory lubricators Ask yourself if the note type has helped you remember information for examinations
Concept maps		
Flash cards		
Posters		
Ceiling maps		
Audio notes		
Grids/tables		
Time lines (useful not only for History students but for when you have to know about the progress or development of an innovation, etc.)		
Other (see Price and Maier, 2007, Chapter 2.1 for ideas)		

What sort of notes you produce and how you distil a whole series of lecture notes into revision notes is to some extent personal preference. There is a variety of ways of producing effective notes which you may want to consider. It is vital, however, that whatever system you choose it provides **you** with **useful notes** and is an **efficient** use of your time and effort.

Hot Tip

Remember, revision should not be a passive activity. Making your revision notes, by whatever technique or combination of techniques you choose, is only a means to an end: effective tools for memory stimulation and ultimately obtaining better examination grades. However, these notes are merely one part of the whole process. Sitting back and admiring your notes will not get your desired outcomes. It is the interaction between your mind, the information (subject context), memory stimulators and your examination systems which gets results.

If you always do the same things to revise, how do you know if they are really working? Could you be more efficient? Could you have remembered the information if it had been presented to you in a different format? It is just as important to evaluate what you did linked to your results. The type of information you are dealing with will also have a bearing upon your success or otherwise. For example, trying to remember the intricacies of the respiratory system, with its high level of difficult subject terminology, might be best approached using labelled diagrams rather than linear, bullet-point notes.

How good are you at customising your notes for revision purposes?

ACTIVITY 6 Customising your notes

Grade your effectiveness judged against past examination performance, where 1 = very useful, 2 = useful, 3 = just adequate, 4 = not effective.

Revision notes	Allocate grade
1 I only use the notes I made for an assignment/essay on this topic.	
2 I only use my lecture notes.	
3 I put all my notes from different sources together in a file.	
4 I only use my lecturer's handouts and downloaded electronic information from the departmental intranet.	
5 I make a new set of notes from all my sources.	
6 I do not have revision notes.	

If you only use one source of notes, you have to be confident that they are comprehensive. Remember that notes made for another purpose, e.g. for an assignment/essay, may not be right for the job of revision. If you gather all your notes from different sources into one file or section, you must be careful that there is not repetition of information. This can cause a drag on your time and sap your energy and memory.

If you make a new set of notes having gone through all your sources, do you end up with more or fewer notes? In these circumstances, more is not necessarily good, as you will see. Besides, if your revision notes are greater than your other notes, you need to ask yourself whether the increased volume helps or hinders memory.

Some students find that they have amassed a lot of lecture notes and notes made from books and articles for a specific assignment. It may seem rather daunting to try to consolidate these a couple of weeks before the examinations. It may be an impossible task and as a result you are immediately put off doing what is a very important aspect of revision that involves not only memory techniques but understanding.

If you have organised your lecture notes carefully, at the end of each topic/ unit you might find it useful to make revision notes while things are fresh in your mind. It is often a good idea to place your revision notes at the beginning of the section and identify them in a different colour so that they stand out when you come to the final stages of revision in the build-up to the examinations. Many students use different coloured paper for this or a range of coloured pens or coloured fonts.

You can customise your revision notes in many ways. Broadly speaking, you can start by drawing up a big route map (concept mapping notes) or you can draw small, detailed maps (information notes). You must decide which is the best way for you to work. There is no right or wrong way, simply personal preference.

How to customise your revision notes

If you want to provide the best support for your memory and retrieval systems so that they can work at speed under pressurised, timed conditions, you need to categorise and compartmentalise information into different maps.

Revision maps

At different times in your examination you will need to draw upon different parts of information to show off your knowledge and understanding to the examiners. There will be occasions when you need to use the **subject terminology** correctly and with confidence. For this you will need to have **key words** with your definitions at your fingertips. Sometimes you will gain marks for factual detail which is accurate. You will be drawing upon your store of **important facts/theories**. If you want to demonstrate the depth of your knowledge and understanding you will need to be familiar with key **theorists**, **leading figures** or **important innovations**. Being able to draw from a selection of **snappy and relevant quotations** is impressive. At other times your examiners want to find out how well you really understand the topics/subjects and will set questions whereby you will be expected to select and assemble information to bring out the connections. **Revision** or **concept maps** enable you to perform in this way.

During the course of your lectures and seminars it is always good to have an eye out for creating your revision maps.

Key words/subject terminology

Whether you set up a dedicated file on your computer or whether you prefer to work using paper and pen, it is vital that you have an ongoing list of key terminology. Business and management studies subjects have a wide array of terminology and acronyms that you need to become familiar with. Don't just list the key words; you also need to make sure you know what they mean. Copying a definition out of a dictionary will not aid memory recall. The definitions need to be in your own words so that you can understand them. This will give you confidence and speed when using the terminology under pressure in examinations.

A simple two-column table is the most effective way of gathering the information as you go along and is clear and easy to read when you get to the memory stage of revision (see Activity 7).

ACTIVITY 7 Key word map notes

Choose one of the topics/units which will be examined. Start to fill in the table. Keep this in your revision file.

Key word/phrase	Your brief definition (if unsure of this, check the accuracy with a knowledgeable friend)

As part of the ongoing nature of revision, this is a two-stage process:

- **Stage one**. Collect the most important key words and terminology as you go along throughout the lectures and seminars. This will be a random activity.
- **Stage two**. Can the lists be regrouped in any way? This might help you to look again at the terminology to make decisions about how to mentally map the information. Some students use colour at the regrouping stage so that they are preparing for memory storage and map connections later on.

Factual information

If your revision notes are to be of any use, you must distil the information you have. As soon as you have come to a natural pause or finishing point with one of your units, you need to distil your information into manageable revision notes. Summarising notes or handouts into **distilled notes** (key words, phrases) should take up no more than two sides of A4 for each topic.

If you look at some of your notes from different sources, you will find that some of the information is repeated, though in different words.

1. Read through all your notes/sources of information on a topic.

2. Identify the parts where repetition has occurred.

3. Shorten this information into your own words.

4. Pick out the key points first, followed by examples or subsidiary information.

You will have to choose a revision notes system which is suitable for your information, so try out different systems. The type of format you use will depend upon personal preferences to some extent but is often triggered by the type of information with which you are dealing.

Which note format do you prefer?

Here is some information in two frequently used formats: mind mapping and linear. Look at both and see which one makes sense to you.

An example of linear/branch notes

Family: family perspectives[1]

Feminist perspective

- Black feminists
- Radical feminists
- Feminist Marxists
- Liberal feminists
- Marxist feminists
- Common themes:
  - patriarchal institution
  - familial ideology
  - power structures
  - women's experiences
  - division of labour

New Right perspective

- Promotes traditional family
- Opposition to lone-parent families
- Boys suffer from absent fathers
- Dysfunctional families in underclass

---

[1] With grateful thanks to David Bown, Sociology lecturer, for supplying these helpful mind maps and branch notes.

Functionalist perspective

- Loss of functions theory:
  - Talcott Parsons: two 'basic and irreducible' functions
  - George Murdock: four universal residual functions
- Multiple functions family:
  - Ronald Fletcher: 'multifunctional family'
  - Eugene Litwak: 'non-bureaucratic functions'
- William Goode: movement to nuclear family
- Dysfunctions:
  - Vogel and Bell: emotional scapegoats

Marxist perspective

- Michelle Barrett: docile workforce
- Christopher Lasch: haven in a heartless world
- Reproduction of labour

Interpretive studies

- Studies of ordinary family life
- Meanings of family life

An example of mind-map notes

As you can see in Figure 8.1, information in mind-map notes is categorised by colour (or shade) rather than as a separate linear branch. The five main headings are in bold so that they stand out as the main branches or stems from the central theme.

An example of a table/grid format for recording: theories/famous people/innovations/inventions

Depending upon your subject and your topic, you can gain marks in examinations by showing off your knowledge about how development and progress has been made. For Education students, it is important to be aware of the educational system and how it has evolved to become an inclusive education system. You would need to know key names and dates; you would have to be able to state ideas and theories as well as solutions. Law students have to be aware of the Criminal Justice System, its development to today's system, and who the key players were and are. Engineering students may need to know about processes: who invented such systems and what is involved, or the theory upon which the system is based. Psychology students may have to have knowledge of the measurement of intelligence and would need to know the different theories of what makes up intelligence.

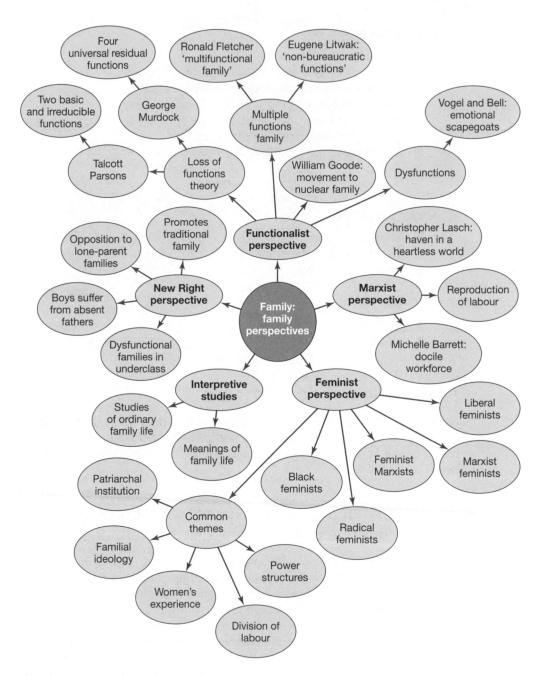

Figure 8.1 An example of mind-map notes

This type of information is often given along the way during lectures and in the course of your background reading. It is as well to establish a separate section in your revision file to keep this type of information all together. Using grids and tables is often one of the most efficient methods of gathering this type of information. It enables you to memorise the facts but also to obtain an overview of information from which to compare and contrast (see Activities 8 and 9).

ACTIVITY 8 Key theories and people map notes (1)

The table below is part of a worked example to demonstrate how you can record this type of information.

Theory	Definition	Named person(s)	My comments
One general intelligence	'g' factor: general ability to reason. Many common abilities classified under this. To do with neural processing speeds. Linguistic, logic and spatial skills.	Cattell Spearman	Cattell – introduced 'fluid' and 'crystallised' intelligence. 'Fluid' – is memory dependent and deteriorates with age. Abstract reasoning and problem-solving abilities. 'Crystallised' – increases with age; attributes can be taught. Performance on culturally loaded tasks. Spearman – developed factor analysis.
Three stratum	Built upon Cattell and Spearman's foundations. Incorporates reaction time.	Carroll	Three layers. Hierarchical layers. Notion of the quicker the reaction time, the higher the IQ.
Multiple	Humans have combinations of different types of intelligence. Not limited to single/one general theory.	Gardner	Reaction to 'g' factor and its components. Multiple – started with seven and then identified nine types of intelligence, e.g. musical, interpersonal, intrapersonal, mathematical, logical, linguistic, spatial, kinaesthetic, naturalistic.
Triarchic	Componential theory of analysis of intelligence.	Sternberg	Opposed Gardner. His categories are analytic (academic) and practical.

The development of thinking relating to the notion of intelligence and comparisons and differences can be drawn out of this table. Thus, the basic framework of information is given together with personal commentary. These notes are the foundations for a compare and contrast type of essay; yet the information could be used more generally as background information to a debate about nature versus nurture.

ACTIVITY 9 Key theories and people map notes (2)

Now try this out for yourself with one of your units by using one of the two grids provided.

Theory	Definition	Named person(s)	My comments

Name a theory or concept related to the chosen topic	Who supports this theory or concept?	Who opposes this theory or concept and why?

Relevant quotations

During the examination, if you can give a punchy and relevant quotation to back up and strengthen what you are writing about and the point you are trying to make, you can gain some valuable extra marks. However, you have to balance up whether (a) you have the time to search them out and learn them and (b) you have the memory capacity to remember quotations. Writing an inaccurate or irrelevant quotation is just as bad, if not worse, than not quoting at all. Your choice of quotation is also crucial because it must be linked to an important point or a unique saying/idea. Thus, it is vital that you remember the accurate quotation but also that you know what point it is making.

Hot Tip Taking into account the above advice, it is better to learn short quotations or phrases which will do the job you want. You should be on the lookout for these while you are conducting your research reading and while you are going through various handouts. It is worth alerting your consciousness to pick up on these when they are given in lectures. Often they are throw-away remarks but can be used most effectively in examinations.

Revision/concept maps

No revision notes section should be without an A4 or A3 revision/concept map of the whole unit. These maps are invaluable for ensuring that you make the connections with all your information. These will help you to obtain a greater depth of understanding of your subject. They are most useful to help you forge links between ideas in a theme or topic. These maps tend to be fairly complicated, depending upon your topic. Figure 8.2 gives an example of a simplified map to show you how the general ideas are linked together.

Having a concept map at the beginning of each section of your revision notes can fuel your final countdown. You can also use it to test yourself in the final stages of the revision process.

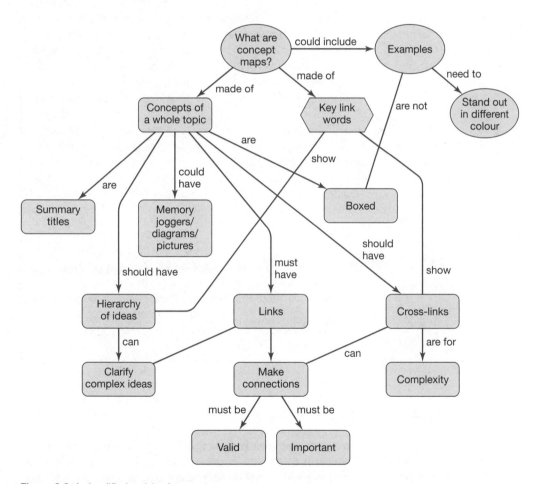

Figure 8.2 A simplified revision/concept map

Source: Adapted from Mesa Community College (www.mc.maricopa.edu/dept/d43/glg/Study_Aids/concept_maps/conceptmaps.html).

Hot Tip

Strategic revision

Look back at Activity 4, 'Knowing what to expect', where you were asked to find out what your examination papers will be like. You can make good use of past papers in many ways. Obviously, your tutors would like you to learn everything connected with the unit. However, you need to be ready for the format of the examination. You have to apportion time properly and be ready for the way in which the tutors word the questions. You will not have much time to figure out what a question is getting at and what information is required under the pressure of the actual examination. Therefore, your preparations should cover all eventualities over which you have control.

Time allocations

If your paper consists of essay-type answers, then it is important to work out how much time you should spend on each question so that you can pace yourself in the examination. You will need to take into account allowing yourself reading time and choosing the best questions for you as well as allocating some time for checking your answers. Some papers do not allow you to do any working for the first ten minutes. This ensures that students read the paper through and start to make decisions about which questions to answer. Some departments assume that students will do this and do not ring-fence or protect any time within the examination. Make sure you know what happens in your subject so that you can calculate the amount of time you have for actually writing your responses. If your paper is a mixed response type (one short section, with short answers or multiple-choice type, followed by a couple of essay-type responses), you also need to consider matching time allocation to maximum marks per question. It would be foolish to spend a lot of your precious time on a question which gives you only a few marks.

Question spotting

Many students look at papers which have been set over the previous two or three years so that they can get a feel not only for the topics which come up (patterns) but also for the wording of the questions (manipulation of information). For example, you may have learnt all about the Industrial Revolution and the question on this topic requires you to weigh up the impact of this upon a certain sector of people. This could have an effect upon the way you make up your revision notes in readiness for memory learning and recall.

Poster displays

These are similar to concept maps but on a larger scale. The best type of poster display for revision purposes is on A3 paper. This size allows you to incorporate visual information which could stimulate memory later on. Posters should be kept in a prominent position.

I always put one on my ceiling above my bed so that when I'm lying in bed forcing myself to get up, I gaze up and see the poster. It's sort of like a subliminal thing to help me remember.

If you have managed to work through all the 'Tricks of the trade' section, you will now have a well-organised revision file which is properly compartmentalised. It will provide you with all the information you need to move on to the next stage in your revision, which is making sure that you can memorise all that is contained in your file sections.

6 Memory stimulators

However effective we are at preparing and organising revision and gaining an understanding of the material, we have to commit it to memory for an examination. The more thoroughly we understand a topic, the more easily we can deal with unexpected and/or complex examination questions. So, it is important not to rely totally on pure memory recall or rote learning (learning chunks of information by heart). We need to develop strategies to help us remember.

Why do some people seem to have good memories and others struggle to remember what day it is? Perhaps those with good memories have developed strategies for remembering and they have worked out ways of remembering which suit them best. **Rote learning** may have worked in the past for some examinations but at university this is not a sensible strategy because of the volume of information you will have to deal with and because you are overloading your memory without understanding the subject. This type of learning uses up a lot of brain capacity, and, in particular, memory capacity. The problem with this is that it leaves little spare capacity for other activities which go on during an examination. It is difficult to remember isolated strings of information, but when you have found a way to connect them, you have a deeper understanding of the material (concept maps will support this) and this makes it easier for you to recall the information you need.

Wouldn't it be wonderful to cast your eyes over a page of information and automatically be able to remember everything on the page? There are very few people who have got a photographic memory to enable them to do this. Most students have to work at developing memory capacity and, as one gets older, it is necessary to keep the memory lubricated through constant practice. Many students have a negative view of their memory. You will be surprised how much you can do if you use the right stimulators. There are different types of memory, and knowing how the memory operates can help you make strategic choices to get the most out of the time and effort you put into memorisation at revision times.

How the memory works

The brain is like a living computer. It relies upon hard disk storage (long-term memory), portable storage facilities (short-term or working memory) and a robust operating system. The operating system has to be able to make decisions about where to go for information and to ensure that linkages and connections are made smoothly between the different parts of the system.

The memory system needs you to stimulate it effectively. Using the computer analogy, Figure 8.3 illustrates the various stages of memory interaction.

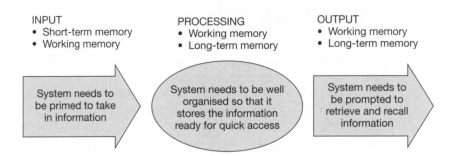

INPUT
- Short-term memory
- Working memory

PROCESSING
- Working memory
- Long-term memory

OUTPUT
- Working memory
- Long-term memory

System needs to be primed to take in information

System needs to be well organised so that it stores the information ready for quick access

System needs to be prompted to retrieve and recall information

Figure 8.3 The stages of memory interaction

This system has to be finely balanced to get the most out of it. If you over-load one part of the system, then you reduce the effective working and processing of other parts of the system. Just like a computer, this reduction will lead to sluggish operation and retrieval. Many of you will, at one time or another, have complained bitterly that your computer takes for ever to load up stored information. Some have said that it is possible to go away and make a cup of coffee while the computer chugs on and displays the irritating hour-glass to let you know that it is loading and retrieving your information from within its filing and operating systems. Rote learning, mentioned previously, clogs up your systems. It saps a lot of the energy from your processor and output systems. Consequently, if you are taking in further information, such as reading a part of an examination question, the balance of your system is skewed and everything starts to slow down – just what you do not want in timed, pressurised conditions.

For optimum working the memory system needs:

- Motivation
- Minimal stress distracters
- Concentration surges.

Therefore give your memory system a chance to work well by ensuring that you are in control of your stress levels, cut out unwanted distractions and utilise memory joggers to provide the concentration surges and lubrication for your memory system.

What sort of memory strategies (joggers) do you use?

Think about how you remember. Answer the following questions:

- What was your first day at school like? (episode)
- What is your home postal code? (fact)
- Where did you have your last lecture? (episode)
- How do you open a document on the computer? (procedure)
- What is a key concept in your favourite topic? (knowledge)

Our long-term memory is organised so we can remember facts, episodes, knowledge and procedures. These use different aspects of our memory. In addition, how facts and knowledge are remembered (written text, diagram, mind map, etc.) could reflect your ability to recall that information. Certain subjects can be remembered effectively by drawing and labelling diagrams, e.g. the intricacies of the blood system, but this would not be suitable for learning the causes of poverty in the last century, where a grid chart may be better. However, if you have set up revision files you are well on the way to strengthening better storage in your memory system.

You may find yourself better at remembering some types of things than others. Can you identify your memory strengths and weaknesses? See Activity 10. Check the feedback section at the end of the chapter to see a sample of two topics and the strategies appropriate for each topic. These strategies help you to prime your memory input system so that you give it the best chance to work. They will also provide effective organisation systems for storage during the processing stage.

ACTIVITY 10 Memory strategies/joggers

List two topics you will be studying (select quite different types of topics):

TOPIC A _____

TOPIC B _____

Memory strategies	Topic A	Topic B
Mind mapping, diagrams and flow charts		
Associations – making links with the information (revision concept map)		
Writing out information		
Remembering information in lists – rearranging the order of the list so that the first letters of each word on the list make up something silly or amusing – a memorable mnemonic		
Using shapes and colour		

Memory strategies	Topic A	Topic B
Saying the information – to yourself or out loud		
Poster display – similar to a concept map but incorporating visual clues as well		
Customised fridge magnet displays		
Chunking or grouping information		
Devising a story about the facts		
Flash cards		
Anything else you have found useful		

Of course, controlling your environment will also ensure that you give the whole system the best chance to operate. Distractions will weaken the effectiveness of the memory system so it is imperative that you evaluate what distracts you and how you are going to eliminate these (see Activity 11).

ACTIVITY 11 Controlling distractions

	Your answer	Ideal? Better to ...?
Where do you revise?		
Is it noisy?		
What about comfort factors?		
Do you take regular breaks?		
Do you set realistic targets for what you can memorise in a specified time?		
Do you prefer to revise alone or with friends/both?		
Do you need to spread out your notes?		
Do you walk around when you are memorising information?		
What is likely to distract you?		
What time of day do you prefer to revise/study?		

Bursts of concentration are better than setting aside long periods to revise. Research suggests that we can sustain **productive** concentration levels for only 40 minutes at a time. The memory retains more when you concentrate for short periods of time. If you have set aside a three-hour chunk of time for specific revision and memory learning, make sure that you split it up into small 15-minute chunks and then take a brief break – stretch your legs, make a drink (preferably not containing caffeine or alcohol) and do some relaxation exercise.

How do you prepare for timed conditions? The output stage

If I had plenty of time, I could recall loads of information.

Emma, second-year Environmental Science student

I can produce a really good essay which flows if I had more time.

Andrew, first-year History student

Most of us would agree with these students at some time during examinations. However, the trick is to ensure that you are prepared for the real circumstances and that you can trigger your brain to recall information from the different storage areas at speed. It is no good having all the information to answer a question if you do not show it off in the examination itself. It is well worth reminding yourself of the time you have apportioned for each examination response (see 'Hot Tip: Strategic revision', above).

Once again you need to give your memory the best chance for success and this will mean a two-staged attack.

Stage 1: Getting the information to stick in your long-term memory

The memory is better lubricated when it has small chunks of information to deal with initially. So break down your facts, etc. into bite-sized portions. Go over them regularly to imprint them and then see what you can remember. Gradually put the chunks together so that your memory makes the connections and so that you can recall larger and larger sections.

Stage 2: Retrieving or recalling the information at speed

The knack in examinations is bringing the information out of the depths of your memory. This means that you must set aside time to rehearse this. Practising recall of facts and timing yourself is important. On the day not only will you have to do this but in response to a specifically worded question, you might have to pull out parts of one of the storage drawers or files in your long-term memory and combine these with others. This slows the process down so you need to make sure that your speed and accuracy of recall are good. Many students practise recalling information at speed by getting hold of previous examination papers and timing themselves with specific questions. Try out a number of strategies in Activity 12.

ACTIVITY 12 Recall speed strategies

Try out some of these strategies. Remember that your subject matter may determine which ones are the best.

Recall speed strategy	Recall time	How to improve
Labelling a diagram		
Drawing a cycle of information		
Listing main facts/events		
Drawing and labelling how things work (e.g. for procedures)		
Constructing an essay plan for specified questions (e.g. for take-home examinations; questions from past papers)		
Writing out prepared essay questions		

7 Controlling the pressure

The mind and body function well on a certain amount of stress. Levels of adrenaline can keep you ready for action which is needed during the examination. Certain levels of stress can keep you on your toes, more alert and ready for action. Stress also means that your motivation is stimulated so that you have a positive attitude to your revision. However, too much anxiety and adrenaline can be counter-productive. To keep a check on your levels, go back to Chapter 2, 'Managing your stress'. This provides excellent advice and guidance. Learn to recognise your stress levels and carry out some of the suggested solutions. Here are some reminders for you.

Stress-busting techniques

1. **Exercise**. This will help the physiological aspect of stress and the release of endorphins will give you a feeling of euphoria as well as help your heart. It is also ideal for getting rid of anger and frustrations. If you want to choose only one stress-busting technique, then choose this one. It is important not to remain static while you are revising. Many students walk around while using their memory strategies.

2. **Relax**. When you are feeling stressed out it is difficult to unwind. You may find you have to make a big effort to do this. It may be better to go to classes such as yoga or tai-chi. Exercising also helps you to relax. If you want to develop your own relaxation techniques then try deep breathing or meditation. While you are revising, make sure that your shoulders, neck and hands, in particular, do not tense up. Regularly do some relaxation exercises for these areas while you are sitting. See if relaxation tapes can help you to unwind.

3. **Eat well**. Avoid junk food and too much alcohol – both of these can sap your energy and make you feel low. During revision time, some students drink excessive amounts of caffeine which can be found in coffee, tea and cola-type drinks. There is the popular idea that drinking coffee will keep you awake so that you can revise all through the night before your examination. Whilst this liquid intake may keep you awake, it has an adverse effect upon your memory capacity and functioning.

> *I kept myself awake all night with mugs of coffee so that I could learn and memorise my notes the night before my exam. The coffee certainly kept me awake but I had a memory blank in the exam and felt exhausted. I did worse in that exam so I'm not going to do that again.*
>
> Peter, second-year Chemistry student

Of course, if you have paced yourself in the weeks before examinations, you should not need to take these drastic measures.

E-day pressure countdown

Examination day or e-day has finally arrived. This is another source of stress and anxiety. Remember that anxiety can cut down your memory's performance, so carry out the following countdown checklist to give yourself the best possible chance in the examination.

> ### Checklist: e-day countdown
>
> - Make sure you get a good night's sleep the night before the examination.
> - Think positively: your hard work in the build-up to the day will pay off.
> - Avoid groups of friends who want to talk about what they have learned. This can be a source of worry. Panic rises when you listen to what they have done because it is different from you. If you have carried out the stages of revision set out in this chapter, you will be well prepared. Anyway, who is to say that your friends are right?
> - After the examination it is better if you avoid groups of friends who want to talk about what they did in the examination and what they wrote. This is another source of anxiety. There is nothing you can do to change what you wrote in the examination. Besides, who is to say that your friends are right?

8 Last-minute countdown

Rushing around at the last minute or on the day of the examination places you under unnecessary pressure. Go through this routine, it will keep you calm and positive as e-day approaches.

- Double-check the day, place and time of your examination.
- Check that you have a good pen and at least one spare ready for use.
- Check that the other equipment you can take into the examination is in good working order.
- If you are allowed to take in notes or a textbook, make sure that you have followed the regulations. Some departments require you to erase all your supplementary notes on textbooks so that they are 'clean' for the examination.
- Minimise your personal belongings – money and mobile telephone.
- Switch off your mobile telephone before entering the examination room.

9 The examination: ten-point plan

Stress can be minimised by getting into routines which take your mind off your anxiety levels. This section looks at what to do at the beginning of the examination, during the examination and at the end.

The beginning

1. Remind yourself of your worked time allocations. If necessary, jot these down on your answer booklet in pencil.

2. Read through all the questions carefully.

3. Categorise the questions:

   (a) the ones you can do;

   (b) questions for which you have some of the information;

   (c) questions which you cannot answer.

4. Decide on the order in which you will answer the questions. Start off with the ones you are most confident about and which will give you a chance of gaining the most marks.

During

5. Now take each question in turn.

6. Read the question carefully and do the BUG technique (see Chapter 13) to work out exactly what information you need to include and how to handle the information.

7. For essay questions, do a framework plan or a mind map. This means that you download all the relevant information before you start writing. This will take pressure off your memory and enable you to produce a more coherent and cohesive response.

8. Remember your reader – get to the point and then expand upon it.

After

9. Try not to do a post-mortem of your performance.

10. Do **not** check with others about what they did. Remember, if it is different from what you did, who is to say that they were correct?

10 Special examination arrangements

Some students can be granted special arrangements for examinations. These students will need some sort of proof of entitlement. Usually, this is provided when eligible students have applied for the Disabled Students' Allowance (DSA). In these circumstances, the student's needs are known well in advance and are unlikely to change over time. There may be occasions when something unexpected happens which could affect examination performance: for example, breaking a hand or arm, family bereavement, etc. Your institution can respond to these circumstances but it needs to know as far in advance as possible to organise the best arrangements for you.

What are special arrangements?

There is a variety of types of arrangements:

- Additional time
- Separate room
- A reader
- A scribe
- An amanuensis (reader and scribe)
- A computer.

If you think you are eligible, you need to discuss how special arrangements can be organised. Your personal tutor, the Disability Officer or the Dyslexia Coordinator are usually the best sources of information.

NOTE Do **not** leave this to the last moment or you may be told that nothing can be organised at short notice.

11 On reflection

This chapter has focused upon revision and examinations. You have been taken through suggestions, advice and guidance for ways to tackle the whole process. Some sections may have challenged the way you currently work and you may find that your skill levels and working habits have changed. It is vital that you constantly reappraise the way that you go about your revision and preparation for examinations to make sure that you maximise your efforts to gain the best marks and grades.

Summary of this chapter

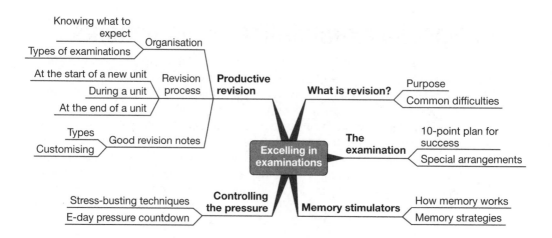

ACTIVITY 13 Update your personal development planner

Now reflect on your current abilities and consider what you need to do to improve. You may want to transfer this information to your own institution's personal development planner scheme.

Grade your confidence on a scale of 1–5 where 1 = poor and 5 = good.

My developing skills	Confidence level 1–5	Plans to improve
I can manage and organise the whole revision process effectively.		
I can recognise which revision notes systems to use for different purposes.		
I understand how to control pressure and stress.		
I understand the characteristics of productive memory strategies.		
I can use effective strategies during the examination.		

Date: ————————————————

Getting extra help

- Go to the students union to find out where to go for skill development. Many universities and colleges have tutors who provide this service.
- Some departments organise special revision sessions. Check to see if these are available.
- Revision buddies: some students find that getting together with others on the course is a useful and interactive method of revising. To get the most out of this, you need to plan this with your friends so that you all are at the same stage of revision when you meet. It is frustrating if you have worked on a section but the others haven't.

The following books will help you to improve your examination technique:

Buzan, T. (2006) *The Ultimate Book of Mindmaps*. Harper Thorsons.
Buzan, T. (2006) Brilliant Memory: Unlock the Power of your Mind. BBC Active.

Feedback on activities

ACTIVITY 2 Common difficulties with revision

Which of these apply to you?	Tick ✓
1 I am often frustrated at examination times.	
2 I am often **very** nervous at examination times.	
3 I often find that I can't sleep properly at examination times.	
4 I seem to spend a lot of time revising and not getting good results.	
5 I am not sure if my techniques are the most efficient.	
6 I mainly leave revision until it is almost too late.	
7 I put off my revision and find myself looking for other things to keep myself occupied.	
8 I have vast amounts of notes to help me revise.	

If you have ticked one of these then it is time to start thinking about how to improve your revision strategies.

If you ticked '1'

You have not perfected an efficient system of revision. Your memory strategies may not be the most effective. You need to try out different techniques. (Read this chapter carefully to identify where you could make improvements.)

If you ticked '2'

Most people are nervous at examination times. However, if you are excessively nervous, you may need to learn how to control your examination nerves more effectively (see Section 7, 'Controlling the pressure').

If you ticked '3'

This may be a sign of your growing anxiety. It is also an indication that you may not be using the most productive strategies for revision (see Section 3, 'Productive revision', Section 5, 'Tricks of the trade', Section 6, 'Memory stimulators' and Section 7, 'Controlling the pressure').

If you ticked '4'

Your revision may be without a proper focus and plan of campaign. You may not know how to prepare for revision. You need to try out different techniques (see Section 4, 'Countdown not meltdown', Section 5, 'Tricks of the trade' and Section 6, 'Memory stimulators').

If you ticked '5'

You are stuck in a rut and no one has told you how to revise properly. You need to try out different techniques (see Section 3, 'Productive revision' and Section 5, 'Tricks of the trade').

If you ticked '6'

Your time management is in need of an overhaul (see Section 4, 'Countdown not meltdown' and Chapter 1, 'Managing your time').

If you ticked '7'

This is often a sign of procrastination. Of course, it may be that revision has been an unpleasant experience in the past. It may be that you are dithering because you don't have a plan of campaign or you don't know how to revise.

If you ticked '8'

Having large files of notes is not necessarily appropriate for revision. It takes time to search through lots of information to find what you need. This may be time you do not have. For some students, a thick volume of revision notes is like a security blanket. However, you need to ask yourself if your notes are time efficient. Remember that it is quality not quantity that matters! You need to explore ways in which you can distil your information (see Section 5, 'Tricks of the trade').

REMEMBER! If you always do what you have always done,
You will always get what you have always got.
Now is the time to take stock of your revision habits.

ACTIVITY 10 Memory strategies/joggers

List two topics you will be studying (select quite different types of topics):

TOPIC A The cardiovascular system

TOPIC B Handover procedures on the hospital ward

Memory strategies	Topic A	Topic B	Uses and relevance
Mind mapping, diagrams and flow charts	✓	✓	Topic A: Labelling a photocopied diagram. Topic B: Numbered flow chart helps to remember procedure.
Associations – making links with the information (revision/concept map)	✓		Topic A is interconnected while B is more sequential.
Writing out information	✓	✓	Write out either the diagram or flow chart to help make mental links.

Memory strategies	Topic A	Topic B	Uses and relevance
Remembering information in lists – rearranging the order of the list so that the first letters of each word on the list make up something silly or amusing – a memorable mnemonic			Not relevant for B – correct order is essential.
Using shapes and colour	✓		Topic A lends itself more readily to colour associations for flow of blood, etc.
Saying the information – to yourself or out loud	✓	✓	Useful to reinforce most information.
Poster display			
Customised fridge magnet displays	✓		Pictures of different parts of the system more easily displayed than text.
Chunking or grouping information	✓		Topic B procedures can be grouped.
Devising a story about the facts Flash cards	✓		Photocopied pictures of parts of system and definitions of terminology can reinforce memory.

Reference

■ Price, G. and Maier, P. (2007) *Effective Study Skills*. Harlow, Pearson.

3 Apply your thinking skills

The connection between studying at Higher Education level and thinking might seem obvious, but the ways in which you will be developing your thinking skills are not so self-evident. One of the great surprises to many students is that in addition to *what* you think or know, the reasoning that goes into **why and how you know it or think like that** is also important.

In 1956, a group of American psychologists led by Benjamin Bloom established a comprehensive framework for learning. The cognitive dimension to this framework identified both lower-order and higher-order thinking skills. It is higher-order thinking using the skills of **analysis, synthesis** and **evaluation** that distinguishes the most successful graduates from the rest. So, although your studies at university will be full of 'content' (i.e. the knowledge in your subject) that you have to learn, alongside this you will also be expected to learn new and challenging ways of thinking.

Although the technical abilities you may develop during your degree are important, many employers of graduates will equally value the thinking skills you will develop. Your graduate career will be enhanced by applying yourself to the development of these higher-order skills.

This section of the book looks at three key areas relevant to developing higher-order thinking skills: critical thinking, reflective thinking and approaching numerical problems. These are key skills that will make a big difference to your results.

9 Thinking critically

According to the UK's Council for Industry and Higher Education, intellectual ability is one of the top four things that matter most to employers (Archer and Davison, 2008). Intellectual ability is not the same as being able to recall strings of facts. It is the ability to reach informed and valid judgements in complex situations through the use of rigorous analysis and evaluative skills, frequently with the explicit purpose of solving a problem. The nature of that problem may vary between your university work and future graduate employment, but the ability to think critically is **the** common underlying process in both these settings. This chapter explores some of the essential components of critical thinking which, if you commit yourself to developing them, will help you to achieve higher grades and give you an employment advantage.

In this chapter you will:

1. learn what critical thinking is;
2. find out about argument and some common thinking process and inference errors;
3. explore critical approaches to real-world problems;
4. examine the relationship between critical thinking and professional behaviour.

Study Skills for Business and Management Students

USING THIS CHAPTER

Estimate your current levels of confidence. At the end of the chapter you will have the chance to re-assess these levels where you can incorporate this into your personal development planner (PDP). Mark between 1 (poor) and 5 (good) for the following:

I understand what the principles of critical thinking are.	I can analyse other peoples' arguments and evaluate their strengths and weaknesses effectively.	I can construct and support my own arguments using evidence and reasoning to reach sound conclusions.	I know what 'critical engagement' with my subject is.	I understand how to synthesise knowledge and ideas as a critical thinker.

Date: _____

1 Why critical thinking is important

I think, therefore I am

René Descartes – (French philosopher, rationalist and mathematician, 1596–1650)

Today's highly interdependent world increasingly requires business students to recognize and understand diverse perspectives. And … requires … an understanding of the assumptions on which one's thinking rests (Neville, 2008).

Thinking critically in business and management is important because it is how you rationally question, test and challenge assumptions about the way things are done, then innovate and create new understanding and new solutions to problems. Yet Alter (2006), for example, found 'inadequate critical thinking' in real-world business-oriented system analyses to be one of the shortcomings even in his professional, working MBA students. The way you approach thinking is important if you are to demonstrate the rationale and evidence for your judgements, recommendations and actions. Your lecturers and current/future employers will expect this from you. If you get feedback on your work that says 'You need to be more critical' or 'More critical evaluation required' then you need to stretch and tone your ways of thinking. To get the best from this chapter, you first need to look at Chapter 7 'Reading critically' and Chapter 4 'Getting the most out of lectures', section 7 'Critical listening'. After this section you may then want to (re)visit Chapter 14, 'Improving your business and management studies writing' to develop how you express yourself as a critical writer.

2 What is critical thinking?

In Chapter 7, 'Reading critically', you discovered SMART (**S**kill **M**anagement in **A**cademic work through **R**easoning and **T**hinking) reading and considered the '**R**easoning' and '**T**hinking' aspects involved. As a **critical thinker** this means that for a given situation or context you:

- recognise alternative perspectives;
- analyse impartially;
- evaluate rationally and evidentially;
- judge objectively;
- embrace and respond to critique of your thinking.

Once mastered, this dynamic process drives continuous improvement in your thinking, learning and understanding. Critical listening, critical reading and critical writing are components of this dynamic process and the interaction between these and critical thinking is modelled in Figure 9.1. But 'doing' critical listening or 'doing' critical reading is only part of the bigger picture. Of themselves they are necessary but not sufficient solutions to the challenge of developing critical thinking skills, as the rest of this chapter will explore.

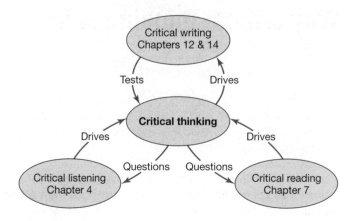

Figure 9.1 The dynamic process of criticality

Being 'critical'

I don't think I can be critical, as I don't like being criticised myself.

Steve, part-time Masters Human Resource Management student

Some business and management studies students confuse academic criti-cality with *criticism*. Criticism (of someone else's point of view or a friend's preference in music, for example) is usually a negative process of what's not liked about something. Many students assume that being critical means they must find fault, any fault, in the work they are studying. Thinking criti-cally is neither of these: it is a process applied *equally* to all supposed knowledge in a subject area. This process is the constructive, rigorous scrutiny of the strengths and weaknesses of that knowledge (such as the-ories, models and evidence). The purpose of this is to establish whether and/or how those theories and methods contribute to our broader under-standing of, and the solving of, the problems within that knowledge area. So, critical thinking is about demonstrating rigorously to our audience the grounds and reasons as to why we either reject *or* accept something.

I had this, like, sudden flash of inspiration when I was doing a business scenario analysis ... being critical was applying the same questioning framework to different explanations in the literature, trying to judge which provided the better explanation and then showing that in my writing!

Paul, final-year Business Systems student

The right mind frame

We take much every day knowledge for granted. For example, '2 + 2 = 4' is a real-world bit of knowledge that doesn't require constant demonstration of proof (although there will have been a time in prehistory when it was a revolutionary concept!). Some students don't recognise that at degree level they need to distinguish between 'obvious' or 'common sense' knowledge and knowledge which is open to question. If you are a part-time business or management student in employment, you may take for granted the way *your* business/organisation does things. Consequently you may not think outside the box when critically evaluating operational process improvement strategies, for example. Even 'obvious' knowledge in a context may be no more than a deeply embedded belief that has never been questioned, or a legacy from previous changes that no one has thought to review.

> *The other day I heard the saying 'if you do what you've always done then you'll get what you've always got'. As none of my family has ever been to university before I didn't have any experience of other ways to look at the world.*
>
> Serena, first-year Leisure and Tourism student

Many students, like Paul and Serena, discover that thinking at university changes them. The willingness to participate in this change is an important part of the mind frame you bring to your studies as it will push you out of your comfort zone in a number of ways. Look at Chapter 7, 'Reading critically' to review the sorts of approaches you need to develop. Critical thinking is an *'effort applied = results achieved'* relationship where attitude and motivation are important: if you don't put the effort in, then you can't expect to get high grades for your work.

The right thinking skills

The difference between information and knowledge is subtle but important. Knowledge is what you do with information. Knowledge is how you make meaning out of information. And, usually, you gain knowledge through an interactive process – by interacting with someone or by doing some critical analysis or further exploration of information.

(Hilton, 2006)

> *In my first year, for some of my modules I had to learn facts and information, which was fine. In others I thought I'd be told the theory I needed to know and then just write about that. I didn't expect to have to discuss alternative explanations, evidence and points of view and then weigh them up.*
>
> Mark, second-year Management student

There is a big difference between being taught what to think as opposed to learning ways of thinking in order to approach a thinking task. The first requires you to accept that certain things are held as absolutely true under all circumstances, whereas the second demands that you verify the validity of things in their context and test whether they remain valid beyond that context. Activity 1 lets you examine your approach to thinking skills and to consider where you might currently be between these two points.

ACTIVITY 1 Examine my approach to thinking skills

For each of the four **key statements** in the left hand column of the table below, circle the statement in the **response** column that most closely matches your current approaches to thinking about your subject knowledge.

Key statement	Response			
1 How I know about my subject is best described by:	Knowing all the facts.	Knowing what is certain and what is uncertain.	Knowing that everything is uncertain.	Knowing that things might have different meaning depending on context or situation .
2 Where academics have different explanations for something in my subject, this is best described by:	Some of the facts are wrong.	The academics don't agree because some of the facts are uncertain.	The academics all have different points of view.	The academics analyse and evaluate the evidence to reach their conclusions.
3 What I have to do as a student to learn is best described by:	Learning what my tutors tell me.	Applying my understanding of what my tutors tell me.	Developing my own opinions and points of view.	Considering different points of view to analyse and solve problems.
4 Showing my learning is best described by:	Memorising and repeating what I have been taught.	Showing I understand what I have been taught.	Asserting and defending my point of view.	Being able to analyse and evaluate the arguments of others.

Activity 1 is based on Baxter-Magolda's original (1992) Stages of Development of Knowing model and it offers you one way of thinking about your current perception of knowing (about a subject) and the process of learning within it. Baxter-Magolda used research she conducted with US college students to identify four stages of knowing: Absolute/Transitional/Independent/Contextual. While Baxter-Magolda found certain gender differences, the most successful students **at university** tend to be those who have developed what Baxter-Magolda calls 'contextual knowing'. Contextual knowing is a product of critical approaches to your subject and the topics within it.

See the feedback section for further guidance on what your response pattern to this activity may suggest before continuing with this chapter.

3 Making an argument

Science is built up of facts, as a house is built of stone; but an accumulation of facts is no more a science than a heap of stones is a house.

Henri Poincaré – (French mathematician, physicist and philosopher, 1854–1912)

There is no absolute right or wrong in many of the topics you will study in business and management. There are boundaries set by legal requirements, and there are ethical or social responsibility drivers that will also impose constraints (which is why ethics are considered in Chapter 12). Outside these, you are faced with a range of theories/models and methods that seek to explain business and management phenomena. These theories and models may totally disagree as to the causes or reasons for those phenomena. They may also totally disagree about the solutions or practices necessary to deal with them. However, what these theories and models will each do is make their case on the basis of an 'argument' to seek to persuade an audience (i.e. you or other readers of the text) of their worth. If you and I could each take one of Poincaré's 'heap of stones' and build houses from them, we would likely both end up with different-looking houses. We would then judge each house on how the foundations were laid, how the stones were selected and put together, and how the resultant structure meets expected standards or requirements. An academic argument is in some respects similar to this and has a structure that we can talk about to help us understand how other people have 'built' their arguments.

The structure of an academic argument

At university, 'argument' has a precise meaning and a clear goal which is to present a conclusion based on an argument. When we make an *academic* argument, we combine three components: a starting **assertion**, the **evidence** to support it and the **reasoning** that shows the relationship between the assertion and the evidence (see Figure 9.2). Success at university requires you to understand the difference between these components. Success also depends on you learning how to combine these components as a **process** to show *how* you have approached the thinking tasks most of your assignments will demand of you.

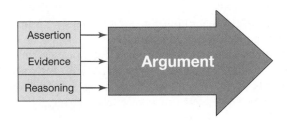

Figure 9.2 Components of an argument

I got very confused when our tutors told us in the first semester that they weren't interested in our opinions. I thought, how can I write anything if they don't want to know what I think?

Suzie, first-year Marketing student

Assertion

Whenever we make a statement about something, we usually say what we think it is, say something about its cause, effect or consequence, or make a judgement about its value or worth. For example: 'Internet shopping will kill off the high street'; 'without some regulation, market principles cannot produce socially responsible outcomes'; 'flexibility is more important than expertise in a modern workforce'. On their own, such statements are *assertions*. An assertion may be based on observation, belief, abstract thinking or research, but even so it is still no more than an opinion expressed by one person. This is really what's behind Suzie's tutor's comments. If you want an opinion on something, you can ask anyone, anywhere, what they think about it and they'll probably tell you. But what they won't do is put effort into researching the evidence and then demonstrating the steps of reasoning that underpin their opinion. All arguments will contain one or more assertions, but it is the further effort of building the argument that turns an assertion into a case to be made. A well-made case, with demonstrated grounds for the conclusion, puts you well on the way to getting good marks. Activity 2 helps you to think a bit more about the nature of assertion.

ACTIVITY 2 Considering assertion and opinion

This activity lets you examine the nature of assertion and opinion.

- First, select a current news topic that is politically, economically or socially significant.
- Second, select three newspapers that are aimed at different audiences and have different political editorial positions. (For example, in the UK, the *Daily Mirror/ Sun/Daily Mail* are tabloid papers aimed at the so-called blue-collar audience and the *Guardian/Independent/Times/Telegraph* are broadsheet papers aimed at the so-called white-collar audience. Here they are grouped very approximately to their political persuasion. You might choose one tabloid and two broadsheet papers for example.)
- Next, read how the three different papers present their editorial or 'leader' comments about the news topic you have chosen.
- Now consider the differences in their coverage, perhaps in relation to what they identify as the cause, consequence or solution to the news topic. Use the following **question words** to interrogate what has been written.

Question word	Example
Who	Who are they? E.g. what sort of political agenda might they have? What sort of vested interests might they represent?
What	What are they stating/claiming happened? What do they conclude as an answer?
Why	Why have they picked this issue/topic as a 'leader' item? Why do they reach the conclusions they do?
How	How do they reach these conclusions? How do they present their evidence?
Where	Where else do they get evidence or support for their conclusions?

■ Finally, ask yourself what the different papers want you to accept, to what extent they agree or disagree and what might explain any difference of opinion you observe.

See the feedback section for further comment on this activity.

Evidence

To begin with many business and management students are unsure what is meant by 'evidence'. Whilst there will be some discipline differences, evidence in business and management subjects can be wide ranging. The table below summarises some of the main types and sources of evidence that you might be expected to use in your work.

Type	Examples
Quantitative data	Numerical data and figures from government, academic and trade association sources.
Qualitative data	Surveys, questionnaires, focus groups, observation.
Case studies	Those published in texts, or your own summary and analysis of the business/organisation you are employed in.
Academic texts	Citation from textbooks, journals.
Organisation and business documents	Citation from policies, procedure documentation, memos, meeting minutes.
Professional regulatory bodies	Citation from standards, protocols, codes of behaviour.
Professional/trade journals or magazines	Citation from editorial leaders, articles.
Personal communications	Citation from emails, memos and letters between you and another person.

See Chapter 12, 'Understanding academic integrity: learner ethics and plagiarism' for more about accurate citation.

Hot Tip Your university library will be your major source of good quality evidence; however, online sources are available to widen your research. Use this online tutorial to explore internet research for business and management students: www.vts.intute.ac.uk/tutorial/business/

I didn't pass my first assignment because I hadn't done enough reading, actually I only read the textbook chapter. My personal tutor said: 'If I see only a couple of sources listed in the Reference section of an essay, then I know that no matter how well a student writes, they won't have much to write about'. She was right.

Liu, direct entry second-year International Business Studies student

As Liu found, the type and source of evidence you put into your work will immediately reveal how much or how little independent study and research you have done. You will also reveal much about your skills as a critical thinker from the selection of evidence you use in your work. Be aware that how you *select* your evidence is not the same as being *selective* of your evidence. The critical thinker uses evidence that is relevant and current, and that shows the full range, breadth, depth and authority of evidence about a subject (see Figure 9.3). A non-critical thinker tends to be selective and uses only evidence that 'fits' what they want to say without too much concern for whether it is authoritative, relevant or of sufficient breadth and depth.

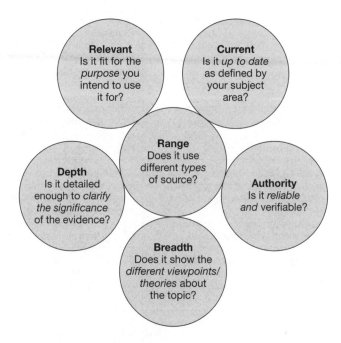

Relevant
Is it fit for the *purpose* you intend to use it for?

Current
Is it *up to date* as defined by your subject area?

Range
Does it use different *types* of source?

Depth
Is it detailed enough to *clarify the significance* of the evidence?

Authority
Is it *reliable and* verifiable?

Breadth
Does it show the *different viewpoints/ theories* about the topic?

Figure 9.3 Six criteria for critical evidence

Hot Tip

If to begin with you are unclear about what *is* appropriate evidence in your subject area, **ask your tutors for guidance**. They will prefer this to having to write it on your assignment feedback and mark sheet.

Try Activity 3 to identify use of evidence in your subject.

ACTIVITY 3 Using evidence

Choose a text from your subject area. First, look for the types of evidence it uses. Next, use the questions in Figure 9.3 to critically test the evidence. Finally, ask yourself the question: 'Does the evidence presented give me confidence about what the author wants me to accept?'

Reasoning

One way to think about reasoning is to think of it as the glue or cement that holds the evidence together. In doing this it also connects things in certain ways: it shows the *relationship* between things. If we take three of Poincaré's stones, we can assemble them (or not at all!) in a number of ways. Figure 9.4 shows some of these.

There is nothing 'wrong' with any of the combinations in Figure 9.4, but for building purposes some combinations will be better for a certain job than others. There is a relationship between purpose and combination. When we consider the relationship *implied* by the connections, things get a bit more difficult. For example, if on the basis that it rained yesterday and it is raining today I reason therefore it will rain tomorrow, I am connecting my evidence together in a certain way *and* claiming a relationship between two days of rain and what will happen tomorrow. If, however, from the same basis I reason that I cannot predict what will happen tomorrow, I am connecting my evidence differently *and* claiming that there is no relationship between the days of rain. Reasoning is a complex process and there are a

Figure 9.4 Some ways of assembling three stones

number of errors that can creep into it. We look at this a bit more in Section 4, 'Common errors in thinking'.

The argument process

When we put these components of assertion, evidence and reasoning together we can think about the argument *process* as pushing a ball (the assertion) up a slope (the argument to be made). We could then see evidence (one or more pieces of the type identified above) acting like a brake at key points to move the assertion, reasoned step by reasoned step, towards the conclusion at the top of the slope. See Figure 9.5.

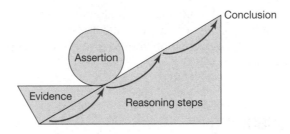

Figure 9.5 The argument process

(This diagram is based on the classical myth of Sisyphus who was destined to eternally repeat the task of pushing his boulder to the top of the slope only to see it roll back to the bottom again)

So an academic argument has three key parts: assertion, evidence and reasoning. We can apply the **A**(ssertion) **E**(vidence) **R**(easoning) approach to test an argument critically to see whether it meets the minimum requirements for an academic argument. Figure 9.6 summarises the AER approach.

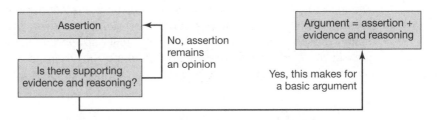

Figure 9.6 The minimum AER requirements for an academic argument

Use Activity 4 to look at the AER approach in a bit more detail

ACTIVITY 4 Apply the AER approach to argument construction

Here is a short argument. Read it and then look at the analysis.

'In February 2008 house prices in the UK were at an unsustainable price to income ratio and the market had to readjust. The historic average ratio is around 3.5 (Times, 2006), suggesting the historic ratio is a long-term indicator of what the market can sustain. The last major UK house price cycle saw the ratio peak at 3.9 before falling to 2.1 (Nationwide Building Society). The aggregate UK ratio grew from 3.5 in August 2002 to 5.4 in December 2007 (Nationwide Building Society). Evidence from previous cycles suggests that when the ratio goes beyond certain limits this indicates instability that will lead to adjustment (OED, 2004). Therefore, based on the evidence, the house price market had to readjust.'

Elements of the argument	Analysis
In February 2008 house prices in the UK were at an unsustainable price to income ratio and the market had to readjust.	Assertion
The historic average ratio is around 3.5 ...	Evidence
... suggesting the historic ratio is a long-term indicator of what the market can sustain.	Reasoning
The last major UK house price cycle saw the ratio peak at 3.9 before falling to 2.1.	Evidence
The aggregate UK ratio grew from 3.5 in August 2002 to 5.4 in December 2007.	Evidence
Evidence from previous cycles suggests that when the ratio goes beyond certain limits this indicates instability that will lead to adjustment.	Reasoning
Therefore, based on the evidence, the house price market had to readjust.	Conclusion

This activity looks at how an assertion can be built into an argument to reach a reasoned and evidenced conclusion and shows the process of 'pushing the ball up the hill' in a number of steps to achieve this. While this example may appear to be a sound argument, in reality from a critical perspective there are a number of flaws, some of which will be explored later in Activity 7.

My first proper essay got marked down: I was told all I was doing was expressing an opinion, and that I needed to put more critical argument and citation evidence in my work.

Gemma, first-year Business Strategy student

Gemma was not developing her assertions in a rigorous fashion; she was failing to make an argument and therefore to demonstrate a deeper approach (see Chapter 7, 'Reading critically') to her understanding of the subject matter. Furthermore, by not citing evidence sources she wasn't capitalising on the studying effort she had invested in her essay preparation.

> **Hot Tip**
>
> It is a common fallacy that citing other people's work shows you don't know things. On the contrary, it shows that: you've done wider research than just the textbook; you've understood what those other sources are saying in the context of the question set. If you then build arguments based on that understanding, it shows that you can apply that understanding. All these things get marks.

As soon as we are presented with an argument, we can start to examine it in detail. Expert thinkers develop a set of cue questions that they use to test other people's arguments. According to Saaty (2008), the quality of professional decision making also relies on the nature of the information gathered. A systematic method of generating information from reliable, interrogative questions is a transferable skill common to both critical thinking and effective professional decision making. You can use and adapt those questions in Chapter 7 to start to build your own set.

ACTIVITY 5 Develop my critical cue question toolbox

Using the questions from Activity 7 in Chapter 7 as triggers, expand the following toolbox. Some suggestions and prompts are made to help get you started.

Trigger question	Critical cue questions
Who is the author's audience?	Is the audience purely academic, or is it professional or trade? *Consider what the relationship is between the author and audience. Is the audience likely to question or accept the author's authority? How might the audience use the work?*
What are the central claims/ arguments of the text?	Are these about solving a problem, identifying new opportunities or proposing new theories? *Consider what stake the author has in the claim/argument. Are they trying to settle an outstanding question or raise new questions? Are they repeating what other people have done? If so, what reason do they give for this?*
What is the main evidence?	How recent is the evidence presented? *Consider its context. Might the regional/cultural origin of the evidence affect its validity in this text? Is the evidence new primary research or is it previously published material?*
How is this substantiated?	Does the author have a wider range of supporting evidence? *Consider the method(s) used to collect that evidence. Is it comparable/relevant to the type of argument being made? Does the author just list other evidence without discussing how or why it supports their main evidence?*

Trigger question	Critical cue questions
What assumptions lie behind the evidence or arguments?	Are these assumptions made clear and discussed in the text? *Consider whether the author has a preference for a particular model or theory. Are they ideologically influenced? Are they sponsored by an organisation with a vested interest in the conclusions reached?*
Is adequate proof provided and backed up with examples of evidence?	Does the author include real-world examples? *Consider the choice of examples. Are they recent? Are they relevant to the context?*
What are the general weaknesses of the threads of the argument/ evidence?	Does the author discuss alternative interpretations of the evidence that might not agree with their final conclusion? *Consider how the author deals with contradictory or 'awkward' evidence. Do they clearly show why they have rejected different explanations? Do they leave threads unconnected? Do they actually answer the question(s) they said they intended to answer?*
What do other leading authors say about the same subject?	Are these leading authors discussed by the author? *Consider the areas of agreement and disagreement between authors on this subject. What conflict or contradictions are there between the authors?*

See the feedback section for comment on this activity.

4 Common errors in thinking

So far we have talked about the process of academic argument. But we haven't talked about the quality of the argument itself. Sometimes arguments appear sound, but it is only when you take a deeper look that flaws are seen. This deeper engagement is vital when dealing with others' work and it is vital that you apply the same approach to your own thinking processes.

> *'When I use a word,' Humpty Dumpty said in a rather scornful tone, 'it means just what I choose it to mean – neither more nor less.'*
>
> Lewis Carroll, *Through the Looking Glass*

Unlike Humpty Dumpty who can make it up as he goes along, critical thinking is about accurate communication of what we mean. We cannot choose and then change what something means when we are making an argument. To communicate clearly and accurately, we also need to be accurate and clear in our thinking process. This is a complex area, but there are some common thinking 'errors' that students make. These errors can get in the way of achieving the advanced expert reading stage 8 (see Chapter 7, 'Reading critically') and of producing critical, written assignments (see Chapter 14, 'Improving your business and management studies writing'). Looking out for these thinking errors will improve your critical thinking and be helpful to your critical reading and writing.

Generalisation

My seminar tutor told me that I generalised all the time and that it frequently sounded as though I had read something without any thought.

Sally, final-year Business Studies student

One common error is that of generalisation, for example: 'All good leaders are good managers.' If this is supported by evidence and reasoning then it becomes an argument, but as an argument it remains weak. If someone can find a single case of a good leader who actually isn't a good manager, then the argument falls over. You can recognise generalisations in your own thinking and in other people's work as they tend to be introduced by words or phrases such as: 'All ... ', 'It is commonly believed ...', 'It is a well-known fact ...', 'Many people would argue ...'. None of these provides clear or accurate communication as far as the critical thinker is concerned. The table below considers the problems with these phrases.

Generalisation	Issues
'All ... '	'All' is generally an unverifiable term. It can be accurate only if it can be guaranteed that every instance of something has been examined. Most of the time this is not achievable.
'It is commonly believed ...'	'Common' is an imprecise term. For it to have a sense of accuracy it would have to be a quantifiable majority. But then this quantity gives a more accurate way to refer to the subject. 'Believed' is also unclear as the evidence and reasoning for the belief are not clear.
'It is a well-known fact ...'	Like 'common', 'well known' is imprecise. A fact is an indisputable thing. In business and management studies, 'facts' tend to be questioned and argued about in the texts.
'Many people would argue ...'	'Many people' is also imprecise. Who those people are, how many there are of them and why they would make the argument are important questions that aren't addressed.

Sometimes a broad assertion is a starting point for an argument, particularly if the topic or subject matter is contentious or uncertain. It can be a device some advanced thinkers use to set up a target against which they then argue. This tends not to be encouraged among undergraduates as it pre-supposes an expert level of knowledge, but you might come across it in some of your texts. If so, ensure that you apply the trigger and cue questions from your toolbox to test out the author's case.

If you do have to start with a broad assertion, one way to support it is to provide both necessary and sufficient evidence. Take the example of the generalisation 'It is commonly believed that taxation in the UK is too high'. To make this an acceptable assertion would require the *necessary* citation of credible, authoritative source and *sufficient* number of such sources to demonstrate the extent of the 'common belief'. The argument still has to be made though!

Hot Tip

Generalisations tend to suggest to your tutor that you haven't given much thought to the subject and/or that you haven't bothered to undertake sufficient reading to fully inform yourself about the subject. It can lose you marks.

Chapter 14, 'Improving your business and management studies writing' looks more closely at the critical writing skills that help you to avoid generalisation and express yourself more clearly.

Cause and effect

Another common error is to simplify or misunderstand cause and effect. The statement 'The implementation of the new business strategy has boosted profits by 12 per cent' sounds very impressive and clear, and might even get its author a pay rise! Figure 9.7 shows this apparently simple cause and effect.

Cause: New business strategy

Effect: Profits up by 12%

Figure 9.7 A simple cause and effect

However, the critical thinker would ask a key critical question:

> *'How is the observed effect (profits up by 12 per cent) linked to the apparent cause (the new business strategy)?'*

It might be that other factors, for example an unrelated change in consumer behaviour or unrelated changes in personnel, caused or contributed to the increase in profits. The critical thinker will start with the observed effect or consequence and then examine the evidence and reasoning in respect of any apparent cause. In the example given, the critical thinker may identify that the suggested cause (the new business strategy) is in fact *not* the only cause. They might produce a very different analysis that reveals a much more complex set of cause and effect events such as that shown in Figure 9.8.

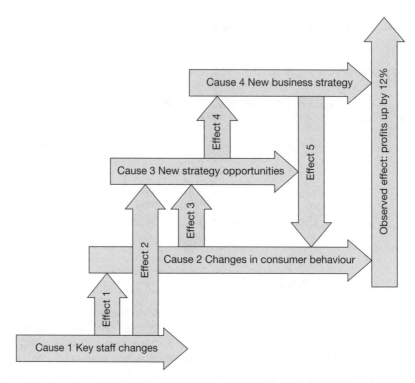

Figure 9.8 A more complex cause and effect

The analysis there shows that the underlying cause, i.e. that of key staff changes, is not *directly* linked to the increase in profits. But it had two effects:

- a related change in consumer behaviour, which can be directly linked to the change in profits; and
- new strategy opportunities (this scenario doesn't examine these, but this would be another set of chained cause/effect events in its own right).

These effects become new causal factors. Changes in consumer behaviour have an effect on new strategy opportunities, and these new strategy opportunities lead to what was seen as the initial *apparent* cause, the new business strategy itself. This in turn had two effects:

- one being a contribution to the increase in profits; and
- one being further changes in consumer behaviour.

This last effect also impacted on the final *observed* effect, the 12 per cent increase in profits. This is a fictitious example, but it demonstrates that one of the key characteristics of a critical thinker is to never take things at face value.

The critical thinker deals with complex chains of events. This is always demanding, but this is precisely where the stretch and challenge of university learning and the resulting personal development opportunities occur for you. Chains of arguments involve more complex thinking approaches and these will be considered in Section 5 below. One final note: sometimes cause and effect may be straightforward: the critical thinker however will ensure that they can demonstrate this by showing the steps they have taken to examine the situation to be able to reach such a conclusion.

Hot Tip Generalisation and causality statements are common in essay assignment questions. These are designed to test your critical thinking skills by asking you to 'discuss' or 'critically evaluate' the statement (see Chapter 14, 'Improving your business and management studies writing', and for general guidance see Chapter 13, 'Taking control of the writing process'.

Logical conclusions

Logic is a study in its own right beyond this book, but one common logical error some students make is to offer a conclusion that doesn't logically follow from previous statement(s). Consider the following sentence: 'CO_2 (carbon dioxide) is a greenhouse gas as it is emitted from burning carbon fuels.' What is accurate is that CO_2 is accepted as a greenhouse gas and CO_2 results from burning carbon fuels such as coal, oil and petrol. There is a connection between these two, but the relationship needs to be *methodically* demonstrated for the conclusion to be logically linked to the opening statement, as Figure 9.9 shows.

So the problem with the sentence is that it actually says CO_2 is a greenhouse gas *because* it is emitted from burning carbon fuels. The leap to the conclusion has completely missed out the more complex sequence of argument necessary to show the proper relationship. The short-cut results in an illogical and meaningless sentence.

This type of error occurs either because something is not fully understood, or because not enough attention is paid to the way in which it is expressed, or just through laziness. Whatever the case, if you make this type of error in an essay you will lose marks and receive feedback such as: 'You have misunderstood the principles here' or 'You haven't given enough thought to what you are trying to say' or 'You need to critically engage more with this topic.' Activity 6 lets you test your thinking error-recognition skills.

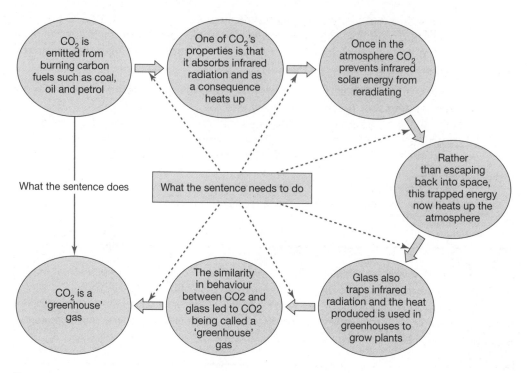

Figure 9.9 Producing a logical conclusion

ACTIVITY 6 Test my thinking error-recognition skills

Analyse each statement, decide whether it contains any error in thinking and identify what needs to be done to correct any error. Note: some statements may contain more than one type of error. The context you assume for the statement may affect your judgement as to the type of error present (or not). In this case you will need to consider how your assumptions have been made and what alternatives exist.

Statement	Error type?
It is generally accepted that communication skills are essential to successful organisational change.	
Assessing the external environment to any organisation is important due to SWOT analyses.	
An increase in scheduled flights has led to a growth in tourist activity.	
All SMEs need to review their IT procurement annually to ensure they have the most cost-effective procedures in place.	
No one under the age of 25 has experienced age discrimination; therefore the company's equal opportunities policy is working.	

See the feedback section for more comment.

5 Developing argument

In the last section we looked at some common thinking errors. These are all based on the key factor that critical thinking at university is about seeking to go beyond what we know using rigorous and systematic means and methods of thinking. Arguments need to be developed in detailed and layered ways using such thinking. And in the process of developing them, we encounter opportunities not just to learn more about what we already know but also to start to see new connections between topics and fields in our discipline. Innovation in business and management depends on the same process.

Chains of arguments

Most academic arguments are built up from a number of chains of arguments. The colloquial saying 'Big bugs have smaller bugs upon their backs to bite them' gives a hint of what this is about. For example, you might need to test some major pieces of evidence (and show your audience this process) before you can rely on it for your own argument. Or, a piece of reasoning needs to be argued for and established before you can apply it to evaluate some evidence. Equally, your main assertion may well be built from a number of contributory assertions. When, in Figure 9.8, we considered a possible cause and effect chain we were actually beginning to build an argument chain (the 'big bug'). And in Figure 9.9 we were actually developing the argument chain to make clear the steps in reasoning (a smaller bug) to support our conclusion. In order to tackle most assignments as a critical thinker you will have to build a clear sense of the whole argument chain that will allow you to answer the question set or the problem posed. Figure 9.10 is an illustration of the argument pathways and branches that a critical thinker might develop for a particular argument.

> *I keep getting summative feedback which says 'You need to show more critical engagement' with the topic. I don't know what they mean.*
>
> Terry, first-year Hospitality Management student

It is the process of identifying and developing these chains of arguments that will help you to show your critical engagement with a topic. To do this, you will typically:

■ identify and summarise the alternative argument(s);
■ demonstrate the grounds for accepting/rejecting alternative arguments;
■ show the possible limits/implications acceptance of any specific argument implies.

Activity 7 looks at an example of how a chain of argument and critical engagement can be developed.

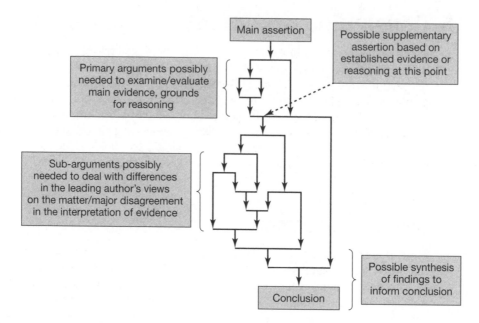

Figure 9.10 A representation of a fictitious argument chain

ACTIVITY 7 Developing chains of argument

Let's have another look at the argument we explored earlier in Activity 4. Let's take one of the pieces of reasoning we used there: '*The historic ratio is a long-term indicator of the sustainable position.*' As critical thinkers we know to use one of our critical trigger or cue questions to test out reasoning. Let's try: 'What assumptions lie behind the evidence or arguments?' By asking this question we're prompted to ask further questions such as: 'Who says so?', ' What's the basis for the assertion?', 'Do authors agree about this?' At this level of analysis, what passed before as 'reasoning' now looks very much like an assertion!

When we answer our critical trigger and cue questions we develop a sub-argument to show our audience the *grounds* on which the reasoning is based. If you refer back to Figure 9.9, you can see how this activity example could be one of the sub-arguments that contributes to the bigger argument chain.

Original 'reasoning'	Elements of a more developed argument chain	Analysis
… the historic ratio is a long-term indicator of what the market can sustain.	Whilst the historic ratio has been generally accepted as a reasonable indicator of the sustainable relationship between house price and earnings, there are a number of factors that are assumed by this.	Assertion
	For example, some observe that the ratio is based on assumptions about average tax or interest levels, but that these need not be taken for granted (OECD, 2004).	Identify/summarise argument

Original 'reasoning'	Elements of a more developed argument chain	Analysis
	This suggests that average interest rates over the last 10 years, if maintained, *could* result in a higher sustainable house price to earnings ratio.	Inference
	This is offset by a view that such short-term analysis of interest levels is the result of temporary monetary and fiscal policy opportunities that are subject to great variability over a longer term (IFS, 2005).	Identify/summarise argument
	On this basis, and without clear evidence that such policy changes may become sustainable,	Rejection/acceptance grounds
	The 3.5 ratio is the best empirical benchmark currently available to judge a sustainable position.	Conclusion with limitation acknowledgement

Now select a text of your choice, analyse it in the same way and make a critical judgement as to how the authors have developed their argument.

See the feedback section for further comment.

Synthesis

I have heard several lecturers say that they don't just want us to present theories and say why one is better than another or why one particular framework would work well here, but another one there. They say they want us to achieve a 'synthesis' – what does that mean?

Asmi, second-year Business Enterprise student

According to a dictionary definition, synthesis is a 'combination of components to achieve a connected whole' (OED). While this answers Asmi's question as to *what* synthesis is, it leaves the process of *how* to synthesise unanswered. Synthesis is opposite to analysis. Analysis is a process of examining something and taking it apart in a systematic way to understand what it is, how it works, why it is like it is, and what its strengths, limitations and weaknesses are. Synthesis is when we are faced with the task of putting something back together from that analysis. Figure 9.11 is a very simplified model of what this might look like at the point we have applied critical analysis and evaluation (in this example) to two theories. At this point we have also evaluated (weighed up) each element against other evidence, explanations or theories to judge how they stand up.

This model suggests that we produce two main results. First, elements of the theories that haven't stood up to our analysis and evaluation, and that we reject. Second, elements of the theories that have stood up to our scrutiny and that we accept. If the thinking process stops here, then the assignment based on it will have some critical engagement. But the assign-

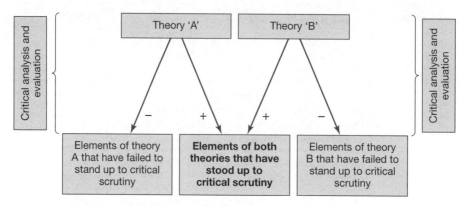

Figure 9.11 The product of a critical analysis and evaluation

ment won't achieve the best marks because it doesn't go on to show the significance or consequence of the *output* of the analysis and evaluation. This is what happens when we 'synthesise'. As an *outcome* of the critical thinking process, synthesis could be one of a number of things, as the table below summarises.

Possible outcome of synthesis	Explanation
Clarification …	… of the core, important factors that different theories do agree about and identify what is less (or not at all) important for your purposes.
New grounds …	… to support the use of thinking or evidence from a related or comparable topic area to the specific one you are working in. This might not otherwise be apparent and which may be innovative.
'Middle way' …	… alternative to the existing positions leading authors hold on a subject.
Confirmation …	… of a different theory or approach that you have already examined, or support your rationale for moving on to consider such a different approach.
Insight into …	… a new way of understanding or explaining a problem or issue (although this is unlikely to happen at undergraduate level except perhaps in the very best final-year dissertations).

Figure 9.12 maps one way of seeing how synthesis is part of a 'system'. Synthesis is probably the hardest idea to grasp in this chapter, as in many respects it is not tangible. Think about getting together the ingredients and utensils for a meal. You can easily define these as *inputs*; they are tangible. Then think about the recipe and activities to prepare and cook the ingredients: you can define the *process*; it is tangible. The product of this process is the cooked meal on the table. The *output* is tangible. The *outcome*, how-

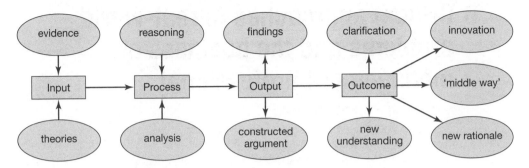

Figure 9.12 Synthesis as part of a critical thinking 'system'

ever, is to do with enjoyment, satisfaction, fulfilment and a range of other real but subtle things about the meal that may vary from person to person; these are less tangible. This is a common, everyday experience, yet even so it shows why synthesis is the ultimate challenge for any critical thinker.

In practical terms, particularly if you are working on an operationally based assignment, synthesis may be the way in which you make the case to 'bespoke' or combine purely theoretical problem solving, analytical or decision-making tools to work for you in a specific real-world context.

ACTIVITY 8 Examining synthesis

Choose a text in your subject that people acknowledge is innovative or offers a new, exciting approach to an existing problem. Using the guidance from all the previous sections, critically analyse and evaluate how the author develops their perspective and how they propose and justify the innovation or new approach they offer in their work.

Chapter 14, 'Improving your business and management studies writing' looks at writing strategies and practices that can enhance your use of synthesis in your assignments as a business or management studies student.

6 Critical approaches to real-world problems and the business or management professional

Real-life problems are messy.

Halpern (1997)

So far we have looked at aspects of critical thinking without thinking about the real world. Real-world problems are complex, with many dimensions, and in business and management terms will frequently involve conflicts of interest. These conflicts may come from competing pressures of a psychological, social, political, legal or regulatory nature that prevent us from acting in certain ways. Some subject areas (in the sciences, for example) avoid 'mess' by not letting real-world consequences interfere with their theorising and experimental demonstration of proof. Business and management students, however, have messiness right at the heart of most of their subjects. Success in your discipline is frequently about understanding and then dealing with the compromises that conflicts of interest force on to business or management practices.

This does not mean that critical thinking has no relevance; in fact, it is even more relevant if you are to achieve the best balance between competing demands *and* be effective. All the critical thinking principles explored so far directly contribute to this. Try Activity 9 to examine a real-world-type problem using a critical thinking approach.

ACTIVITY 9 Rightsizing the sales team

Due to recessionary pressures, you are tasked with restructuring the sales team of the organisation you work for. It is a very successful team of five, but you need to reduce the team to four staff. You must observe legal boundaries in terms of a non-discriminatory approach. Based on the following profiles, and assuming all team members have equal length of service, who would you make redundant and why?

Employee **T** has no dependants and his sexuality is the subject of speculation. He has a wealth of detailed knowledge about the sector and intuitively spots new sales opportunities.

Employee **S** is divorced. She has recently remortgaged her house to support her daughter's university education. Her attention to detail and communication skills make her the best deal-closer in the team.

Employee **Q** has a young family. He previously worked for a blue-chip company in corporate information systems. When this was outsourced, he volunteered for a redundancy package. He is particularly strong in selling to black and minority ethnic-run businesses.

Employee **Z** is 55. He has been in sales all his life and has no formal qualifications. As his wife is disabled, his is the sole household income. He has a portfolio of smaller accounts and meets his targets by spending many more hours on the road than other team members.

Employee **X** is the youngest team member. He is highly motivated and consistently exceeds his monthly targets. He has a cocaine habit.

See the feedback section for further comment on this activity.

For the business or management professional, critical thinking will directly affect how they perform in the tasks and activities of their role, and how they move ahead and stand out for promotion and career progression. Critical thinking offers the business or management professional a systematic method of approaching problem solving and the following observation on methodology is worth considering:

> *Knowledge organised in a discipline does a good deal for the merely competent; it endows him with some effectiveness. It does more for the truly able; it endows him with excellence. (Drucker, 1964)*

7 Critical thinking: putting it all together

In Figure 9.1 we introduced you to critical thinking as part of a dynamic process. Its role 'manages' the connection between the sources of knowledge and information on your course (for example lectures, seminars and texts) and the assessed assignments (for example essays, reports and presentations) you complete to demonstrate your progress as a student.

The central part of Figure 9.1 does not contain convenient linear connections that give you a simple template or set of instructions about critical thinking. Figure 9.13 below represents more closely what it might look like as a 'cloud' with key ideas and elements loosely aligned. The final activity in this chapter is for you to construct your own concept map of the components of critical thinking.

ACTIVITY 10 Your own critical thinking concept map

Using Figure 9.12 and your notes from the activities you have completed in this chapter, construct your own detailed concept map of critical thinking. Make it a 'rich' map with your own ideas and other sources that build it as a personal framework for your understanding. To help you develop your concept mapping, this web link will prove useful:

http://users.edte.utwente.nl/lanzing/cm_home.htm

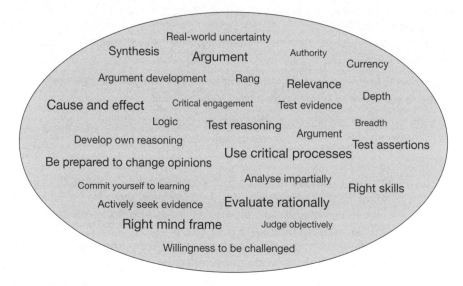

Real-world uncertainty
Synthesis   Argument   Authority   Currency
Argument development   Rang   Relevance   Depth
Cause and effect   Critical engagement   Test evidence
Logic   Test reasoning   Breadth
Develop own reasoning   Argument   Test assertions
Be prepared to change opinions   Use critical processes
Commit yourself to learning   Analyse impartially   Right skills
Actively seek evidence   Evaluate rationally
Right mind frame   Judge objectively
Willingness to be challenged

Figure 9.13 The critical thinking 'cloud'

Above all, critical thinking is what Higher Education at university and college is about. How you develop your thinking skills whilst at university, and what this does to your ability to perceive, analyse and interpret the world around you, is the single most marketable skill you will take away with you when you graduate. No book can teach you to be a critical thinker, it can only signpost the way. You have to make the journey.

8 On reflection

If you want to get a good degree and stand out in your graduate career, then this chapter is vital reading. You must develop and enhance your critical thinking skills to allow you to critically apply your learning and show how you connect and construct knowledge in your subject to successfully undertake the assignments you will be set. Knowing **what** and **how** to do something is important. But knowing **why** that something is what it is, the conditions and circumstances under which that holds true and **when** to apply it rather than an alternative, are the essential critical thinking skills that will contribute to your success as a business or management studies student and as a professional. This chapter has introduced you to some of the ways of thinking you need to continue to practise and develop to ensure that in your professional career you are master of your plan for yourself rather than being part of someone else's master plan for you.

Summary of this chapter

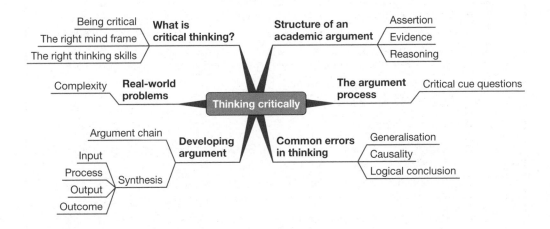

ACTIVITY 11 Update your personal development planner

My developing skills	Confidence level 1-5	Plans to improve
I understand what the principles of critical thinking are.		
I can analyse other people's arguments and evaluate their strengths and weaknesses effectively.		
I can construct and support my own arguments using evidence and reasoning to reach sound conclusions.		
I know what 'critical engagement' with my subject is.		
I understand how to synthesise knowledge and ideas as a critical thinker.		

Getting extra help

- Go to the students union to find out where to go for skills development. Many universities and colleges have tutors who provide this service.

- Be proactive with your seminars or group tutorials. Prepare and participate. These learning opportunities let you practise your critical thinking skills. Direct feedback from peers and tutors is some of the best help you can get.

Consult the following:

- Bonnet, A. (2001) *How To Argue: A Student's Guide*. Harlow, Pearson Education.

- Sussex University's study skills website has helpful information about critical analysis: www.sussex.ac.uk/languages/1-6-8-2-3.html#crit

- Hong Kong University has an extensive website which looks at critical thinking, logic and creativity: http://philosophy.hku.hk/think/critical/

- The Institute for Human and Machine Cognition website gives you an extended background to concept mapping: http://cmap.ihmc.us/Publications/ResearchPapers/TheoryCmaps/TheoryUnderlyingConceptMaps.htm

Feedback on activities

ACTIVITY 1 Examine my approach to thinking skills

If your responses are mainly on the **left-hand side** of this table then you need to review in detail the section on 'Learning in Higher Education' at the beginning of this book and then work through Chapter 7, 'Reading critically' before you continue with this chapter.

If your responses have **no particular pattern** then you need to review Chapter 7 in detail before you continue with this chapter.

If your responses are mainly on the **right-hand side**, then you are already thinking contextually and critically and you should use the rest of this chapter in conjunction with materials from your own independent reading to deepen your approach.

ACTIVITY 2 Considering assertion and opinion

This activity has no right or wrong answer. It sets out to demonstrate that different interpretations/opinions/judgements can exist about something when the **only** point of agreement is that something has happened. The importance of the approach is that you are invited to apply some simple but effective question words (**What/Why/How/ Who/ Where**) that should always inform your critical questioning of any published materials.

ACTIVITY 5 Develop my critical cue question toolbox

The important thing about any toolbox is that it grows to contain a range of tools to deal with a variety of situations. A mechanic sometimes needs a screwdriver and a spanner, at other times a hammer. Sometimes they might need all three, at other times a specialised tool. In all cases they need to know how to use the tools and what to use to complete a particular task successfully. Your critical thinking toolbox is similar to this, and it will grow and develop as your studies progress. You will become more skilled in the use and selection of questions to read, listen and think beyond the words in a text or discussion. This is one of the main things you will learn at university, but this depends on you putting in the effort to maximise this aspect of your learning: no one else can do this for you.

Aim to add a new critical cue question every week. This may come from your reading or from the types of questions that your lecturers pose when they are talking about a topic.

ACTIVITY 6 Test my thinking error-recognition skills

Statement	Error type?
It is generally accepted that communication skills are essential to successful organisational change.	As it stands this is a **generalisation**. If the assertion of 'general acceptance is supported with authoritative citation then this sentence is OK.
Assessing the external environment to any organisation is important due to SWOT analyses.	This sentence does not have a **logical conclusion** as it makes SWOT analyses causal to the importance of assessing the external environment.
An increase in scheduled flights has led to a growth in tourist activity.	As long as **cause and effect** have been established then this sentence is OK.
All SMEs need to review their IT procurement annually to ensure they have the most cost-effective procedures in place.	This sentence is a **generalisation**. As in the first sentence above, it could be 'rescued' with suitable supporting citation.
No one under the age of 25 has experienced age discrimination; therefore the company's equal opportunities policy is working.	This sentence does not have a **logical conclusion** for two reasons. First, the grounds are suspect (*No one under the age of* 25) and second, absence of evidence is not evidence of absence, i.e. even if no one (whatever age) has experienced age discrimination, this does not of itself support the conclusion.

Note that many of the above sentences also need a citation to be acceptable.

ACTIVITY 7 Developing chains of argument

Your examination of the text of your own choice demonstrates that critical engagement is actively going *beyond* what might be seen as the right answer, to show the *basis* upon which it is judged to be the right answer. It demands more of you in terms of research and reading. You have to develop your understanding from that reading. Then you need to write (or verbally present) clearly to communicate that understanding. This is what it takes to get the best marks in your assignments.

ACTIVITY 9 Rightsizing the sales team

This activity demonstrates that there are no absolute answers to many real-world problems; rather, there is a range of possible solutions. The appraisal of those solutions, and the final decision as to what to recommend and/or implement, demands consideration of competing proposals and clarity of rationale. It also illustrates that what is theoretically rational and what is practical or feasible in the real world may be very different. Sometimes the existing frameworks aren't uniquely or singularly up to the job, and this requires a rigorous, critically judged synthesis of such frameworks to fit a new scenario.

References

- Alter, S. (2006) 'Pitfalls in analyzing systems in organisations', *Journal of Information Systems Education*, 17 (3), 295–302.
- Archer, W. and Davison, J. (2008) *Graduate Employability: what employers think and want*. London, CIHE.
- Baxter-Magolda, M. (1992) *Knowing and Reasoning in College*. San Francisco, CA, Jossey-Bass.
- Drucker, P. (1964) *Managing for Results: economic tasks and risk-taking decisions*. London, Heinemann.
- Halpern, D. E. (1997) *Critical Thinking Across the Curriculum*. Mauwah, NJ, Lawrence Erlbaum.
- Hilton, J. (2006) 'The future for higher education: sunrise or perfect storm?', *Educause Review* [electronic version], 41(2), 58–71.
- Neville, M. G. (2008) 'Using appreciative inquiry and dialogical learning to explore dominant paradigms', *Journal of Management Education*, 32 (1), 100–17.
- Saaty, T. L. (2008) 'Decision making with the analytical hierarchical process', *International Journal of Services Sciences*, 1 (1), 83–98. Available at http://inderscience.metapress.com/media/mftaqnqwxp4t69xrkc3u/contributions/0/2/t/6/02t637305v6g65n8_html/fulltext.html [last accessed October 2009]

10 Understanding the value of reflection

When we are asked to reflect on our developing skills, an event or a particular theory, we know it is difficult and generally feel 'what's the point?', even though we may know deep down that it is an essential skill. The pressure on managers to keep moving, to drive their plan forward and come up with new ideas is what we generally consider a manager should be doing. However, if we just *do* things without reflecting on the consequences then we are essentially a non-thinking and non-strategic learner and in later life a similar kind of manager.

By three methods we may learn wisdom: first, by reflection, which is noblest; second, by imitation, which is easiest; and third by experience, which is the bitterest.
Confucius – Chinese philosopher 551–479BC

In this chapter you will:

1. understand the value of reflection as a strategic tool;
2. know how to use several frameworks for reflection;
3. work through some of the models of reflection.

USING THIS CHAPTER

Estimate your current levels of confidence. Mark 1 (poor) and 5 (good) for the following.

I know why reflection is a strategic tool.	I know some of the frameworks for reflecting.	I can work through a structured framework of reflection.

Date: _____

1 Introduction

There is usually a big sigh when we are asked to reflect on something. Reflecting is not easy and it is more than just being in a reflective mood or daydreaming. In order to reflect on an event, you have to be able to describe the event as it occurred and state how things could have been done differently to create a better outcome. If the outcome is perfect, knowing why is equally important so that you are able to repeat the success. If you are reflecting on your skills, you need to describe how well you can do something now and what you need to do to improve. Reflection therefore enables you to verbalise (externalise) what has happened/how things are so you are able to capture the event or activity. It is an essential strategic tool.

Consider the following questions:

- What is it that turns experience into learning?
- What specifically enables you to gain the maximum benefit from the situations you find yourself in?
- How can you apply your experience in new contexts?

(Boud *et al.* 1985)

Boud *et al.* (1985) suggest that structured reflection is the key to learning from experience, and because reflection is difficult, we could do with some support.

2 What is reflection?

According to the *Encyclopaedia of Informal Education (InfED),* the American philosopher and educationalist John Dewey (1859–1952) is considered to be a significant figure in progressive education. How we think and reflect in the process of learning was key to his ideas. For Dewey, reflection was both active at the time an event is occurring, referred to as 'incidental reflection', and then later through making sense of that experience through 'systematic reflection', as without systematic reflection the learning can be lost. The poet T.S. Eliot wrote in *The Dry Salvages* (1944 and the third poem of the Four Quartets), 'We had the experience but missed the meaning', and this should be a pertinent reminder of the value of reflection.

The work of Dewey also influenced Donald Schön (1930–1997), another American philosopher. He is known for his work on the value of reflective practice in organisations and the term 'reflective practitioner'. Schön's position on reflection is not dissimilar to that of Dewey and Schön refers to *reflection-in-action* and *reflection-on-action*. *Reflection-in-action* refers to thinking and adjusting what we do 'on the hoof'. Being able to do this enables us to respond flexibly to a given situation and prevents us from sticking to rigid plans. *Reflection-on-action* refers to thinking about an event: what happened, how other people reacted, what the outcome was and the interrelationship between certain actions that affected the outcome. This is what we commonly think reflection is when we are asked to do it. For both Dewey and Schön, making sense of or making explicit what we have learned is the key value of reflection. Much of Schön's work concerned how society, organisations and individuals learn and develop.

How organisations learn became the research area of Peter Senge (1947–) and from him we have the concept of the 'learning organisation'. Learning organisations reflect the ability of individuals within that organisation to openly reflect on what has been learned and take that forward collectively to resolve issues and achieve common goals. Reflections from all individuals within the organisation are considered valuable. Senge refers to this work as the Fifth Discipline, and you may be asked to look at his work in your studies.

3 Why should we reflect?

Most of the time, we are thinking about things without being aware of it, or regarding it as 'reflection' at all. Your reflection at this point is IMPLICIT, it has value, but it is not captured or made explicit. Once you are asked to reflect or critically reflect on something, you start to make it EXPLICIT (i.e. you become conscious about what happened/is happening) and use it strategically. Take a look at Activity 1.

Hot Tip Search on the internet using the search term 'conscious competence' and it will provide you with a series of informative sites that can help you realise why reflection is an essential strategic tool for a learner, whether as a student or an employee learner.

ACTIVITY 1 Why don't you like reflecting?

If you have already been asked to do some reflection or reflective writing, do you want to scream *WHY*? If you do, you are like many other people (not just students) who feel the same way. So, why are we generally so resistant to reflecting on our learning? One reason is because we have to confront something we may feel uncomfortable about and going back to look at it is not always pleasant. Also, we are not sure how to analyse what happened or what to do with the information we uncover. Look at the table below and tick the views that you have regarding reflection.

What I feel	Usually me	Why do you feel like this?
I find reflection difficult because I don't know what I am supposed to write.		
I find it a waste of time and it just takes too long.		
I can't see where I'm developing skills in my courses so how can I reflect on it?		
I don't know what to do with my PDP when I complete it		

Check the feedback section at the end of the chapter for more information.

This exercise is itself an example of reflection. You possibly had some difficulty getting started, but once you relaxed into it, I am sure you were able to tap into how you felt.

4 What skills do we need to reflect effectively?

Reflection is about you:

- understanding what happened or where you are now with an issue;
- being perceptive enough to 'see' what happened;
- recognising how you felt.

Being perceptive enough to 'read' what has happened and be in touch with your feelings about it will depend a lot on your emotional and social intelligence (see below).

Emotional intelligence

Daniel Goleman, author of the popular book *Emotional Intelligence* (1995), claims that intellectual IQ alone does not give us all the skills needed to be successful in everyday life. We need to develop self-awareness and recognise what others are feeling (empathy), know how to handle our emotions and to have self-discipline. This, Goleman claims, is emotional intelligence (EI). Group work projects, for example, if taken seriously, develop our interpersonal skills (emotional literacy). Similarly, the personal development planner is a tool that enables us to reflect on our progress and personal development. These aspects of your curriculum therefore have good reasons for being there.

According to the Emotional Intelligence network (www.6seconds.org), EI comprises, in essence, three areas: *know yourself, choose yourself, give yourself.*

Emotional intelligence categories	Questions	Application to your studies
Know yourself	■ What makes you think and feel the way you do? ■ What parts of your reactions are habitual or consciously thought through? ■ What are you afraid of/anxious about?	Being honest with yourself enables you to reflect on your qualities and faults. You learn from your experiences. Reflect on this through your studies. This reflection should alert you to habitual actions such as how you behave in groups or how you are at public speaking. When you become aware of this you can then try to prevent yourself being a hostage to previously learned negative reactions.
Choose yourself	■ How do you know what's right for you? ■ If you were not afraid or anxious, what would you do? ■ Can you increase your awareness of your actions?	Manage your feelings. If something starts to stress you, identify exactly what it is and objectively assess why this is a stressor for you. Can you manage it yourself or do you need help?
Give yourself	■ Am I helping or hurting people? ■ Am I working interdependently with others? ■ Have I developed empathy? ■ Do I work by a set of personal standards?	Be aware of your fellow students. When working together be alert to their needs as well as yours (be empathic).

Source: Adapted from the Emotional Intelligence Network (http://6seconds.org/index.php)

By developing your emotional intelligence, you have the grounding to develop your self-belief and self-confidence, which gives you the insight to see the value of reflection. You also become aware of your own behaviour and you may start to reflect how this impacts on the outcome of an event.

Social intelligence

In 2006 Daniel Goleman wrote another book, about social intelligence. For Goleman, emotional intelligence is concerned with how we handle ourselves and manage our emotions, while social intelligence is about having empathic skills, motivating and inspiring others and generally knowing how to work most effectively with others. We are all aware of people who give us a 'buzz' and make us feel good and those who just seem to drain us.

Social intelligence is about your:

- feelings of self-respect, self-worth;
- ability to use language effectively;
- understanding of social and organisational contexts;
- confidence in being honest (but not impolite!) which others will appreciate;
- empathic qualities, i.e. your ability to 'connect' with people.

In companies, staff appraisal can be carried out using the 360 procedure where everyone you deal with, above and below you, appraise you. As a student this doesn't happen, but your friends may give you feedback (and you them) as well as your tutors. Feedback is a good source for your reflection and you should use it positively.

NOTE   If you search 'Daniel Goleman' on the Internet you will find many references to him as well as small videos of him talking about his ideas.

5 Are there frameworks to help me reflect?

There is no one technique for reflection, but very often if you have been asked to reflect you will be given a series of questions to answer. It is important to know the purpose of your reflection and have a structure on which you can focus. Is your reflection concerned with personal development or is it concerned with a particular learning event? Take a look at the lifecycle of the reflection process in Figure 10.1.

Your tutor will probably give you a structure to work from, but if you are left to devise your own then you will need to develop a framework that follows the reflection lifecycle in Figure 10.1. Below are some other frameworks that you could use to help you develop your own reflective cycle.

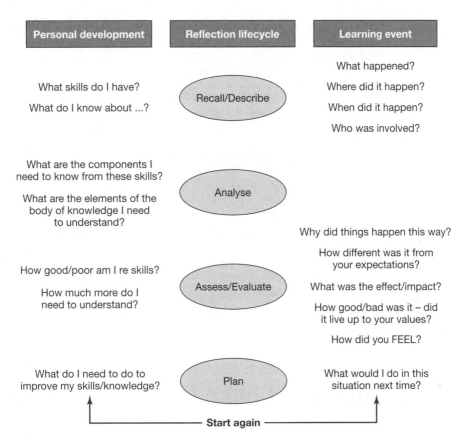

| Personal development | Reflection lifecycle | Learning event |

What skills do I have?

What do I know about ...?

Recall/Describe

What happened?

Where did it happen?

When did it happen?

Who was involved?

What are the components I need to know from these skills?

What are the elements of the body of knowledge I need to understand?

Analyse

Why did things happen this way?

How different was it from your expectations?

How good/poor am I re skills?

How much more do I need to understand?

Assess/Evaluate

What was the effect/impact?

How good/bad was it – did it live up to your values?

How did you FEEL?

What do I need to do to improve my skills/knowledge?

Plan

What would I do in this situation next time?

Start again

Figure 10.1 The reflection lifecycle

Gibbs (1988) Reflective Cycle

Description *describe what happened*

Feelings *describe what were you thinking/feeling*

Evaluation *identify what was good/bad about the experience*

Analysis *identify a sense/meaning you can make out of this*

Conclusion *identify what you could have done differently*

Action *what would you do differently next time?*

This is a fairly straightforward framework for reflection. Ideally you could use this model to reflect on group work or an oral presentation. If you keep each of your reflections from various group work projects, you can complete several cycles of this reflective framework. Why not start by taking one of your key skills, for example group work, and see how your 'Action' stage works (or not) with the next group project. If you are asked to write a reflective journal then this model would work well. You can repeat the cycle several times during a group project for example; this can be seen as *reflection-in-action*.

Rolfe *et al.* (2001) Reflexive Practice Framework

This framework uses three stages: WHAT?, SO WHAT? and NOW WHAT?

WHAT?	What was the purpose of this event? Describe the event and the people involved. What did I observe? What roles did others play? What was the most difficult/challenging part? What surprised me/was unexpected?
SO WHAT?	What did I learn about myself and those I worked with? What did I do that I thought was effective or not effective? Why was it effective? Could I have done anything differently? Have I improved my understanding of the event/situation? What are the general issues that I can take from this event/situation?
NOW WHAT?	What changes would I make if I repeated this experience? How do I take what I have learned forward – what do I need to do? Are there any areas where I feel it is difficult to make changes/move forward?

You can also apply this to a personal situation or an (critical) event like an oral presentation.

6 When will I need to use reflection on my course?

Reflection can occur in many ways during your studies, with some more formal (as described above) and others more informal and much shorter. One of the important characteristics of being a graduate will be this ability to be a reflective practitioner when you leave.

> *Critical reflection is taken to mean a deliberate process when the candidate takes time, within the course of their work, to focus on their performance and think carefully about the thinking that led to particular actions, what happened and what they are learning from the experience, in order to inform what they might do in the future (Qualifications Curriculum Authority, 2001, 8).*

Reflecting on your key skills

One generic area for reflecting on practice is via your personal development planning document and this is very often concerned with the current state of your knowledge and your developing key skills. If you have to do this, you will usually be given a structure for the document – see Activity 2.

ACTIVITY 2 Reflecting on your key skills

Take time to consider your key skills at this point in time. This table offers some suggestions, but feel free to use your own.

Key skill	Confidence level 1–5		■ Evidence of your competence ■ Plan progress
	Now	Aspire to be at end of the year	
Writing – I have the ability to write a variety of essays and reports clearly, accurately and coherently. I can write these documents with the correct structure and appropriate vocabulary.			*e.g. through tutor feedback*
Referencing material – I have the ability to correctly reference sources I use.			
Oral presentations – I have the ability to structure my talk so that it is focused and well organised. I use effective visual aids and engage with the audience through good eye contact.			
Working with others – I understand how groups work together and the issues involved in successful group work. I am developing my ability to work effectively in groups.			
IT – I have the ability to use standard office software effectively and software appropriate for my technical area.			
Application of number – I have the ability to carry out simple financial calculations, basic statistical techniques and use mathematics as needed for my course.			
Solving problems – I have the ability to solve more complex problems within my subject area.			
Improving your own performance – I have the ability to reflect on my progress and understand how to improve.			
Comment on skills you want to improve and why, and also on those skills you are happy with and say why.			

Commenting (a less emotionally loaded word than 'reflect') on your skills' development allows you to identify precisely where you need to improve and how to action that. How you *action* improvement is key to reflective practice.

Being able to work in a group and become a real team is also a key skill you need to develop and reflect on. See Activity 3.

ACTIVITY 3 Reflecting on your group working skills

Working in a team: reflective log

Setting up the team

Describe how you went through the stages of forming a team: eliciting strengths of individuals, forming ground rules, understanding the task and defining areas of responsibility. Could you identify team members with different roles? Check Chapter 5, 'Working in a real and diverse team'. What role did you play in the group?

Reflect

What would you do differently next time when forming a team? Reflect on how effectively the team worked together as a group. Reflect on how YOU could improve your role in a team.

Working to plan

Describe any working schedule/plan you may have developed for your project. How did you identify roles and tasks in order to complete your plan? Did you have structured meetings/agendas? Chair person? Minute-taker? Were there any problems getting the group together? How focused was the team? Did everyone take part? Were the actions from meetings clear? What do you feel about the outcome of your group project?

Reflect

What procedures did you have in place that worked or didn't work? What have you learned from the procedures you put in place? How would you change it next time (if necessary)? If your procedures were good, say why. Comment on how you would improve the team to make it function better as a real team. Also reflect on why the good points were good and how you can make sure you repeat this next time. How did YOU FEEL in the group?

Assessing the output of the group

Describe and **reflect** on your output from the group. Was the output to the standard required by the lecturer? Was the output at a lower standard than you wanted? How could you improve standards in a group next time? Did you feel YOUR output was far higher than expected and how did you feel about that?

Overall

What would you change next time in terms of your behaviour and group processes?

NOTE Remember, if you are being assessed on your reflection of group work or another learning event, you will get good marks for your ability to reflect and *not* whether you got something right or not. This kind of assessment is about you being honest and perceptive enough to see where the mistakes are and how you would deal with it in the future.

End-of-unit/module evaluation

Your tutor will probably give you a form to complete at the end of the course and there will be a space to offer your views on the delivery of the course. Take time to think about this in a truly reflective way and do not just enter comments based on your like/dislike of the tutor or the subject.

Giving feedback to your department/school in a more formal setting

Many institutions have something similar to a staff–student committee that enables student representatives for the year to put their views forward in a more formal setting. Once again, truly reflect on how your year is developing and give your comments to your representative. Try to consider all aspects of the issue you raised so that you are not moaning because things are not just how you like them.

Focus groups and surveys

Sometimes an issue may arise in your department/school and they want to find out your views. In order to do this they can (a) talk to you all as a group, (b) send out a questionnaire or (c) hold a focus group. A focus group is a sample of students from your department, who comment on the issue under discussion and give their views. Take this opportunity again to reflect on the improvements your department is trying to make.

Using feedback to reflect on your development

Feedback from your tutor – be that on your coursework, in class generally, or a one-to-one meeting – is an ideal opportunity for you to reflect on how you are developing. If you are not getting the feedback you need, why not make a note on your coursework to your tutor asking for a specific kind of feedback. This would really show your maturity.

Work-based learning and placements

This will be a more formal aspect of reflection. You will probably be given a learning agreement which will comprise a set of learning outcomes. You will be expected to show, with evidence, how your placement has achieved these learning outcomes. Your ability to reflect on the skills and knowledge you are developing at this time will be crucial.

7 On reflection

Reflection is essentially a strategic thinking tool that enables you to externalise an experience in order to learn from it. Being able to reflect is a skill that you need to learn and it doesn't always come easily. We need to become more observant during a critical learning event (here we are using 'critical' to mean important) in order to process what happened.

The exercises at the end of each chapter in this book are also a small reflective activity and the more you get used to doing these, the more comfortable you will be with reflection in general. Remember, this is a life skill you are developing and as a future business leader it is non-negotiable.

ACTIVITY 4 Upgrade your personal development planner

Grade your confidence on a scale of 1–5 where 1 = poor and 5 = good

My 'reflecting' skills	Confidence level 1–5	Plans to improve
I know why reflection is a strategic tool.		
I know some of the frameworks for reflecting.		
I can work through a structured reflective framework.		

Date: _____

Getting extra help

- Using the internet and searching on 'critical reflection', 'critical thinking', 'reflective practitioner' etc. will bring more information than you can deal with.
- If at all in doubt about any kind of reflection you have been asked to do, clarify what is needed immediately with your tutor.

Summary of this chapter

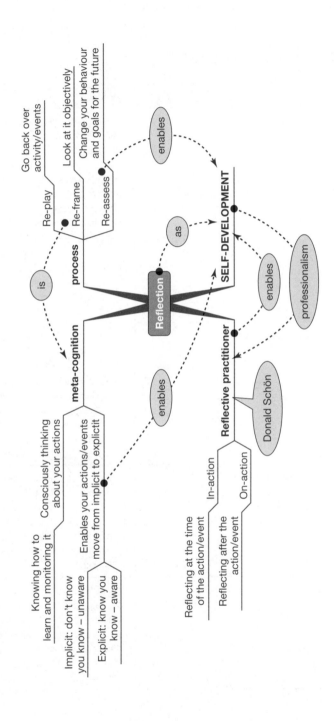

Reflection

process
is

Re-play — Go back over activity/events
Re-frame — Look at it objectively
Re-assess — Change your behaviour and goals for the future

meta-cognition

Knowing how to learn and monitoring it — Consciously thinking about your actions

Implicit: don't know you know – unaware — Enables your actions/events move from implicit to explicit

Explicit: know you know – aware

enables

as

SELF-DEVELOPMENT

enables

professionalism

Reflective practitioner

Donald Schön

In-action — Reflecting at the time of the action/event

On-action — Reflecting after the action/event

enables

Feedback on activities

ACTIVITY 1: Why don't you like reflecting?

What I feel	Usually me	Think again
I find reflection difficult because I don't know what I am supposed to write.		Sometimes it is difficult when you first start to be objective about your own behaviour or the skills and knowledge you have. Work with a friend – you may want to exchange views about each other. Or, if you are reflecting on group work, do the following. Everyone places an envelope with their name on it and puts it on their chair. Members of the group write a comment ('you are good at', 'you could improve') on separate pieces of paper (anonymously) which are put it in that person's envelope. You then open your envelopes in private. This will give you something to consider for your reflection.
I find it a waste of time and it just takes too long.		OK, don't call it 'reflecting', sometimes the word can put you off. Make a list of some important key skills or things you need to know and note whether you can do them *well, OK or poorly* and work out how you can improve. If someone asked you in an interview if you were a good team player, how would you answer? If they asked what makes a good team player, what would you say?
I can't see where I'm developing skills in my courses so how can I reflect on it?		Each course/unit should have a description of what you'll be expected to do along with the assessment. Check the learning outcomes and the assessments (these should include a list of skills you're learning) and from this you can see what skills and knowledge you are developing.
I don't know what to do with my PDP when I complete it.		Your PDP should be part of every year in your degree. In some degrees it is built into the first year and then vaguely mentioned in years after that. Try to keep it up-to-date – this is for you and you can use it to adjust your CV and keep you prepared for those interviews, even for part-time work.

References

- Boud, D., Keogh, R. and Walker, D. (eds) (1985) *Reflection: Turning Experience into Learning*. London, Kogan Page.

- Eliot, T.S. (1944) 'The Dry Salvages' from the *Four Quartets*, available online at: www.tristan.icom43.net/quartets/ [last accessed September 2009].

- Gibbs, G. (1988) This work is now out of print, but you can access it from http://distributedresearch.net/wiki/index.php/Gibbs_reflective_Cycle [last accessed September 2009].

- Goleman, D. (1995) *Emotional Intelligence*. New York, Bantam Books.

- Goleman, D. (2006) *Social Intelligence: The New Science of Human Relationships*. New York, Bantam Dell Publishing Group.

- *InfED The Encyclopaedia of Informal Education*, www.infed.org/ [last accessed September 2009].

- QCA (2001) Guidance on Key Skills Qualifications at Level 4, *Publication of the Qualifications and Curriculum Authority*. London [online] www.qca.org.uk/pdf.asp?/nq/ks/ks_guide.pdf [last accessed 12 December 2001]

- Rolfe, G., Freshwater, D. and Jasper, M. (2001) *Critical Reflection for Nursing and the Helping Professions*. Basingstoke, Palgrave.

- Schön, D. A. (1983) *Reflective Practitioner: How Professionals Think in Action*. New York, Basic Books.

- Senge, P. (1990) *The Fifth Discipline: The Art and Practice of the Learning Organisation*. New York, Doubleday.

11 Approaching numerical problems

The ability to tackle and solve numerical problems is an essential life skill to improve your employability whatever your career aspirations. Technology has made many numerical tasks easier, but the price we pay is that we lose both skills and understanding of the principles of how to approach numerical problem-solving. For your future employers, however, these skills are real assets. In order to be competitive and successful, business has to manage numerical data. While technology addresses many routine aspects of this, it is the human contribution in terms of non-routine problem-solving and true innovation that can make or break a business. Employers expect graduates to be able to rapidly appraise data, discern trends and inform strategic decisions with number-based arguments and business cases.

At university, making sense of numerical data is vital to thinking critically about the research in your subject. Having these skills will improve your grades at all levels of study.

In this chapter you will:

1. consider the types of numerical problem you will meet at university;
2. define what you find hard about solving numerical problems;
3. think about how the kind of numerical questions you meet will change as you progress through your studies;
4. consider how to improve your strategic approach to numerical problems.

If you want to dip into the sections	Page	If you want to try the activities	Page
1 What sort of numerical problems will you find at university?	308	1 Map out the types of numerical problem you will have to work with	308
2 Thinking about numerical problems	311	2 Using estimation	310
3 Preparing yourself to solve …	317	3 Levels of accuracy in your calculations	310
4 Keeping a useful record	319	4 Problems with problems	312
5 On reflection	320	5 Reconsider your problems with problems	317
		6 Steps to success	318
		7 Update your personal development planner	321

Estimate your current levels of confidence. At the end of the chapter you will have the chance to re-assess these levels where you can incorporate this into your personal development planner (PDP). Mark between 1 (poor) and 5 (good) for the following:

I am aware of how I currently think about and approach numerical problems.	I am aware of how the kind of numerical problem I might meet will change as progress through my studies.	I know what a successful strategy needs to be for me to approach numerical problems with confidence.	When I revise a topic I remember what I learnt the first time I worked through it.

Date: _____

1 What sort of numerical problems will you find at university?

We had to do some marked statistics worksheets in class quite early on. I hadn't expected that!
Tammy, first-year Business Studies student

The numerical problems you will encounter will involve:

- **Calculation:** applying specific arithmetical operations, formulae and processes to produce results.
- **Summarisation:** using visual and arithmetical methods to represent key themes and trends from data and results.
- **Interpretation:** using the products of calculation and summarisation, along with critical and logical thought processes, to analyse and evaluate consequences, findings and implications.

Although it depends on your degree subject and the elective unit or module choices you make, you will encounter some of the following types of problem:

- specific problems where you will have to use arithmetic manipulation with, for example, accounting or economics principles and formulae (such as working out depreciation or marginal costing);
- budget management, such as monitoring actual against planned expenditure, or forecasting and informing corrective actions when an overspend looks likely;
- calculating averages and percentages from raw data to identify trends (for example year-on-year changes in tourism levels, or average customer spend on products);
- interpreting and making judgements about the significance of such trends and changes (this links to thinking critically: see Chapter 9, 'Thinking critically');
- analysing, interpreting and evaluating other people's numerical research data (this also links to critical thinking processes: see Chapter 9);
- summarising complex and/or large amounts of data in a meaningful way and using visual methods (graphs or tables, for example) in order to present key findings and trends accurately and concisely.

ACTIVITY 1 Map out the types of numerical problem you will have to work with

Use the list of numerical problems given in this section. Closely read all of the unit/module handbooks for your current term/semester to identify the types of numerical problem you will be working with. Now find a real-world example of each type of problem so that you can relate it to a memorable case or scenario. (You may want to research this online, in the business sections of newspapers or by listening to business reports on the radio or TV.)

See the feedback section for further comment on this activity.

NOTE There are many different types of numerical problem and a study skills book such as this cannot examine their solution methods in detail. There are, however, many good examples of specific subject textbooks that do this well. Ensure that you purchase the recommended texts on your reading lists and ask your tutors for further suggestions if a particular book's style is less suited to your learning preferences.

The next sections consider two general issues that arise whatever type of numerical problem you are approaching: calculator use and number rounding.

Using a calculator

A big question that arises immediately when working with numerical problems is: when should you use a calculator? In most situations you can make that judgement yourself, but you need to check whether your college or university has a policy on calculator use in class test or exam situations. Some of your course units may not be run by your 'home' department within your faculty or in some cases even by the same faculty. In other words, there may be different policies that you have to work across.

If you can use calculators, don't assume that this guarantees accuracy. Bear in mind the **RIRO** (rubbish in rubbish out) principle. If you put all of your trust in the calculator and you make a simple input error (for example, missing out a numeral, putting the decimal point in the wrong place), you will get the wrong answer but probably not question it. Of course, performing 'long-hand' manual calculations can also result in errors, but there is a better chance that you will 'trap' the error when you work manually step by step through the process.

Estimate>Calculate>Compare

To minimise the risk of error in either case, you need to practise 'estimation' whenever you are performing calculations. This lets you establish roughly what the answer should be first so that you can then compare this estimate with the calculated result. Comparing the two for approximate agreement allows you to accept the answer, or recalculate it if they don't compare. If you've ever had to jump across a stream or river to continue a walk, you'll know exactly what this is about: you'll estimate how far you've got to jump to avoid getting wet feet, *before* you jump!

To estimate the result of a calculation you will need, first, to simplify the numbers involved by rounding them up or down as appropriate. Then you apply the calculation to these more manageable numbers. The point of approximation is to get the **right magnitude** and a **rough value** for the answer using figures that are easier to manage quickly, mentally. Read Activity 2 to follow an approximation process.

ACTIVITY 2 Using estimation

Work out the following calculation: what is 48% of 171,320?

To perform this calculation mentally is fairly challenging. However, to estimate the answer, first you might round 171,320 down to 170,000. Next you might round the percentage up to 50 per cent. The **estimate** calculation is then a more manageable 50 per cent of 170,000, i.e. 85,000. So your final, accurate figure will be in the vicinity, in terms of magnitude and value, of this estimate. When you calculate the answer using the actual numbers, you produce a whole figure answer of 82,234. This is close enough to the approximation to give you confidence in the result. If you had mistakenly keyed 117,320 when calculating this, you would have produced a whole figure answer of 56,314. This is significantly different to your approximation and you might be prompted to question it and redo the calculation before committing it to paper.

Hot Tip

On some calculators a key may have more than one function and you need to remember to use the shift key to access the alternative function. Always read the instructions that come with the calculator and practise using it on some simple calculations.

Rounding and levels of accuracy

In Activity 2 the decimal points and fractions of whole numbers have been 'rounded'. One of the things that lecturers find frustrating is that some students calculate to meaningless levels of accuracy, whereas others don't calculate to sufficient levels of accuracy. For example, if 171,320 was the **number** of cars a country exported in a month and 48 per cent was the percentage that came to the UK, the arithmetic answer to full decimal point accuracy is 82,233.6. However, 0.6 of a car is meaningless in this context and you have to make a judgement as to whether you round the figure up (82,234) or round it down (82,233). However, if 171,320 represented the **tonnage** of car exported, then the 0.6 may be meaningful. A **meaningful** answer requires **understanding of context and your judgement** as to what is appropriate in that context. Use Activity 3 to explore this.

ACTIVITY 3 Levels of accuracy in your calculations

1. How would you round the figure for the number of cars shipped to the UK: 82,234 or 82,233? Why have you judged it this way?

2. What level of accuracy would you use in analysing the level of national debt in the UK? How would this compare with analysing individual levels of personal debt?

3. Add your own examples. (These might range from levels of accuracy when estimating your likely shopping bill as you go around the shop, to thinking about levels of accuracy for different purposes in relation to corporate/national data you read about in newspapers.)

To begin with you should find that you are given guidance as to the level of accuracy required in any context. If you are uncertain, ask. In the longer term, as an independent learner, you will be expected to recognise context and apply your judgement accordingly.

Hot Tip

The underpinning arithmetical operations of addition, subtraction, multiplication and division, the concepts of fractions, decimals and percentages, and practices such as estimation are essential tools. If you are rusty, there are several interactive tutorial websites you might want to use: see the 'Consult the following' section at the end of this chapter.

NOTE   Many colleges and universities offer maths support facilities to help with maths and statistics-related questions. However, they are unlikely to offer basic numeracy teaching. If you think you need such help then discuss this with your personal tutor to see if there are any specific facilities in your department or faculty. Alternatively, you can independently contact external organisations such as your local Adult Education provider, learndirect (http://www.learndirect.co.uk/browse/mathsenglish/) or other providers of National Certificates in Numeracy via the Move-on website (www.move-on.org.uk/findatestcentre.asp) to see what course(s) they may be able to offer you.

2 Thinking about numerical problems

*Many students I tutor don't recognise that they need a **strategy** to deal with their approach to any quantitative problem. They either tend to dive in and produce answers without any thought as to their meaning, or they freeze and can't get past first base.*

Tutor's comments.

You will find that your lecturers and tutors often give you a worksheet with a set of example problems so you can check your understanding of a new topic. These can provide you with useful formative feedback about how well you have understood the new material you are learning. However, many of you will be familiar with that feeling when you look at a problem on a worksheet and you just can't think how to begin. You think you understood the lecture but you can't see how to apply your knowledge to get to a solution. Understanding why this can happen may help you to avoid many hours staring at your worksheets with little or no progress. Use Activity 4 to help you start to understand this.

ACTIVITY 4 Problems with problems

Think about a worksheet or problem set you have found difficult during your course so far. What happened? Tick any of the statements below that describe how you felt. Do you want to add any further scenarios to the table?

	✓
1 I looked at the problems and I just didn't know how to begin to tackle them.	
2 I knew how to do the problems but I made errors in arithmetic as I worked, so I never got the right answer at the end.	
3 I knew what I was trying to find but I didn't know how to go about it.	
4 I could do the problem sheet when it was set, but when I came to revise for my exam I had forgotten how I did it.	
5	
6	

See the feedback section for further comment on this activity.

Spending hours staring at the same problem and not getting anywhere or else doing all the problems on a worksheet but getting them all wrong are not efficient ways for you to learn. Getting everything right but then forgetting how you did it later is also frustrating. So how do these problems arise and what can you do about them?

In the next section you will consider the levels of difficulty of different kinds of problems and examine one strategy you might use to manage the development of your approach to numerical problems.

How problems change as you progress

One change you will notice as you progress through your course is that the numerical problems you are set get harder. Whilst this might sound obvious, some students assume that the numerical problem-solving techniques they learnt as beginners will continue to work effectively as their studies progress. To improve your numerical problem-solving skills, a good first step is to understand how the kinds of problems you are given change and how things that are difficult now become routine as they become more familiar to you. Figure 11.1 shows a simplified model of how the type of problems you will be set change and how this relates to a learning cycle.

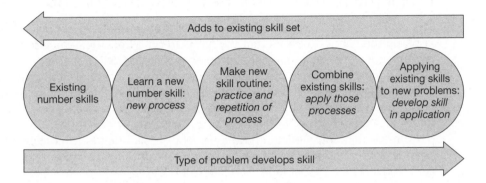

Figure 11.1 How numerical problems change as your studies progress

Problems to develop numerical skills and memorise relationships

Your early school number skills will have concentrated on numeracy and arithmetic. The idea was to teach you relationships between different numbers, such as their products and sums. The problem sets you were given most likely consisted of a lot of very similar examples and the aim was to embed these relationships between different numbers in your memory for later use.

There are many number skills that are useful to remember. You need to be able to recall them instantly while you are trying to solve harder problems as they make your toolkit of what to do. An example from your early schooling is multiplication tables. To begin with you need to learn them, and later you need to have them at your fingertips so you can multiply numbers easily without a calculator. Learning this kind of information often involves a lot of repetition, which some people find tedious. However, it is worth it in the long run because when you are solving harder problems, the arithmetic is second nature and you don't need to think about what or how to do it; you are free to concentrate on the more complex aspects of your problem without getting bogged down. The same will apply to the numerical problems you will encounter on your course. You need to learn the processes of what to do and how to do it through repetition so that you can then move on to thinking about the principles and consequences of the product/answers from those processes. Figure 11.2 visualises this first strategic step in the approach to numerical problem-solving.

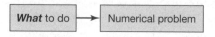

Figure 11.2 Approaching numerical problems: Step 1 'What'

Problems to make new skills become routine

The next step in developing your numerical problem-solving skills involves applying the 'what' to do so that the 'how' to do it becomes embedded as part of your developing numerical problem-solving toolkit. Let's take a very straightforward example in which you are asked to calculate the amount of Value Added Tax (VAT) on something. If you know *what* to do and *how* to do this, you will be able to calculate this every time with little conscious thought. Assuming the VAT rate is 17.5 per cent, *what* we have to do is perform certain arithmetical operations. Your toolkit needs to consistently provide you with the skill of *how* to do the relevant multiplication and division to calculate a percentage. See Figure 11.3.

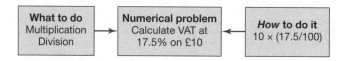

Figure 11.3 Approaching numerical problems: Step 2 'What' and 'How'. An example.

When you first met percentages you solved problems where the objective was simply to find percentages. Now you are starting to apply those tools to deal with more complex numerical problems. If the requirement is to calculate the total retail price of an item including its VAT, this is a (slightly) more complex problem. It still uses the same basic toolkit (in this case addition, multiplication and division) so the 'what' to do is clear, but the *how* to do it needs to be developed before it can become an embedded skill. Again, **repetition** is one of the key things you need to do to achieve this progression and the familiarity that will come from repetition will facilitate understanding the principles of how those tools actually work.

Problems that bring together different known skills

Once you have a good basic toolkit, you solve problems by **applying** your known skills, facts and theory in the right way. You may be told what method to use in the question or statement of the problem. In doing this you are bringing together things you have memorised, things you have practised and some recently learned theory to get a feel for how the new theory works or how it may be applied.

You may have started to solve this kind of problem during your pre-degree studies and you will be expected to develop your ability further to solve similar problems during the early stages of your degree programme. This is the point where you really need to make a transition in how you work. Simply learning numerical problem-solving methods as if they were recipes will eventually lead to poor marks as you need to focus on 'why' the solution works. This is knowledge that takes time and practice to develop and it marks the major difference between study at university and pre-university levels. See Figure 11.4.

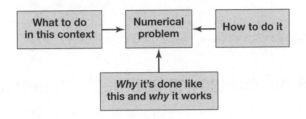

Figure 11.4 Approaching numerical problems: Step 3 'What', 'How' and 'Why'

Problems that require application of known skills to new situations

Even harder problems involve the application of your existing skills and theory to unfamiliar situations. You know the necessary facts and you have the necessary skills and concepts, but you need to learn about the situation before you can proceed.

Once you have understood how your existing knowledge applies to the new circumstances, you need to develop a strategy to solve the problem. In these problems you are not expected to be able to find a solution straight away. These are advanced problems. You need to consider how the unfamiliar situation might resemble a situation you are more familiar with and learn to ask yourself relevant questions to work towards a solution:

- Can you make any valid assumptions about the situation described in the problem statement?
- Which of the theories you already know about might apply?

This may be unknown territory for you, but perhaps someone has published the information you need to make the link. You need to work out how to track it down. Solving these less well specified problems takes persistence and patience, but once you have found a solution to any given problem you are well on your way to also considering this type of problem as routine. To achieve this you are using the same principles and skills of critical thinking that we explored in Chapter 9, 'Thinking critically' and applying the same toolkit of basic questions to break down the numerical problem into its constituent parts. See Figure 11.5.

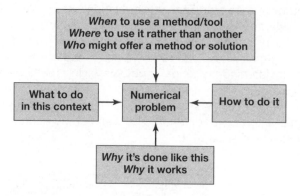

Figure 11.5 Approaching numerical problems: Step 4

A full strategy to approach numerical problems

The key thing the previous sections emphasise is that you need to be prepared to **practise**, through **repetition**, the numeric processes and procedures that will build your toolkit at each stage of your learning. You also need to be **patient** and **persistent** at each step. Albert Einstein is reputed to have said: 'Do not worry about your difficulties in Mathematics. I can assure you mine are still greater.' The inference from this is that whatever threshold of numerical problem-solving skills development we are at, a constant, rigorous strategy will help us build from what we know to move towards where we need to go.

A complete strategy to approach numerical problems in the quantitative subject areas you study requires a developmental framework, such as the one outlined in the previous sections, *and* the consistent application of the right attitudes and behaviours. Figure 11.6 represents this diagrammatically.

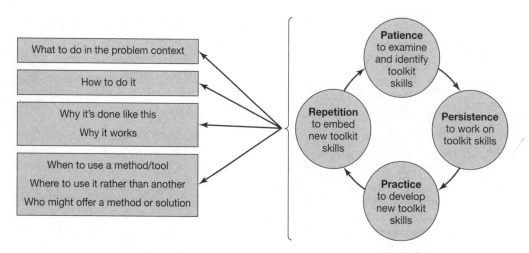

Figure 11.6 One way to visualise a strategy to approach numerical problems

ACTIVITY 5 Reconsider your problems with problems

Go back to your responses to Activity 4, 'Problems with problems' and review the further scenarios you added at that point. In the light of what you have now examined, consider what new scenarios you should add in, particularly in relation to your attitude, behaviour and expectations of yourself when faced with a worksheet or numerical problem. Be absolutely honest! For example, are you *really* **persistent** in your approach: do you do one example, get the right answer and then just leave it at that? Are you **patient**: if it doesn't come right first time, do you convince yourself that it's OK and that you'll come back to it later? Do you really commit as much time to **practice** and **repetition** as you need (and we are not talking about 5 minutes here, but nearer to 50 minutes of real application)?

A word about numerical and logic problems

One area that some students find difficult is distinguishing between number problems and logical problems. While numerical problems require *logical* thinking and many logical problems involve numerical processes, there are some problems that are pure logic. See Figure 11.7. An everyday example of this is Sudoku; even though it 'uses' numbers, solving the grid is a problem of pure logic. If you need convincing of this point, replace each number 1–9 with a different type of fruit and then continue to solve the logic problem with these symbols instead.

If you really are not making progress with a specific type of problem, it is worth considering whether you have identified the problem correctly.

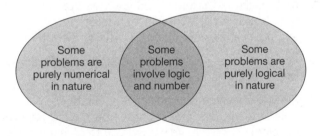

Figure 11.7 Numeric and logic problems

3 Preparing yourself to solve ...

Most lecturers in number-based subjects provide example questions, either from worksheets or from a recommended textbook. These will be based on the kinds of questions you are expected to solve for the assessment. Tackling these problems during the course will help you to judge how you are progressing. Your solutions may also be marked to give you some credit towards your final grade. Activity 5 encouraged you to think more deeply about your strategic approach to numerical problems. Let's look at the actions involved in this in more detail.

The temptation for many students is to rush into an attempt at solving the problems as soon as they are given the sheet. However, you can't solve the problems if you haven't got to grips with the basics of the theory you need to do the job. To get the most from a set of example questions you need to prepare, so it's worth taking a bit of time to do some groundwork before you dive into the worksheet. It will pay off in the long run.

1. Read through the printed notes and your own notes from the lecture. You don't need to try to understand everything at this stage – just get a feel for the main points of the topic.

2. Work through the worked examples in the notes. Don't just read them – try to do the examples yourself using the notes as a guide. Can you see how and why each step is taken?

3. If you have difficulty following the steps and ideas in the example problems, are they to do with the new material or missing background knowledge (e.g. basic arithmetic skills)?

4. Can you find a textbook or a friend to help you with any difficulties? Even if your example problems are to be assessed, it is fine to ask a friend to help you understand the underlying theory or to explain the examples given in the lecture. (Make sure, however, that the final solutions you submit for assessment are your own individual work. [See Chapter 12, 'Understanding academic integrity: learner ethics and plagiarism])

5. Make a list of the questions you need to ask at a tutorial. Try to be specific about what you don't understand. Mark the step in the worked example where you got stuck. Attend the tutorial and ask the questions.

6. Once you feel you have understood the topic reasonably well you are ready to start on the worksheet.

7. Finally, after you complete the worksheet, read the lecture notes again. This time you are making sure you have grasped the detail. Solving the problems should have helped you to gain a more in-depth understanding of the topic.

ACTIVITY 6 Steps to success

Consider the questions below. Are you taking every possible step to help yourself to success? If you give yourself a low score on any of the questions, what might you do about it?

Do you ...	Mark along the line where you feel you are				
	Never				Always
	1	2	3	4	5
Attend all your lectures and tutorials every day?					
Make notes in lectures about worked examples even when you are given printed notes?					
Study regularly, sorting out problems as they arise?					
Work through notes and worked examples noting what you do and don't understand?					
Go prepared to tutorials and ask questions?					
Attempt all the problems on the worksheets?					
Find extra examples in textbooks from the library?					

See feedback section.

4 Keeping a useful record

You may find that you can do a problem when the topic is new, but when you go back a few weeks later you can't make sense of it any more. When you revise your work, it is often difficult to recall the method you used and the steps you took. You can help yourself prepare for an assessment if you take a little extra time to think about your solutions after they are completed and to make notes about this. After all, you wouldn't read a textbook or journal article without making notes to help you make sense of it later. In the future, when you are in the work place, a clear record of what you did and why is essential to professional practice, so get into good habits now. Make sure you write down what you are doing at each step of solving your problem. It doesn't take much extra time to make the notes and in the long run it saves you time trying to puzzle out what you meant when you come back to the problem in the future.

Once you have solved a problem, take a moment to reflect on the solution. You can help yourself even more by making extra notes next to your solution to remind you. You can use the trigger questions below to help you structure these notes:

- Was it hard or easy? Why was this?
- If you had to look anything up or get help: with which bit? What did you find out?
- Were there any particularly tricky bits? Did they relate to new material or gaps in your basic skills (e.g. arithmetic or algebraic manipulation)?
- How was it different to the previous example? Or to the next example?

Jotting these things down next to your solution can really help when it comes to revision. The solution you write is there for you to **learn** from in the future. These notes add enormous value to the effort you have applied – don't waste that effort, or the learning opportunity it represents, by failing to persist just a little bit more.

5 On reflection

This chapter has asked you to consider the approach you currently have to numerical problems and has discussed the different types of problem you might meet. The kinds of problems you are presented with become gradually less well defined and rely more on your own creativity the deeper you go into your chosen area of study. It's no use just diving into a numerical problem and expecting to be able to work out how to do it; you need to prepare yourself by understanding the topic from the notes a little first. Once you have gone to the trouble and hard work of sorting out how to do your problems, you can make it easier to revise by writing down what you got wrong or found hard. The key to approaching numerical problems successfully is to have a rigorous strategy that requires you to think about your attitude and behaviours just as much as about the 'functional' skills to do such problems.

Summary of this chapter

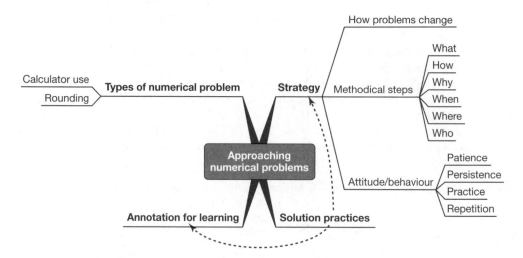

ACTIVITY 7 Update your personal development planner

Reflect on your current abilities and consider what needs to improve. You may want to transfer this information into your institution's personal development planner scheme.

Grade your confidence on a scale of 1–5 where 1 = poor and 5 = good.

My developing skills	Confidence level 1–5	Plans to improve
I am aware of how I currently think about and approach numerical problems.		
I am aware of how the kind of numerical problem I might meet will change as I progress through my studies.		
I know what a successful strategy needs to be for me to approach numerical problems with confidence.		
When I revise a topic I remember what I learnt the first time I worked through it.		

Date: _____

Getting extra help

- Make sure you know when your timetabled tutorials are and attend them regularly.
- Is there a study centre or a system of drop-in tutorials for maths that you can access when you need extra advice?
- Your department may maintain a register of post-graduate students who offer private tuition if you are consider that you need additional help.
- Your university or college may have specific tutorial software on its intranet that you can use independently.

Consult the following

- The BBC Skillswise website offers interactive essential basic number skill content: www.bbc.co.uk/skillswise/numbers/
- The mathcentre website can help if you need to develop or refresh arithmetic and math skills: www.mathcentre.ac.uk/students.php
- Your tutors will recommend subject-specific books. If you wish to get a head start, there are some helpful quantitative methods books, for example: Morris, C. (2008) *Quantitative Approaches in Business Studies* (7th edn). Harlow, Pearson Education.
- You can try a daily Sudoko challenge by going to the Daily Sudoko website: www.dailysudoku.com/sudoku/play.shtml?today=1

Feedback on activities

ACTIVITY 1 Map out the types of numerical problem you will have to work with

This activity gets you to identify the range and type of numerical problems you will have to tackle on your course. It also encourages you to think about such numerical problems in a real-world context that makes sense to you. As a future business leader you will not be solving 'pure' numerical problems, they will be problems with very real, tangible impacts. Seeing this early on helps you to keep a broader perspective when, as will happen, some of the quantitative problems you have to engage with start to challenge you.

ACTIVITY 4 Problems with problems

1. You may need to do some more work understanding the topic before you start to solve the problems. If you have grasped the topic then you may need to do more work to understand the problem itself. Developing a systematic approach to the problem will help with this.

2. You can lose a lot of marks through poor accuracy with numbers of algebra. You need to work on accuracy just as much as you work on new topics.

3. You need to develop some tools to help you find solution strategies. There are some standard approaches that are worth trying when you can't see a way forward.

4. You need to work on the way you record your progress and the challenges you meet as you practise solving problems.

ACTIVITY 6 Steps to success

Do you ...	Feedback ...
Attend all your lectures and tutorials every day?	In number-based units/modules, each section builds on your previous knowledge. It is important to keep up steady progress with your work. If you miss a lot of sessions, through illness for instance, make sure your tutor knows in case you struggle to catch up.
Make notes in lectures about worked examples even when you are given printed notes?	If the printed notes aren't clear about a complete method or approach, write additional comments on them during the lecture.

Do you ...	Feedback ...
Study regularly, sorting out problems as they arise?	This makes it much easier to prepare for exams at the end of the term or semester – revision really is re-vision then.
Work through notes and worked examples noting what you do and don't understand?	You will be actively helping yourself by sorting out problems as they arise, not leaving them until later in the course.
Go prepared to tutorials and ask questions?	There are almost always other students wanting to know the answers to the same questions you have. If you are in a big group you may feel more comfortable asking the lecturer face to face at the end of the session.
Attempt all the problems on the worksheets?	Number-based subjects are learned by doing problems. The problems help you learn the formulae and techniques you need to know, as well as improving your problem-solving prowess.
Find extra examples in textbooks from the library?	In number-based subjects, practice in using new methods, theories and techniques is the only way to really grasp them. The more the better.

Reference

■ Mathcentre: www.mathcentre.ac.uk [(last accessed December 2009].

4 Develop your business writing

Having chosen to study a business-related subject, you may be surprised at how much emphasis your tutors put on your writing skills. In this section we are looking at how you can **improve** your writing to meet your tutor's expectations and to make it more professional.

Once you have graduated, however your graduate career develops, you will need to communicate your ideas to a variety of colleagues and clients. A major part of that communication will be through reports and structured documents where you will be expected to write with clarity and precision. Communication skills are a top skill employers want in graduates; if you develop your written communication skills at university or college then you will impress your future employers.

At university you will be set certain assignments that ask you to reflect on your learning and later, as a professional graduate, you may need to write documents and accounts to support your ongoing professional development. This will call for a reflective style of writing.

The chapters in this section will help you develop these lifelong skills and enable you to take control of the writing process so you can handle all aspects of an assignment, understand about student ethics and academic integrity, and develop your business and reflective writing abilities. These are all key skills for success.

12 Understanding academic integrity: learner ethics and plagiarism

Academic integrity is an aspect of learner ethics and is a code of practice which is strongly adhered to in any type of academic writing. You must ensure that you are able to give recognition to the work of others in your own writing. To do this effectively, you need to understand the rules of referencing your work and how to cite others' work within your text. If students do not reference their work properly they are in danger of being accused of plagiarism. Learning how to reference the work of others demonstrates your background reading.

In this chapter you will:

1. learn that there are different forms of plagiarism;
2. learn steps to prevent plagiarism;
3. learn how to cite references in your written work;
4. learn how to build up a bibliography or reference list;
5. find out how to organise and manage your bibliographic data.

USING THIS CHAPTER

Estimate your current levels of confidence. At the end of the chapter you will have the chance to re-assess these levels where you can incorporate this into your PDP. Mark 1 (poor) and 5 (good) for the following:

I know the variety of ways in which plagiarism can take place.	I know the difference between presentation of in-text citations and references at the end of my written work.	I know the difference between a bibliography and a reference list.	I know the rules for presenting different types of references.	I am able to manage the collection of references in a systematic manner.

Date: _____

1 What is learner ethics?

Understanding learner ethics, academic integrity and how it can manifest itself in us as learners is very important. This is all part of our personal development as professionals to understand that our integrity impacts on our personal and professional lives and that it is something we must be vigilant about all through our lives.

Ethics and the individual

In order to understand learner ethics, it is necessary for us to explore what we mean by 'ethics'. As you think about the concept of ethics you might say, 'it's a gut feeling' and you just know when something is right or wrong. Or you may say it is something that religious people deal with and is part of their moral code. You may also think it is much more concrete and related to abiding by the law. Ethics can, of course, be all of these things, but saying exactly what it is is very difficult. A country's laws, for example, can be considered unethical; we just need to think about South Africa's apartheid laws and Germany's laws in the 1930s regarding Jewish people. It is also legal in some countries to experiment on live animals, devastate rain forests, uproot indigenous people and kill murderers. Which of those do *you* regard as unethical?

So what makes us feel that something is ethical or not? Is it our upbringing, our culture or our personal value system? Behaving within our own value system enables us to have a free conscience, but as soon as we do something outside our value system, we start to feel uncomfortable. We make moral judgements, large and small, all our lives and working within our own value system is a start, but as you have probably realised, we all have differing sets of values that vary within and across cultures. This is one of the aspects that contribute to our stereotyping of people from different cultures and different value systems within our own society.

If ethical decisions cannot be based on our laws, individual values, cultures or religions, then how can we make ethical decisions? Ethicists and philosophers have contributed significantly to this area. From this work we have five approaches to ethical standards that can be used to test our decisions:

1. **Utilitarian approach** (John Stuart Mills) which says that an ethical decision should do the most good and the least harm.

2. **Rights approach** (Immanuel Kant) which says that an ethical decision should result in respect of one another.

3. **Fairness/Justice approach** (Aristotle) which states that we should treat people equally.

4. **Common good approach** (Plato, Aristotle) which says that an ethical decision should be the best one to serve the community.

5. **Virtue approach** (Plato, Aristotle) which says that an ethical decision is one where it is in line with the kind of (good) person I am.

NOTE   There is a great deal of public information about these five standards; this section has simply introduced them in order to alert you to their existence. If you need to learn more about ethical decision making, start with these concepts.

There are some rules, informed by the five standards, that can be applied when we have to make decisions that could have an ethical dimension:

REVERSIBILITY: Would I think this a good choice if I were among those affected by it?

PUBLICITY: Would I want this action published in the newspaper?

HARM: Does this action do less harm than any available alternative?

FEASIBILITY: Can this solution be implemented given resource, interest and technical constraints?

Can you recognise which of the five approaches to ethical decision making are represented by these four simple rules?

ACTIVITY 1 Ethical decision making

We probably all agree that theft is unethical in principle, so take a look at the following and (a) from your gut feeling say if you would be happy doing this or not (be honest) and then (b) apply the four rules of ethical decision making and see if the outcome is different. Say which of the rules was the strongest for you. (c) If your gut feeling said it was not OK but you still felt you would do it, can you say why?

You may regard the decisions below as trivial and in some ways they are. However, their simplicity is deceptive and used here to illustrate that even at quite a trivial level, we are continually making ethical decisions, consciously or not. This exercise starts to make the unconscious process conscious. There is no criticism implied here, but analysing why you do some things and not others when you know them to be, in principle, unethical is valuable and kick-starts your awareness of ethical decision making.

Action	Gut feeling/ generally I would	Ethical rule
1 Stealing something from a shop.	OK/not OK/depends	OK/not OK/depends *which rule?*
2 Borrowing a book from a friend and failing to return it.		
3 Borrowing a pencil from a friend and failing to return it.		
4 Borrowing your friend's car and failing to return it.		
5 Using your friend's ideas on an assignment and not telling them.		
6 Finding a paper on a table in a room that had the answers to a mathematical assignment you had to do.		

NOTE   There is of course one overarching rule which is referred to as the 'Golden Rule' and that comes from the Ethics of Reciprocity and states: 'Treat others as you want to be treated' (Harry Gensler, Philosophy Department at John Carroll University, USA). The Golden Rule features in most of the world's moral teachings and religions.

Ethics and team work

William Frey, Professor of Philosophy at the University of Puerto Rico, has looked into the ethics of engineering and business practices. He also teaches undergraduates and has developed a unit looking at the ethics of team work and within this he expects students to record their group processes with respect to the following four ethical principles:

JUSTICE	How is the work between the team members distributed? Is there a fair distribution of work? How has the team ensured this happens?
RESPONSIBILITY	How has the team allocated tasks? How does the team deal with those who don't work (don't fulfil their responsibilities) and those who do more than their share? Is this work recognised and recorded by the team?
REASONABLENESS	How does the team ensure participation, resolve conflict and make decisions?
HONESTY	How does the team ensure their actions are honest (not corrupt) and that their work is the result of honest endeavour with no cheating?

You may want to look at these criteria in relation to Chapter 5, 'Working in a real and diverse team'. These criteria relate quite well to the set of personal values (see below).

Ethics and professional conduct

In business you will be faced with ethical decision making all the time. How far would you cut corners to make a deal? If you did that, how would you feel if this was made public, if it had been done to you (reversibility) or what harm would it cause you? As a case study you may want to look at the Bhopal gas explosion of 1984 at Union Carbide's pesticide chemical factory where poor decisions regarding safety and plant maintenance, due to saving money, led to the death of thousands.

Although the examples from Activity 1 are fairly insignificant, the more you think about it, the more you realise that you are working with a set of values that allows you to make both ethical and unethical decisions. The degree of harm to another was probably a key factor in your decision making that would tip you over that unethical edge, or not.

Ethical behaviour is closely related to professional conduct and social responsibility.

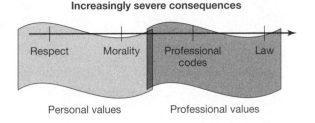

Increasingly severe consequences

Respect   Morality   Professional codes   Law

Personal values   Professional values

Companies that don't have staff that work professionally, i.e. uphold a set of personal values as well as company values, are a liability to their employer. Companies that have staff that are prepared to 'bend the rules' are seen at best to be unprofessional and at worse corrupt and possibly outside the law. Companies with such a reputation also find it difficult to recruit good staff. A company will have a statement of professional conduct and social responsibility, but it is up to the individuals it employs to carry this through.

This may seem a long way from you as a learner, but let's look at this model.

Respect:

- being polite and considerate to your fellow students and tutors;
- turning up on time to lectures and tutorials;
- not talking or disturbing others during class.

Morality:

- not cheating;
- not faking your project results;
- not stealing work from others.

Professional code:

- academic integrity which states that the work is your own and any use of other people's work is fully acknowledged through the referencing system.

Law/regulations:

- rules of your university with regard to the sanctions placed on students who are found cheating or plagiarising. Sanctions usually start with a warning, then move on to a reduction in grade.

Universities have increasing severity of sanctions for students found cheating or plagiarising.

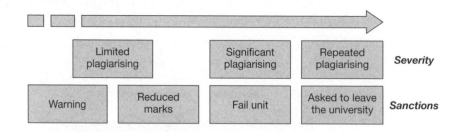

Some understanding therefore of ethical behaviour and decision making is a fundamental value for you as a student and later a business manager. Increasing your awareness of this now alerts you to an important dimension of decision making.

2 What is academic integrity?

Integrity is another aspect of ethics and represents a value system. Academic integrity is a code of practice and a set of professional rules for academia. The ethical dimension is simply not taking the work of others as your own; in essence respecting the work of others.

Your tutors set great store by academic integrity, and two essential ingredients of this are plagiarism and how you reference your written work. Referencing your work properly will substantially ensure that you are not accused of plagiarism. However, some students are genuinely unaware that they have plagiarised work because they do not understand what plagiarism is. Nowadays, it is much easier to inadvertently plagiarise because of the ease of access of information. Andrew Hammett, the principal of Strathclyde University, stated that many students are part of the 'Google Generation' (Universities UK, 2006), which results in the authorship boundaries being blurred, leading to more frequent instances of plagiarism.

Academic integrity is a code of practice which is strongly adhered to in any type of academic work. It relates not only to essays but to PowerPoint presentations, examinations, dissertations, team work and theses.

3 What is plagiarism?

'I didn't know that I'd plagiarised things. I took words and phrases on the internet and rearranged them into my own sentence. I was shocked and humiliated when I was told to go to my tutor about cheating.'

Chris, first-year Geography student

Plagiarism can take many forms. The *Oxford English Dictionary* gives a straightforward definition:

'PLAGIARISM: to take and use as one's own, the thoughts, writings or inventions of another.'

It cannot be stressed strongly enough that plagiarism is grounds for failure on your course. All universities and colleges have regulations which can be found on the main institutional website or translated in your course handbooks and departmental guidelines. The wording is strong to emphasise the severity of the offence.

'A student who is suspected to have committed an act of plagiarism in any element of work presented for assessment shall be subject to the implementation of academic procedures as detailed in the University plagiarism policy. A student who is found to have committed an act of plagiarism will incur a penalty in accordance with the penalty guidelines listed in the University policy. The severest cases of plagiarism may result in the reduction of class of degree award, deprivation of a University qualification, termination of course, and/or the implementation of disciplinary procedures. (University of Southampton)

Many students like Chris, the first year Geography student above, are not aware that they have plagiarised. However, trying to establish your innocence when you are being questioned by your tutor may be difficult. Therefore, it is vital that you are aware of what plagiarism is and its many forms.

ACTIVITY 2 What constitutes plagiarism?

Look at these statements and answer Yes or No or Possibly.

Which of the following are considered plagiarism?	Yes/No/Possibly
I quoted the words from my textbook in my essay.	
I used inverted commas around the words I took from a text I was reading.	
I used different phrases from different sources and put them into a sentence in my essay.	
I used information from an internet page which did not have a title or author so it is not plagiarising.	

Check the feedback section at the end of the chapter to find out the answers.

Patchwriting

The term 'patchwriting', penned by Howard (1995), aptly conjures up what you may be doing when writing. When you are drafting your ideas, you look at information from a variety of sources: books, articles and information which your tutors have given you. You may alter the odd word from lots of sources. This is termed paraphrasing. Some students think that since they have written the sentence, it is not plagiarism. Much depends upon how close your text is to the originals and how you have referenced your work.

Patching together other people's ideas, without some overarching concept of your own, is not a good way of demonstrating your understanding and knowledge. This type of writing can appear to be disjointed and fragmented.

Plagiarism defined

You will be accused of plagiarism if you:

- borrow or copy words from texts;
- copy words/phrases word for word from texts;

- do not identify and acknowledge all your sources of information;
- download text from the internet and do not acknowledge the source;
- play around with (paraphrase) the text of others to create your own text, without acknowledgement;
- copy another student's words without acknowledgement;
- use someone else's ideas or theories without acknowledgement;
- download pictures and diagrams from the internet without acknowledgement.

Fiona Duggan, manager of the Plagiarism Advisory Service (PAS), is convinced that many students in the early part of their studies are not aware that they are committing an offence against academic integrity (Curtis, 2004).

Steps to prevent plagiarism

Sticking too closely to the words of others without acknowledging or referencing the source can be avoided. Problems stem from weak reading techniques as well as inexperienced writing strategies.

ACTIVITY 3 Problems and solutions to plagiarism

Students often lack confidence in their ability to write authoritatively, which is understandable. Look at the following statements and reflect upon which ones apply to you. They could be the precursors to plagiarism.

Do any of these statements apply to you?	YES or NO
I can't possibly write this better than the author.	
When I look at the notes I've made on the texts I've read, I can't remember which are my words and which are ones from the author's text.	
I can't remember where I got the information to make my notes so I can't check whether the notes are in my own words or not.	
My sentences and paragraphs are like a patchwork quilt. That's how I write up my information.	
I think I can avoid plagiarism just by listing every single source in the bibliography at the end.	

Check the feedback section to find out the solutions to your problems.

Although plagiarism is detected at the final stage of your writing, prevention measures have to be taken much earlier on in the writing process. It often begins unwittingly at the note-making stage. Thus, it is vital that you distinguish in your notes direct quotations and your own paraphrasing.

ACTIVITY 4 Can you spot which texts contain plagiarism?

Read the original text and the following samples and identify which are cases of plagiarism.

Original text:

The cognitive resources used in the writing process are considerable, and memory capacity and storage are often overloaded by competing, simultaneous operations. The ability to synthesise information is one of the essential skills required by HE students (Price, 2006).

Version A:

The cognitive-resources used in the writing process are great and memory capacity and storage are often overloaded by many mental, simultaneous operations.

Version B:

In Higher Education, the cognitive resources used in the writing process are often overloaded by competing, simultaneous operations. One of the essential skills needed is to synthesise information.

Version C:

As Price (2006) indicates in her research, writing is complex and draws upon many of the mind's resources. One of the difficulties is that at times the writer runs out of memory space because of the need to do many tasks at the same time.

Check the feedback section to find out which texts would be considered to contain plagiarism.

Hot Tip

You can prevent plagiarism occurring by:

- **organising** the way in which you collect information for your essay or written work;
- developing good **summary skills** so that you put information in your own words and are not tempted to use the words of others;
- getting into a routine of **accurately recording your sources** – either using your own lists or an electronic reference manager software program.

The key to success is management and organisation right from the start. Efficient strategies will support your way of working. To ensure that you develop skills, techniques and strategies, explore the chapters on reading and writing where you will find information to help you to develop methods for recording information systematically which will cut down your chances of plagiarising work.

Many students find referencing confusing, but once you understand the logic and principles you will be able to work it so that you do not lose valuable marks in your essays and project work.

4 Referencing your work

Referencing your work accurately is a means of demonstrating the ownership of information. It is also a way of showing off the background reading which you have undertaken in order to formulate your ideas on a subject. Citing references provides your tutor with confirmation that you are aware of what is going on in your subject and the research field. Thus, it has a positive effect if it is carried out properly.

Referencing is complicated because there are three different systems which are closely related:

- citations within the text (in-text citations);
- references: a reference list at the end of your essay;
- bibliography: a list at the end of your essay.

In-text citations are short but are linked to the reference list or bibliography at the end of your essay. The latter should provide the full information about the item which has been cited within your text.

Is a reference list different from a bibliography?

A reference list and a bibliography serve similar purposes. Some departments use the two terms interchangeably and make no distinction between the two. Some departments have a preference for one or the other, while others like to see both included at the end of your work. You must check your department's guidelines about this.

A **reference list** is a full and accurate description of all of the citations which are found in your text. Some departments prefer these to be listed chronologically. Thus, each item in the list is in the order in which it occurs in your text. This means that it is NOT alphabetically presented but rather the items appear in a numbered list which is cross-referenced with each in-text citation. However, many departments ask students to prepare 'References' at the end of the essay, and these are formatted in alphabetical order.

A **bibliography** has a different purpose. It contains an alphabetical list of **all** the books, articles, internet information, etc. you have used in the process of formulating your ideas and thoughts about the subject. Not all of the items in this list will be given an in-text citation. For example, you might have read a chapter in a book which has helped you to understand a difficult concept but you do not use this as a specified citation in your essay. In a sense it is a hidden resource which helps in the accumulation of your knowledge.

In-text citations, references and bibliographies

Why bother?

These can be used to good effect and can give your writing the academic integrity it needs.

1. They give the reader of your text the opportunity to read the original source for themselves.

2. They provide a record of what you have used in your piece of work, so that you can easily find it in the future – there is nothing worse than knowing you once found something really useful, but you cannot remember where to find it.

3. They give authority to what you are writing and are an excellent way of strengthening your point or argument – if you are making reference to other people's research, it shows you are not just making it up.

4. You avoid the risk of plagiarism. By giving your information sources, you are making it clear that you are not pretending that someone else's work is yours.

5. It is only courteous and polite to acknowledge the work of another person.

When to use?

We have just examined *why* you should use in-text citations and references. The question now is, '*when* should you use them?'

Here are some possible answers:

1. When you have quoted directly from someone else's work.

2. When you have paraphrased the work of another author rather than quoted directly from them.

3. When you have referred to previously published work of your own.

4. If someone's work or ideas are the source of a particular theory, argument or viewpoint.

5. When you have used specific information, e.g. statistics or case studies.

6. When you have used something as background reading, but where it still has influenced your thinking towards your piece of work.

How to present citations and references

The key purpose of any citation and its corresponding reference is to enable you, or someone else who is reading your work, to identify and locate the original text. So, be accurate and give full details. There is a variety of conventions for the compilation of in-text citation and references for bibliographies. Two of the most common are the Harvard system and the British Standard Numeric system.

In-text citation rules: The Harvard system

The Harvard system is the most commonly used. In this system in-text citation must contain the author's name and the year of publication together with page numbers if a direct quotation is used.

For example, Price (2006) states that … or

In a recent study, Price (2006, p.21) demonstrated that 'memory capacity and storage are often overloaded by competing, simultaneous operations'.

As an example of the British Standard System, let's take a book reference with three authors – note that it is a numbering system so we need the number 1.

1. Cowen, M. Maier, P. and Price, G. *Study Skills for Nursing and Healthcare Students,* Harlow, Pearson Education Limited, 2009.

In-text citation possibilities: as indicated/noted by [1] or As … by Cowen, Maier and Price [1]

Hot Tip   Always check with your department or tutor what referencing system they want you to use.

What information is needed for referencing

For each reference which appears in your reference list or bibliography you must record specific pieces of information. It is vital, therefore, that you get into a routine of noting down this information in a safe place. This will be dealt with later in this chapter. The presentation of the information has to be carefully punctuated, and the source of your information will have a different method of presentation. However, the main details which you need to collect are:

- Author's or editor's surname and initials
- Title, with any sub-titles
- Year of publication
- Edition if other than the first
- Location of the publisher
- Name of the publisher
- Name, volume number, part number and pages of the journal
- For electronic resources, the web or email address.

The remainder of this section contains information and examples of how to record a wide range of resources and draws upon the Harvard system because it is the most widely used. You may choose to practise creating references for the types of resource that you feel you will need to use in your studying. The most common sources for students are books, chapters of edited books, journal articles and websites.

Books

Author's NAME and INITIALS
Year of publication, in brackets
Title of the book, underlined or in *italics*
Edition, if other than the first
Place of publication
Publisher

e.g. Smith, P. and Jones, W. (2006) *The art of academic referencing* (2nd Edition) London, Make-up Publishing.

Chapters of edited books

Some books contain chapters which are written by a number of authors. These books will have an overall editor who has compiled the book.

- NAME and INITIALS of author of the chapter
- Year of publication, in brackets
- Title of the chapter
- Title of the book, underlined or in *italics*
- Edition, if other than the first
- Place of publication
- Publisher

e.g. Smith, P. (2005) The role of punctuation in referencing. In Smith, P. and Jones, W. (2006) *The art of academic referencing* (2nd Edition) London, Make-up Publishing.

Note that the main source, i.e. the book, into which you have dipped is still the part which is in italics, NOT the name of the chapter.

Journal articles

Author's NAME and INITIALS
Year of publication, in brackets
Title of the article (not underlined or in italics)
Title of the journal, underlined or in italics
Volume no. and (Part no.)
Page number(s)

e.g. Price, G. A. (2006) Creative Solutions to Making Technology Work: three case studies of dyslexic writers in Higher Education. *ALT-J Research in Learning Technology,* 14 (1), 21–28.

Electronic information

There is a wide variety of types of information which you might use from electronic sources. The main ones are:

- Internet pages (Uniform Resource Locators or URLs)
- Articles in electronic journals
- Electronic books
- Articles in internet journals
- Photographs and images
- Information from your department's virtual learning environment, e.g. Blackboard
- Online newspaper articles
- Personal email correspondence (with a leading researcher, for example)
- Course discussion board information.

As a rule of thumb it is important that you provide the URL address and the date when you accessed the information. The rules for books and journal articles remain the same with the additional URL and accession date.

Referencing a website

Author or source
Year
Title of web document or web page
[medium]

Available at: include web site address/URL (Uniform Resource Locator) and additional details such as access or routing from th ehome page of the source.

[Accessed date]

e.g. Business Ethics Network, 2010 *World Water Day 2010* [Online], Available at: http://businessethicsnetwork.org/article.php/list=type&type-176 [Accessed 10 January 2010]

Referencing a paper from a website

Name/s of authors of paper/article
Title of paper/article
[Online]
Publisher
Available at: url
[Accessed ...]

e.g. Borkowski, Susan, Ugras, Yusuf, J.1998 *Business Students and ethics: A Meta Analysis* [Online] SpringerLink, Available at: http://www.springerlink.com/content/q082t898u7r41274/fulltext.pdf [Accessed 10 January 2010]

Quick overview of components of references

	Author	Year of publication	Title of publication	Title of article/ chapter	Issue
Book	✓	✓	✓		
Chapter in book	✓	✓	✓	✓	
Journal article	✓	✓	✓	✓	✓
Internet	✓	✓	✓		

	Place	Publisher	Edition	Page no.	URL	Date accessed
Book	✓	✓	✓			
Chapter in book	✓	✓	✓	✓		
Journal article				✓		
Internet					✓	✓

Punctuation of citations and references

There is nothing more irritating to your tutor than to have to correct incorrectly punctuated citations and references. It is imperative that you are meticulous in this to maintain your academic integrity. It is also important to ensure that you do not lose vital marks because of silly errors, omissions and lack of proofreading. The examples above provide you with the correct punctuation so it is worth spending a bit of time looking carefully at these and using them as templates for your own work.

In-text citations

Short quotations – single words or short phrases – are included in the body of your text and brought to the reader's attention by single inverted commas. For example, Price (2006, p.21) intimated that a person's capacity, the 'cognitive resources', are significant …

Longer quotations are best delineated from your text by placing in a separate paragraph which is indented. The reader is alerted to the fact that you are going to use others' words by a colon:

For example:

The centrality of using language in particular ways in subject disciplines is at the heart of the sociolinguistic theory relating to discourse:

> 'The student who is asked to write like a sociologist must find a way to insert himself into a discourse defined by this complex and diffuse conjunction of objects, methods, rules definitions, techniques and tools … In addition he must be in control of specific field conventions, a set of rules and methods which marks the discourse as belonging to a certain discipline.'

> (Ball *et al.*, 1990, p. 357)

Note that the quotation was taken from a book by Ball ***et al.*** '*Et al.*' is Latin for and all of the rest. This is a shorthand method of referring to a number of different authors. Note also the punctuation of this.

If you have paraphrased information and ideas which are related to your reading of a specific author, you can strengthen your statement by letting your tutor see that you have read a relevant text. It is important to note where this is located in your text in order to avoid confusion.

For example: Expert writers need to be able to multi-task when they are drafting their ideas (Price, 2006). They have to draw upon …

Notice that the full stop does not come until after the brackets, thus indicating to which sentence the reference is related.

Hot Tip Make sure that the minute you put a citation in your own writing, you also take time to put it into your reference list or bibliography.

5 Frequently asked questions

Do I have to name every author or just the first one in my essay?

It depends upon the location. In-text citations require the first author only followed by '*et al.*' if there are more than two authors (see example above). If there are only two authors, it is usual to name both in your text. For example, Smith and Jones (2006) state …

How do I cite and make reference to something which is referred to in a book or chapter which I have read?

These are called **secondary sources** and the rules for dealing with these are slightly different. The important thing to remember is that you are showing, by your citations and references, which sources you have actually used. If a secondary source is not properly identified it will be taken that you have read the original text or research – which clearly you have not. This would be less than honest.

In-text citation

According to a study by Smith (2001, cited in Jones, 2005).

When you transfer this into your reference list or bibliography, you can only include the Jones (2005) reference because this is the only one which you have actually read. You have not read Smith's original research but rather Jones' interpretation of it. Thus, Smith is a secondary source.

Do I have to keep repeating a citation from the same book?

If you have used the same reference on a number of consecutive occasions in your text then a way round this would be to use the Latin term **Ibid.** which means 'from the same place'. However, it is often not used with the Harvard system.

What if I want to refer to a number of books by one author?

One method of getting around this with your in-text citation is to use the Latin term **op. cit.** which literally means 'in the work cited'. It is often used to refer to the work of the same author which you have last cited. However, it is often not used with the Harvard system.

6 Bibliographic reference management

Remember that your bibliography should include all the resources you have used to complete your assignment. This means both resources you have referred to in the text of your document and relevant background materials that you have used, but not necessarily discussed. It is essential that you keep meticulous records. A little time spent recording the details of a book, a chapter, an article or an electronic reference will be time well spent.

> 'What advice would I give to future students? It's simple. Keep a record of everything you read in the proper format so that you can use it for your written work. I know my tutors kept impressing on us the need to do this but you know how it is. I was in a rush, didn't think I had time to get out my list and update it. I was convinced that I would remember the reference anyway. So what happened? Yes, when it came to using the reference for my essay I didn't have the correct information. I could not believe how much time it took me to find that one single reference.'
>
> Natasha, third-year Fine Arts student

Natasha's experience is important to remember if you want to become an efficient student and prevent the disproportionate amount of time it takes to search for vital references.

There are different ways of recording your information and much depends upon what you prefer. However, if you are doing a lengthy project which will depend upon a lot of references, it is often well worth spending time learning how to manage software which is dedicated to this purpose, such as EndNote or Reference Manager. While such programs can be used in a simple way, they nevertheless take time to master. If your third-year project starts in the summer term of your penultimate year, it is worth setting aside the Easter vacation get to grips with using the software; it will save you much time and stress later on.

Whatever system you use, it is imperative that you record all the details accurately following the system used by your department. Check with your tutor or the course handbook if there is a preferred style and look carefully at the rules which govern this system.

Low-tech management

You can use either a handwritten list or a separate card index system. The handwritten list has the advantage of being accessible at all times if you carry this paper around with you. However, the disadvantages are that the lists are not automatically put into alphabetical order and you will have to enter the separate items into a word document eventually.

Writing out separate index cards is another option. The key to success of this system is that each reference is written on a separate index card. There is usually sufficient space to jot down page references and useful quotations. The advantage this system has over the handwritten list is that you can shuffle them around into alphabetical order manually before you enter the separate items into a word document.

Dedicated bibliographic software systems

If you are using or would like to use a bibliographic database software like EndNote (see below and/or Using Endnote Guide) or Reference Manager, this is an ideal way for you to keep track of your notes and references. Although it does not always appeal to those who are not comfortable with computers, it is nevertheless a time-saving method once you have mastered some of the basics. The advantage of this type of system is that the software will allow you to take notes you can search, add in key words, sort out your lists into alphabetical order, select various types of referencing systems and cite-while-you-write.

Disabled students' allowance

Remember, if you are eligible for this allowance, ask for EndNote or Reference Manager software to be purchased for your sole use. This means that it will be installed on your machine and you will be entitled to individual software training.

Tips for management

- Put everything you read for a topic into your software.
- Key word the items in your database so you can find a group of references on a related topic you are working on.
- Store the hard copies (if photocopies or paper articles) in alphabetical order, but always make a note in the software if you have a hard copy and where it is.
- Finally, if you make notes on something you've read, also record where your notes are on your database entry.

What will electronic bibliographic managers do for me?

The specific program that you choose will depend upon:

- the preferred system used by your department – for example, many medical departments use Reference Manager;
- personal preferences;
- the system to which your university or college has subscribed – many institutions now provide a cut-down version of EndNote for under-graduates which is found on the network system at workstations around your university. It is worth looking into this before you rush out and purchase the costly full program out of your own money.

This sort of software is very powerful and can save much time, providing that you have set it up for your personal use. Many students (and tutors) do not use the full potential of these programs but rather are content to select the features of most use to them.

Common features

You can:

- create a separate reference 'library' for each of your essays;
- add information for each entry – this can be personalised to include key words (for later grouping of references);
- choose the referencing style you need to use (most software provides extensive lists from which to choose);
- see an example of what each item in the list will look like at the end of your writing;
- sort the items in your 'library'. There are many options available for sorting your data so that you can extract the specific items for any written assignment;
- search for authors or key words (if you have meticulously put these in);
- automatically create term lists from the author, journal title and key word fields;
- use term lists which are particularly useful if you regularly consult specific journals, and to ensure that key words are being used con-sistently as an additional research tool;
- use the system with Word so that you can select a reference from your database and cite-while-you-write. This means that the referenc-ing and cross-referencing are carried out by the software, and it can save you time;
- sort your selected bibliography into alphabetical order at the touch of a key;
- import references from electronic sources, provided you have set up your system correctly. This can save time typing in each individual reference.

These are just some of the basic tools available in these systems. However, like all technology, you must set aside time to become familiar with its workings and use it frequently so that you do not forget the procedures for carrying out specific operations

Hot Tip

A comprehensive and accessible booklet on the subject of citing and referencing is 'Cite Them Right' by Pears and Shields (2005). It is inexpensive and provides a wealth of examples of different types of references which might be applicable to your subject.

7 On reflection

Being aware of the pitfalls and the regulations for referencing your written work will ensure that you are less likely to be guilty of plagiarism. An awareness and understanding of the principles behind the regulations is essential. With this knowledge you can begin to appreciate why your tutors are so particular about your referencing.

The essence of this is to organise and manage your time and efforts effectively. Getting into good routines early on in your studies will reap rich rewards and higher grades.

Summary of this chapter

Having read this chapter, you can see that organisation and management play key roles in the way you reference your written work. Knowing the rules for in-text citations and compiling accurate bibliographic data will ensure that you do not plagiarise work.

Summary of this chapter (*continued*)

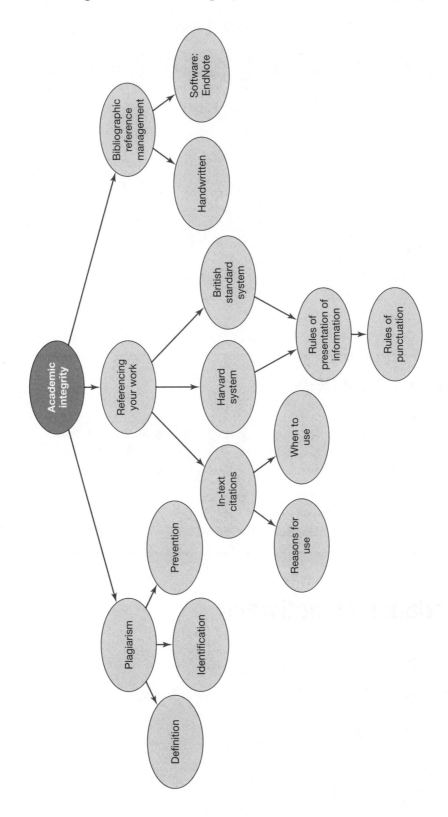

ACTIVITY 5 Update your personal development planner

My developing skills	Confidence level 1–5	Plans to improve
I know the variety of ways in which plagiarism can take place.		
I know the difference between presentation of in-text citations and references at the end of my written work.		
I know the difference between a bibliography and a reference list.		
I know the rules for presenting different types of references.		
I am able to manage the collection of references in a systematic manner.		

Getting extra help

- Go to the students union to find out where to go for skill development. Many universities and colleges have tutors who provide this service.
- Closely examine your department's guidelines to make sure that you are aware of the rules and regulations.

Consult the following:

Pears, R. and Shields, G. (2005) *Cite Them Right: Referencing Made Easy.* (2nd edn) Newcastle, Pear Tree Books.

Feedback on activities

ACTIVITY 2 What constitutes plagiarism?

Look at these statements and answer Yes or No or Possibly.

Which of the following are considered plagiarism?	Yes/No/Possibly
I quoted the words from my textbook in my essay.	YES
I used inverted commas around the words I took from a text I was reading.	Possibly
I used different phrases from different sources and put them into a sentence in my essay.	YES
I used information from an internet page which did not have a title or author so it is not plagiarising.	YES

'I quoted the words from my textbook in my essay.'
If you quote the words of others and do not acknowledge that you have used the words of others, this is considered plagiarism.

'I used inverted commas around the words I took from a text I was reading.'
Just because you have put inverted commas around the quoted words does not mean that you have not plagiarised work. If you have not stated your source as well, this is considered plagiarism.

'I used different phrases from different sources and put them into a sentence in my essay.'
Patching together lots of phrases from different authors and sources without showing the reader that these are not your own words still constitutes plagiarism. Just because you have put the words into your own sentence does not exempt you.

'I used information from an internet page which did not have a title or author so it is not plagiarising.'
Many students think that because there is no obvious author or title to the work they can use such internet information freely. This is not the case. You are still expected to indicate where you got the information.

ACTIVITY 3 Problems and solutions to plagiarism

Do any of these statements apply to you?	YES or NO	Solutions
I can't possibly write this better than the author.		A. Read what the author has said. B. Cover up the text. C. List the key words/ideas in your own words. D. Try to explain it simply in your own words.
When I look at the notes I've made on the texts I've read, I can't remember which are my words and which are ones from the author's text.		There are two solutions to this: 1 Colour code your notes so that you can immediately 'see' which are the notes written in your own words. 2 Improve your summary skills by following A–D above.

351

Do any of these statements apply to you?	YES or NO	Solutions
I can't remember where I got the information to make my notes so I can't check whether the notes are in my own words or not.		The solution to this problem is to adopt a more organised routine to recording your notes. You need to record not just the 'what' but the 'where' – using cards/software/electronic lists will help. See the section on 'Referencing your work' in this chapter.
My sentences and paragraphs are like a patchwork quilt. That's how I write up my information.		First, develop your reading skills in getting the global picture. Second, become a more critical and active reader of information. See the section 'Taking a critical look at a text' in Chapter 7.
I think I can avoid plagiarism just by listing every single source in the bibliography at the end.		You need to incorporate your acknowledgements into what you are saying to avoid plagiarism. Go to the section on 'Referencing your work' for examples of how this is done effectively

ACTIVITY 4 Can you spot which texts contain plagiarism?

Read the original text and the following samples and identify which are cases of plagiarism.

Original text:

The cognitive resources used in the writing process are considerable, and memory capacity and storage are often overloaded by competing, simultaneous operations. The ability to synthesise information is one of the essential skills required by HE students (Price, 2006).

Version A:

The cognitive-resources used in the writing process are great and memory capacity and storage are often overloaded by many mental, simultaneous operations.

Comment: This is clearly plagiarism. Even though there has been some attempt to substitute some words, the original author's sentence structure is intact and no acknowledgement has been given.

Version B:

In Higher Education, the cognitive resources used in the writing process are often overloaded by competing, simultaneous operations. One of the essential skills needed is to synthesise information.

Comment: This is still plagiarism. Although the writer has moved the sentences around a little, it is too close to the original and this version does not acknowledge the source. In addition, this version does not use inverted commas to identify the original text: e.g. 'cognitive resources used in the writing process', 'overloaded by competing, simultaneous operations', and 'to synthesise information'.

Version C:

As Price (2006) indicates in her research, writing is complex and draws upon many of the mind's resources. One of the difficulties is that at times the writer runs out of memory space because of the need to do many tasks at the same time.

Comment: There is no plagiarism with this version. This version clearly indicates the source and appropriate paraphrasing of the original has taken place.

References

- Ball, C., Dice, L. and Bartholomae, D. (1990) 'Developing discourse practices in adolescence and adulthood.' In Beach, R. and Hyndes, S. (eds) *Advances in Discourse Processes.* Norwood, NJ, Ablex.

- Curtis, P. (2004) 'Quarter of Students "plagiarise essays"' [Online], The *Guardian*, Available at: www.guardian.co.uk/education/2004/jun/30/highereducation.uk1 [Accessed 13 January 2010].

- Frey, W.J., Ethics of team work, http://cnx.org/content/m13760/latest/ [last accessed 28 October 2009].

- Gensler, H., The Golden Rule, www.jcu.edu/philosophy/gensler/goldrule.htm [last accessed 28 October 2009].

- Howard, R.M. (1995) 'Plagiarism, authors and the academic death penalty', *College English*, 57, 788–806.

- Price, G. A. (2006) 'Creative solutions to making technology work: three case studies of dyslexic writers in Higher Education', *ALT-J Research in Learning Technology, 14(1), 21–8.*

- Universities UK (2006) 'Conference to tackle university plagiarism problem' [Online], *Education Guardian*, Available at: www.guardian.co.uk/education/2006/oct/17/highereducation.uk1, [Accessed 13 January 2010].

13 Taking control of the writing process

Writing essays, reports, literature reviews and a variety of other documents is an essential part of your studies. Not only do you learn the subject by writing about it, you also learn to convey what you know in a logical and coherent manner that is appropriate for those going to read your work.

In this chapter you will:

1. learn to manage the writing process effectively;
2. know how to unpack a question or title so you can focus your answer;
3. develop a technique for categorising and recording information;
4. know how to effectively edit and proofread your work.

USING THIS CHAPTER

Estimate your current levels of confidence. At the end of the chapter you will have the chance to re-assess these levels where you can incorporate this into your personal development planner (PDP). Mark between 1 (poor) and 5 (good) for the following:

I know how to manage the writing process effectively.	I can analyse what is required of a question or title correctly.	I have a system for collecting relevant information linked to a title or essay question.	I know how to effectively edit and proofread my work.

Date: _____

1 Becoming a writer

Being able to write is much more than writing the way you speak and much more than just knowing the grammar of a language. Being able to write well is a series of demanding intellectual processes where you need to decipher the question or title you have been given, know how to break that down and collect the relevant information, categorise the information you have, plan a structure, start writing, edit and revise. This is definitely not a simple activity, which is why you read books like this and attend writing classes.

In this section we shall briefly look at the characteristics of expert and novice writers, recognise the writing process and understand how to decipher that question in order to get the marks you deserve. Misreading the question or not writing 'on target' is one of the most common errors for poor marks in student work.

Recognise expert and novice writers

Researchers Bereiter and Scardamalia have spent the past 30 years exploring what makes a writer an expert writer. They have examined how schoolchildren and academic writers go about the process. One of the interesting findings is that expert writers manage their writing process differently from novice writers (Bereiter and Scardamalia, 1987). Novice writers adopt a linear approach to their writing and tend to take each of the writing process elements in turn (see Figure 13.1). The reason they do this is because they are not at the stage of managing and controlling more than one element at a time, and for example may gather information for a document without giving thought as to how they are going to use the information at a later stage in the writing process.

Expert writers keep in mind a mental map of the finished product or essay while they are gathering information and writing a draft. They keep moving

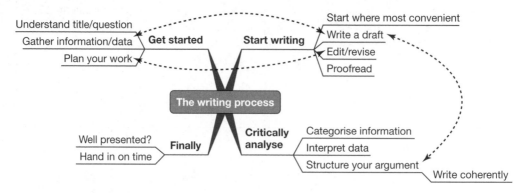

Figure 13.1 Understanding the writing process

backwards and forwards through the various activities in the process with ease and skill, and with practice, so will you.

ACTIVITY 1 Do you have novice or expert writer characteristics?

Novice writer	Mark along the line where you feel you are					Expert writer
	1	2	3	4	5	
I don't read very much.						I read as much as I can to gain an overview.
My reading is mainly from websites.						My reading is from books, articles and websites.
I often read something, take a few notes and then start writing.						I read, take notes, plan a structure (even if it changes later).
When ideas come to me while writing I just fit them in as I write.						I make a note of ideas that come to me while writing so I can fit them in in the correct place.
When I write, I usually just paraphrase what I've read.						I paraphrase and critically challenge or evaluate what I've read.
I never need to make a draft copy. I can hand my work straight in.						I usually write several drafts before handing it in.
I never or rarely proofread or edit my work.						I always proofread and edit my work – often several times.

See the feedback section at the end of the chapter.

How do you rate yourself? Check the expert writer characteristics and use this book to improve yourself as a writer.

Understand the writing process

It is easy when writing something to get wrapped up in the small detail and forget the larger picture. It is important to understand and take control of the whole writing process in order to stay on top of your work. Figure 13.1 gives you an insight into the writing process.

To get started, the first things you will have to do are:

1. **Understand the title given**. The title you are given provides the framework and focus within which to work – see 'Crack the code' below.

2. **Gather information and data**. You will need to have done some research and read key texts.

3. **Plan your structure**. You may not get the exact plan at the beginning, but it is a plan for you to start from, even if you make changes later. Starting without a plan or a structure will make it more difficult for you to structure your thoughts and your reader will feel that your work is incoherent and rather random. This is the most common criticism of students' writing – see Chapter 14, Section 3.

Once you get the first three steps sorted out, the other aspects of the process will be up to you and you will find yourself shifting between the writing, drafting and editing activities. Like expert writers, you will also develop a more sophisticated way of working to respond to the more complex needs of writing at university.

Crack the code: unpacking the title or question

When you have been given a title to work with, it is important that you are able to 'decode' it effectively so that what you write is 'on target'. If you are able to write 'on target', i.e. answer the question **asked**, you will gain good marks. Most lecturers complain that students haven't answered the question properly, so take time to fully understand the title and focus your research and answer.

Understanding the question or title

Fully understanding the title and 'cracking its code' will help you to:

- narrow your research and enable you to focus your reading more carefully;
- look for the right evidence and information to include in your work;
- Answer exams questions effectively.

If you are not sure what you are supposed to do when you read the title, you need to develop some strategies to help you to decipher just what it is getting at and what is expected of you. The BUG technique can help you do that. This stands for:

Box Put a box around action words. These are words in a title that tell you what you have to do, e.g. 'Explain', 'Evaluate', 'Analyse', etc. These are important words because they are telling you something about the type of structure expected for your work.

Underline Underline the key words in the question. This will not only help you sort out the content expected but will also tell you any limitations, e.g. only a specific time scale or one facet to be analysed.

⬅━━━━━

Glance back to check Have you missed out any words which are important and change what you have to do?

The BUG is a system developed by Geraldine Price in response to concerns expressed by university students (Price, 2001). It has been used successfully by hundreds of students in different subject areas. Here is what a student had to say:

> *I used to frequently get comments like 'you have not answered the question' from my tutors. I couldn't understand what they meant because the way I read the essay title, I thought I **had** done what was asked. When my tutor told me I wasn't tuning myself into the language academics use and showed me the BUG, I found that at last I had something which I could use for any essay title or exam question. It's brilliant and saves so much time.*

Dave, second-year Mechanical Engineering student

The reason it is important to **box** and underline specific words is that it helps differentiate the function of the language used. It is easy to pick out the type of essay or question required because the clue word(s) is boxed. This also serves as a quick reminder when you come back to the title at different times.

If you go through the process of **underlining the key words**, you will have had to weigh up which words you think are important and also eliminate words which are not so vital. By doing this activity, you will have started the thinking process and will be analysing the language that will help you get to the heart of what is required. Similarly, the physical act of underlining chosen words helps them to stand out so that they act as memory joggers later on when you are embroiled in your sentence construction and writing – a time when you could forget your way and wander from the point.

The ⬅ **'glance back'** is the part which is often overlooked by students anxious to get started with the essay. However, this is the part which helps you to develop critical skills. More importantly it is a self-check to ensure that you have not got stuck in a 'thinking rut' and taken things for granted. This makes you check that you have done the job properly.

Unpacking your essay title: BUG in practice

Let us explore how this works with some illustrative essay titles across some business and management subject areas.

1. Compare and contrast the benefits of the HR function.
2. Assess the viability of BPR as a change method in the not-for-profit sector.
3. Analyse the potential for growth in one tourist sector studied in this unit.
4. Describe the UK's potential for the generation of renewable energy.
5. Is continuous economic growth sustainable?

Let's take essay title 1: *Compare and contrast the benefits of the HR function.*

The first thing we do is to BOX the action words and in this example they are: **compare and contrast**. This tells you immediately how to structure your essay. You know you have to look at various HR roles and weigh up the pros and cons. It will be important therefore for you to know how you are going to structure your argument and how you are going to possibly group different roles so you can tell 'your story'.

Next we **underline** the key words in the title and these are the HR function. This tells you the subject area where you will do your research. Many students would have compared and contrasted the different roles and not got many marks because they failed to see other key words, namely, 'the benefits of'. When you **glance back** that is when you would pick up 'benefits of' if you had not spotted it earlier.

1. In this essay you need to know what the HR function is, but the key aspect for getting good marks will be how you structure your argument in relation to the 'benefits'. You should get some clues from your lectures. However, if you don't you will need to define how you are going to deal with this. You may want to consider the benefits, for example, in relation to a specific role of the HR function, showing how it makes it less or more beneficial for a particular use. This essay title could be made more explicit, for example: *Compare and contrast the benefits of the HR role in SMEs and global corporations.*

Hot Tip

It is worth spending time solving the language of the title – the key to good marks starts with cracking the code of the essay title. **Remember to also use this in exams.**

Clarifying the 'instruction words' in an essay or exam question

As a general guideline the following definitions give an indication of what you are expected to do and what sort of essay you are supposed to be structuring. The list below gives some of the most frequently used terminology. It gives general guidelines for working out what kind of essay is required. You are advised to check with your department, as some terminology is used in a very specific way by different departments.

Account for	Give the reason for. Don't confuse this with 'Give an account of' which is asking only for description.
Analyse	Identify the main ideas in depth, showing why they are important and how they are connected.
Assess	Discuss the strong and weak points of the subject. Put your own judgement clearly in the conclusion.
Comment	State your views on the subject clearly. Back up your points with sufficient evidence and examples.
Compare	Look for similarities and differences.
Contrast	Show how the subjects are different.
Criticise	Give your opinion/judgement about the merit of theories/facts; back this up by discussing the evidence or reasoning involved.
Define	Give clear, concise meanings. State limitations of the definition.
Describe	Give a detailed or graphic account of how something is or how it works.
Discuss	Give reasons for and against; examine implications.
Evaluate	Weigh things up; look at the strengths and weaknesses and assess.
Examine	Look closely at all aspects of the topic.
Explain	Give reasons for something.
Illustrate	Make clear by the use of examples/diagrams; clarify points.
Interpret	Express in simple terms. You are usually expected to include your own judgements.
Justify	Show adequate grounds for decisions/conclusions/ideas/theories.
Outline	Give the main features or general principles of a subject – should not include all the details.
Prove	Establish that something is true by presenting factual evidence or giving clear, logical reasons.
Relate	Show how things are connected to each other; how they affect each other.

Review	Make a survey of something.
State	Present brief, clear information.
Summarise	Give a concise account for the main points – should not include details.
Trace	Follow the development of a topic.
To what extent …	Another way of saying evaluate but suggests that you bring out how much (or how little).

Sometimes the action word may be missing and you have to make a judgement yourself (or clarify with your tutor) as to what is meant. The essay title above '*Is continuous economic growth sustainable?*' lacks an instruction word. Typically the 'hidden' action word here is *discuss* or *evaluate,* which you can assume at the end of the question, e.g. '*Is continuous economic growth sustainable? Discuss.*'

ACTIVITY 2 Debugging the question or title

Look at the essay titles above and complete the following:

- Apply the BUG technique on the titles.
- Identify what you should do to get good marks.

See feedback section.

You can do this exercise **even if you don't know about the subject**. You are expected just to unpack the title and see what would be expected of you.

Having worked out what your tutor wants in the essay, it is important to develop efficient ways of gathering information so that you group and categorise information/ideas/arguments at an early stage. Doing this systematically will help you join up your thinking and enable you to write coherently.

2 Gathering information

Some students spend too much time and effort on this part of the writing process. It is easy to get stuck at this stage as you may feel you need to keep reading to understand more before you can start writing. Try to make sure that you streamline this activity and then have the CONFIDENCE TO STOP.

In this section you will identify how you gather and record your notes and then discuss a structured way of categorising and recording information that maps on to your question or title.

ACTIVITY 3 How do you gather information in preparation for writing?

Ask yourself:

1. Do you spend a lot of time gathering information for an essay?   Yes | No

2. Do you find that you have gathered information that is
   irrelevant or wandering off the point?   Yes | No

3. Do you find it difficult to decide what is needed from the
   information you have?   Yes | No

4. Do you end up with lots of notes and spend too much time
   picking out information that you need when you come to write?   Yes | No

5. Do you feel overwhelmed by the amount of notes you have made?   Yes | No

6. Do tutors comment that you have not answered the question and
   that there are irrelevant sections/information in your work?   Yes | No

See feedback section for some help.

Categorise and record information using a matrix

To overcome some of problems listed above, you need to develop a system. One system you can use employs the matrix or a grid which can:

- help you categorise and compare information;
- help prevent copying out word for word what is in books and journals because there is a limited space available for making notes;
- prevent plagiarism if you do not copy out word for word information into your matrix;
- develop your summary skills;
- be useful for those who like to see an overview of information;
- be very good for those of you who have difficulty with sequencing and structuring your work because once you have your information in this format you can then order the information as you wish.

Link the matrix to an essay question or title

Let's use the title which was used earlier to unpick the language.

Compare and contrast the benefits of the HR role.

Your 'evidence' can be collected from different sources and as you find information on the various roles you can place your summarised bullet points in the most appropriate part of the grid.

The HR role

Keep this title in mind so you remember what it is you have to focus on.

Criterion/focus for your comparison e.g. *in SMEs*			
The HR role	**Pros***	**Cons**	**Short reference** to remind you where this is from.**
1			
2			
Your quick summary/overview/observations***			

NOTE   * The pros and cons will depend on the criteria that you select – you may not be able to decide that until you have done sufficient reading. Your lectures should also indicate the focus you should be taking.
** Remember that all your notes should have the full reference. See Chapter 12.
*** Adapt your grid to suit your question and how you work best.

It is important to use the language of your question in your matrix. This will act as a constant reminder of what you are supposed to be finding out and keep you on track. Set up the grid BEFORE you start your information gathering and reading so that you can focus better. This means that as you conduct your background reading, you can decide which box the information goes into.

If you are using printouts of e-articles from your university website, you can colour code the information so that it fits into your matrix or grid. For example, all HR roles could be highlighted in a specified colour, which then gets transferred to your grid. This way you can quickly identify and categorise information from an article or chapter to suit your purpose.

If you are concerned about how to get your ideas to hang together in paragraphs, you might like to see Chapter 14 'Improving your business and management studies writing' where more detailed information about writing is discussed.

3 Making changes and spotting errors

Having made up a comprehensive matrix of evidence for your essay you are now ready to manage the drafting and editing stages. Are you aware that these are different activities? Some students start to compose or draft their ideas into prose and at the same time edit what they are writing. For novice writers, it helps to keep these activities separate. Some students have said that they don't have the luxury of time to go through the drafting process and then go through the whole essay again editing what has been written. It is **not** a luxury. Students who try to combine these activities are often unaware of the purpose of the two processes. Trying to cut corners by combining these activities may lead to a drop in the quality not only of your sentence and paragraph structure but also in terms of the overall structure of your essay. Go back and see how you responded to Activity 1.

In this section you will recognise the importance of editing and proofreading your work. This is a task that many students avoid, but which is such an essential stage for the expert writer.

Draft

Drafting is often referred to as the composing part of the writing process. At this stage you are ordering and structuring your ideas. It should be considered as the first stage of your finished product. During the drafting phase you have the chance to get your initial thoughts into sentences and paragraphs. When you are writing your draft, it can be enough of a struggle just getting the ideas down in the right order. Do not add to it by worrying too much about finding the right word or a particular reference. In fact, when you're stuck, it is often better to leave a gap and fill it in later. If you do this, you must develop a consistent technique that enables you to quickly spot where you have left unfinished parts. You can use the highlighter function in a word processor and then visually go through to see where the gaps are. Alternatively, you can use letters or symbols, for example XXX is ideal as no word has three consecutive Xs and therefore you will pick up your gaps easily using the 'search' function. After XXX you can always put a note to yourself to remind you what it is about. Remember to devise a method that will best suit your working style.

Edit and proofread

Editing and proofreading are very similar and often carried out as one process when it is your own work. Proofreading is simply going through your work and detecting errors and does not necessarily involve any rewriting or major editing work. Generally, the nature of errors is grammatical, spelling or formatting. Editing, meanwhile, involves not only correction but also a reorganisation of ideas or a rewriting of parts to make it flow better.

When you edit, you are refining your work and when you proofread you are searching out 'surface' errors.

In order to edit or proofread your work, you need to get some distance between you as the writer and you as the editor; do this by leaving your work for a day or two and coming back to it (build this into your time management). Many people find it helps to print out the first draft and mark it up in a different coloured pen. That way you can choose the alterations you would like to make without losing sight of the original text. Read the essay as if someone else had written it. Now is the time to check that you have included all the references you need and filled in any blanks that you left in your draft. When you are happy that you have marked up all the changes which you can cope with, go back and edit the document.

Checklist for editing and proofreading

This is a complex activity and you will find you are switching between macro concepts, such as 'is this relevant to the question set?' and micro activities such as grammatical error spotting. When you carry out this activity, decide whether you are working at macro or micro level as switching between the two is less productive and you could miss things. This will mean of course, reading and rereading several times. Use the questions in the table below to guide you.

Macro level (editing)	**R**elevance	■ Is my analysis of the topic correct? ■ What can be deleted as it is not relevant to the topic?
	Organisation	■ Is this the best way to structure the sections? ■ Can I move paragraphs/sections around for more clarity?
	Coherence	■ Does the information flow well between sentences? ■ Do the first two sentences of a paragraph develop the idea within that paragraph? ■ Do the paragraphs link well?
Micro level (proofreading)	**G**rammar +	Have you checked: ■ spelling ■ grammar (read aloud to hear grammatical errors) ■ abbreviations (do you say what they stand for?) ■ labelling (figures, equations, diagrams?) ■ contents page if necessary ■ references ■ Your name, and title of work

Using the checklist above, carry out some proofreading on your own work. For small samples of text just work at the 'C' and 'G' levels.

How to spot your errors

You can of course use word-processor functions to spot grammatical and spelling errors. However, do check as sometimes the program does get it wrong for your context. Generally Microsoft Word, for example, will tag words as misspelled if they do not conform to American spelling. Similarly, the program does not like the use of the pronoun 'which', which is used in UK English grammar and offers 'that' instead. Overcome this by setting your system to UK English. To do this go to the top menu in an open document and select the button marked **Tools**, then **Language** then **Set Language** (for a Microsoft Word document) to UK English.

In addition to a word-processing program you can always read your work aloud. By reading aloud you slow down the speed of reading and because you can HEAR what you say, you can detect errors better. This is particularly true for grammatical errors or where your line of argument is disrupted. Of course, you could let the technology help you. Using voice-recognition software can be useful for those who prefer to work alone. You can listen to your sentences and paragraphs being read aloud to you by the computer so that you can hear whether your work makes sense.

Proofreading 'buddies'

These may be difficult to find, especially from your own year group because of the work pressures of your fellow students. However, it may be a useful service that you and a group of friends can provide for each other. You have to decide on a mutual deadline and place to get together to form a proofreading group to critically examine each other's work and make helpful suggestions.

Get a proofreading 'buddy' to read your work aloud while you listen for errors in construction and structure. You have to really trust your buddy and not feel embarrassed or threatened as they read your work while you are sitting next to them. This often appeals to auditory learners who can spot their own errors when they hear what they have written.

Learning from errors: frequency patterns

If you want to improve your writing, you need to reflect frequently upon your writing. It is frustrating and time consuming to keep making the same errors. Therefore, you ought to reflect upon the types of errors you make so that you can make a difference in the future. Look for spelling error patterns – do you frequently get certain words incorrect? Do you often miss off the endings of words or the middle bits? By findings patterns of errors you will get a focus on what you need to tackle to improve.

If you know you have persistent problems with spelling, you may want to invest in software that can help you. The student support services at your institution should be able to give you advice. It is also good to identify those words you consistently misspell and devise a way of trying to remember their spelling. Take care to master everyday words that you tend to misspell as tutors get particularly irritated by this, e.g advice/advise – practice/practise. It gives a bad impression to your tutors who are marking your work. Finally, really get to grips with the correct spelling for the technical words in your field. If they are not spelled correctly, the quality of your work (whether correct or not) is put into doubt.

Hot Tip

Remember a 'noun' represents a THING and a verb an ACTION. Sometimes words look alike but they have a different function:

AdviCe is a noun, e.g. The advice you gave me was excellent.
AdviSe is a verb, e.g. I was advised well.

Trick to remember

'**C**ent' is a noun, so is advice, practice.
'**S**ent' is a verb, so is advise, practise.

Now devise a way to remember the difference between: *effect* and *affect*, *stationery* and *stationary*.

---

4 On reflection

If you explore how you take control of the writing process, you will be well on your way to becoming an expert writer. Taking the pragmatic approach set out in this chapter will make a difference not only to the quality of your work but also to your time management.

Excellent writing relies upon your organisation and management of the whole process and not just on digging out the information. If you take control of the process from the moment you are given the title, you give yourself a better chance of producing coherent and critical work (see Chapter 14 for writing critically and developing coherence).

Summary of this chapter

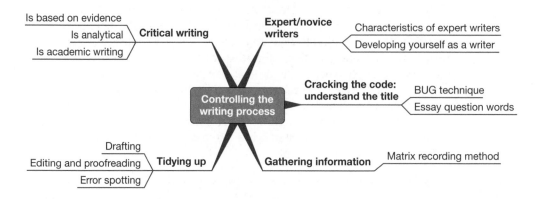

ACTIVITY 4 Update your personal development planner

Having read this chapter, you can see that organisation and management play key roles in academic writing. From the moment you receive an essay or report title to the time you hand it in, you need to be in control of the process. Using the personal development planner below, reflect on how you can take control of the writing process and how you intend to change and adapt your habits so that you can spend your time more expertly. You may want to transfer this information to your institution's personal development planner scheme.

Grade your confidence on a scale of 1–5 where 1 = poor and 5 = good.

My developing skills	Confidence level 1–5	Plans to improve
I know how to manage the writing process effectively.		
I can analyse what is required of a question or title correctly.		
I have a system for collecting relevant information linked to a title or essay question.		
I know how to edit and proofread my work effectively.		

Date: _____

Getting extra help

■ Go to the students union to find out where to go for skill development: this can cover all aspects of writing from grammar to spelling, and proofreading to assignment preparation. Many universities and colleges have tutors who provide this service.

■ If you are unsure about what you have got to do, make an appointment to see the academic tutor who set your essay title. Make sure you have given some thought to the possible ways of interpreting the question so that you have specific questions to ask, and it does not look as if you want them to help you write your essay.

Feedback on activities

ACTIVITY 1 Do you have novice or expert writer characteristics?

Novice writer	Mark along the line where you feel you are					Expert writer
	1	2	3	4	5	
I don't read very much.	If you don't read much, it will be difficult to form arguments and write properly.					I read as much as I can to gain an overview.
My reading is mainly from websites.	If all your references are from websites, your lecturer will know that you are not getting to grips with the topic. Your reading should be a mixture of websites (properly referenced), books and articles.					My reading is from books, articles and websites.
I often read something, take a few notes and then start writing.	Resist reading and writing in one sitting. Read and take notes, collect your notes and from that plan what you want to say. Give yourself a reading limit, read key texts and then work out what you want to say. Make sure all your notes are fully referenced.					I read, take notes, plan a structure (even if it changes later).
When ideas come to me while writing I just fit them in as I write.	It is very obvious to your lecturer if you are coming up with ideas while you write. It is so obvious it almost jumps off the page and can disturb your flow. When you have a good idea, make a note of it and when you edit, see whether it fits in properly. Or, if it is a really good idea, stop and reassess your plan.					I make a note of ideas that come to me while writing so I can fit them in in the correct place.

Novice writer	Mark along the line where you feel you are					Expert writer
	1	2	3	4	5	
When I write, I usually just paraphrase what I've read.	*Novice writers tend to limit their writing to paraphrasing what they have read, that is, being simply descriptive, while more experienced writers will take a more critical look at what they are reading and evaluate in the light of evidence. This is a premium graduate quality skill. Look at the section on critical writing in Chapter 14, 'Improving your business and management studies writing'.*					I paraphrase and critically challenge or evaluate what I've read.
I never need to make a draft copy. I can hand my work straight in.	*No writer worth his or her salt would dream of handing in the first draft of their work. You have to build in time for editing and refining your work. It always shows.*					I usually write several drafts before handing it in.
I never or rarely proofread or edit my work.	*Without proofreading you will hand in work with silly and annoying mistakes. You will not have checked the formatting so it will also look messy. As above, build in time to do this.*					I always proofread and edit my work – often several times.

ACTIVITY 2 Debugging the question or title

Let us explore how this works with some essay titles across science and engineering.

1. *Compare and contrast the benefits of the HR role.*
   Already analysed.

2. *Assess the viability of BPR as a change method in the not-for-profit sector.*
   The action word is '*Assess*' where you need to look at the arguments and develop your own judgement, given the evidence. You need to research the evidence in relation to BPR use in different contexts and the characteristics of the not-for-profit sector in relation to this. The key to success in this essay is your analysis of the **viability** of this change method. How will you 'measure' viability and what does the literature say about that?

3. *Analyse the potential for growth in one tourist sector studied in this unit.*
   The action word is '*Analyse*' where you will be expected to identify the main ideas in depth and show why they are important and how they are connected. The topic is the potential for growth in a particular tourist sector. You will focus your essay on the specific sector you select and find information about this sector.

4. *Describe the UK's potential for the generation of renewable energy.*
   The action word is '*Describe*' which means you have to give an account of what is available. You are not expected to make any evaluative comment or compare and contrast information (although do check with your tutor as sometimes they use 'Describe' but also mean 'Evaluate') . The key here is the **potential** for generating renewable energy which may be different from what is actually happening currently.

5. *Is continuous economic growth sustainable?*
There is no action word, but as we discussed earlier, by default you can assume it is *'Discuss'* or *'Evaluate'*. However, do check with your tutor. You need to find out information on the key elements of the topic (continuous economic growth), group these 'themes' in some way so they are easier to deal with and then **discuss** (i.e. give reasons for and against; examine implications of) the general and specific issues they raise in the context of **sustainability** in each case. You may also want to state how you are interpreting 'sustainability' in this context.

ACTIVITY 3 How do you gather information in preparation for writing?

Ask yourself	Possible solution
Do you spend a lot of time gathering information for an essay?	*This sounds as if you are not really sure what you are looking for. Carry out the BUG to clarify what your tutors want.*
Do you find that you have gathered information which is irrelevant or wandering off the point?	*Go back to the title and do the BUG to find out exactly what you need to find.*
Do you find it difficult to decide what is needed from the information you have?	*Check back to the underlined words in your title. Ask yourself how relevant your notes are and whether you have information to answer the question.*
Do you end up with lots of notes and spend too much time picking out information that you need when you come to write?	*You have no system for gathering notes. You need to be more efficient. Consider the different ways of making notes.*
Do you feel overwhelmed by the amount of notes you have made?	*You have no system for gathering notes. You need to be more efficient. Look at the next section.*
Do tutors comment that you have not answered the question and that there are irrelevant sections/ information in your work?	*This is probably because you have not carefully analysed the wording in the essay and conducted the BUG.*

References

- Bereiter, C. and Scardamalia, M. (1987) *The Psychology of Written Composition*. New York, Lawrence Erlbaum.
- Price, G. A. (2001) *Report of the Survey of Academic Study Skills at Southampton University*. Southampton, University of Southampton.

14 Improving your writing in business and management studies

Once you are in control of the writing process you can focus on how to improve your writing as a Business or Management Studies student. Although you probably didn't consciously think about this when you chose your subject, by choosing to study at a Higher Education institution such as a university you have also signed up to learning how to write **formally** in an academic style. The good news is that being able to write complex documents in this way will equip you to write the sort of professional and operational documents your future employers will expect from you. Sooner rather than later, clear and effective writing will be one of the most powerful tools of communication you will use in your future career.

To get the most out of this chapter you should work through Chapters 7, 'Reading critically', 9, 'Thinking critically' and 13, 'Taking control of the writing process' before starting here.

In this chapter you will:

1. compare essays and reports;
2. examine some helpful document and sentence-level writing practices;
3. look at writing about the literature and case studies

USING THIS CHAPTER

Improving your writing in business and management studies

Estimate your current levels of confidence. At the end of the chapter you will have the chance to re-assess these levels where you can incorporate this into your personal development planner (PDP). Mark between 1 (poor) and 5 (good) for the following:

I know what my English language skills are and know what to do to improve them.	I understand the elements of an essay and report and can use these effectively.	I write clearly and accurately and achieve coherence and cohesion in my writing.	I understand how to move beyond descriptive writing using paraphrasing and summary.	I understand what case studies are and how to approach writing about them.

Date: _____

1 The business or management studies student as a writer

All writing sets out to persuade its reader of something. For example, Chapter 9, 'Thinking critically' sets out to persuade you that (amongst other things) critical thinking is an important skill that employers value highly and that the process of critical thinking is a major way in which your learning takes place. As a business or management student writer you are being asked to show that you can take part in academic debates and, possibly, produce operationally relevant recommendations based on those debates. You will be judged on:

- how you state your argument/evidence/information;
- how you back up your argument/evidence/information;
- how you analyse the issues;
- how you evaluate all the evidence, both supporting and opposing your claims;
- how you support and reach your operational recommendations.

In other words, you are being asked to produce critical, written assignments that will persuade your markers to give you marks. Over the duration of your course, the threshold levels you have to meet to 'persuade' your lecturers will rise. This means that what gets good marks in year 1 might be only a bare pass in year 2 and would probably fail in the final year. Just as learning to read and think critically takes time to develop, so does critical writing and this is something you will have to continue to work at.

In my gap year I got a lot of experience writing brief reports for my boss, and she wanted bullet points. When I did this in my first essay at university I was told this wasn't good essay writing and lost some marks.

Errol, first-year Business Studies student

One particular challenge business and management studies students face is that they commonly have to write assignments that demand different styles ('genre') for the different subject areas that their degree may include. Whilst these assignments use the same rules of grammar, spelling, criticality and use of sources that are common to all academic writing, in order to gain good marks you need to be aware of the *genre* requirements.

Hot Tip Your tutors will have very clear ideas about the *format* they are expecting. This will include whether or not you can submit assignments printed on one or both sides of the page, the font size to be used (and preferred font type) and the line spacing. Carefully read the unit or module guidance, or the assignment briefing, as frequently these requirements will be specified. If not, then ask the person setting the assignment before you start working on the assignment.

But as you probably realise, writing is also a complex activity for other reasons. A simple search on the Web, using the search strings for example 'online writing laboratory' (known as OWLs) or 'report writing', demonstrates this. This is because writing is a complex *cognitive* (i.e. thinking process) activity and is an interplay between many systems. These include the systems for grammar (sentence level), document structures (known as text grammar), genre and finally making sure that the whole document hangs together and tells 'a story' (its coherence). Figure 14.1 gives you a visual representation of this.

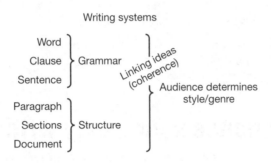

Figure 14.1 A representation of the systems involved in document writing

Characteristics of formal writing

I am increasingly receiving emails, from students who barely know me, that open with 'hey!'. I am concerned that they don't see the need to be more formal in some aspects of their writing and communication.

Tutor's comment

If you are writing a novel or marketing literature, your style is going to be quite different from a formal essay or report. A novel is designed to keep us, the readers, in suspense and surprise us. Marketing literature is there to convince and influence us to buy. In each style, or genre, you use a different set of vocabulary; you express yourself differently and present material in a different way.

Written academic essays and formal reports use what is known as **Standard English**. This can vary considerably from our colloquial (everyday) use of spoken and informal written language. Our own dialect and colloquial language is to be celebrated in its own right; it represents our common values and sense of community with other people who share this language. The world has many variations of English, but as English is the global language of business there is a need for people to be skilled in accurate communication using Standard English. This ensures precision and clarity of meaning. Your tutors are tolerant of many things but, like the tutor above, they will be irritated by lack of clarity or sloppiness in your written use of language. In Activity 1 you can self-assess your language proficiency using DIALANG (DIALANG is an EU-supported development based on the Council of Europe's Common European Framework of Reference).

ACTIVITY 1 Self-assess your Standard English proficiency

Whether English is your first language or not, understanding your strengths and weaknesses in reading, writing, grammar and vocabulary is essential to help you plan to improve. The DIALANG website (www.dialang.org/) offers you a comprehensive self-assessment tool. Select 'English' as the language option and follow the instructions to download the software. Full instructions are given to help you do the self-assessment.

See the feedback section at the end of the chapter for further guidance as to how to respond to your findings.

2 Enhance your essay writing

An essay has an 'implicit' structure, in other words it doesn't have obvious headings to create its structure. A report, meanwhile, has an 'explicit' structure: it uses headings to create its structure. In this section we shall look at the structure of the essay, writing better paragraphs and some sentence-level writing skills.

One of your *responsibilities* as a writer is to present your audience with well-structured writing, and you will be expected to arrive at university being able to write a coherent essay and understand how they are structured. If your work is badly structured, your tutor will comment on this and expect you to take note of the feedback given. If you are unclear about how essays are structured, read through the next section.

The basic essay structure

The basic framework for any essay is that it has a beginning, a middle and an end. Within this framework there will be a number of sections. These sections will be made up of one or more paragraphs. Paragraphs are sentences which are grouped to provide a mechanism for communicating your thoughts and ideas in a logical and structured manner. These paragraphs need to be linked coherently so that the document you write hangs together and develops a thread of ideas or line of argument. Novice student writers often ask how many paragraphs/sections an essay should contain. The only proper answer to this is that it depends on what you have to write and the word limit set by your tutors. However, based on our experience, it is possible to say that a 1500-word essay, for example, *might* have between seven and nine paragraphs in total.

As a general guideline, the five-section model is a useful one (see Figure 14.2). This is a diagrammatic representation of the essay and, depending on the word limit and the task, its sections can run across many more paragraphs. Sections 1 and 5, the introduction and conclusion, tend to be smaller than the main body sections 2, 3 and 4 where, most of your argument lies.

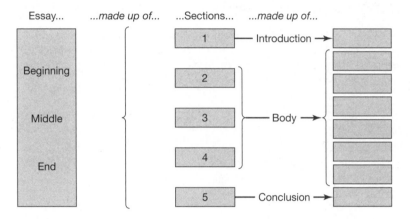

Figure 14.2 The five-section essay model

The introduction to an essay

Section 1 is the introduction. The role of the introduction is to show the reader the ideas which will be discussed and developed in subsequent paragraphs. The introduction provides the reader with a clear overview of what the essay will cover and the structure it will take. It will also identify the areas or topics which will be written about and explained in detail later. It is not uncommon for the introduction to be worth 10–20 per cent of the marks for an essay assignment: *an essay without an introduction will lose all of these marks immediately*. One way of writing an introduction is to use a topic task treatment thesis approach. See Figure 14.3.

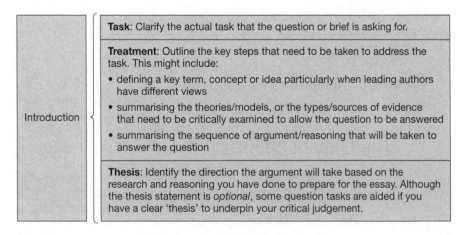

Figure 14.3 The topic/task/treatment/thesis introduction model

In the next activity you can explore this model in a bit more detail.

ACTIVITY 2 Analyse a sample introduction using the topic/task/treatment/thesis model

We are going to look at one student's introductory paragraph in response to the question '*To what extent do theories of motivation help us understand how to manage a work team through a period of change?*' First read the text, and then identify the topic, task, treatment and thesis elements of the paragraph.

Sentence	Topic/task/treatment/ thesis?
It has been recently estimated that at any one time more than 85% of businesses in Europe are in the process of implementing change that directly affects their workforce (Smith, 2007).	
Understanding how to manage work teams through change successfully is likely to be a major issue in any business context.	
It is reasonable to ask whether, and if so how much, motivational theories may assist this process.	
To answer this question, firstly the notion of 'motivation', and agreement as to what it is, will be examined to establish a definition to underpin the rest of the discussion.	
Next a critical analysis and evaluation of the leading theories of motivation will be undertaken to test their relevance and applicability to the change management process.	
The findings from this will then be briefly reviewed against two cases, a large corporate organisation and an SME.	
Finally, the extent to which motivational theory contributes to understanding work team change management will be considered.	
The literature suggests that other factors such as group/team dynamics and communication are important; motivational theories alone are unlikely to be the most important way of managing such change.	

See the feedback section for further information.

The body of an essay

Sections 2, 3 and 4 form the body of your essay. The body of the essay is where you discuss the topics and develop your argument, in the sequence you indicated in the introduction. Some students lose marks unnecessarily because whilst they have good content, they don't follow the sequence they set out in their introduction. Many marking schedules allocate

5–10 per cent of the marks for an essay assignment to structure and presentation. Losing such marks is likely to mean that someone who could have got 65 per cent based on content and good structure ends up with 58 per cent simply because they didn't structure their work well. If you don't see why this matters, look back at Figure 14.1 to see how structure is an essential part of the writing systems you have to manage.

Section 2 is your first topic for discussion. You will have indicated this in your introduction, so the reader is prepared for this. The topic for Section 2 may be concerned with looking at the debates around definitions such as in Activity 2, or it may map out the general range of thinking in a topic area. Or, it may be an examination of the relevance of the topic to an operational issue. It could be many other things that are determined by the specific question and the reading and research you have undertaken.

Section 3 could be a sub-topic of Section 2. You could use this section to discuss further some aspect of the topic mentioned in Section 2. However, you may wish to introduce another sub-theme and strengthen what you say by giving examples and using evidence and reasoning.

Section 4 could be used to link back to your introductory section, or a broader statement about the topic in Section 2. Alternatively you may wish to introduce another sub-theme and strengthen what you say by giving examples and using evidence and reasoning.

There is no simple template for the body of an essay. Your ability to plan and structure an essay is part of your learning process because it is here that your reading, thinking and writing about a topic integrate. Your essay structure is the way in which you *represent* the framework of the argument chains you have developed, a process we considered in Chapter 9, 'Thinking critically'. Ultimately this is why the essay is a core part of your assessment, even though you probably then won't ever have to write an essay for your future employer.

The conclusion to an essay

Section 5 is your conclusion and will sum up key factors of the topics discussed and relate back to issues in your introduction. Never introduce new topics in this section. The conclusion is also where you answer the question set: this question might be explicit (such as the 'to what extent … ' example used earlier to which the answer is going to be somewhere along the spectrum of *'not at all–sometimes–totally'*) or implicit (such as when you are asked to *'discuss'*, or *'analyse'* and the answer is going to be based on your synthesis of thinking – see Chapter 9). Conclusions tend to attract a high share of the marks in any essay assignment; this can be as high as 25 per cent. The reason for this is that it is here that you show as a writer that you can **construct** meaning and sense out of a range of material. A bicycle is not a bicycle until all its component parts are put together in the right way. In a similar way an essay is not an essay until its component parts are put together in a way that persuades the reader it is more than just a pile of its parts; the role of the conclusion is to 'lock' everything into place.

One way of thinking about the conclusion is that it is almost a mirror of the introduction. You are **reminding** the reader of the purpose of the writing, you are **summarising** the key findings that support the argument or case you have made, and you are **answering** the question on that basis. See Figure 14.4.

Conclusion	**Remind**: purpose/task undertaken
	Summarise: the key findings from the body of the text in their logical order. These findings might include: • summary of key evidence that supports the argument • summary of the critical analysis/evaluation of texts and theories/concepts or models discussed • summary of any synthesis of thinking arising from the discussion
	Answer: the question, or confirm the thesis argued for, as a consequence of, and on the basis of, the findings presented.

Figure 14.4 The remind/summarise/answer conclusion model

The five-section structure is simply a model for the role of paragraphs/sections in an essay. Making paragraphs work in your writing is the next key document-level contribution to improving your business and management studies writing.

3 Making paragraphs and sentences work: coherence and cohesion

You've got some good ideas, but they lack coherence.

Tutor's comment

Expert writers produce paragraphs where the messages are clear and the reader is able to understand the points that are being made. Good paragraph writing ensures that the train of thought flows. This is the 'coherence' factor your tutors will be looking for.

You may have been told by your tutors that your assignments are disjointed, or that they lack structure. If so they may be referring to the way you write paragraphs and the way you sequence them. Novice writers often overwhelm the reader with detail, without first telling the reader what the topic is or what point is going to be made. If you point someone in the right direction first, they are then much more likely to see what you see. By using the topic sentence approach to writing paragraphs you are pointing your reader in the direction you intend to go. First you flag up the main idea and then you develop it with supporting or complementary ideas, evidence and reasoning.

ACTIVITY 3 Does my essay hang together?

Take a recently marked assignment and consider the following statements. Decide whether any apply to your work. This will give you indicators for future development.

Ask yourself …	Commentary to look out for
Is there a logical sequence to my paragraphs?	Your ideas are muddled. Your paragraphs do not follow on. Your essay structure is weak.
Is my train of thought obvious to my reader?	A question mark in the margin. What are you getting at?
Is the thread of my argument obvious?	Can't follow your argument. This section is jumbled/muddled.
Are my paragraphs well structured?	Your paragraphs do not seem to follow on from each other. Your ideas are all over the place. Your sentences are muddled within this section.

If you find any of the commentary identified in Activity 3 in your work then you probably need to do some work on your paragraph writing.

Paragraph structure

The topic or summary sentence approach to paragraph writing is one way to improve the clarity of your writing. Let's open up one of the paragraphs from Figure 14.2 to see how sentences can work inside a paragraph – see Figure 14.5.

Novice student writers often ask a similar question about the number of sentences in a paragraph as they do about the number of paragraphs in an essay. The answer is similar: it depends on what you are writing about and what you intend your paragraph to do in relation to other paragraphs. From a theoretical point of view, a paragraph can be as short as a single sentence or as long as a whole section of writing. However, these extremes can rarely be justified. In practice, if novice writers aim for paragraphs that range between 4 and 12 sentences, this is a good starting point. Activity 4 examines an example paragraph.

	Link sentence from previous paragraph: Although this is **optional**, if you can make links between paragraphs your essay will hang together more effectively. It might be the further development of the previous paragraph topic, but from a different perspective. Or it might be a comparison with a related topic that makes the link.
Paragraph	Topic sentence: This is always **essential**. This tells your reader what to expect from your paragraph.
	Topic development sentences: This is always **essential**. This is where you develop your topic sentence. It might be several bits of evidence (possibly 3–4 in a typical paragraph) and/or reasoning necessary to establish the point.
	Summary or lead-out sentence: Although this is **optional**, if you can summarise the findings from the topic development and indicate where this is going to go this helps the reader understand your sequencing. It may also be the point that you reiterate in your conclusion when you summarise all your findings.

Figure 14.5 Elements in a topic sentence paragraph

ACTIVITY 4 Exploring paragraph structure

Let us look at a paragraph written by Michael, an Education student, and examine the way he ensures there is coherence to his paragraph.

Sentence	Function/purpose
1 Newell and Simon (1972) were the first to propose that there was a computational workspace between the Short-Term memory and the Long-Term Memory, which they termed the Working Memory (WM).	This is the **topic sentence**. It introduces the reader to the main idea which is to be explained in the paragraph. Notice how he succinctly tells the reader the main ideas so that the reader is primed for the rest of the paragraph and what follows will make sense.
2 It is here that the reader stores the theme of a text, where the reader's own representation of the situation is referred to and major syntactical elements, from the surrounding sentences, are accumulated.	**Develop the topic**. This sentence gives an explanation of what the Working Memory does. By using the word 'here', the writer links back to the previous sentence to provide strength and cohesion (cohesion will be discussed in a later section).
3 In this way, the individual can make sense of the text.	**Develop the topic**. This sentence is further explanation of the topic sentence.
4 The Working Memory is also the space where the reader can temporarily store earlier parts of a sequenced story in order to relate them to later sequences.	**Summary sentence**. This sentence draws the paragraph to a close.

Writing your topic sentence

One way to think about topic sentences is that if you *could* write essays just with bullet points, then the main bullets would be the key topics you need to cover and the indented bullets the evidence related to the topic. Indeed, some people use this approach to plan their essay structure before they write it as a continuous text. See Figure 14.6.

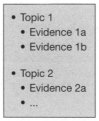

Figure 14.6 A bullet point outline

The problem with bullet points, however, is that they tend to be 'closed' statements and closed statements, like closed questions, leave little room for development. Figure 14.7 compares an open and a closed question.

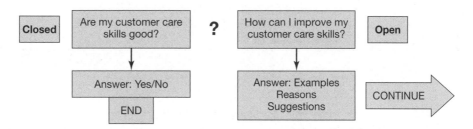

Figure 14.7 Open and closed questions

Like open questions, open statements lead to further exploration, illustration and discussion. Closed statements lead to, well, closure!

Good topic sentences tend to have the quality of openness: they clarify the issue but in a way that paves the way to further development and further enquiry. The topic sentence in Activity 4 might look a bit closed at first sight, but the choice of words (e.g. *propose*) and the introduction of a new concept (*the Working Memory*) provide plenty of opportunity to develop the topic. Try Activity 5.

ACTIVITY 5 Capturing the reader's attention: topic sentences

Look at these topic sentences. Can you identify why one of each pair is a good statement and the other is a poor statement? They have been taken from University of Toronto, *Advice on Academic Writing*, available at **www.utoronto.ca/writing/advise.html.**

A.		
Poor	Shakespeare was the world's greatest playwright.	**Why poor? Why is it difficult to develop from this point?**
Better	The success of the last scene in *Midsummer Night's Dream* comes from subtle linguistic and theatrical references to Elizabeth's position as Queen.	**Why good? How could you develop from this?**
B.		
	Having an official policy on euthanasia just causes problems, as the Dutch example shows.	**Why poor? Why is it difficult to develop from this point?**
	Dutch laws on euthanasia have been praised for their attention to the principles of self-determination. Recent cases, however, show that they have not been able to deal adequately with issues involving technological intervention of unconscious patients. Harmackian strategies can solve at least the question of assignation of rights.	**Why good? How could you develop from this?**

To begin with you are likely to make the first sentence of a paragraph a topic sentence, but as Figure 14.5 suggests, you will encounter texts written by expert writers where they start with a link sentence and follow this with the topic sentence. Their expertise is such that you are aided by this process, not hindered. This takes time to develop.

Developing your topic sentence

Supporting evidence shows that you are looking at the evidence and findings of other researchers and writers in support of your main/topic statement. Of course you will do this critically, and **any conclusions you come to are due to the evidence you discuss**. This is what your tutors call 'your voice' in the essay. Through critical discussion, and the choices you make from the range of ideas in the texts and other sources you have read and researched, you **demonstrate** what you want to say. Sometimes tutors give feedback such as 'Don't tell me, show me'. They are asking you to demonstrate the way you got to a conclusion through an evidencing and reasoning process, not just the conclusion itself. See Chapter 9, 'Thinking critically' for further guidance on such processes.

Making your writing work: cohesion

Many students know the meaning of the words cohesion and coherence in isolation but do not know how they can be achieved when they are writing. Signalling to your reader what your thoughts are will achieve coherence. Similarly, ensuring that your sentences and paragraphs link together into one large whole will help to communicate your ideas to others more effectively.

> *I had one tutor in my first year who kept going on about sentence 'cohesion' separating the excellent from the very good essays. I didn't have a clue what that meant! I saw my personal tutor who looked at my work and said that I either wasn't using link words or when I was I wasn't using them right, like using 'and' when I should've used 'but'.*
>
> Samantha, second-year Business Administration student

Coherence and cohesion are closely linked. An essay which has logical sequencing and guides the reader through the ideas and thoughts will have coherence and make sense. Cohesion is applied by making sure that all the parts fit and stick together. This is done by careful choice of language to point the reader in the direction you want them to go.

Signal words – making links across sentences

If you state a new idea or give an example in a paragraph, it is a good idea to use 'signal words'. These are words or phrases that prepare the reader for what is to come. This could be an example, a comparison with what went before, a contrast, a continuing description, or a logical move.

Signal words help the reader through the text. They act as small, mental arrows that keep the reader on track. Without signal words, a text is quite difficult to read and can seem stilted. Some common signals are shown in the table below.

Purpose of the signal	Link word/phrase examples
Comparison or similarities	Similarly/Likewise/In the same way/In comparison
Contrast or differences	In contrast/On the other hand/Not only … but also/In comparison/But/Even though/However,

Purpose of the signal	Link word/phrase examples
Cause and effect	As a consequence (effect)/Because (cause)/ Consequently (effect)/As a result of(effect)/Due to(effect)/The reason for … (cause)/Therefore (effect)/If … then/With the result that
Listing	A major development …/ To begin with/ Next …/ Later …/ Furthermore/In addition/ Afterwards/Finally/In conclusion
Problem solution	The dilemma facing …/ The problem facing …/ A major difficulty …/ A resolution to this …

ACTIVITY 6 Look at how signal words are used

Select a text in your subject area and, unless you own the original, photocopy it. Closely read it to identify and underline/highlight the signal words/phrases it uses. Then use the following questions to analyse what the author is signalling and make brief notes in the margin.

What is the purpose of the signal word/phrase?
Why is the author using it here?
How does the author's choice of signal suggest they will move their argument/case forward?
How closely does your 'prediction' of what the author is signalling match what they actually do?

See the feedback section for further comment.

Cohesion within sentences: coordinating words

There are other ways in which the writer achieves cohesion *within* the sentence and the first of these is using coordinating words such as *and/but/ or/so/yet*. Such words give you greater flexibility in how you move your reader forward with your thinking: you are subtly 'coordinating' small steps of thinking development for them. It is possible to write in short, staccato sentences without such coordinators, but this produces child-like writing that rapidly becomes irritating to read. It also means that you have to work harder to show the connection you intend between statements. The table below shows how these words can coordinate statements within a sentence and move the reader forward, along with some brief examples. Try Activity 7 to practise using different coordinating words.

Purpose	Coordinating word	Example
Connection/addition	and	The unreformed Common Agricultural Policy was a major drain on the enlarged EC budget *and* was unpopular with member states who were net contributors to the budget.
Contrast	but, yet	The unreformed Common Agricultural Policy was a major drain on the enlarged EC budget *but* it had worked well for the founder members of the EEC.
Link/alternative	or, nor	The unreformed Common Agricultural Policy was a major drain on the enlarged EU budget *or* it was a reasonable price to pay depending on which group's interests are considered.
Conclude/cause or effect	so,for	The unreformed Common Agricultural Policy was a major drain on the enlarged EU budget *so* its review and revision was inevitable.

ACTIVITY 7 Linking within sentences – using coordinating words

Use this website to practise using coordinating words: www.bbc.co.uk/skillswise/words/grammar/interestsentences/compoundsentences/factsheet.shtml

You may also want to use the interactive quiz and games from the tabs on this page.

NOTE   In formal academic writing there is a general principle that you don't start a sentence with coordinating words.

Cohesion within sentences: working with clauses

Just as documents are made up of paragraphs, sentences are made up of clauses. A simple sentence has one clause, that is, a subject, a verb and some information about the subject. As we saw in the last section, when you want to write about a more complex idea, you can join simple sentences using words like *and, or* and *yet*. This would give you a sentence with two independent clauses. For example:

'The detailed data from this study indicate that students with a vocational school background used on average more time for their studies and achieved their target grades better than those with an upper secondary school background.' (Kolari *et al.*, 2008)

See also examples 1 and 2 below.

You can also add clauses that are dependent on that simple sentence, using words such as *if, although, whereas, since* and if you do that, you have then added a dependent clause. All sentences have to have at least an independent clause, while compound sentences have a series of clauses that have a relationship to that independent clause. For example:

> *Second year Civil Engineering students on a health and safety courses felt that advice given by their team-mates was better than that from post graduate students teaching them, <u>even though</u> they would expect them to be more knowledgeable than year two students.* (Petersen et al., 2008)

In the sentence above *even though* triggers the independent clause and once that is written it has to either be preceded or followed by a dependent clause in order to make a complete sentence.

Compound sentences will:

- link ideas of equal importance (coordinate clauses);
- link additional information to the main idea (add dependent clause/s to add information);
- show a relationship between the main idea and other ideas (using, e.g., which, that, who, whose).

Each of these links has trigger words that show how the clauses are linked. Let's look at some examples.

Example 1. A compound sentence (two clauses)
(a) *European countries have their own standards for the remediation of brown-field sites <u>although</u> there is a need for a unified Europe-wide set of standards.*

Notice that the second clause starting with 'although' could not stand alone because the 'although' triggers that it belongs to an independent clause. Words that trigger joining like this are called subordinating conjunctions (see the following table).

(b) *Since home broadband access hit critical mass, high street retailers have had to work hard to maintain their competitiveness against low cost-base internet operations.*

Notice that the dependent clause is at the front of the sentence and triggered by the subordinating conjunction, 'since'. The independent clause begins with *high street retailers have.* Also note that if you start with a dependent clause you need a comma before the independent clause. You can also reverse the order of these clauses.

Example 2. Another compound sentence (two clauses)
(a) *The 4Ps concept of marketing mix, <u>that considers product, price, place and promotion</u>, is usefully extended by considering people, process and physical evidence.*

Notice that the word 'that' refers back to 'the 4Ps concept of marketing mix'. It also triggers a clause that has pushed into the middle of the independent clause: *The 4Ps concept of marketing mix is usefully extended by considering people, process and physical evidence.*

Improving your writing in business and management studies

The following table lists trigger words that show how clauses are linked together to form sentences.

Coordinating words ▢	Subordinating words △	Relative words ◯	Function
and			Adds additional information or something similar.
but, yet	although even though unless		Shows a contrasting idea.
or, nor	while		Shows sometimes different, an alternative.
for, so	if since because		Shows a cause and/or effect.
	since while when as after		Show a time relationship.
		who	Refers back to a person. For example: *A number of researchers have since developed content theories of motivation, but it was Maslow <u>who</u> first proposed a hierarchy of needs theory.*
		which, that	Refers back to a thing or the whole of the previous clause. In this case 'the submitted essay': *He submitted an essay <u>which</u> cited an impressive range of book and journal sources.*
		whose	Shows possession. For example: *Skinner, <u>whose</u> work on operant conditioning using rats, contributed to the development of Behaviourism.* Main clause interrupted by relative clause. Main clause is: Skinner contributed to the development of Behaviourism.
		where	Refers back to a place. For example: *The Hawthorne Works in America, <u>where</u> the original research took place, gave its name to the alleged effect researchers can have on subjects.*
		when	Refers to and expands on a time. For example: *The UK economy became governed by monetarist principles, <u>when</u> its financial markets were deregulated in 1986.*

To help you visually, you may benefit from looking at this diagrammatically by using symbols to illustrate the different trigger words that link clauses (see the next table below).

Key	
▬▬	An independent clause that stands alone as a sentence. For example: *Most networks are organised as a series of layers.*
▢	This is a word that joins independent clauses and allows you to add similar or show contrasting information. For example: *Most networks are organised as a series of layers and each layer is built upon its predecessor.* ▬▬▢▬▬ Note: you can use a coordinating conjunction to join two dependent clauses as well.
- - - - -	A dependent clause. This means that it can't stand alone as a sentence. For example: *…. because this helps to reduce the design complexity.*
△	This is a word that allows you to link a dependent clause to an independent clause. For example: *Most networks are organised as a series of layers because this helps to reduce the design complexity.* ▬▬△- - - - -
◯	Examples of these words are: who, whom, where, which, that. Like subordinated clauses, they cannot stand alone. For example: *Most networks are organised as a series of layers which are dependent on their predecessor.* ▬▬◯- - - - -

All sentences must have at least a main, independent clause and you can build them up to be more complex. See if you can use this to build your own.

ACTIVITY 8 Linking within sentences – working with clauses

Using the key above, take the patterns of the sentences here and write your own sentence below. You may want to look at the feedback section first to get some ideas before you try your own.

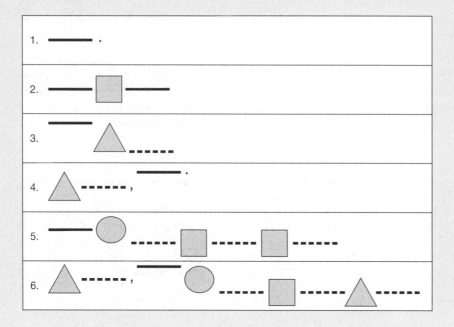

As you can see, the more clauses you link, the more difficult it can become to read. A classic error that many students make is around example 6 above. Students often start a sentence with a subordinator, e.g. *although,* and then start linking other ideas at that level and forget to finish the sentence off with an independent main clause. Remember that good academic writing is characterised by clarity, so don't make long compound sentences that are difficult to process.

A word on spelling and grammar and vocabulary

Good writing requires accuracy with spelling and grammar, the use of accurate punctuation and a good general and subject-specific vocabulary. Word-processing packages provide direct support to you as a writer with built-in spelling and grammar checks. Be aware that unless you specify British English, you will be accepting spelling and grammar changes that may not be welcomed by your tutors as these may conform to US English standards. These differences may seem minor, but they will attract critical feedback. Also be aware that the software is not 'context-aware'. For example, if you type 'their' when you mean 'there', the computer will not spot this as a problem because as far as it is concerned the spelling is correct. Your tutor however will spot this and probably suggest you need to give more attention to proofreading your work.

Punctuation, particularly the use of the apostrophe and the comma, is another common area of difficulty for many students. If you do not know the rules of usage for apostrophes and commas, use one of the many excellent websites available to learn and practise these. (See the 'Getting extra help' section at the end of this chapter.)

Finally, some students use a thesaurus to expand their vocabulary. In principle there is nothing wrong with this, but you need to be cautious as the detailed meanings of the words in a thesaurus entry are not necessarily interchangeable in an academic context. It can also reveal that someone is trying to sound 'academic'. If there is a straightforward word to say something, use it.

Hot Tip If you are concerned about your knowledge or understanding of English grammar and how to write effective sentences, find out what additional skills support is available at your university or college. This may range from specialist programmes for English as second-language students, to group or individual tutorials run by academic skills tutors for first-language students.

---

4 Enhance your report writing

In this chapter we have looked at the essay and its constituent parts, and some specific writing practices that can enhance your formal writing. We identified earlier that unlike an essay, a report has an explicit structure. The purpose of such structure is to create a consistent framework that will be familiar to its audience and which possibly reflects the professional standards or expectations of the work environment in which the report is to be read. Unlike an essay, a report is also much more likely (but not always) to be based on primary (i.e. first-hand) evidence that *you* collect. This might be, for example, through observation, case study or conducting a survey. A report is also likely to present recommendations, for example changes in practices or new process implementations. In other words, some proposed action based on the analysis and discussion of findings. There is also likely to be a critical review in its conclusion of the methods and research undertaken that led to the report's recommendations. Knowing what it takes to prepare and produce a formal report is a key skill **all** business and management graduates will need in graduate-level employment.

Report writing uses the same underpinning good writing practices (such as topic sentence paragraphs and Standard English) as essays, and of course a report also has a beginning, a middle and an end. Essays and reports share common standards of presenting evidence and use of sources, and they are both written with the reader/audience in mind. Figure 14.8 compares and contrasts some of the main characteristics of the two.

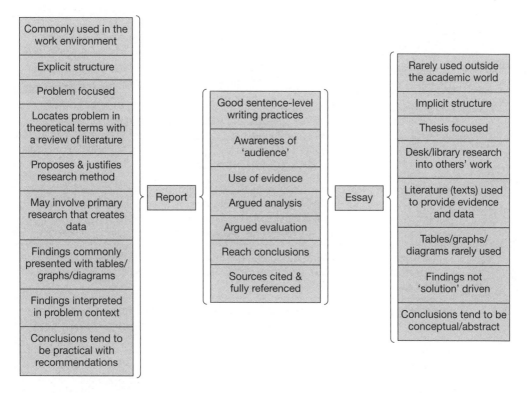

Report		Essay
Commonly used in the work environment	Good sentence-level writing practices	Rarely used outside the academic world
Explicit structure	Awareness of 'audience'	Implicit structure
Problem focused	Use of evidence	Thesis focused
Locates problem in theoretical terms with a review of literature	Argued analysis	Desk/library research into others' work
Proposes & justifies research method	Argued evaluation	Literature (texts) used to provide evidence and data
May involve primary research that creates data	Reach conclusions	Tables/graphs/diagrams rarely used
Findings commonly presented with tables/graphs/diagrams	Sources cited & fully referenced	Findings not 'solution' driven
Findings interpreted in problem context		Conclusions tend to be conceptual/abstract
Conclusions tend to be practical with recommendations		

Figure 14.8 Reports and essays: some characteristics considered

NOTE In reality, expert writers will synthesise certain aspects of essay writing into their reports to achieve the most fluent outcome. For example, advanced reports at Masters level will have extended reviews of literature, and these tend to explore, develop and substantiate the thesis the writer may seek to test to assist their solution appraisal.

Core elements of formal reports

In a subject area such as Business or Management Studies, there are common, core elements to reports, but exactly *how* your tutors want you to structure a report assignment in detail will be specified by them. This will be either discussed in class and/or written in the unit/module/course handbook or guidance. Make sure you understand this. If you aren't sure, ask. However, some elements are general and the table below outlines these.

Title page (essential). The report title may be given to you, or you may need to make up a title. Remember that the title should be as short as possible yet be sufficiently informative to tell the reader about the report's subject/problem focus. On your course you will probably need to put your student refernece rather than your name on the title page, whereas an employer would expect the report to be dated and for your course you need to put the submission date.

Acknowledgements (optional). This is where a report author gives recognition to individuals (or organisations) who have offered 'generous consultancy' to the report author. For example, an individual may have offered informal verbal guidance on some aspects of the work, or an organisation may have provided some service or facility without asking for payment. This is not the same as attributable sources, which go in the **References** section.

Abstract (refer to your course handbook/tutor). An abstract is a brief summary (typically between 150 and 350 words) which tells the reader what problem is under examination, what the author(s) did to examine it, what they found and what the key recommendation is. Novice writers find abstracts hard to write. Fortunately you probably won't be asked to write one until your final year.

Table of contents (essential). The main sections of the report listed in the order they appear in the report, and the page number at which they start. The section title should appear exactly in the table of contents as it does in the body of the report.

Table of figures (essential if diagrams/graphs/tables appear in the report). A complete list of figures in the order in which they appear in the report: numbered with the exact caption it has in the body of the report, and with the page number on which it appears.

References (essential). A complete list of all the sources that have been cited in the body of the report using the referencing protocol your course/department requires. See Chapter 12, 'Understanding academic integrity: learner ethics and plagiarism'.

Appendices (refer to your course handbook). If you are allowed to use appendices you will use them to include descriptive content (such as an organisational context, the chronology of a policy development, your role in the organisation). You will use them to make any 'raw data' generated by research available to the reader. You will also use an appendix to make available documentation that is not in the public domain, such as an internal communication, but which is relevant to your case and in which the extra detail will be of help to your reader's understanding (be aware that confidentiality may apply and you will need to seek permission to make such material available). You 'cross refer' (e.g. '*See appendix 2*') to the relevant appendix from the body of your report.

The main body of the report will then have an introduction, review of literature, methods, findings/data, analysis/discussion, conclusions and recommendations. You may be asked to do these all as separate sections or you may be asked to do some of these in combined sections. Figure 14.9 models these possibilities with those sections that are more commonly combined placed side by side. As you can see, the report may have only four main parts in its body, or up to seven. This is why you **must** check the assignment requirements.

- The **introduction** tells the reader the context of the problem. This may include the background to the problem, the impact the problem has/will have and what may have been done previously to address the problem. The introduction specifies the aim or purpose of the

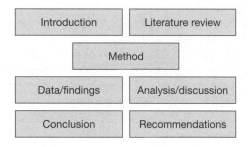

Figure 14.9 Components of the main body of a report

research/work to be done to understand and address the problem. It will also specify the objectives by which the success of the work will be measured. You may be required to include a review of the literature in the introduction.

■ Whether the **literature review** is part of the introduction or a separate section in its own right, its purpose is to show what the current evidence and thinking are in relation to the report's topic or focus. The review seeks to identify what is agreed, what is subject to debate and what trends or themes are shown by the literature evidence. You are using the literature review to demonstrate the significance and relevance of your report activity, and how your aims and objectives relate to current published work. The sources of literature in Business and Management studies are wide: see Chapter 9, 'Thinking critically' for examples of text and literature 'evidence'. Your literature review will also consider what types of method are generally used for this type of problem examination and what factors may contribute to the decision you make about your choice of methodology.

■ The **method** section will typically outline the specific methodology chosen. Partly this is descriptive as the reader needs to be clear about how you went about researching/undertaking the work for your report, but be brief. However, you also need to show your reader the rationale for selecting the method chosen as against other possible approaches. This is a brief 'critical' discussion and you should connect with the literature review findings in the previous section to justify your approach. Remember, your methods can range from library-based reading to collecting empirical data in a variety of ways. If you are unsure what approach to take, discuss this with your tutor.

■ The key thing about the **data/findings section** is that you do not 'throw' a mass of information at the reader, you are presenting an *interpretation* of the *key trends/themes/messages* that the raw data suggest. This might be averages of numerical data, or commonly repeated views/statements in interview/survey question responses. You may use graphs or tables or diagrams to summarise these key points for your reader. Your connecting text should not describe the table/graph/diagram contents but **show the significance** of those contents in relation to other possible interpretations of the same data.

The analysis/discussion is commonly combined with this section as this can seamlessly link to a more detailed discussion in relation to the literature review findings.

■ The **analysis/discussion** section puts the data interpretation into the context of the bigger picture, for example the key things the literature review established. It considers how these together inform possible answers to the research questions that the report's aims and objectives set out to answer. This is a critical process and may look at how the findings confirm or contradict what the literature suggests. You are building your case in this section so you will need to use all of your critical thinking skills – see Chapter 9, 'Thinking critically'.

■ The **conclusion** section typically answers the report's research questions, based on the previous section's discussion. If it is an operational report it may also consider what real-world constraints apply. For example, the 'best' solution may not be viable, so the conclusion needs to consider what compromises are needed to implement successful solutions to the problem. It will also look critically at the research/work you undertook. You will consider things such as what may have limited the range of the findings, what unexpected problems affected the whole process, and the confidence that can be placed in the findings. You may also be asked to write some personal reflection: see Chapter 10 'Understanding the value of reflection' and Chapter 15, 'Developing your reflective writing'.

■ If you are required to make **recommendations**, this section will set out the specific actions, changes and so on that the report process indicates should be made. These should be clearly supported by the evidence, the analysis and the conclusions previously presented. Don't 'invent' solutions, or propose unrealistic solutions, as your tutors will see through this immediately.

Get synergy into your report

Writing a report isn't just bolting together a number of separate sections. Covey's 7 *Habits of Highly Effective People* (2004) lists habit 6 as 'Synergise', in other words making the sum of the whole of something greater than the sum of its parts. The very best, expertly written reports achieve synergy because they maintain a critical process **across** the report's sections. Novice writers initially find this hard to grasp because it requires an 'embedded' approach to thinking **about** thinking whilst writing. A good comparison is with learning to drive. When you first start driving you have to consciously think about each action (for example, steering, indicating, braking, gear changing and clutch work, appraising the external environment, trying to predict other drivers' likely behaviours and so on) and it takes some time for this to all be 'embedded' sufficiently to become a proficient driver. Guidance, feedback and practice make for proficiency.

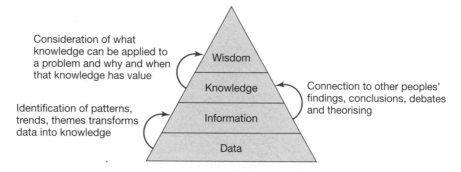

Figure 14.10 One way of applying the DIKW model (attribution uncertain, see for example www.erm.ecs.soton.ac.uk/theme2/how_does-data_become_knowledge.html

One way to visualise this process of expert report writing and 'thinking about thinking' is to consider a variation on the **Data_Information_ Knowledge_Wisdom (DIKW)** model in the way shown in Figure 14.10.

- **Data** on its own tell us little. It is only when we ask the question 'What patterns/trends/ themes and relationships does it reveal?' that it becomes useful **Information**.
- **Information** in isolation is interesting. It is only when we ask questions such as 'Who else has discussed this issue?', 'How does this relate to other people's findings?', 'What different ideas or theories are proposed to explain such information?' or 'How might this be used?' that it becomes useful **Knowledge**.
- **Knowledge** alone doesn't solve problems. It is only when we ask questions such 'Why is this knowledge useful in this context?' or 'When does the existing knowledge suggest doing 'X' rather than 'Y'?' that we start to approach **Wisdom**.
- **Wisdom** is truly powerful but *what* it is is the subject of much debate. Einstein (n.d.) is attributed with the saying 'Wisdom is not a product of schooling but of the lifelong attempt to acquire it'. Your degree studies are only the beginning of your journey in this respect.

Many students write excellent, individual report sections but then fail to connect them sufficiently by not considering the types of questions above. A lack of synergy can also come from not referring back to the literature at key points. At the heart of any report are the literature findings (see Figure 14.11). If you take time to consider how these findings link with what you are saying in each section of the report and mention this, then you will start to show you are in control of the report writing process and your grades will improve.

Developing professional, expert report writing skills takes time, effort and practice. Your tutors will offer you feedback that will help you to develop what will be one of the most essential communication skills your future career will need.

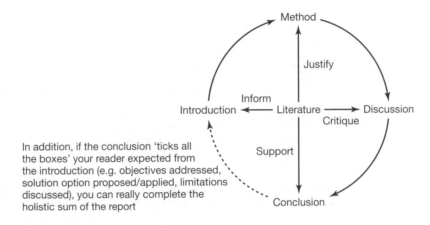

In addition, if the conclusion 'ticks all the boxes' your reader expected from the introduction (e.g. objectives addressed, solution option proposed/applied, limitations discussed), you can really complete the holistic sum of the report

Figure 14.11 One way to show how the literature links sections of a report

ACTIVITY 9 Explore report writing

Use this website link to explore report writing in more detail:

www.learnhigher.ac.uk/learningareas/reportwriting/betterreportwriting.htm

This activity uses an online resource developed by the LearnHigher Team at Reading University and is the work of Dr Michelle Reid and Dr Kim Shahabudin.

Hot Tip

Always pay attention to the marking criteria for your report assignment as they appear in your course/module/unit handbook or guidance. These will make very clear what the markers are looking for and the way in which the marks are distributed across the various sections of the report. Typically the literature review, analysis and conclusion sections attract most marks. However, just because the method section may have a smaller percentage of the overall marks than each of these other sections doesn't mean you can ignore it. If you can't demonstrate a well-constructed approach to your methodology, this is a strong indicator to your tutor that you haven't put in as much effort as you could have done. Further, poor methodology produces poor information and this will make it difficult for you to write the other sections effectively.

5 Moving beyond descriptive writing

'If you're not making mistakes, you're not learning.'

Campaign for Learning (n.d.)

As a Business or Management Studies student you are faced with a range of texts and published work (the 'literature') that your tutors expect you to include when writing essays and reports. The challenge you face as a novice writer is to show that you are **learning** about the topics in your subject and not just repeating things that your reader could read for themselves in the original texts. This challenge of avoiding pure description, yet accurately identifying the core issues or characteristics of key ideas, is one of the biggest hurdles in moving from novice to expert writer.

Many novice writers are also uncertain how to phrase their use of others' work to their audience. This section will look at some of the ways you can move beyond descriptive writing through the use of a writing *process*.

> *In my second semester I don't seem to be able to get over the problem that my markers keep saying that I am being descriptive and not analytical enough in what I write. Help!*
> Anu, first-year Business Studies student

> *I tell my students that writing about theories, or models or whatever needs them to see the whole forest, not just the individual trees within it.*
> Tutor's comment

One way to think about the issue of descriptive writing is to consider how you would explain the concept of a car to someone who didn't know what a car was. If you describe a particular make and model of car in great detail, then they might be able to tell you about that particular make and model of car. However, if you identify the key **characteristics** of what a car is, i.e. those things that all cars have in common, then they are much more likely to grasp the car **concept**. In this process you do something significant. That is, you analyse something very detailed and distil the important factors that define it. As a novice writer this is hard. You are grappling with new ideas and information which you have to understand in order to write about them. The natural response is to write descriptively about what you have just learnt, in other words all of the detail, because you haven't yet thought about the bigger picture this detail creates.

Developing writing practices to avoid unnecessary description

The writing process is as much part of the learning process as a result of it: when you write you are trying to express what you think you know. This challenges what you actually understand. This 'challenge' can then help you better find what to write. See Figure 14.12.

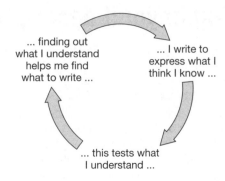

... finding out what I understand helps me find what to write ...

... I write to express what I think I know ...

... this tests what I understand ...

Figure 14.12 A virtuous writing/thinking circle

We have called this a 'virtuous' circle because it lets us say two very important, related things about academic writing. First, some novice writers forget that they need to think about what they write and just write 'straight to page' from their reading without any further thought (this also runs the risk of plagiarism, see Chapter 12, 'Understanding academic integrity: learner ethics and plagiagrism'). Second, consistently successful academic work is based on an iterative 'draft and redraft' strategy. This creates the opportunity to systematically review and revise **what** you have said, **how** you have expressed yourself, **what** is important to say and questioned **why** this is important in your written assignment. Critical thinking skills are as important throughout the whole process as when you are first reading your texts. See Figure 14.13 for one way to illustrate this process.

- **Rough draft**. The rough draft is just that, rough, and no one else need ever read it. It does not attempt to be grammatically accurate. It will be incomplete in terms of coherence. It will have gaps in reasoning and evidence. The point of it is for you to test out **how** your understanding is developing and to identify **what** further reading and research you need to do to start to make a coherent and seamlessly argued piece of work. Some of what you have written will be fine, some will need to be reworked and some will disappear completely in the next draft. These last two types of writing are likely to include unnecessary description that is a result of your first attempt to express your understanding.
- **First draft**. After you have done the further reading and research your rough draft identified, you will do your first draft. This will be your first go at being more accurate and complete. For example, you will ensure that citations are included for sources and evidence. You will aim for coherence (although you will still have some minor gaps in flow). You will start to think about cohesion. You will concern yourself with the balance between description and critical analysis. It is still work in progress, however, and it will probably identify what final reading and research are needed to clarify your understanding and/or that you need to include to support your analysis, evaluation and reasoning.

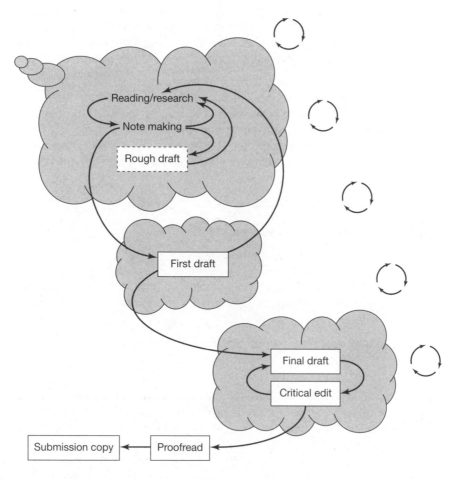

Figure 14.13 A draft & redraft writing model

- **Final draft**. This is nearly, but not quite, the copy for submission. You will ensure that your writing is accurate and complete: it will include the final reading and research and you will have spent time on coherence and cohesion. Your **critical edit** will ensure that you have answered the question and that you haven't got any major gaps or errors in argument or evidence. You will check the learning outcomes and mark criteria for the assignment to ensure that you have addressed the things that get marks. You may hear a tutor talking about developing 'critical distance' from your work: this is where you apply objective, critical thinking to your own work.
- **Proofreading**. This is the last read-through to check and amend spelling and grammar. You will also check that all citations have a corresponding reference and that both are accurate. You will ensure that the format conforms to the requirements of your department. See Chapter 13, 'Taking control of the writing process' for guidance on the proofreading process. Once you are satisfied on all points, print

out your submission copy. Check that all pages have printed and that you have them in the correct page-numbered order before securing them together. Complete any assignment submission documentation, attach to your assignment as required by your department. Submit.

For many students, simply recognising that there are a number of distinct steps to a successful submission copy is an immediate solution to the descriptive writing problem as it highlights the need to plan time more effectively and not leave assignment writing to the last minute. For many others, actually doing the redrafting takes them around the virtuous circle a number of times and enables them to think, and then write, **beyond** description.

ACTIVITY 10 Review a piece of your own work

Take a piece of your work that has been marked, reread it and read all the feedback closely (both on the mark sheet and any further comments the marker makes on the assignment). You need to be very honest with yourself and decide where in your draft/redraft writing process, based on the marker's comments, you made shortcuts or didn't apply enough effort.

See the feedback section for more information.

Hot Tip	Although your tutors will have certain expectations about your writing skills when you arrive at university or college, they will not expect you to have fully mastered critically analytical and evaluative writing. They will offer you feedback designed to guide you as to how to improve. If you need further help, your university or college may have study or academic skills tutors, or a writing centre which can help you to understand this feedback about your work and to develop a strategy to enhance your academic performance.

6 Writing about 'the literature'

Another common problem that novice writers face is knowing how to include the literature in their writing. Sometimes this is about knowing how to reference sources (see Chapter 12, 'Understanding academic integrity: learner ethics and plagiarism') but mostly it is about what to actually do with the words and ideas in those sources. Many novice writers use direct quotes all the time in their writing. To begin with, as long as you reference your sources, this is a safe way to demonstrate that you have done reading and further study. However, your tutors will quickly start to give you feedback such as 'You need to paraphrase the theories and spend more time analysing them' or 'too descriptive, summarise the key points'.

Using paraphrase and summary

Too often I have to mark work where the student has just written quote after quote. It doesn't contain anything that lets me make a judgement about whether they know what it means or whether they've just 'got lucky' with random choice of a good quote.

Tutor's comment

Although the original words are sometimes the only way to make the point, mostly this is a poor way to show your understanding. Your 'voice' (see earlier) develops by paraphrasing and summarising other people's work. This is how you show that you understand authors' ideas and arguments and can use them to support and construct your own argument, analysis, evaluation and critical judgement. The table below considers this by comparing some of the consequences of quotation, paraphrase and summary.

	Quote	Paraphrase	Summary
Word count efficiency	Low. Key points(s) may need extended quotation *and* description to clarify.	Medium. May not improve on quote.	High. Distils the key point(s).
Shows understanding	Low. Unless quote is clearly the key idea, it just repeats what someone else says.	Medium/High. Based, at least, on some analysis.	High. Based on analysis/ evaluation.
Supports criticality	Low. Focus tends to be on description rather than argument.	Medium/High. May still tend towards description.	High. Is embedded in the argument being made.

To explore this, let's show an original piece of text as a diagram – see Figure 14.14.

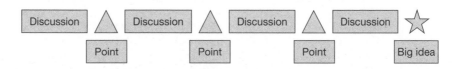

Figure 14.14 Diagrammatic representation of a paraphrase of the original text

If you wanted to write about this just using quotation, you would have to either give lots of shorter, separate quotes, or give one long, extended quote. This still leaves you with the task of demonstrating the significance of the big idea from the *what, why, how, where, when* perspectives (see Chapter 9, 'Thinking critically').

If you paraphrase the original text **accurately**, you are immediately showing understanding of the discussion and how this leads to/supports the points that are made. Figure 14.15 shows this.

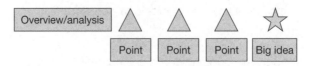

Figure 14.15 Diagrammatic representation of a paraphase of the original text

The main advantage here is that you have added some of your 'voice' to the use of the source. However, you are still left with the task of evaluating this critically and you may find that your writing coherence is affected because you are still following the original author's structure. This is where summarisation wins out. If you **accurately** summarise the big idea, you can move straight on to draw on other authors to engage in a critical analysis and evaluation of the big idea. The significant shift in writing like this, compared with the paraphrase, is that the focus is on the 'big' idea and your 'voice' is now fully part of the debate about this big idea. See Figure 14.16.

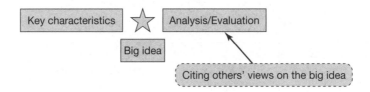

Figure 14.16 Diagrammatic representation of a summarisation of the original text

NOTE   You must always fully cite and reference other people's work irrespective of whether you quote, paraphrase or summarise. See Chapter 12, 'Understanding academic integrity: learner ethics and plagiarism'.

ACTIVITY 11 Compare and contrast quote and summary

The two short extracts below are from two different students' work citing the same original text. Read each one in turn. First, identify which is the extended quote and which is the summary. Second, judge which one you think best demonstrates that the writer fully understands the original text and can use this understanding to develop their own argument. Finally, if the rest of the assignment these extracts came from were written similarly, how would you grade them?

[A]. Ramsay, Maier and Price (2010) say there are four sentence types in a successful essay paragraph.

'**Link sentence from previous paragraph:** Although this is optional, if you can make links between paragraphs your essay will hang together more effectively. It might be the further development of the previous paragraph topic, but from a different perspective. Or it might be a comparison with a related topic that makes the link. **Topic sentence**: This is always essential. This tells your reader what to expect from your paragraph. **Topic development sentences:** This is always essential. This is where you develop your topic sentence. It might be several bits of evidence (possibly 3–4 in a typical paragraph) and/or reasoning necessary to establish the point. **Summary or lead-out sentence:** Although this is optional, if you can summarise the findings from the topic development and indicate where this is going to go, this helps the reader understand your sequencing. It may also be the point that you reiterate in your conclusion when you summarise all your findings.' (p. 382)

[B]. Ramsay, Maier and Price (2010) suggest a model of paragraph structuring which clarifies key constituent sentence types as linking, topic focus, topic development and summary (p. 382). They argue this model allows the writer to achieve coherence and, more broadly, to present evidence and reasoning which permits what they call the writer's 'voice' to be present (p. 384). They acknowledge, however, that 'novice writers' will have a concern about getting this right (p. 405), and this has some similarity to Hood's idea of 'representing an evaluative stance' (2004, p.24) which will now be considered in more detail.

See the feedback section for comment on this activity.

Some novice writers understandably express the anxiety that if they 'get it wrong' when paraphrasing or summarising then they will lose marks. However, the greater risk to your marks is if the marker cannot see evidence in your writing that you have attempted to understand the source(s) you are quoting. To use a business metaphor, your tutors are looking for evidence of your attempts to 'add value'. The table below summarises, compares and contrasts paraphrase and summary.

Paraphrase	Summary
Rewritten in student's own words.	Rewritten in student's own words.
Tends to reduce unnecessary words from original text.	Eliminates unnecessary words from original text.
Tends to follow original text's structure.	Restructured to suit context/function in assignment.
Tends to presents the original text's major and minor points without critical evaluation as to its 'big' idea or significance. This demonstrates some understanding of the original text.	Presents the key points that characterise the text's 'big' idea or significance. This demonstrates critical engagement and evaluation with the original text.

7 Writing about a case study

'Cases quickly put theory into practise by presenting realistic management dilemmas for students to solve.'

Harvard Business Publishing, 2008

As the marketing statement above suggests, case studies are likely to be used on your Business or Management Studies course to get you to look at real-world problems. Knowing how to approach this type of text and write about it, and possibly at some point in your studies to write a case study yourself, is a skill you will need to develop to maximise your grades.

Understanding case studies

'When we were given a case study as a group work assignment, although the brief for the assignment was clear, none of us actually knew how to deal with the case study itself!'

Sian, second-year Business Administration student

Case studies are written to present the key features, with evidence and data, of a real-world problem situation. A case study might be a summarised account of one business, organisation or team or it might be constructed from a number of such settings which have common, key features (see Figure 14.17). The purpose of this is to give scenarios that pose real-world problems or dilemmas in a manageable form so that students can apply theory and knowledge to these in an analytical way. The outcome of this is the identification, evaluation and appraisal of different solution options to the case study problem or dilemma. All of the critical skills we look at in Chapter 9, 'Thinking critically' apply to this process and Activity 10 ('Right size the sales team') in that chapter is a *very* simple example of a case study. You will be given much more detailed and comprehensive case studies to work with than this; nevertheless that activity does illustrate the point of a case study.

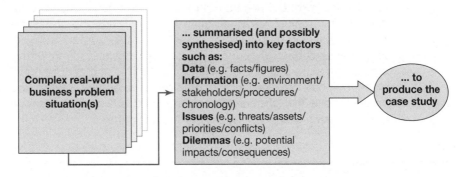

Figure 14.17 The relationship between the real world and the case study

Working with case studies

'One of my main concerns with the case study assignments I set is that many students just regurgitate the detail that's written in the study itself. I want them to stand back from the detail, see the patterns or themes the detail shows, filter out the unimportant things and focus on what matters. I tell them: get this and you will get ahead of other graduates when it comes to getting that job.'

Tutor's comment

As a **means of learning**, the case study can substitute for your lack of personal experience; it can also be used to test out your existing experience in new situations. When you apply critical processes (for example, analysis and evaluation) to understand and suggest solutions to the case study problem, you are also developing the skills which will improve your employability prospects, as Figure 14.18 illustrates.

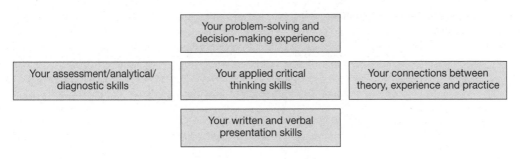

Figure 14.18 Some of the skills that working with case studies can develop

However well written, a case study is only a *representation* of the real-world situation it is based upon. This means that there will be some gaps in the data or information it supplies, so don't expect the scenario to tell you everything. You may have to do further research or make certain assumptions to deal with the scenario. In either case you will need to have a good *rationale* (i.e. logical reasons) for the research actions or assumptions you make. To develop this rationale you need to use content from your lectures and texts, and possibly prior real-world experience, along with all the critical thinking skills considered in Chapter 9, 'Thinking critically'. All real-world situations pose challenges of incomplete data or information. You are being forced to face the complexity the real-world business or management professional faces every day, as part of the assignment.

Hot Tip

Analysing a case study is deceptively hard. If you have been given a case study to prepare for a group discussion or seminar, **don't leave it until the day before**. If you do this, even if you accurately identify the problem, you will probably have only a superficial grasp of the scenario. Spread the reading and thinking over a number of days: this way you will increase the likelihood of improving your marks and enhancing the skills a future employer will look for.

ACTIVITY 13 Begin to analyse a case study

Choose a text from your course that uses a case study. Read it and identify the problem it illustrates. Now use the matrix tool below to begin to develop your analysis/diagnosis of the problem. Note: you will need to make your own copy of this matrix as you are likely to need much more space to fill in the detail.

Factor	A theory/model that can help me to understand this	Alternative theories/ models that might help me to understand this	Possible synthesis (you might find the 'Synthesis' section in Chapter 9 helpful here)
Identify relevant **Data**			
Identify relevant **Information**			
Identify relevant **Issues**			
Identify relevant **Dilemmas**			

To develop your analysis, you will also probably need to use a range of analytical tools such as a SWOT or PEST or stakeholder analysis or fishbone diagrams. To help you develop and inform decisions you may need to use various decision-making tools (for example, a decision-making matrix or Pareto-style analysis or some method of decision pathway analysis). Your tutors will give you guidance on their expectations. The most important thing to remember when you are working with a case study is that you need to show how you are **integrating** your understanding of the theories, concepts and methods of your subject with the facts and circumstances of a real, or real-type, situation to produce well-argued, evidenced and workable solutions.

It is common for case studies to be set as group or team work. In this case you will be given clear guidance on how you are expected to present your work and how that will be assessed and marked. For example, you may be asked to give a verbal presentation, to write a collaborative group report or to write an individual report. If it is a collaborative report, you need to ensure that you are working effectively as a team (see Chapter 5, 'Working in a real and diverse team') to allocate writing responsibilities to deliver the end report, and that you understand what sort of peer assessment may contribute to the overall mark. If you all have to write your own, individual reports then you must ensure your report is your *own* work. No matter how great the temptation, do not copy someone else's work or allow them to copy yours: you will both be penalised for plagiarism (see Chapter 12, 'Understanding academic integrity: learner ethics and plagiarism').

Writing about case studies

The first way you might write about a case study is to produce a report that analyses the problem the case presents and which leads to recommendations to solve the problem, with a possible plan to implement the solution(s). The exact format of the report will be specified by your tutors, but whatever the exact structure, the writing skills considered earlier in this chapter will be relevant. The table below identifies some of the main do's and don'ts when writing a case study report.

Do	Don't
Refer to the particular data or information that supports the analysis, decision or conclusion you make.	Just repeat the data or information contained in the case study. (*This is descriptive writing.*)
Cite theories/models and discuss why or how they may or may not apply in relation to the data/information/issues of the case.	Describe theories/models in detail, or fail to show why they are relevant. (*This is just telling what something is, not why or how it is important.*)
Clarify what assumptions you may have had to make, and on what grounds you have confidence in the validity of the assumptions.	Hope the reader won't spot your assumptions, or present them as 'obvious'. (*This reveals lack of critical engagement.*)

Do	Don't
Use relevant analytical/decision-making tools and show how the results inform your analysis/evaluation/judgement.	Use relevant tools but then expect the reader to guess what the results mean. (*You are not showing your applied skills at all.*)
Discuss the alternatives at key points in your analysis, interpretation, decision making and strategising.	Focus on the 'right' answer. (*It reveals lack of critical application of theory, knowledge, skills and experience. The whole point of tackling real-world problems is that there are always several possible ways forward.*)
Be concise and accurate and offer evidenced conclusions and recommendations for solutions.	Waffle and offer personal opinion. (*This is evidence that the writer hasn't really attempted to read or understand the case study.*)
Ensure that any action or implementation plan is realistic and logical in context of the rest of the report.	Suggest a plan that either has no basis in the evidence or analysis offered, or solves a different problem entirely from the one in the case study. (*This shows you've missed the point or haven't taken the case study seriously.*)

NOTE   If you have jumped straight to this section and are uncertain about the writing skills referred to, we recommend that you review the rest of this chapter now.

There is a second way in which you are likely to write about case studies. Case studies commonly appear in the texts you read for your course. In this context, case studies either inform the reader of the key factors of the situation being examined in the text and/or supply empirical data which the authors use as part of their analysis. In either case you may be citing such case studies as part of your use of other people's work when you develop your own argument chains. If so, you need to apply the same skills of critical thinking (see Chapter 9, 'Thinking critically'), critical writing (see previous sections in this chapter) and referencing (see Chapter 12, 'Understanding student ethics and academic integrity: learner ethics and plagiarism') as to any other published text you use in your own work.

So writing about case studies uses the same skills of thinking and writing you use to write about other people's research or theoretical work. However, there may be a need in your studies to write a case yourself. The next section briefly considers the key aspects of writing a case study to support an assignment.

Writing a case study for an assignment

'I found writing a case study for my 'Improving team communication' operational report quite difficult. I knew the work context intimately, but I struggled to write a clear, concise yet sufficiently full case study to support my report.'

Jan, postgraduate Human Resources Management student

Most Business and Management undergraduates will not need to write a case study until their final year and perhaps only then if their independent study project or dissertation is based on work placement experience. Students studying professional postgraduate programmes may find this is expected sooner in their studies. The main purpose of this activity is likely to be to provide the reader with a clear understanding of the context and background to the problem-based task. Depending on the type of written task, you may need to provide a 'case' as an appendix to which you cross-refer, or you may be required to include this as part of the background/ introduction/ context/overview section to support your rationale for the investigation you are undertaking.

When writing about a case study you are looking from the case study, as a representation of the real world, outwards to the real world. When writing a case study you are looking from the real world, inwards, to the representative case study. This shift of perspective can create the difficulties Jan found: she knew so much that she found it hard to *summarise* the key factors.

The ability to filter out frequently interesting but often unnecessary detail is quite an advanced skill. It requires you to achieve 'critical distance' from a familiar thing in order to see the key themes, trends and issues and identify the specific data and information that best represent those features.

ACTIVITY 14 Create a draft for your own case study

This activity helps you to develop case study writing. It assumes that you have some detailed knowledge of an organisational or business problem context. Using the organisational or business problem context that you wish to summarise as a case study, apply the following sequenced approach.

- Clarify your purpose for writing the case study.

  - Develop and write a brief two-sentence purpose statement. It won't appear in your actual case study, but it will help you to focus on the important elements for your writing.

  - Write a single sentence defining the identified problem.

- Your case study will include, among others, some the following elements: context (for example mission), chronology, internal/external environment (for example customer/ provider relationships, infrastructure, legal constraints), relevant procedures/policies, formal/informal decision-making processes, existing and emerging threats/opportunities, primary stakeholders, past responses to comparable problems and outcomes.

  - Try making a concept map (see Chapter 9, 'Thinking critically') to map out and identify the connections between the key elements you select. You can then develop this by visually scaling the elements according to your evaluation of their significance: this is one way to start to identify the key factors that your case study should include.

- Write a single sentence that captures what each key element is about and what might specifically characterise it.

- Now try to write a single sentence for each connection that captures what each connection is about and what specifically might characterise it.

- At this point you should have a rough draft of the 'big picture' in words.

- Revisit your initial purpose and problem statements. Using these, review the single-sentence statements you have written and review your initial judgement as to what is significant and what you have identified to represent/summarise that.

- If you are happy with the big picture you have roughly drafted, turn it into a first draft. If not, go back to the concept mapping to reformulate the elements and connections to get closer to what you need to represent.

See the feedback section for further comment.

8 On reflection

This chapter has looked at some of the things that you can do to improve your business and management studies writing. These things can improve your grades and equip you with effective written communication skills to help you impress future employers. These skills include aspects of language use, methodical and systematic approaches to the writing task, incorporating evidence in your work to provide critically argued documents that carry authority, and some specific types of writing you may be asked to do while studying. While you may begin your course as a 'novice' writer, an important part of the learning on the course is related to you becoming a more expert writer, both in general terms and in specific genres. This is a journey without a given end: only you will determine the end point. Your course will give you writing practise and experience opportunities, right up until you graduate, to get on with this journey. Don't opt out before that point.

Summary of this chapter

ACTIVITY 15 Update your personal development planner

My developing skills	Confidence level 1–5	Plans to improve
I know what my English language skills are and know what to do to improve them.		
I understand what the elements of an essay and report are and can use these effectively.		
I write clearly and accurately and achieve coherence and cohesion in my writing.		
I understand how to use paraphrasing and summary and avoid descriptive writing.		
I understand what case studies are and how to approach writing about them.		

Getting extra help

- Go to the students union to find out where to go for skills development. Many universities and colleges have tutors who provide this service.

- Your tutors will encourage you to look at good examples of how experts write in your subject. Ask them to recommend texts that show this.

- If there is a suggestion that you might have a specific writing difficulty (associated with dyslexia, for example), make immediate contact with your university or college disability advisers for further advice.

Consult the following

- Purdue University's Online Writing Laboratory (OWL) is a widely respected online writing centre: http://owl.english.purdue.edu/owl/

- Goldsmiths University of London website has helpful information about essay writing: www.real.gold.ac.uk/essayguide/index.html

- Manchester University's 'Academic Phrasebank' is a very useful resource for academic writers: www.phrasebank.manchester.ac.uk/

- The BBC's Skillswise website has good interactive resources to assist your grammar and punctuation development: www.bbc.co.uk/skillswise/words/grammar/

- The Colorado State University Writing@CSU website provides a helpful overview of writing an executive summary for a report: writing.colostate.edu/guides/documents/execsum/index.cfm

Feedback on activities

ACTIVITY 1 Self-assess your Standard English proficiency

DIALANG gives you further advice about specific strategies you might follow to improve your language skills. (Note: you can also check your proficiency in 13 other European languages, useful if you plan to go on holiday!)

ACTIVITY 2 Analyse a sample introduction using the topic/task/treatment/thesis model

Sentence	Topic/task/treatment/thesis?
It has been recently estimated that at any one time more than 85% of businesses in Europe are in the process of implementing change that directly affects their workforce (Smith, 2007).	**Topic focus**. This sentence offers an interesting/relevant citation to get the reader's interest.
Understanding how to manage work teams through change successfully is likely to be a major issue in any business context.	**Task understanding**. This is spread over two sentences. Not
It is reasonable to ask whether, and if so how much, motivational theories may assist this process.	necessarily a good thing, but indicative of the writer's personal style.
To answer this question, firstly the notion of 'motivation', and agreement as to what it is, will be examined to establish a definition to underpin the rest of the discussion.	**Treatment**. This is appropriately spread over a number of sentences. Note the
Next a critical analysis and evaluation of the leading theories of motivation will be undertaken to test their relevance and applicability to the change management process.	use of ordinal words: 'firstly', 'next', 'then', 'finally'. This gives the reader a clear map of
The findings from this will then be briefly reviewed against two cases, a large corporate organisation and an SME.	how the topic will be dealt with. This outline also
Finally, the extent to which motivational theory contributes to understanding work team change management will be considered.	suggests the progression of a critical method.
The literature suggests that other factors such as group/team dynamics and communication are important; motivational theories alone are unlikely to be the most important way of managing such change.	**Thesis**. An indication of the writer's views on what they have found from their research.

Whilst this may not produce the best essay answer to the question (that depends on what the writer actually writes!), the writer *is* using the introduction to demonstrate that they have given thought to how they are going to tackle the question in a structured way.

ACTIVITY 6 Look at how signal words are used

You will have identified a number of signal words and phrases in the text you chose. If you have done this activity thoroughly, you will also have made brief notes in the margins. You should have a very clear picture of the author's logical flow. You will also have some good examples of the use of signalling and what results from this that you can use as models for developing your writing skills. A good learning point from this activity is that when you read texts, remember to read not just for content but also for how the content is presented.

ACTIVITY 8 Linking within sentences – working with clauses

1. _____ .

Carbon dioxide is the dominant contributor to current climate change.

2. _____ ▢ _____ .

Carbon dioxide is the dominant contributor to current climate change _and_ **its atmosphereric concentration has increased from a pre-industrial value of 278 ppm to 379 in 2005.**

3. _____ △ - - - - - .

There is a variety of renewable sources of energy _although_ most of them still require more technological or commercial development.

4. △ - - - - - , _____ .

Unless we make significant efforts to reduce our emissions of greenhouse gases, **the global climate will continue to warm rapidly over the coming decades and beyond.**

Notice the comma if you start a sentence with a subordinate clause.

If you start a sentence with a subordinate clause, notice the comma.

5. _____ ◯ - - - - - ▢ - - - - - ▢ - - - - -

Greenhouse emissions from post-consumer waste make up almost 5% of the total global greenhouse gas emissions _which_ can be reduced not only by recovering the gases emitted from landfills, _but_ also through improved landfill practices _and_ engineered wastewater management.

Notice that when coordinating clauses can share the same verb (here '_be reduced_') you don't need to repeat it.

6. △ - - - - - , _____ ◯ - - - - - ▢ - - - - - △ - - - - -

Although it is too early to predict the future climate agreement, **it is possible to identify guiding principles to be included in an extended regime** _that_ provide incentives for developing countries to limit their emissions and adapt to the impacts of climate change _while_ safeguarding socioecoomic growth and poverty eradication.

You can see that, as a reader, the more clause links you have, the more complex they are to process.

ACTIVITY 10 Review a piece of your own work

This is a hard activity as you are being critical of yourself by trying to understand the marker's comments in the context of the words you wrote. Too often students skim over the feedback or don't bother to read it at all. This is a sure way to both repeat the same mistakes in your next piece of work (that really bugs your tutors) and miss the point that it's the feedback that matters more than the mark in terms of your learning. Make this activity your normal behaviour with **every** piece of returned, marked work.

ACTIVITY 11 Compare and contrast quote and summary

Extract B is the summary. Extract A is the extended quote.

Whilst you don't have a detailed knowledge of the other source used in this activity, extract B clearly demonstrates that the writer has engaged with the big idea. The actual model is acknowledged briefly, but the significance and consequences of it *form* the discussion. There is consideration of the first source's critique of its own model, which is used as a link to the next step in the writing. Note the use of a further source to strengthen the case for this next step. Extract A leaves the reader asking 'so what?'. The reader is none the wiser as to the writer's intentions, or indeed if they have understood what the quote is saying.

How we would grade the assignments they came from (if they continued in a similar way) is that B would pass and providing B shows full understanding of the sources and makes a good case, it would pass well. We would struggle with A: if it was a first assignment it might just pass. Subsequently, though, writing like this just wouldn't reach the pass threshold.

ACTIVITY 12 Explore phrases to write about the literature

The main point about this activity is that a resource bank like this provides you with prompts and suggestions, not answers. It can suggest ways to help you express yourself academically in ways that you may not previously have thought of. It also, in the way it is structured, models key critical steps in academic writing. You should bookmark it and use it to prompt and stimulate your thinking.

ACTIVITY 14 Create a draft for your own case study

There is no single prescription for writing a case study. The process in this activity is very similar to the draft/redraft model we considered in the 'Moving beyond descriptive writing' section earlier in this chapter. This is not surprising as the common underlying factor is developing critically analytical and evaluative writing. Like many other aspects of writing, experience and practice lead to improvement once you apply a systematic approach. You may well add to or amend the steps this activity asked you to follow as you become more experienced.

References

- Campaign for learning (n.d.) www.campaign-for-learning.org.uk/cfl/yourlearning/making_it_stick.asp [last accessed 22 September 2009].
- Covey, S. (2004) *The 7 habits of Highly Effective People* (2nd edn). New York, Simon & Schuster.
- Einstein, A. (n.d.) http://thinkexist.com/quotation/wisdom_is_not_a_product_of_schooling_but_of_the/171910.html [last accessed 9 October 2009].
- Harvard Business Publishing (2008) http://hbsp.harvard.edu/product/cases [last accessed 2 October 2009].

15 Developing your reflective writing

We ended Chapter 10 saying that reflection is a life skill that you should develop as a future business leader. Reflective writing ought to be easy, but as many students and professionals will say, it can be one of the hardest types of writing to do successfully. You have to have a high degree of self-awareness, write with a degree of self-disclosure, and have well-developed critical thinking skills. You then need to use these to integrate theory and practice with your thoughts, feelings and behaviours. Typically this makes us explore our 'soft' skills and it is these interpersonal attributes that make the difference in the real world. This is the reason why Business and Management Studies students are set reflective writing assignments. The importance of soft skills over technical or 'hard' skills in a global business environment is increasingly acknowledged as essential to getting that first graduate job and important in achieving career success. Developing your reflective writing skills will directly contribute to your asset development.

To get the most out of this chapter you should first work through Chapters 9, 'Thinking critically', 10, 'Understanding the value of reflection' and 14, 'Improving your business and management studies writing'.

In this chapter you will:

1. consider what types of assignment ask for reflective writing;
2. compare reflective writing style with other academic writing styles;
3. examine some helpful reflective writing techniques.

USING THIS CHAPTER

Estimate your current levels of confidence. At the end of the chapter you will have the chance to re-assess these levels where you can incorporate this into your personal development planner (PDP). Mark between 1 (poor) and 5 (good) for the following:

I understand why I am asked to write reflectively on my course.	I know what types of reflective writing I may be asked to do.	I understand what makes better critical reflective writing.	I understand how to include evidence in my reflective writing.

Date: _____

1 When will you be asked to write reflectively?

*'I know that reflective writing is difficult and I could make my life much easier by not setting the reflective assignment. But those students who stop whingeing about it and **really** give it a go tend to go on and accelerate their learning impressively.'*

Tutor's comment

As we saw in Chapter 10, 'Understanding the value of reflection', you will be asked to use a reflective process on a number of different aspects of your learning progress. The ways in which you write about this will vary. The table below considers some of these.

Aspect of learning progress	Type of assignment
Chronological development (*e.g. reviewing the semester/year overall*)	Learning log + critical reflective essay
Specific learning event (*e.g. using the university library for the first time/a group work experience/comparing learning expectation with learning outcome from a lecture, seminar or key note speaker*)	Critical reflective account or essay
Work placement/real-world incident (*e.g. considering how theory and practice-based models informed your understanding of the experience*)	Learning log + critical reflective essay
Application of learning and professional skills (*e.g. problem solving and implementing operational improvements*)	Separate critical reflective section in an operational report (or included in the report's conclusion section) or in a professional development portfolio

There will be other aspects of your learning that you may have to write about reflectively and you may be set other specific writing tasks that aren't mentioned above. However, the two important points the table shows are that first, you may have to maintain a log (to capture and record data and information) and second, you will definitely need to write **critically** to analyse and evaluate such information along with other sources of information. We will look at sources of information/evidence for reflective writing later. If you have worked through Chapter 14, 'Improving your business and management studies writing' you should be familiar with the ideas of critical analysis and evaluation, so what is different about reflective writing?

2 Comparing reflective writing with other academic writing

In many respects there is no difference between reflective and other academic writing. You need to:

- use correct grammar and spelling;
- fully reference other people's work;
- include evidence;
- focus on analysis and evaluation rather than description;
- produce a cohesive and coherent piece of work;
- produce logical and supported conclusions.

When you write an essay, the subject is determined by the question and this is usually something quite abstract or theoretical. When you write a report, the subject is the problem or situation that you have chosen to investigate. Where reflective writing differs is that the *subject* of the writing is not an external thing, it is you or rather you in a specific context. You have already explored what reflection is and some models that explain this in Chapter 10, 'Understanding the value of reflection'. Reflective writing also differs in so far as **the conclusion is focused on what the evidence and reflective reasoning suggest for future self-improvement**. Because of this focus there is a genre writing difference. The next section explores this difference.

Using the 'first person'

'I got really worried when we were told we could use the 'first person' when writing reflectively. I wasn't sure what that was.'

Maria, second-year International Business Relations student

Many students are surprised that a lot of reflective writing, unlike other academic writing, is done in the first person. You will have been told that your academic writing should avoid the use of 'I', 'me', 'my' and you have probably been told that you should write **impersonally** (or in the 'third person') to achieve this. When writing reflectively it is hard to avoid the first person as it is you who has the 'expert' knowledge about yourself. The table below looks briefly at the difference between personal and impersonal forms of writing.

Writing	Example
Personally	*'I knew that in interpersonal communications there is a difference between hearing and listening (for example, Stuart, Sarow & Stuart, 2007), and I found that I was just hearing and therefore missing the full message.'*
Impersonally	*'Models of interpersonal communications suggest that there is a difference between hearing and listening (for example, Stuart, Sarow & Stuart, 2007), and it was found that just hearing meant the full message was missed.'*

Technically the personal form is known as writing in the first person and writing impersonally is known as writing in the third person. (There is also the second person but this is rarely used in academic writing except to give instruction or direction. For example, we use it in this book to talk directly to you when we are offering you guidance on how to do something). These forms subtly say something about the 'presence' of the writer in a text, and we can liken it to the writer's voice in the sense we discussed in Chapter 14, 'Improving your business and management studies writing'.

The reflective writer's presence appears in two ways: through the immediacy of the writer (that is, you in the first person) and through the writer's voice as in critically evaluating and reflecting on the evidence. Figure 15.1 illustrates this with a simple example.

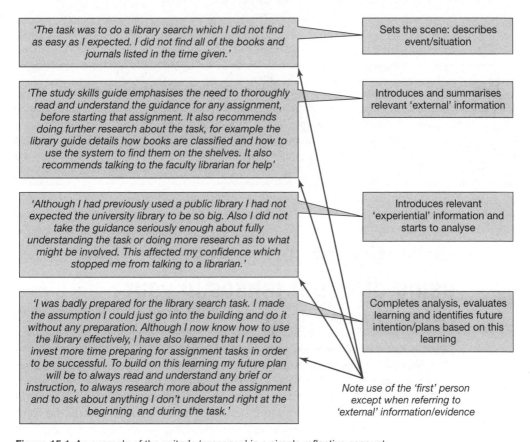

Figure 15.1 An example of the writer's 'presence' in a simple reflective account

NOTE Some tutors may ask you to avoid the use of 'I', 'me' but to use phrases such as 'the author' or 'the writer' instead. If you are not clear about exactly what your tutor wants, ask for an example.

Although the example in Figure 15.1 is a bit 'lightweight', it demonstrates some basic writing steps that a novice writer might use to produce a reflective piece. Use Activity 1 to try out these steps.

ACTIVITY 1 Write your own brief reflection

Select a recent experience at university, college or work that required you to do something new, or to do a familiar task but in a totally different way. Use the steps from the model in Figure 15.1 to write a brief (no more than 250 words) critical reflection about that experience. (Note the example in Figure 15.1 is approximately 240 words long.)

See the feedback section for further comment on this activity.

Hot Tip If you are concerned about your understanding of the grammar principles behind the points covered in this or the next section, your university or college may have academic or study skills tutors who can help you develop your understanding. Alternatively if you search online using the search string 'writing labs' or 'online writing labs', you will find a number of helpful websites.

3 Reflection as a process over time: using different tenses in your reflective writing

When you write reflectively you need to be in control of what was in the past, what is in the present *as* you write and what is in the future in terms of proposed actions or plans. The time frames that reflection addresses (Schön's ideas about reflection-*in*-action and reflection-*on*-action are one example of this) need you to use the correct *tense*, in other words the form of the verb words that tell us whether something happened in the past, is happening now or will happen in the future. This helps you to manage the complex flow of ideas and time lines that an expert reflective writer uses to produce good, clear reflective writing. The table below summarises tense use over the time frame of a piece of reflective writing.

Tense	Use
Past The point at which the situation/event/occurrence that is the focus of the reflection **took** place.	*You will use this to write a **brief description** of the situation/event/incident and your 'reflection-in-action', and **when referring back** to a specific part of that situation/event as **evidence** in your current reflection.*
Present The point at which the reflective writing **takes** place.	*You will use this to write your current **critical analysis and evaluation**, the 'reflection-on-action', that **integrates** theory and experience/evidence from the event into a **conclusion**.*
Future The point at which the proposed action plan **will take** place.	*You will use this to write your **proposals** to develop/improve the aspects of your understanding/behaviour/practice skills that your critical reflective conclusions identified.*

ACTIVITY 2 Manage the time frames in a piece of reflective writing

Read through the following example of reflective writing, based on part of one student's critical reflection about a group work assignment, to identify where and how the tense changes are used to keep the time frames clear.

Verbs in text identified	Commentary
'It ***was*** at the point that the group ***failed*** to react that I ***realised*** we ***had not*** given enough consideration to how far we ***had developed*** as a team. My previous work experience ***was*** in an established team, so this ***was*** a new and uncomfortable experience for me.'	■ Use of **past tense** to refer back to specific issues in this examination of a 'reflection-in-action'. ■ *Note how the writer brings in a brief, but relevant, piece of previous experience to develop the analysis. They then summarise its impact as a feeling.*
'Looking at this particular incident it ***is*** apparent that the process of team formation ***was not*** given enough attention. For example from Tuckman's (1965) model of 'forming/storming/norming/performing', it ***is*** clear that the team ***was still at*** the storming stage. The team ***had not*** sorted out each team member's role, although because of my previous experience the others ***assumed I was*** a leader. Belbin's (1993) team-roles model **suggests** that **I have** a strong 'monitor-evaluator' tendency when **I consider** my previous experience, whereas the team saw me as a 'coordinator'. So it ***is*** likely that the discomfort **I *experienced was*** a result of role conflict arising from that ambiguity (Rizzo *et al.*, 1970).'	■ Use of **present tense** to engage in 'reflection-on-action', to cite relevant theory, and to undertake some analysis. ■ Use of **past tense** to refer back to relevant factors from the event itself. ■ *Note how the writer attempts to use evidence from the event, their own previous experience and relevant theories. They are trying to analyse both what was happening and why, the impact they had on the situation, and the impact the situation had on them.*
'Based on this aspect of the group work assignment, it ***is*** clear that **I *will have to*** read more about how teams develop and team roles. Also **I *will have to*** experience a wider range of roles that ***will help*** me to develop a broader skill set. A good way to achieve this ***will be to*** find some volunteer work that ***will involve*** working with others to get tasks done.'	■ Use of **present tense** to complete analysis. ■ Use of **future tense** to indicate proposed actions/action plan. ■ *Note how the writer links the findings with the proposed actions and tries to identify a practical, real-world way to achieve them.*

4 Writing about the actual event/situation/incident

> 'When I got my assignment back, the main thing the tutor said was that it was a good story but it had no analysis.'

Tomas, third-year Business Enterprise student

One of the main problems with reflective writing is that although many students are used to writing about themselves on social networking sites such as Facebook, they don't have a model for writing about themselves in a *focused and constructive learning* way. This usually results in the wrong balance between initially describing the event, circumstance or incident, and the subsequent analysis and evaluation of it in a reflective way. As a rough guide you should aim to spend no more than 10–15 per cent of the word count describing 'what' happened. For example, the introduction in Figure 15.1 is 33 words long, well within this range.

One way of starting to focus on the important points to include in an introductory paragraph is to ask a set of specific questions. One example of how to do this is to think about the following five components: **P**eople_**A**ntecedent_**O**ccurrence_**I**ssue_**C**onsequence (PAOIC). See Figure 15.2.

NOTE   It is not possible to specify a universal template to do this task as the specific questions or the specific components are likely to change with each event or incident. The important point is the use of a **question-based** approach, as it is this that will help you to find focus and filter out unnecessary detail.

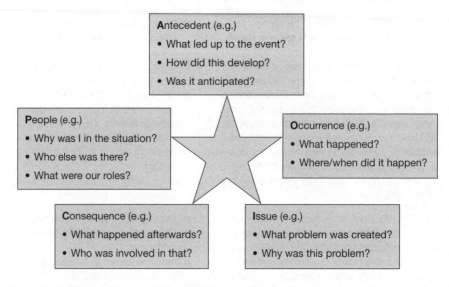

Antecedent (e.g.)
- What led up to the event?
- How did this develop?
- Was it anticipated?

People (e.g.)
- Why was I in the situation?
- Who else was there?
- What were our roles?

Occurrence (e.g.)
- What happened?
- Where/when did it happen?

Consequence (e.g.)
- What happened afterwards?
- Who was involved in that?

Issue (e.g.)
- What problem was created?
- Why was this problem?

Figure 15.2 One possible use of the PAOIC approach with example cue questions

ACTIVITY 3 Achieving a more focused reflective introduction

In this activity you will do more work on the event or experience you chose in Activity 1 and move towards writing a focused introductory paragraph.

1. Take the PAOIC approach from Figure 15.2 and add in any further cue questions you think are relevant to your context. You may also find that some of the example questions in Figure 15.2 won't work in your context so omit those.

2. Using a concept map approach (see Chapter 9, 'Thinking critically'), write one brief sentence that answers each question. (For example: Why was I in the situation? '*I was in the library to search for specific books and journal articles as an assignment.*' What happened? '*I didn't complete the library search task.*')

3. Remember that the reader of your introduction will not know anything about the situation, context or your role in it. You must now turn this concept map into a focused, written introduction. You will need to identify what is necessary and relevant from your map, what can be 'synthesised' from your map to eliminate repetition, and what else might be needed to complete the picture. Your challenge is to write this in no more than 200 words.

See the feedback section for further comment on this activity.

Remember, your main objective when writing an introduction to any critical reflective writing is to ensure that the description of the event outlines:

- enough detail for your reader to understand the context;
- the key issues/characteristics which frame the reflection triggered by the event.

A well-written introductory paragraph provides a framework for the empirical evidence (i.e. gained by your observation and experience) that underpins more detailed analysis and evaluation. To achieve this and get the best marks you have to get a range of evidence into your reflection to make it a *critical* process.

5 Getting evidence into critical reflective writing

'While there is not a formula that guides learners to write reflectively, most effective reflective writing will begin with some form of statement of the subject of the reflection. It will include some notion of the direction or purpose for the reflection plus some additional ideas about theory and observations.'

Moon (1999)

Many novice reflective writers miss the opportunity to make the most of the rich range of information generated by the event they are reflecting on. If you apply critical questions and use your critical thinking skills, you can analyse and evaluate the event at a deeper level. In Chapter 14, 'Improving your business and management studies writing' we looked at the **DIKW** model, part of which looks at how information becomes knowledge. It is this 'information into knowledge' step that gets you the best marks in reflective writing assignments. To understand what we mean by 'richness', look at Figure 15.3, which represents some of the sources of information diagrammatically.

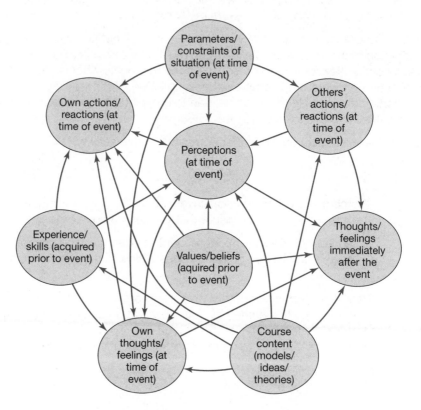

Figure 15.3 A network representation of some of the rich evidence generated

What Figure 15.3 shows is that we can identify specific types of thoughts/feelings/actions and behaviours and we can identify the connections between these. Once we do this we can then analyse and evaluate the origin, influence, impact and consequences of these connections. Figure 15.4 illustrates this, in a bit more detail, for one part of the network above.

The event itself generates a rich range of empirical (i.e. your directly observed) evidence which you need to identify, analyse and evaluate against the framework of other evidence in the texts and literature of your subject area. When you do this, you are transforming the information into *knowledge* that is meaningful to you.

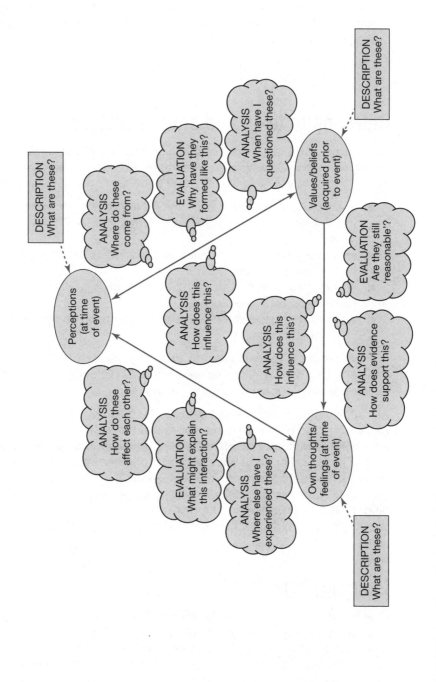

Figure 15.4 Some of the critical questions that can unpack rich information

ACTIVITY 4 Develop critical reflection

For this activity you can either do more work on the experience/event you chose in Activity 1, or you can select another significant learning or work-based incident. Use the model in Figure 15.4 to identify and write not just a summary of *what* your thoughts/values/perceptions were but an analysis and evaluation of them. In other words, think about the *how, why, where* and *when* dimensions to your thoughts/values/perceptions as Figure 15.4 suggests.

See the feedback section for further comment on this activity.

Referring to texts and other literature

As we said at the beginning of this chapter, one of the goals of reflective writing is to show **how** you are integrating experience, practice and theory. So at key points you will need to show evidence of giving critical thought to:

- **how** relevant theories and models improve your understanding of the incident/situation/event, both during it (*in-action*) and after it (*on-action*);
- **why** you judge those theories and models to be relevant in the context of your reflection;
- **where** your understanding or application of those theories and models can be improved;
- **what** further experience or research you need to pursue to improve your understanding.

For this process, you will need to use the same academic standards and principles of critical writing that we explored in Chapter 14, 'Improving your business and management studies writing'.

Although there is no specific activity for this section, when you tackle Activity 5 at the end of this chapter, reflect more deeply on how this will be incorporated into your overall PDP. In particular, **start to think about the bigger picture that all of your personal planner updates throughout this book have created for you**. You will benefit from reviewing all of these as they have started to create a unique source of evidence for you as a beginning, reflective practitioner. The next section looks briefly at learning logs: you might like to consider how these might fit with your PDP.

Learning logs

One final source of evidence is the learning log. Writing a learning log is a task that you may be set if you are doing a placement, engaged in some group work activity or a project that runs over a period of time, for example. Your tutors will have a number of reasons for setting this task and they may require you to submit the learning log in support of a critically reflective essay. The table below outlines some of the reasons a learning log is used.

Possible context	Possible log content	Some reasons for its use
Placement	Day-to-day summary of new work-based experience, issues/problems encountered, solutions tried, personal observations on the work environment, personal observations on self-development and plans/intentions.	Diary-based account. Supports retrospective review of significant formative events and key influences; insights into personal/professional development needs.
Group work/project	Detailed account of activity/project development, research undertaken, possible theories/models to aid development of ideas/proposals, issues/problems encountered, solutions tried, observations on group dynamics and skills sets used to facilitate progress, personal observations in respect of strengths/weaknesses.	Notebook account. Supports detailed recording of process and progress towards achieving assignment goal. You can then use this record as evidence in your critical reflection. If the task is a group work task, then the log also provides unique data to avoid risk of plagiarism if an individual assignment is to be written by each group member.

You may be given a template for a learning log. If not, you can start by using the framework in Chapter 10, 'Understanding the value of reflection' Activity 3 and add some of the 'content' ideas from the table above.

Many students fail to see the importance of keeping a log during an assignment or task and make it up from what they can remember at the end. Your tutors will spot this as you are likely to include things at a time when you couldn't possibly have known about them. This will probably mean you will lose marks, both for not having a true record and because it will limit the range of your critical reflection. The skill of writing ongoing contemporaneous (i.e. *at the time* something happened) records will be important to you as a future business leader as you are likely to be called upon to evidence/justify decisions and outcomes on the strength of those records. You may also find that your professional graduate career requires you to keep a continuing professional development (CPD) portfolio backed up by a learning log.

6 Sometimes reflection is celebration

The thing to remember in **any** critical process is that we are not just finding fault, we are examining the evidence and reasoning for something (see Chapter 9, 'Thinking critically'). Reflective process is no different. In fact, **being able to critically reflect on why things worked or went well is probably harder** than when they didn't. One of the reasons for this is that when things go well we don't remark on them and there tends to be no pressure to ask why.

An indicator of your developing reflective skills is that you are able to write in an objective and evidenced way about success as well as less successful events. This isn't the same as boasting or selling yourself. You are engaged in **analysing** what factors contributed to that success and **evaluating** what further actions you should take to enhance them. This is where reflection really contributes to soft skill development. It is also the start of genuine professionalism: the commitment to continuing professional development demands acceptance that each of us can always do better than we currently do.

7 On reflection

Shall I not reckon among the perfections of the human understanding that it can reflect upon itself? ... In this power of the mind, and the actions thence arising consists the whole force of conscience, by which it proposes laws to itself, examines its past and regulates its future conduct.

Richard Cumberland (English philosopher and theologian, 1631–1718).

If you want to take control and maximise your learning opportunities whilst at university, you will approach all reflective writing assignments seriously and rigorously. It will also give you a head start over other graduates if you start to develop reflective practices whilst at university. You are then well placed to continue to build your soft skills as your graduate career progresses. As Cumberland's words demonstrate, critical reflection is a time-honoured and significant process. The best way to develop the skills required by this process is to engage with the **virtuous writing cycle** we examined in Chapter 14, 'Improving your business and management studies writing'. Reflective writing is probably the hardest type of academic writing to master and to do well. If you don't accept this challenge, you are accepting second best for yourself.

Summary of this chapter

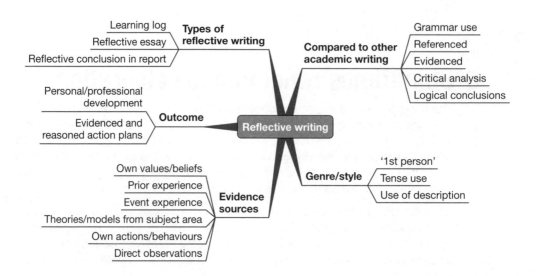

ACTIVITY 5 Update your personal development planner

My developing skills	Confidence level 1–5	Plans to improve
I understand why I am asked to write reflectively on my course.		
I know what types of reflective writing I may be asked to do.		
I understand what makes better critical reflective writing.		
I understand how to include evidence in my reflective writing.		

Getting extra help

- Go to the students union to find out where to go for skills development. Many universities and colleges have tutors who provide this service.
- Your tutors may be able to offer you examples of the type of reflective writing they expect from you. Ask them.

Consult the following

- Do a simple Web search using the search string 'reflective writing introduction' to find further helpful examples of university-level guidance on reflective writing.

Feedback on activities

ACTIVITY 1 Write your own brief reflection

You may find this hard to begin with and you may have followed the example in Figure 15.1 closely. While this is probably a good place to start if you have no experience of writing reflectively, you will need to start to make such writing 'your own'. One way to do this is to come back to this first attempt to write reflectively once you have worked through the other activities in this chapter, **and reflect on it**. Remember, the reflective process is not a one-off activity. You will start to develop new insights and understandings, and begin to see better ways to express those in writing, if you make a point of regularly reviewing significant past events and actions in the light of new experience.

ACTIVITY 3 Achieving a more focused reflective introduction

This activity encourages you to think critically about what the reader really needs to know so that the rest of your analysis and evaluation makes sense. It also suggests that using a concept map approach helps you to see a bigger picture before you try to write. It really uses the same range of skills and techniques of writing that we examined in Chapter 14, 'Improving your business and management studies writing' applied to a slightly different purpose.

ACTIVITY 4 Develop critical reflection

This activity is difficult as it requires you to get behind things that might as yet be unknown to you. The use of cue questions helps this process, but it does need practice to become both comfortable with it and to start to see the payback and benefit from it.

Reference

■ Moon, J. (1999) *Reflect on the inner 'I'*. www.timeshighereducation.co.uk/story. asp?sectioncode=26&storycode=148442 [last accessed 20 October 2009].

Index

Index

Index

Index

Index

Index